David Mamet

DAVID MAMET

A LIFE IN THE THEATRE

IRA NADEL

palgrave
macmillan

DAVID MAMET

First published in hardcover in 2008 by
PALGRAVE MACMILLAN®
in the United States—a division of St. Martin's Press LLC,
175 Fifth Avenue, New York, NY 10010.

Where this book is distributed in the UK, Europe and the rest of the world, this is by Palgrave Macmillan, a division of Macmillan Publishers Limited, registered in England, company number 785998, of Houndmills, Basingstoke, Hampshire RG21 6XS.

PALGRAVE MACMILLAN is the global academic imprint of the above companies and has companies and representatives throughout the world.

ISBN: 978–0–230–37871–1

Library of Congress Cataloging-in-Publication Data

Nadel, Ira Bruce.
David Mamet: a life in the theatre / by Ira Nadel.
p. cm.
ISBN 0–312–29344–5
1. Mamet, David. 2. Dramatists, American—20th century—Biography.
3. Screenwriters—United States—Biography. I. Title.

PS3563.A4345Z82 2008
812_.54—dc22
[B] 2007024287

A catalogue record of the book is available from the British Library.

Design by Newgen Imaging Systems (P) Ltd., Chennai, India.

First PALGRAVE MACMILLAN paperback edition: June 2012

10 9 8 7 6 5 4 3 2 1

Transferred to Digital Printing in 2012

For Dara, Ryan,
and
Anne

Robert: How do you want it?
John: Give it to me straight.
Mamet, *A Life in the Theater*

Everybody loves to be fooled.
David Mamet, 2000

CONTENTS

ABBREVIATIONS

AB	*American Buffalo*. New York: Grove Press, 1996.
ACT	Richard Boleslavsky, *Acting, The First Six Lessons*. 1933; New York: Theatre Arts Books, 1949.
ALT	*A Life in the Theatre*. New York: Grove Press, 1978.
AOT	John Lahr, "David Mamet, The Art of the Theatre XI," *Paris Review* 39 (1997): 51–76.
AP	Aristotle, *Poetics*. Tr. S.H. Butcher. Intr. Francis Fergusson. New York: Hill and Wang, 1961.
BBCP	Bertolt Brecht, *Collected Plays*. Ed. John Willett and Ralph Manheim, Vol 1. London: Methuen, 1970.
BBP	Bertolt Brecht, *Plays*, Vol. II. London: Methuen, 1962.
BG	"Bambi v. Godzilla, Why art loses in Hollywood," *Harpers Magazine* (June 2005): 33–37.
BM	*Boston Marriage*. New York: Vintage, 2000.
BMW	Martin Esslin, *Brecht, The Man and His Work*. Garden City, N.Y.: Anchor Books, 1961.
BOT	Bertolt Brecht, *Brecht on Theatre: The Development of an Aesthetic*. Ed. and tr. by John Willett. New York: Hill and Wang, 2000.
BVG	*Bambi vs. Godzilla, On the Nature, Purpose and Practice of the Movie Business*. New York: Pantheon, 2007.
CA	*The Cabin. Reminiscence and Diversions*. New York: Turtle Bay Books, 1992.
CAM	"The Camel Document." Goddard College, 1969.
CO	*The Cherry Orchard*. Adapted by David Mamet from a literal translation by Peter Nelles. New York: Grove, 1985.
CRP	*The Cryptogram*. London: Methuen 1995.
DMB	Christopher Bigsby, "David Mamet," *Cambridge Companion to David Mamet*. Ed. Christopher Bigsby. Cambridge: Cambridge UP, 2004. 1–40.
DMC	*David Mamet in Conversation*. Ed. Leslie Kane. Ann Arbor: Univ. of Michigan Press, 2001.
DOJ	"The Disappearance of the Jews," *The Old Neighborhood*. New York: Samuel French, 1998.

DV	"The Duck Variations" in *Sexual Perversity in Chicago* and *The Duck Variations*. New York: Grove Press, 1978.
E	*Edmond*. New York: Grove Press, 1983.
5TP	*5 Television Plays*. New York: Grove Weidenfeld, 1990.
F	*Faustus*. New York: Vintage, 2004.
FCR	*Five Cities of Refuge, Weekly Reflections on Genesis, Exodus, Levicticus, Numbers and Deuteronomy*. Lawrence Kushner and David Mamet. New York: Schocken, 2003.
FM	John Lahr, "Fortress Mamet," *The New Yorker* (November 17, 1997): 70–82.
FMP	Brecht, "Four Men and Poker Game," *Short Stories 1921-1946*. Ed. John Willett and Ralph Manheim. London: Methuen, 1983: 94–100.
FOM	*File on Mamet*, compiled by Nesta Jones and Steven Dykes. London: Methuen, 1991.
GGR	*Glengarry Glen Ross*. New York: Grove Press, 1984.
GS	*Goldberg Street, Short Plays and Monologues*. New York: Grove Press, 1985.
H	*Homicide, A Screenplay*. New York: Grove Weidenfeld, 1992.
HG	*House of Games*. New York: Grove Press, 1987.
HOFFA	*Hoffa*. Screenplay, 1990.
IDM	Esther Harriott, "Interview with David Mamet," *American Voices: Five Contemporary Playwrights in Essays and Interviews*. Jefferson, SC: McFarland, 1988.
IOW	"David Mamet," *In Their Own Words, Contemporary American Playwrights*. Ed. David Savran. New York: Theatre Communications Group, 1988.
J	"Jolly," *The Old Neighborhood*. New York: Samuel French, 1998.
JAF	*Jafsie and John Henry. Essays*. New York: Free Press, 1999.
LB	*Lakeboat*. New York: Grove Press, 1981.
LUF	"The Luftmensch," *Three Jewish Plays*. New York: Samuel French, Inc., 1987. 35–43.
MA	Karen Kohlhaas, *The Monologue Audition, A Practical Guide for Actors*. Second Edition. New York: Limelight Editions, 2002.
MBT	*Make-Believe Town*. Boston: Little Brown and Co., 1996.
NOA	"The Story of Noach," *Genesis: As it is Written, Contemporary Writers on Our First Stories*. Ed. David Rosenberg. San Francisco: Harper, 1996. 59–62.
ODF	*On Directing Film*. New York: Viking, 1991.
OL	*Oleanna*. New York: Vintage, 1992.
ON	*The Old Neighborhood*. New York: Samuel French, 1998.
OR	*The Old Religion*. New York: The Free Press, 1997.

PHA	Melissa Bruder, et al. A *Practical Handbook for the Actor*. Introd. David Mamet. New York: Vintage, 1986.
ROM	*Romance*. New York: Vintage Books, 2005.
SF	*Some Freaks*. New York: Viking, 1989.
SH	*The Shawl* in *The Shawl* and *Prairie de Chien*. New York: Grove, 1985.
SM	*State and Main*. London: Methuen, 2001.
SMA	Sanford Meisner and Dennis Longwell, *Sanford Meisner On Acting*. New York: Vintage, 1987.
SNK	*South of the Northeast Kingdom*. Washington: National Geographic, 2002.
SP	*Speed-the-Plow*. New York: Grove Press, 1988.
SPC	*Sexual Perversity in Chicago* in David Mamet, *Sexual Perversity in Chicago* and *The Duck Variations*. New York: Grove Press, 1978.
SPR	*The Spanish Prisoner* in *The Spanish Prisoner, The Winslow Boy*. New York: Vintage, 1998.
SQ	*Squirrels*. New York: Samuel French, Inc., 1974.
TF	*True and False, Heresy and Common Sense for the Actor*. 1997. New York: Vintage, 1999.
THR	*Three Uses of the Knife, On the Nature and Purpose of Drama*. New York: Columbia Univ. Press, 1998.
TOO	Richard Christiansen, *A Theatre of Our Own, A History and A Memoir of 1,001 Nights in Chicago*. Forward Brian Dennehy. Evanston, IL: Northwestern UP, 2004.
UV	*Uncle Vanya*. Anton Chekhov, *Uncle Vanya*, Adapted by David Mamet from a literal translation by Vlada Chernomordik. New York: Grove Press, 1989.
VIL	*The Village*. New York: Little Brown, 1994.
W	*The Woods*. New York: Grove Press, 1979.
WB	*The Winslow Boy* in *The Spanish Prisoner, The Winslow Boy*. New York: Vintage, 1999.
WE	*The Water Engine* in *The Water Engine and Mr. Happiness*. New York: Grove Press, 1978.
WIL	*Wilson, A Consideration of the Sources*. Woodstock, N.Y.: Overlook Press, 2000.
WR	*Writing in Restaurants*. New York: Viking Penguin, 1986.
WS	*The Wicked Son, Anti-Semitism, Self-Hatred, and The Jews*. New York: Schocken Books, 2006.
YLC	Richard Christiansen, "The Young Lion of Chicago Theater," *Chicago Tribune Magazine* (July 11, 1982): 8–19.

ACKNOWLEDGMENTS

Many have contributed to this project, beginning with David Mamet, whose curiosity and generosity allowed me to study his life and career. I am especially grateful for his patience and invitation to join him and Rebecca Pidgeon at Ohr HaTorah Synagogue on a sunny Southern California Shabbat. Leslie Kane, the most informed of Mamet scholars, has from the beginning been remarkably generous in sharing with me her knowledge of Mamet's work. Through her scholarly approach to Mamet's plays and films, and groundbreaking and extensive study of his Jewishness, she has established a high standard of research and accuracy. What began as a professional association has become a valued friendship. Richard Christiansen, the distinguished former drama critic of the *Chicago Tribune*, has been unfailingly gracious in answering queries and sharing time with me. His knowledge of Chicago theatre history is as impressive as it is thorough.

In New York, Gregory Mosher has been immensely helpful, ensuring that I get the story right, whether it dealt with the Chicago or New York years of Mamet's career. His clarity sharpened my often obscure sight of theatre events. Glenn Horowitz and his wife Tracey Jackson assisted with long-distance encouragement and news of the New York theatre scene, while Vicky Bijour, my agent, was supportive throughout what must have seemed a lengthy process. Similar thanks are due to my patient editor, Farideh Koohi-Kamali. Two other editors aided at earlier stages: Michael Earley, then of Methuen, and Michael Flamini, now at St. Martin's. Their keen interest started me on the path that led backstage, as well as to front-of-house.

At the Theatre Collection in the Special Collections Division of the Chicago Public Library, located at the Harold Washington Library Center, Sarah V. Welshman displayed extraordinary and expert assistance during my frequent and likely disruptive visits. Not only did she graciously accommodate her hours to aid a distant traveler, but located important material in several archives that made my research time both efficient and enjoyable. Constance J. Gordon, also of the Theatre Collection, offered similar help and a biting sense of humor, which prevented me from becoming too serious about Chicago's past, while offering insightful details about Chicago's theatrical present. Morag Walsh and Lorna Donley also provided welcomed assistance. Glenn E. Humphreys, also of Special Collections, repeatedly shared with me his extensive knowledge of the Theatre Collection, even while rushing for a plane at O'Hare.

At the Goodman Theatre, Chicago, Robert Falls, artistic director, was remarkably generous in providing details of his long association with Mamet and the challenges of directing *A Life in the Theatre.* His grasp of the evolution of the Chicago theatre world, past and present, was immensely useful. Denise Garraty, publicity director of the Goodman, and her staff kindly tolerated repeated requests and queries with a smile, and I thank them. Others in Chicago who helped begin with Mike and Julie Nussbaum for showing me the "real" Chicago and correcting my confusion over the location of the Hotel Lincoln. Mike Nussbaum, distinguished Chicago actor, displayed a profound knowledge of Mamet's career, from his earliest attempts at acting to his first efforts at playwriting. Recalling his roles in early productions of *American Buffalo* and *Glengarry Glen Ross,* as well as later stagings including the world premieres of *A Life in the Theatre* and *The Shawl,* Nussbaum provided remarkable insights that made him an outstanding, as well as debonair, resource.

Linda Kimbrough, actor and Mamet friend for almost thirty years, provided critical details of his acting method and the early days of the St. Nicholas Theatre Company. Richard Pettengill, former dramaturge of the Goodman, offered information on the theatre's activities and, most importantly, the world of Hyde Park. Dominic V. Saracino, director of communications at the Francis W. Parker School, was another willing "researcher" who enthusiastically shared with me the school's history and philosophy. Chris Jones, current drama critic of the *Chicago Tribune,* was also an important resource, as was the staff of the Newberry Library, Chicago.

William H. Macy sat with me on the set of *American Buffalo* at the Atlantic Theatre and addressed Mamet's acting technique and approach to directing. Rabbi Lawrence Kushner sat with me in his San Francisco home patiently explaining the nuances of Torah study and what it meant to write a book with Mamet. Pam Susemiehl, Mamet's assistant, sat with me via the computer to answer a variety of questions. Rabbi Ronald Weiss of Wellesley, Massachusetts, formerly from Chicago's South Side, cleared up any confusions I had about Reform Jewish life in that city, while Naomi Landes and her husband, Rabbi Landes, provided further details about Jewish history in Chicago. Abe Sacks of Vancouver, originally from Chicago, was also instrumental in getting me to think more fully of the Jewish experience on the South Side in general and on Maxwell Street in particular.

Robert Brustein and the staff of American Repertory Theatre, Cambridge, Massachusetts were of great assistance, Brustein taking time to speak to me at a critical period of transition for the theatre. Also to be thanked are Harold Baldridge and Richard Pinter of the Neighborhood Playhouse School of The Theatre in New York, who shared with me their experience with the Meisner method and process of becoming an actor. I was allowed to meet students and staff and tour the space, which was extremely valuable, and I thank them for their encouragement. Neil Pepe, artistic director of the Atlantic Theater, graciously allowed me to attend a rehearsal of *Romance* and then elaborated on Mamet's career as a playwright, while rapidly devouring a sandwich before rushing into the theatre for that night's preview. He also permitted me to visit the Atlantic Theatre's theatre school and discuss Practical Aesthetics with students and faculty.

Pati Cockram, also of New York, kindly took a seat at Mamet and Ricky Jay's "Two Hussies" performance and provided me with details, while often answering sometimes arcane questions about New York street addresses. Harriet Voyt, Mamet's former assistant, and Will Hamlin, at one time Mamet's English professor at Goddard, were also helpful. Carey Perloff, artistic director of the American Conservatory Theatre, San Francisco, was also generous in allowing me access to press and other materials related to their productions of Mamet. The press and archival staff of Lincoln Center, New York and at the National Theatre, London, are also to be thanked. Stephanie Wilson, publicist at Pantheon/Schocken Books was also instrumental in my research.

Others who helped in various ways include the late agent Howard Rosenstone, of Rosenstone/Wenders Agency, New York, who discussed aspects of Mamet's career with me at an early stage in the project; the staff of the River Run Café, Plainfield, Vermont, for insights into the rural life and cuisine of Vermont; and David and Janice Sauer, who have prepared what is now the most up-to-date research and production source book of Mamet's work. Joan Sibley of the Ransom Humanities Research Center in Austin, Texas, new home of the Mamet archive, was also helpful at a late stage of the project.

Academic colleagues whose ideas on Mamet have been challenging as well as insightful include Chris Hudgins, Steven Price, Sherrill Grace, and Jerry Wasserman. I especially want to thank Wendy Moffatt, who alerted me to Pierce Bounds and Jim Lartin-Drake of Dickinson College. Both provided me with wonderful insights to Mamet at Goddard College and the early productions of his plays. I am also grateful to Pierce Bounds for sharing with me photographs of early Mamet productions at Goddard. Jennifer Forhan and Kelly Graham were outstanding research assistants who constantly turned up new leads and forgotten articles, while David Lemon made it possible to complete the book in the wonderful seaside setting of Boundary Bay.

My son Ryan, then in Jerusalem, offered not only encouragement from afar but was able to supply me with details about Mamet's 2002 visit there and was, earlier, an able theatre companion for the premiere of *Romance* at the Atlantic Theatre in New York. Dara, my daughter, became an astute critic, asking such incisive questions as "Shouldn't you be done by now?" The support, patience, and insight of Anne MacKenzie made the completion of this project both possible and pleasurable. Her sense of style has been, and remains, a special quality.

The University of British Columbia and the Social Sciences Humanities Research Council of Canada have both generously contributed support to this project and I am grateful. Of course, any errors remain my own, resisting Chekhov's advice to a would-be biographer: "if you haven't the facts, substitute lyricism."

IRA NADEL

INTRODUCTION

This book shamelessly borrows its title from David Mamet's 1977 comedy, *A Life in the Theatre*. A parody and celebration of the theatre, the play spotlights the egos, jealousies, and camaraderie of two actors, one old, one young, as they perform. It's theatre history and theatre practice tightly presented in twenty-six short scenes revealing careers under strain and underway. It is Mamet's acknowledgement of what the theatre can give and take, its rewards and punishments. And it summarizes his own forty-year love affair with drama.

The subtitle to this biography, however, is misleading. While it summarizes his commitment to the theatre world, it discounts his efforts in other genres. A striking feature of Mamet's long career is his success with forms outside the theatre, while never really leaving it. His work—whether in screenwriting, film directing, television, or teaching—continually encompasses the theatrical arts. His film work, for example, draws from the acting principles and directorial practice that have defined his theatrical achievements. But no single genre nor format can satisfy his artistic restlessness. Consequently, Mamet explores a series of forms, whether children's stories, fiction, essays, or, most recently, cartoons. The challenge is to balance artistic clarity with moral honesty, which occasionally requires the use of the con. Mamet's artistic diversity is not so much the evolution of an aesthetic as the need to try something new, one of the themes of this narrative.

Another theme is competition. Mamet's world is cut-throat, whether among actors, thieves, or salesmen. They battle each other to get on top, and undermine each other to survive. Driven by the American dream of success, defined most often in materialist terms, his characters turn to sinister behavior: theft, violence, abuse, and secrecy. Whether on the professional level of businessmen or on the personal level of the family, competition destroys trust, self-confidence and intimacy. In this world, triumph can immediately turn to defeat. Elliptical and broken talk struggles for meaning. "All that I'm telling you, it's not always so clear what's going on," Teach explains to Don in *American Buffalo*, summarizing Mamet's world (AB 74).

Mamet is artistically direct but personally oblique, a paradox that may be at the center of his life. From his characters and actors, he demands a brutal honesty, yet he persists in maintaining a wall around himself. His plays are, and are not, autobiographical. He resists revealing himself to interviewers, critics, and even biographers, encouraging them to interpret his works to suggest, if not infer, biographical connections. This condition may be the irony at the heart of Mamet, the contradiction between an aesthetic drive for clarity and a determination to obscure, if not hide, his past.

One artistic explanation for this behavior is his celebration of the minimal. What looks like obscurity is a form of lucidity; leaving out is more valuable than putting in. Robert's request to John in *A Life in the Theatre* that he "*do* less" on stage epitomizes the approach (ALT 41). Mamet first learned this when studying music, being told at one point to leave out the third (the third step in the octave) and concentrate on the missing tone. One hears it anyway, as a musical producer later explained. This equaled a tip from a hustler-instructor Mamet knew at Bensinger's pool hall in Chicago: "If you can see more, *don't shoot*." This is central to Mamet's aesthetic, expressed in this question, "How much can one remove and still have the composition be intelligible?" A history of minimalist drama then follows: "Chekhov removed the plot. Pinter, elaborating, removed the history, the narration; Beckett, the characterization. We hear it anyway." The last sentence is the key. We elaborate, predict, or estimate naturally. Good writers get better "only by learning to *cut*" (ODF xv); "omission is a form of creation."[1]

Mamet demands that his characters be up-front with each other, requiring from them no nonsense, no crap, no misunderstandings. Their acts should be immediate and decisive, even if their language falters. "Action talks and bullshit walks," Donny warns Bobby in *American Buffalo*, announcing a Mamet doctrine (AB 3–4). The writing itself must be pared down and clear at the expense of even the essential. Mamet, impatient and self-assured, prefers action to thought: "Be strong, direct and brave, do not be introspective," he told the opening night cast of *The Water Engine*: "Continue to create rather than interpret."[2]

"Good drama," he believes, "has no stage directions" (ibid). Such directness is, of course, disturbing both for his characters and his audience. Hence, the need to deceive and the reliance on the con. As Joey, an associate of the con man Mike, tells Margaret Ford in *House of Games* when she realizes she was to be conned out of her money, "It's the American Way" (HG 25). Lying in this world is no more than "a gift for fiction" Walt, the director, tells Joe, the writer, in Mamet's film *State and Main* (SM 15). Mamet, himself, never doubted his ability to sustain such a world, whether in theatre or film. According to the actor Joe Mantegna, "Confidence is not one of the things David lacks."[3]

Mamet partly learned this self-assuredness in Chicago, the embodiment of industry and aggression, work and crime. With its history of labor and manufacture, from Pullman railway cars to its meat-packing plants, Chicago's respect for work is unassailable. Accompanying it is the city's "low bullshit tolerance." As a result, "you work a little harder because it's not easy." The only way "to exist is by success" (Man 251). But with this success comes an attitude: "Where am I 'from'? I'm from the United States of kiss my *ass*" Mike declares in *House of Games* (HG 21).

The neighborhoods, voices, and style of Chicago run through Mamet's work as deeply as does London for Dickens or Dublin for Joyce. Mamet's language, characterizations and settings in his drama and film *are* Chicago, from *Sexual Perversity in Chicago*, *American Buffalo*, and *Glengarry Glen Ross* to *House of Games*, *The Untouchables*, and *Homicide*. All find their source in the birthplace of Walt Disney and Gwendolyn Brooks, Edgar Rice Burroughs and Benny Goodman. It was also the home of Harriet Monroe's modernist journal, *Poetry* (Ezra Pound, foreign editor) and *Playboy*, edited by Hugh Hefner. Such incongruities appealed to Mamet, a man who is South Side street-smart *and* well-read.

Mamet presents himself as an average Joe *and* an intellectual. His favorite hat for years was a crumpled baseball cap with "Twelfth Night" written on the front. He will say "ain't" in one sentence and quote Tolstoy in the next. Writing for him is a craft, a job that demands daily practice, discipline, and determination, something Chicagoans understand and respect. Writing is being on the job, commitment the test of a man's character. As he likes to repeat, "Writing is my trade," as though he were making tables or hunting-knives (YLC 11). Writing produces something tangible, but if you're stuck on a play, you turn to an essay, or a novel, or a children's story. It's work and he doesn't stop. The pursuit is not fame or even fortune but to make the writing itself better, to improve and to produce. His work ethic is strong.

Chicago reflected this attitude toward theatre, conceiving of it as "popular entertainment. It was very close to blue-collar amusement, like going to see the Cubs," Mamet recalled. The theatre was both a spectacle and a show and rarely thought of as intellectual as it was in New York. It showed actors at work, doing their best at what they knew how to do. Mamet put on plays, "and if people were pleased, that meant that we didn't have to drive a cab the next week 'cause we could put on another play."[4]

Similarly, playwriting, like acting, is no mystery for Mamet. It emanates out of the Chicago tradition of "writing as a legitimate day-to-day skill, like bricklaying. . . . you need a script. Well, hell, figure out how to write one" (AOT 64). Start by writing dialogue and if you "write enough of it and let it flow enough you'll probably come across something that will give you a key as to structure" (AOT 68).

The other source of the directness that identifies Mamet's work was his family. It was competitive and filled with friction. His father demanded performances each night at the dinner table, the children having to not only speak clearly about their activities but defend them. His mother displayed an intemperate attitude toward anything that did not conform to her wishes. The parents ganged up on Mamet and his sister, Lynn, denying them the security that would come from stability. The parents' divorce in 1959 only led to greater difficulties and a determination on Mamet's part to be honest and frank in expression and emotion. The pain of secrecy was too great.

While Chicago taught Mamet to be pragmatic, he first began to learn this lesson at home, where life was a constant challenge to defend himself from a father who insisted on word games at the dinner table and a mother who could not understand his impulse to dramatize so much of his life. The con was often his only means of survival against the intimidation and threats his parents posed. Later, he would learn its finer points through poker, gambling, and life in the Chicago demimonde, but initially it was an instinctive form of domestic preservation. Ironically, he could be both a street-wise kid and the son of a middle-class family. Later in his writings, the street-tough style would mix with the bohemian. The con, however, suited his purposes, since it allowed him entry into a series of illegitimate worlds otherwise limited or closed.

The home was his first schoolhouse. There, existence increasingly depended on the language of decoy if not deception. At an early age, he understood that language could be a joy and a weapon: "In my family there was always a large premium on being able to express yourself—if only for purposes of chicanery." Early success as a confidence man even tempted Mamet to take up a life of illegal behavior. Without irony he writes, "I do not know how I escaped becoming a criminal" at the opening of his essay collection *Jafsie and John Henry*.[5] He once told the critic John Lahr that if he hadn't found the theatre, "it's very likely I would have become a criminal"—although this, too, might be a con (FM 79).

After his parents divorced in the spring of 1959—Mamet was eleven—he left, with his mother, the ethnic South Side for the colorless and newly minted suburb of Olympia Fields, but in 1962, at fifteen, he moved back to live with his father in the more sophisticated, or at least urban, North Side. There, he learned to meet challenges with action as much as with ideas. The necessity of this Chicago-style self-reliance informed his later remarks that New York writers focus on "What does life mean?" while Chicago writers respond with, "Who the hell cares" and ask instead, "What do you do?" Even more directly, they enquire, "What's going on here?"

This later became his formula for playwriting, expressed as a series of direct questions: "'Who wants what from whom? What happens if they don't get it? Why now?'"[6] Learning to live on the margin, Mamet found compromise with the environment useless: "our lives are a fierce attempt to find an aspect of the world that is not open to interpretation," he claimed (WR 74). The need is to live honestly, not falsely. Correspondingly, Mamet's plays are highly taut and intense dialogues that on the surface seem banal. Underneath, however, there is an intense struggle of meaning and emotion, not unlike Chekhov: conversations that seem ordinary, simple exchanges have a subtext of power and urgency underneath the stammering and repetition.

"Mametspeak" is the name some journalists have coined to describe his dialogue.[7] The rhythm, cadences, and syntax are of the street, as is the vocabulary, often corruptions in aid of clarity. The obscenities and vulgarities in his plays are not there to shock but to communicate reality, reworked through Mamet's "filter." "Dead hard sound" is his characterization of Chicago speech, he once explained: "It's a very harsh song. Chicago has always been a writer's town and perhaps because there was no room for euphemism." Mamet embodies Sherwood Anderson's remark that "for a long time I have believed that crudity is an inevitable quality in the production of a really significant present-day American literature."[8]

Collectively the Chicago writers taught Mamet "the Midwestern tone" which he describes as "very legato," offering an interesting, geographical definition of this musical term: "Perhaps the rhythm of the mid-western seasons—a long, impossibly cold winter, then a long, impossibly hot summer. It was a vast, impossibly big lake, a huge sea of wheat. It has that same rhythm, the same legato rhythm, moved on like that. Things were going to unfold in their own time, kind of like a French movie, except not quite that drawn out (AOT 60)." Ironically, while Mamet appreciated this style, smooth and connected between successive notes, he also reacted against it. His writing is the opposite: a staccato, allegro style bordering on the presto, an accelerating style with explosive repetitions, incomplete statements, and abrupt, broken phrasing.

"Mametspeak" leads to "Mametude," another journalistic term defining the disregard, disrespect and deceit expressed by his tough characters. Richard Roma in *Glengarry Glen Ross*, Bobby Gould in *Speed-the-Plow*, and even Anna in *Boston Marriage* have it. But Mamet is aware of the falsity of such journalist labels, citing another of his heroes, the American-born sociologist/economist Thorstein Veblen, who said that the more jargon and technical language involved in an endeavor, the more we may assume the endeavor is "make believe" (WR 5). Distrust is the defining Mamet attitude.

Mamet loves the arcane talk of Mametspeak, whether the language of shooters, card sharks, or magicians. The secret language of professionals and of specialized work draws Mamet in. "The codes mean to me that something of surpassing interest was in progress" he writes, showing his own membership in such a group through his use of the specialized language of knives. At one point in a discussion of the virtue of knives, he writes, "something was being done up to the Green River which . . . exists nowhere but on the ricasso, between the hilt and the choil" (MBT 5). The Chicago style is harsh because it does not tolerate evasion. Chicago audiences are, in turn, difficult to fool; they want things to be on the level, to hear things straight (Case 29).

But if language is agency, in Mamet's hands, it is also formality. His characters speak in an orchestrated, syncopated style of statement and counterstatement. Beyond the unruly subject matter is order and structure. An Edwardian gentleman lurks within Mamet, displayed not only in the elevated register of his personal conversation and expressed in his love of Kipling and earlier nineteenth century writers, but in the prescribed grace and well-made aspect of his plays. Mamet likes shape and he constructs works that show his craft. His admiration of Aristotle, who repeatedly emphasizes completeness as well as order, is no surprise.

Mamet's characters may have bad manners, but they are still manners. This duality—the slang and obscenity expressed formally and rhetorically—exhibits the way speech camouflages one's secret self, encouraging suspicion. The serious moralist knowingly confronts a deceptive world defined by trickery or the con. Nonetheless, through their language, victims sound, or attempt to sound, like heroes. Examples range from Teach (*American Buffalo*) and Margaret Ford (*House of Games*) to Leo Frank (*The Old Religion*) and Arthur Winslow (*The Winslow Boy*). Not surprisingly, this originates in Mamet's own abused childhood, the parents constantly threatening and on occasion physically harming the children, revealed in his essay collection *The Cabin*, and his play *The Cryptogram*.

One way to outwit victimization, however, is the con, an American tradition. Mamet uses the con to structure his plays and films. He repeatedly opens a play with a dubious action that deliberately obscures the real action. The audience is thus set on edge. When Teach enters *American Buffalo* with his litany of "Fuckin Ruthie" repeated five times, we have no way of explaining his anger. His sixth "Fuckin Ruthie" is a coda to his explosive entrance, the cause of which we learn of only later. Anna and Claire at the opening of *Boston Marriage* similarly deceive not only the audience but each other: they enter in Act I discussing the address and decor of the house they are in as if they were unacquainted, and later, in the play's central plot, conspire like two criminals to mislead a gentleman friend. The very title of Mamet's film *The Spanish Prisoner* refers to a confidence game and opens with an equally deceptive scene. As the character Susan in the film reminds the other characters and the viewers, "You never know who anyone is."[9]

Mamet is himself a confidence man, tricking, misleading, and confusing interviewers as much as audiences—in this way shielding himself and keeping a protective distance from outsiders. It is a form of defense, aggressive and powerful, allowing one to manipulate, if not control, a situation. The con is Mamet's way of keeping everyone both at bay and on guard, as he demonstrates in many interviews in which his questioners are at a loss at Mamet's non-answers. Yet, he knows he's acting "badly," as he confessed to one interviewer *after* he sabotaged a public interview held at the Chicago Institute of Fine Art in the nineties. This is his means of deflecting questions he doesn't want to answer while at the same time accepting his public responsibility to appear before audiences.

The ultimate confidence man is the writer who builds a world of illusion from actual experience, as the two writers in Mamet's *Squirrels* or the producers in *Speed-the-Plow* illustrate. In *The Shawl*, Mamet unexpectedly reveals the tricks of the confidence man, as the older John shares with the younger Charles the techniques of deception. In *Glengarry Glen Ross*, each salesman is a confidence man; Richard Roma's initial scene with James Lingk, one of the finest in contemporary drama, shows the overmastering skill of such figures. Mixing self-confidence with an independent morality and no fear of loss, Roma presents Lingk with "an *opportunity*" and proceeds to show him the brochure on Glengarry Highlands in Florida (GGR 49). Roma then warms up: "look *here*: what is this? This is a piece of land. Listen to what I'm going to tell you now." At that point, the first act ends. We know Lingk is hooked and do not need to see him reeled in (GGR 51). As

Shelley Levene announced earlier in the play, "Our job is to *sell.* I'm the *man* to sell" (GGR 19).

As a con artist, Mamet carefully discriminates between the meaning of words. When Aaronow suggests selling leads to Jerry Graff, Moss assures the nervous Aaronow that they were just "talking" about it. Moss replies they were just "*speaking* about it. (Pause). (Pause). As an idea," not an actual robbery (GGR 39). This gets more complicated, however, as Moss pressures Aaronow to go in and steal the leads, saying he, Moss, can't because he made the deal. He then tells Aaronow that he's already an accessory—because he listened (GGR 46).

Confidence men are highly educated artists who succeed in part because of the dishonesty of their victims, as David Maurer explains in his study *The Big Con.* They operate by first establishing trust and belief in their own integrity. Next, they bring into play irresistible temptations to excite the victim and expand the cupidity of the mark. The lust for profit within the mark then grows until the final trick is pulled.[10] Not surprisingly, Mamet's confidence men are talkers, although some trip over their own ideas and plans.

Mamet's films expand the con: *House of Games, The Spanish Prisoner, Wag the Dog, Heist,* and *Spartan* all concern deception and deflection. Even his play *Faustus* focuses on promises made but not kept, expressed through the Magus, who makes false bargains. In Mamet, morality itself is tenuous as Richard Roma explains. His amoral manifesto is seductive, explaining to Lingk that he deals with things that happen to him on a day-to-day basis: "I say *this* is how we must act. I do those things which seem correct to me *today.* I trust myself" (GGR 49).

Despite the central role of the con in his work, Mamet's acting theory emphasizes the opposite: honest expression of the text. "Just say the words" is Mamet's mantra. Unemotional acting is his goal. This in part may relate to a so-called Chicago acting style, described by Gregory Mosher, former artistic director of the Goodman Theatre in Chicago, as "simple and emotional and without being indulgent. It's never about wearing emotion on your sleeve. It's about getting on with the play." Furthermore, it leaves a lot to the audience's imagination: it's not that one does a play on a bare stage but that "the audience fills it in. They actually do the work."[11]

The honesty and directness Mamet champions comes about, as well, from his Judaism, which is similarly aggressive. He rejects the attitude of the assimilated Jew in favor of that of the tough Jew, the *shtarker.* This is the Jew as fighter, aggressive and in- your-face, as he shows with his character Marty Rossen, film producer in *State and Main.* Confronting the chiseling town councilor, Doug, Rossen exclaims, "There's an old saying, two scariest things in the world, a black man with a knife and a Jew with a lawyer. Now, I am a lawyer and I am *The Jew*. . . . Look in my eyes: I made eleven million bucks last year and I don't like being trifled with" (SM 85).[12] He, like Mamet, does not take "no" for an answer, although he (and Mamet) realize they will always remain outsiders (WR 73).

The definition of Jewish identity has been the catalyst for a number of Mamet's plays and essays, from his early "The Disappearance of the Jews," through his essay collection of 2006, *The Wicked Son*. This began in 1975 with *Marranos*, his play about the failed attempt of Jews to "pass" as non-Jews in sixteenth century Spain. He opposes the idea of assimilation because it's a con that never works, and must be renounced as Jews must reject their "state of being the underdog. . . . We Jews give ourselves a vast amount of bad press" he has lamented.[13] Through his understanding of the Torah and Jewish theology, outlined in *Five Cities of Refuge* and *The Wicked Son*, he roots himself in Jewish texts and laws, finding a natural home in rabbinical debate.

Mamet's belief in the tough Jew originated, again, in Chicago. His labor lawyer father dealt daily with union organizers and enforcers, many of them Jewish, and Mamet admitted that he has always been "drawn to determined people, to people who have something so say" (Kun). By his thirties, Mamet renounced the idea of the disappearing Jew. His rediscovered Judaism renewed his confidence and power to take on anti-Semitism and intolerance. His Jewish characters still struggled with their identity, as Bobby Gold in *Homicide* illustrates, but not Mamet himself. His macho aggressiveness, once expressed through guns, hunting, and gambling, shifted to a strident mixing of Jewish bravado with heroism based on a knowledge of Jewish texts and interpretation. Believing that the world hates the Jews, he counterpunches (WS 4ff). This unites the tradition of the fearless Chicago street kid with a Judaism of purpose and strength.

Mamet's successful TV series *The Unit* blends his interest in the macho world of guns, gambling, and the military with the aggressive Jew. The show is a curious summation of the macho line, with the tough Jew theme expressed through a figure equivalent to the marginality of the Jew: the black, represented by the Unit leader, Jonas Blane, played by the imposing Dennis Haysbert. In the series, institutionalized and approved violence, although covert and unacknowledged, goes on daily under the deception that the group is a logistical studies outfit. It's like the new Jew: present, active, and by necessity antagonistic, but often forced to hide his hand or identity until it's needed.

Mamet's work has not always been admired. Critics alternate between praise and condemnation. In the early days, he was understood in New York as a comic writer, but in Chicago as a serious dramatist. Later work has alternately been vilified as foul and obscene and praised as profound and honest. Critics seem divided, although never indifferent.[14]

Mamet's love affair with language, however, always wins him admiration. His attachment is not surprising given that he actually took on the role of Johannes Gutenberg. At Montreal's Expo '67, Mamet played Gutenberg at the West German pavilion, dressed in a leather apron and running a replica Gutenberg press. He produced black-letter facsimiles of Gutenberg's bible and "shrugged distractedly in response to questions in many tongues" (CA 29). The image is apt: Mamet the actor/author/printer conning the public, while absorbed by his work and committed to creating, appropriately, new texts.

Mamet both loves and fears language. He values its rhythms, its poetry, its sounds but knows it is fundamentally untrustworthy. He's suspicious of its effect, something he learned from the changeable atmosphere and intense response of his family to his own statements, reaffirmed through his own enactment of the con, especially during the time he spent selling questionable real estate from a North Side Chicago office. Sophisticated, complex, and elaborate words were dangerous; better were the clear, simple, one-or-two syllable statements that conveyed more than they said. And, better yet, the reality of doing rather than the mystique of just saying. Action is not questionable; action is the completion of language.

Attention to language is what Mamet has called "'the deep, down, dirty secret of dramatic writing'": "'it's poetry, dramatic poetry. That's what makes a play work, in addition to the plot. As Lewis Carroll said, 'Take care of the sounds, and the sense will take care of itself.'" [15] Language navigates our way and challenges the often deceptive practices of the world. And when it works in his plays, it is because the language "is so direct that the actual rhythm of the line carries the intention of the speaker."[16] Mamet's goal is to make the minimal expressive.

But writing, despite the plethora of essays, plays, books, and stories, does not come naturally to Mamet. "Frankly, I don't feel I have a lot of talent for it, but I love doing it and have a certain amount of hard-won technical ability" (AOT 73). It's a form of building rather than creating, if the latter implies a constant imaginative power at work. He derives a great sense of accomplishment from being able to complete a project. Robert Falls, current artistic director of the Goodman Theatre in Chicago, goes so far as to claim the workplace as the most palpable through-line in Mamet's work. He adds, "work is a trade. You learn from the people who do it. It doesn't matter if you're making a chair or a play. There's no art in it. [Mamet's] learned the craft. He embraces that."[17]

Yet Mamet is parsimonious with words, marshalling language sparingly to achieve its greatest effect. Hemingway, he believes, had the key: "'Tell the story, take out the good lines, and see if it still works' which I find the best advice I ever heard about writing." Mamet echoes this view when he states that good writing is pared down, removing "the ornamental, the descriptive and *especially* the deeply felt and meaningful" (MBT 90; ODF xiv-xv).[18] This minimalist aesthetic duplicates his principles of acting, which stress the immediate: If one just says the words, the emotion will follow. As Mamet's influential drama teacher Sanford Meisner, founder of the Neighborhood Theatre Playhouse in New York, would repeat, "the foundation of acting is the reality of doing" (SMA 16). Mamet's goal is to translate desire "into clean action" (WR 20).

Mamet is unambivalent about what makes a successful play. It is a work that is simple, direct, and clear and follows a set of well-defined steps: drafting, "cutting, building to a climax, leaving out exposition and always progressing toward the single goal of the protagonist," which is often expressed in constant awareness of the through-line by the actor (AOT 57). "To get into the scene late and to get out early is to demonstrate respect for your audience" he adds (ODF 64). Many of his plays begin in medias res. When *American Buffalo* opens, Donny and Bobby are talking about an event that already occurred. When *Glengarry Glen Ross* begins, Shelley Levene has already lost the good leads to the other salesmen.

Mamet is nothing if not prolific. At sixty, he has written some thirty-five plays, three novels, eleven collections of essays, several children's stories, a book of poems and nearly thirty film scripts he has either originated or revised. He is perhaps the first *American* playwright to successfully crack the screenwriting trade, paralleling Britain's Harold Pinter and Tom Stoppard. More recently, he's taken on TV. Some, however, see this promiscuous relationship with the arts as diluting his creative energy. But Mamet has always operated on multiple levels, which *A Life in the Theatre* earlier dramatized.

Mamet is keenly aware of what theatre can reveal, although he rarely permits self-exposure on any personal level. He protects his private life partly because he believes "biography makes rotten drama" and partly because he distrusts it (Case 29). People get things wrong. Facts go astray. Events are forgotten. But at the end of his newest collection, *Bambi vs. Godzilla*, he addresses the artistic responsibility of biography, explaining that it is difficult to "engross the audience . . . as the end is known. It calls for greater skill and imagination on the part of the writer in finding an *internal* story within the generally known historical moment" (BVG 209–10). This is not quite a call for psychoanalysis but the need to identify inner stages of development that unite outward events. Del, in *The Cryptogram*, remarks that "in reality, things unfold" but they must be united at a deeper level (CRP 16). The aim of this account is to align the outer story of Mamet's life with the inner, while not losing sight of his primary rule for good writing: telling the audience "WHAT HAPPENS NEXT" (WR 76).

1

CITY OF FACT

The city of feeling rose out of the city of fact like a definite composition—beautiful because the rest was blotted out.

—Willa Cather, *Lucy Gayheart*

East Hyde Park Boulevard runs west from the Chicago lakefront, bordering the neighborhood of Hyde Park. In 1893, the World's Columbian Exposition in nearby Jackson Park rejuvenated the neighborhood. The Midway Plaisance, at right angles to the White City (the exposition's popular name because of its white painted neoclassical buildings), offered a broad, mile-long avenue. It contained exhibits and amusements, including George Ferris' towering attraction, the first Ferris wheel. The Plaisance would soon become the central green space of another new addition to the area, the University of Chicago. Seven blocks south of East Hyde Park Boulevard at fifty-eight and Woodlawn was Frank Lloyd Wright's modernist Robie House, completed in 1910. Rising at Hyde Park and Greenwood was Congregation Isaiah Israel, built in 1923–24, the imposing Byzantine structure topped with a smoke stack in the style of a minaret.

The White City upgraded the neighborhood, attracting hotels, trains, and new businesses. An artists' colony settled at fifty-seventh and Stony Island in a group of concession stand storefronts left over from the Exposition. The Palace of Fine Arts became the Field Museum of Natural History and then the Museum of Science and Industry. Hyde Park also became a literary neighborhood, as it filled with writers partly drawn by the new university. At the corner of fifty-sixth and Hyde Park Boulevard South was the Windermere House Hotel, where Edna Ferber lived with her mother. Saul Bellow later settled in the area Philip Roth and Richard Stern would celebrate in *Letting Go* and *Natural Shocks*.

Nine-twenty-eight East Hyde Park Boulevard became the home of David Alan Mamet, born on November 30, 1947.[1] His parents, Bernard Morris Mamet and Lenore June Mamet (nee Silver) had married in New York on December 28, 1943, and four years later had their first child, a son. When Mamet was two, in 1949, they decided to move west to 2918 Western Avenue in the newer community of Park Forest where Lynn Mamet was born on January 9, 1951. In 1952, they returned to the South Shore, moving to 6947 Euclid Avenue, where Mamet, then five, would spend his adolescence. The parents were children of Polish/Russian Jews who immigrated to the United States after the pogroms of 1906.[2] Mamet's unproduced screenplay *Russian-Poland* engages this history and old country traditions. His maternal grandparents came from Warsaw, on his father's side from Hrubieszow, a village on the Bugg River near the Russian-Polish border.

When his maternal grandmother took him shopping on Chicago's Seventy-first Street in their Jackson Park Highlands neighborhood, part of the South Shore, a young Mamet would hear Yiddish, Polish, or Russian spoken to friends and shopkeepers (CA 125; DMB 8). This was not entirely surprising since there were more than 20,000 Jews speaking different languages in the South Shore and approximately a dozen synagogues. Jewish schools and community centers were common. Although tracks of the Illinois Central railway ran down the center of the road, Seventy-first Street was home to Jewish butcher shops, bakeries, and delicatessens. At Seventy-first and Phillips was a large youth center sponsored by the Young Men's Jewish Council and two Conservative synagogues.

On his mother's side, the family made money in real estate and insurance, although his maternal grandfather, Naphtali, originally sold underwear. He became a traveling salesman and a great storyteller much admired by his grandson (DMC 140). Mamet's paternal grandparents arrived in 1921, likely from Luck, Poland, as recorded at Ellis Island. Mamet's father, Bernard, was born "right off the boat" and raised during the Depression. Bernard's family had little money and brought nothing from the *shtetl* except a soon-to-be-despised language, Yiddish. Bernard's father, however, left his wife, Calara (Mamet would name his third daughter, Clara, after her), who then had to bring up the family by herself. The poverty transformed the son, Bernard (Bernie), into a driven man: he put himself through Wilson Junior College and "bluffed" his way into Northwestern Law School using a forged transcript. He ended up first in his class, edited the law review, and was inducted into their legal honor society. After graduation, he worked for the law firm then headed by Arthur Goldberg, who would become a Supreme Court Justice and then U.N. Ambassador. At the time, the firm represented the United Steel Workers Union and later the AFL-CIO.

Having been poor, Bernie Mamet wanted to be rich. He worked hard as a labor lawyer, and at one point he represented three hundred unions including the Motion Picture Film Editors Union, the Piano and Musical Workers Union, the Bricklayers Union, and the Laboratory Technicians and Camera Repairmen. He once represented 3500 employees of the Argonne National Laboratory in a pension fight against the University of Chicago.

A handsome man, Bernie Mamet was strong-willed, principled, and a good negotiator. Mamet recalled his father's advice that to conserve good feelings at the bargaining table, it was important "to express a negative concept in a positive form: 'not meaningful' rather than 'meaningless'" (BVG 8). Mamet would later try to follow this process, especially when dealing with moviemaking and studio executives. But Bernie Mamet was also something of a showman. In a 1959 court battle over the right to picket in Marion county, Indiana, he was found in contempt, with bond for the contempt citation set at $50,000. He paid it in $1 bills, delivered in an armored truck surrounded by publicity. He successfully argued a case at the U. S. Supreme Court, averted a strike between two photographers unions and NASA, and defused a violent strike at an Illinois cement plant in La Salle, where he represented Local 657 of the Allied Industrial Workers of America. "He was a *shtarker*, a fighter" Mamet has said, and his powerful will to succeed was inherited by his son.[3]

Mamet's sympathy for the underdog and working stiffs derives in part from his father's identity with a world Mamet saw firsthand. Occasionally, when Bernie went to visit a union leader, the young Mamet would go along, observing the talk, attitudes, and mannerisms of these working men. The family was "comfortably middle class" but Bernie Mamet was conscious of "the fear of poverty," which he shared with his family (SNK 105). At one point in the mid-fifties, having made some money, Bernie Mamet lost a good deal of it in the stock market. But he remained driven: "It was not enough to try hard and do very good work for clients. His job, he said, was to win," his son said about his prominent and successful father.[4]

The Mamets lived in a three-story red-brick house on Euclid when they settled in the South Shore section of Chicago, one block west of Jeffrey Boulevard, the main north south thoroughfare. Mamet's essay "Seventy First and Jeffrey" in *The Cabin* recalls life in the neighborhood. Importantly, as he explains, the area from seventy-first north to Jackson Park was a Jewish neighborhood. He went to Parkside Elementary on South East End Avenue, four blocks west of his home on Euclid, and remembered fistfights, days at the local movie theatres watching cartoons, and enjoying chocolate phosphates with his father at Rosenblum's drugstore soda fountain. With his sister Lynn, born in 1951, he had a rich neighborhood life (see SF 154–57).

The Mamets' home was only a block-and-a-half from the Jeffrey movie theatre, where on Saturday mornings Mamet would take a quarter and spend a good part of the day watching cartoons or staring at the large, blue, dimly lit dome set into the theatre's ceiling (CA 127). The Hamilton, slightly to the east, was another favorite. Fistfights at elementary school were relatively common. And although his parents did not encourage his talents, literary or otherwise, Mamet did begin piano lessons at a four. His first teacher was an Austrian, Isadore Buchalter. However, he became thoroughly frustrated because, as he later discovered, he couldn't see the notes. Literally. He was myopic and needed glasses which he began to wear at age eight but by then he had quit the piano. At sixteen, he restarted his piano study with Louise Gould who taught him triads with the octave. He quickly learned the cycle of fifths during his weekly visits to the Fine Arts Building on Michigan Avenue (WR 70). He also began to read music. With his earlier teacher, he only learned to play, falteringly, by ear but he later attributed his ear for dialogue to his teen-age piano lessons, which gave him a feel for the musicality of speech. He continued to play piano throughout high school.[5]

Judaism, a minor part of his growing up, became a major part of Mamet's adult psyche. The family's home on Euclid Avenue was adjacent to the second-largest Jewish area in the city but the parents sought an assimilated life, separated from at least the outward signs of the old Jewish world. The paradox was notable: surrounded by Jewish life, they sought to deny or at least diminish it. Their synagogue was Temple Sinai, one of the most liberal Reform synagogues in America, located at fifty-fourth and the lake. The congregation practiced what was called "classical" Reform Judaism, holding its main service on Sunday. Critics referred to Temple Sinai as Saint Sinai by the Sea. Support of social progress, however, was a congregational concern.

Such freethinking, however, led to complications when it came time for Mamet's Bar Mitzvah. Reform synagogues in Chicago at the time did not generally offer confirmation, but Bernie Mamet wanted one for his son. It thus became a secret, hidden, almost shameful act. He hired a private tutor and held the Bar Mitzvah in a private room. Only the father, son, daughter, and teacher were present. Mamet's mother did not know of it, nor did his grandmother Calara, with whom he was close and from whom he learned Yiddish. The Bar Mitzvah, when it occurred in November 1960, was a private affair. Mamet would later recall that "in 1960, I was bar mitzvahed. Nothing much else of importance happened to me until 1963," when he began to work backstage at Second City (SF 102).

Judaism to the Mamet family was trouble and best overlooked. The mother never defended the children when they were subject to neighborhood abuse, anti-Semitic remarks, or name-calling. Despite obvious bruises and cuts on her children, Lee Mamet denied that such things ever happened. It was Mamet, alone, who protected his sister from such taunts, instilling in him the need for self-defense. But if the mother "betrayed" the children, so did the father in not supporting or even acknowledging his son's artistic talent and increasing success. In 1975 at the opening night party of *American Buffalo* in Chicago, for example, Bernie Mamet went around castigating his son, the play, and the producers.

Disagreements between the father and son would sometimes mean silence: on occasion they would refuse to speak to each other for months. Until Mamet won the Pulitzer Prize in 1984, Bernie Mamet considered his son's writing merely dabbling. Then he stopped criticizing and late in life they reconciled. Mamet even found a small part for his father as Marv in his 1991 film *Homicide*. He died several months later.

As a labor lawyer, Bernie Mamet was constantly aware of workers' conditions and exploitation. He put in long hours at his law office at 327 S. LaSalle in downtown Chicago, working continuously to secure his situation, always feeling under pressure. The strong, upwardly mobile aspirations of the parents also meant demands on the children to succeed. Bernie Mamet never let them forget how the disadvantaged had to struggle and rely only on themselves to succeed. He expected the same determination and success from his son. He was demanding, even at the dinner table, where he nightly harangued his children's lack of language skills. "The prevailing attitude," Lynn Mamet explained, "was that if you could not express yourself correctly, you were dead meat. My father put an almost pathological emphasis on semantics. . . . There was a best word for everything and God help you if you didn't use it."[6]

Growing up, Mamet went through various exercises instituted by his father to improve his awareness of language. He learned complex children's rhymes from a recording produced by the International Society for Semantics that his father often played. Mamet in middle age still remembered a number of them, and his father insisted that one of the rhymes about a duckling's weather report was the inspiration for *The Duck Variations* (YLC 11).[7] But, his sister says, Mamet did not see the motivation for the father's behavior as pure. Rather, he saw it as "a statement that life is horrible and you better be good at something." The absence of love from his parents alternately explains Mamet's bottled-up anger and his equally powerful affection toward his own children supplementally expressed in the children's plays and books he has written (Freedman 46).

As friction between the handsome Bernie and darkly attractive Lee grew, it was often translated into constant criticism of the children. "You are not living up to your potential" was a frequent complaint. Soon, a debilitating competitiveness defined home life. Lee was a schoolteacher with a quick temper and sharp tongue. Her anger could ignite at any moment, but at other times she would be consoling and caring. To her daughter Lynn she once said, "if only I could have had a pretty daughter"; to her son she said, "I love you but I don't like you" (FM 73). She often played tricks with language and meaning, likely resulting in Mamet's persistent quest for verbal certainty in the theatre, compensation for a childhood of linguistic and emotional evasiveness. The confusions of the young boy, John, in *The Cryptogram* reflect this frustration: he cannot make himself seen, heard, or understood by his self-involved mother. His suicidal tendencies go unnoticed and he is almost never touched in the play. Mamet's parents were similarly undemonstrative, although Mamet has defended them by explaining that they had children when they were in their early twenties and didn't really know how to parent.

As a result of this disaffection, Mamet and his sister became, and remain, close, a reaction to the alienation they felt from their parents. Mamet ironically expressed this when he answered the critic John Lahr's question, was he an only child? "Yes, except for my sister" he said, emphasizing both their isolation and unity (FM 73). Brother and sister bonded as they lived through what Lynn Mamet called "an emotional hurricane," a reference to the unstable emotions of the mother and the anger of the father (FM 73). The resulting volatility led to Mamet's protectiveness of his sister and aggressive self-preservation.

"Jolly," a Mamet play inspired by a lengthy phone call to his sister Lynn during the filming of *Homicide*, indirectly expresses some of the conflicts his sister had with their parents. The failure of the play's parents to love her and her brother spills out in a late speech: "If they had *loved* us. Mightn't they have *known* what we might want? I know what *my* kids want. (*pause*). I know what *my* kids want. It's not that difficult. It's Just Not. I'm sorry" (J 45). When asked by her brother Bob in the play how she's getting on, Jolly answers "We're (*pause*) Hey, what the fuck are you going to expect. From the Sort of a Background That We Come From. It's a miracle that we can Wind our Watch" (J 50).

Dreaming of her mother knocking on the door of her house, the besieged Jolly finally opens it "and there is *Mom*, with this *expression* on her face . . . (*pause*) And she wants to kill me" (J 56). Despite the rejection and censure by her mother, Jolly becomes the solid caregiver for her own children. An unproduced later work by Lynn Mamet, "The Lost Years" (ca. 1996), elaborates some of these dysfunctional issues transferred to the marriage of the male figure in the play, Andrew. One of the recurring themes in the play is that no gesture of love is ever enough.[8] When Andrew asks for kindness, he's told, "you *get* kindness. . . . You just refuse to *accept* it" (LY 17). As the marriage breaks up, the wife claims that Andrew "allowed himself" to be persecuted by his parents and did nothing to prevent it (LY 38).

"Suffice it to say we are not the victims of a happy childhood" Lynn Mamet said in an interview. The greatest violence was "emotional terrorism," she added, in graphic language: "in my estimation we are survivors of a travel route that included a 1950's version of Dachau and Bergen-Belson, and that we both still bear the numbers on our arms. In that sense when [Mamet] writes, he wears short sleeves."

Their outlook toward their parents differed, however. For the most part, Mamet loved and admired their father, who died in 1991, but his sister did not. She, on the other hand, has forgiven her stepfather, Bernard Kleiman, while her brother has not. It doesn't matter who they single out: "there was a devil, and as a result we will never run out of stories. The very thing that could have destroyed us and driven us to silence ultimately led us to open our veins on white bond and make a living."[9] Both children could never escape from the burden of trying to please apparently unappeasable adults and had difficulty with the issue of desertion.

Mamet was told by his parents that he wasn't intelligent, despite an early childhood report card that highlighted his talent and forecasts his abilities. Under "Special Aptitude," it notes his "wonderful imagination" for storytelling, remarkable sense of rhythm and "perfect sense of timing," as well as a strong sense of construction. But his parent's dismissal of his abilities resulted in a lack of confidence and poor school performance. He was a low achiever and by his own admission hardly ever opened a school book. In turn, he was bored by his teachers until he went to the Francis Parker School on the North Side at fifteen. The progressive school, with its student-centered learning, did not assign grades, and he flourished there. Before that time, he took little or no interest in his education, bluffing his way through, rarely studying. His schoolroom was essentially the Chicago Public Library's ornate third floor reading room with its Tiffany-style glass ceiling, and he would often cut school to sit and read in the rotunda of the imposing neoclassical building at the corner of Michigan and Randolph. The city became for him a laboratory in which he studied behavior, action, and language, whether it was at the ballpark or Riverview, a North Side amusement park. There, sex, danger, excitement, and even death occurred—if one believed the apocryphal story of the girl who stood up on the Fireball and was decapitated. Riverview was a "dangerous and thrilling" place, whether it was The Bobs rollercoaster or the Parachute Jump. It was also a carnival where the "fix was in."[10]

Summer was often a time to get out of the city, although his earliest experience of the country was limited to YMCA summer camp on the edge of Lake Michigan but still a kind of paradise for a city kid (CA 51). The highlight was a canoe trip of several days and adventures that meant getting lost, overturning boats in the lake, hikes, and general growing up. Another time, his camp job as a kitchen boy turned out to be not a romantic activity of labor as much as plain hard work, but on his time off he had a chance to read Ayn Rand.

Other youthful memories of Chicago for Mamet include WFMT radio and his favorite radio shows, especially Saturday night's *The Midnight Special*, a program that eclectically united blues, satire, folk, and show tunes. Listening at a friend's home in Hyde Park, he felt connected to what defined Chicago, that tradition of free thought espoused by Thorsten Veblen, Clarence Darrow, Vachel Lindsay, and Theodore Dreiser. Chicagoans *are* the culture, he believed: "it was what the people did and thought and sang." His father use to tell him that New York was "the greatest hick town in the world but here [Chicago] everyone had to figure out everything for themselves." Mamet accepted and celebrated the popular motto of Chicago, "the city that works."

Chicago united the populist and the intellectual, a union that Mamet still praises. It is the citizen's willingness to discuss Nietzsche or Kipling in any bar, and the knowledge that literature is an organic part of the people. Individuality defines its own culture, with the autodidact the ideal, especially when he absorbs the ideas of a "European freethinker" (CA 56). This liberalism, coupled with earlier celebrations of the city's democratic roots—see William Dean Howells or H. L. Mencken on its early life—dominates its literary landscape.[11] Where else, Mamet writes, would the reading out of a phone number on a radio station be like the beginning of a philosophic proposition (CA 57)? Mamet would illustrate this in the phone number scene of *American Buffalo*.

But in contrast to the cultural harmony Mamet sensed in the city, Bernie and Lee Mamet were unhappy for the length of their marriage, as court documents and testimony at their divorce confirmed. "It meant I had a traditionally miserable childhood, which may or may not be part of the kit for chewing the fat as a writer."[12] "Nobody with a happy childhood," Mamet concluded, "ever went into show business" (TF 87).

The hostility and profanity of his plays may in fact originate in the antagonism of the family: "in the days prior to television, we liked to wile away the evenings by making ourselves miserable, solely based on our ability to speak the language viciously."[13] Manipulation, verbal and otherwise, was a way of life, a habit Mamet adopted in many of his prose pieces and on the stage.

After sixteen years of marriage, Lee Mamet filed for divorce on January 7, 1959. According to court documents, the couple had been separated for approximately two weeks, although disagreement and disloyalty had been brewing for some time. The reason given in court papers were two physical incidents involving bodily harm in September and December 1958. In testimony at the divorce hearing held on January 19, 1959, Lee reported running to neighbors in reaction to the incidents. Preceding the hearing, on January 13, 1959, she and her husband signed a settlement agreement giving her custody of the two children in exchange for waiving any present or future claim for alimony. Bernie Mamet agreed, however, to child support until the children reached the age of majority. Lee was also allowed to stay in the house until she chose to leave or change her marital status, Bernie paying all household expenses. She did, however, have to transfer her portion of the title to Bernie Mamet, who granted her all the furniture, including a marble dining room table. He sought only camera and record equipment plus works by three painters he admired.[14] The divorce was officially granted on April 14, 1959. Three days later, Lee Mamet married Bernard Kleiman, a newly divorced, former law associate of Bernie Mamet.

The Old Neighborhood, a trilogy, recalls much of the family hostility. In the three plays that make up the work, "The Disappearance of the Jews" (first produced in 1983), "Jolly" (1997), and "Deeny" (1997), Mamet recreates, through conversation, the Jewish world of the South Shore. The imperfect memories of Bobby, who has left, and Joey, who has stayed, as they try to recollect people and places nevertheless give the audience a tour of Jewish Chicago from the Devon area setting, which he would use in *Glengarry Glen Ross*, to Maxwell and Orchard Streets on the West Side. The play, set between these two old friends, renews rivalries and competitions as the men parry with each other and hide, rather than reveal, their current unhappiness and fear.

When Joey asks Bobby about his wife Laurie, only abuse follows as Bobby admits he never should have married a non-Jew, somehow betraying the code of the neighborhood and the past. But as Bobby tells Joey that he's going to leave her, he worries over his son's Jewish identity. In Mamet's signature, fractured speech, Bobby reveals that even if his son is not formally Jewish because his mother is a non-Jew, he will still suffer from abuse and identification as a Jew (DOJ 15). And a moment later, Bobby shares with Joey Laurie's anti-Semitic remark that "if you've been persecuted so long, eh, you must have brought it on yourself." Joey is incredulous as he repeats the charge: "Wait a second. If we've been oppressed so long we must be doing it." "Yes" is Bobby's reply (DOJ 15).

Mamet's writing may be thought of as mediating between his adversarial home life and his need to establish a secure sense of self. If the former was unstable, the latter was safe because he created it. The coupling of his parents' divorce with the brutal life experienced with the new stepfather resulted in greater determination to establish a world that was under *his*, Mamet's, control. But he also needed support, and this he located, first, in his sister, who encouraged his theatrical efforts, and second, in his acting students, who later became his theatre company at Goddard College and then in Chicago. Even today, Mamet works with a coterie of key actors (Joe Mantegna, Mike Nussbaum, William H. Macy, Patti LuPone, Ricky Jay, Rebecca Pidgeon, and others), an extended theatrical "family." This devoted group have remained with Mamet through the majority of his career. The support, however, is reciprocal, with many actors attributing their success to working with Mamet.

His parents, however, viewed his early dramatic interests with disfavor. Years later, Mamet explained to a reporter his turn to theatre when he said perhaps "I did it because I got bored with the truth or maybe I wanted to be liked."[15] But his father, despite Mamet's evident success in the theatre, would repeatedly ask, "When will this nonsense stop and when will you apply to law school?" Nevertheless, Mamet displayed great self-discipline even as a child. When he was eleven, he felt that his sister, whom he nicknamed "Tuna" because she was always doodling pictures of fish, was reading too many Nancy Drew mysteries and handed her Steinbeck's *Red Pony*. He then locked her in her room until she read it. He would even return her letters, edited (Freedman 50).

Discipline would take another form: punctuality, especially when he was teaching. Both William H. Macy and Steve Schachter recount stories of Mamet's anger at students who arrived late. Macy recalled that if you were one second late for Mamet's acting class at Goddard in 1971–72, he threw you out. Other times, he charged the students money for every late minute (and then burned it in front of them after he collected it). This, he suggested, demonstrated his devotion to art, which he required others to share.[16]

Shortly after the divorce was granted in April 1959, Lee moved out of the house, taking the kids. She quickly married Bernie Kleiman and they resettled in the suburbs. Mamet and his sister learned about the marriage only afterwards, when they came back from a trip to Florida with their own father. To his mother's question about his weekend, Mamet answered, "OK, how was yours?" "We got married" was the reply. Mamet answered, "So what else is new?' and went into the other room (FM 74).

The impact of the divorce was devastating: "it was a very traumatic time. You know it was the—they got divorced in the 50's, and I didn't know anybody who'd been divorced, let alone have it happen to my family" Mamet admitted in 1994.[17] Life, made up of facts, now overturned the fictions that he had valued.

Mamet and his sister had by then moved into a new family home in the suburb of Olympia Fields, twenty-two miles south of Chicago on the edge of a cornfield. The house was the builder's model home, which, with signs throughout announcing all the modern conveniences, was something like a bizarre stage set. Most lots were empty, most streets mud. Even the school they went to was new and still under construction. It was disorienting: "We were in school in an uncompleted building in the midst of a mud field in the midst of a cornfield" (CA 5). Mamet would call this "New South Hell" and sought to sustain familial bonds by spending time with his paternal grandmother: "She was from the shtetl. Real simple, real loving. She adored me and I adored her" (Freedman 42). He would also spend weekends exploring Chicago, sometimes sleeping out in Jackson Park.

The new situation was difficult. When Mamet's sister would not finish her dinner the night she was to play the lead in the school play—she was too nervous to eat—her mother insisted she clean her plate. When she didn't, Lee telephoned the drama teacher and told him her daughter would be unable to perform. She was being punished and kept home because she did not eat her food (CA 6). The impulsive stepfather would often smash the glass kitchen tabletop in anger. On one occasion when Lynn was in the house with her maternal grandfather and parents, she heard a noise and went down to her parents' room for comfort, only to find her stepfather crying, her grandfather on the bed, and her mother in a fetal position on the floor of a closet. Her stepfather was saying, "Say the words. Just say the words. . . . Just say you love her." At that point, the mother moaned louder and the grandfather said, "I can't." Stepping into the room to somehow better understand the situation, Lynn Mamet caught the attention of the stepfather, who, when he saw her, picked up a hairbrush from a dresser as he walked past it and hit her in the face and then slammed the door on her. She continued to hear the words, "Jack, say the words" (CA 7).

Most Sunday evenings, the stepfather would end the evening by beating Mamet's sister for some infraction. Angry after dropping his own kids back at their mother's house, he would find some reason to slap or hit or beat Lynn. Only at the mother's funeral in August 1984 did Lynn learn from an aunt that her grandfather, a traveling salesman, would return and revel in the fiction that Mamet's mother was disobedient and had to be beaten. Every Friday night his first question to his wife on his return was, "What has she done this week . . . ?" Hearing the report, a good deal of it imagined, the grandfather regularly hit her. On one occasion, when the account of Mamet's grandmother was incomplete or inadequate, before she could finish, he grabbed Mamet's mother by the back of the neck and threw her down the stairs (CA 8–9). Domestic violence, it seemed, was inescapable.

On another occasion, when Mamet's sister actually proved the stepfather wrong, he burst into her bedroom where she was studying, battered the book she was reading out of her hand, picked her up, and threw her against a wall where she struck the back of her neck on a shelf. Despite her pain, she was forced to go to school the next morning. She protested that she could not walk because of the pain. But she dressed and made her way to school, where she fainted. X-rays taken some twenty years later showed that she had cracked her vertebrae when she was thrown against the shelf (CA 9).

Going out to dinner was not much better: it often ended with either Mamet or his sister Lynn being banished from the restaurant and told to wait in the car. Happier trips ended with a joke: the stepfather and mother would tell the children to wait at the restaurant entrance while they got the car. They would then drive up, open the passenger door and wait until Mamet and his sister tried to enter and then drive fifteen or twenty feet away, with the children running after. The event would then be repeated. Sometimes, the parents would drive around the block. By then, all would be laughing at what was thought to be a family joke.

Mamet and his sister had the serious responsibility of caring for the lawn. Raking was a task Mamet particularly loathed. One day he got angry and threw the rake at his sister, who was trying to help. It hit her in the face and cut her lip badly. Blood gushed as they ran into the house and to the kitchen where the mother was cooking dinner. Neither would tell her what happened, Mamet out of guilt, Lynn out of concern for the punishment she knew he would receive. The mother, however, made it clear that until one or the other answered they would not go to the hospital—so the family sat down to dinner where Lynn clutched a napkin to her face while blood soaked through and ran down to her food, which she had to eat. Mamet also ate; the two then cleared the table and went to the hospital (CA 11). Mamet would later explain his life in the theatre as a working out and response to these troubling situations.

In the nuclear family home, Mamet unhappily remembered a constant effort to expunge tradition. "Nothing old in the house. No color in the house" (FM 73). The past was to be hidden or invented but never re-lived. In *True and False, Heresy and Common Sense for the Actor*, Mamet wrote, "there is no character. There are only lines upon a page." (TF 18) The same could be said about Mamet: there is no past for him, only events without emotion. The reason for such an erasure is that the past can imperil the present. In his early unpublished play *Marranos* (1975), he explores the very uncertainty and danger of identity as the past entraps the characters, born Jewish, who are living a counterfeit life as non-Jews. The past, reconstructed by others, becomes a new and dangerous reality.

Mamet remembered the walks home from Rich Central High School in Olympia Fields in frigid weather, one side of the road a cornfield, the other, suburbia. Despite its proximity to the city, the development was also part of the prairie. It was a liminal space that could have held beauty; instead, it held terror. At high school, however, he did a great deal of reading, in particular Sinclair Lewis, reading all of his novels (MBT 87). His other favorites, which he would locate at the main branch of the Chicago Public Library, included Elliott Merrick (author of *True North, Northern Nurse*, and the short stories in *The Long Crossing*), Theodore Dreiser, Willa Cather, Sherwood Anderson, and B. Traven (a Chicagoan).

Recalling his early reading, Mamet praised Dreiser and Cather as "the Two Greatest American Writers" because they seem to affect an American style and voice (MBT 88; IDM 86). For Mamet, Dreiser was the quintessential Midwestern writer who faced the city and its challenges and in 1925 wrote what Mamet unabashedly calls "the Great American Novel," *An American Tragedy* (MBT 90). Clyde Griffiths' determination to move up socially meant murder, which Mamet believes is "the tragedy of America: that violence takes precedence over love" (MBT 91). Mamet was long attached to Dreiser's work, later preparing thirty pages of notes for a screenplay of *Sister Carrie*, although it remained unproduced.

In Willa Cather, Mamet saw a Chicago of romantic and artistic possibilities. Through *Lucy Gayheart*, the story of a young piano student who comes to study in Chicago, he found passages that matched his own excitement: "Lucy carried in her mind a very individual map of Chicago: a blur of smoke and wind and noise, with flashes of blue water and certain clear outlines rising from the confusion; a high building on Michigan Avenue where Sebastian had his studio—the stretch of park where he sometimes walked in the afternoon."[18]

A fiercely musical novel that combines Chicago with passion, *Lucy Gayheart* naturally appealed to Mamet. Schubert, Mendelssohn, and Debussy enter and exit easily, as do opera and *leider*. But more important, the city reflects the mood of the hero, who substitutes romantic infatuation and a determination not to return home for her dull, small-town life. She hopes to love Sebastian (despite his wife), but is shattered when she learns of his tragic drowning on Lake Como, an echo of the death of Roberta Alden (Clyde's pregnant girlfriend) in *An American Tragedy* (LG 141–2).

Frontier fiction was another of Mamet's passions, the northwest as found in Cather's *My Antonia* and *O Pioneers!*, Rölvaag's *Giants in the Earth*, and Frederick Philip Grove's *Settlers of the March* and *In Search of America*. The literature of the Eastern United States Mamet found too effete, preferring Sinclair Lewis to F. Scott Fitzgerald: "I am not interested in Art, nor in Fitzgerald's wish to be liked and accepted. . . . The novel of the East is, to me, too pretty . . . I prefer to read about survival" (MBT 88–89). For Mamet, it's Jack London, not Edith Wharton; in fact, his 1979 play *Lone Canoe* originates in London's 1902 short story, "In The Forests of the North." Novels and stories of struggle are his preference, works in the second generation of writers who came to Chicago like Saul Bellow's *Augie March*, Philip Roth's *Letting Go*, and Albert Halper's *The Chute*. In his cherished novels of the North, there is no waiting until the final act to see the knife used: it's applied in every scene (MBT 89–90).

The summer he was fourteen, after a series of flare-ups with his mother and stepfather, Mamet left to live with his father on the North Side of Chicago at 3750 N. Lake Shore Drive. Offered a large and airy room, he chose the much smaller maid's quarters near the back door, perhaps because it made escape easier. That fall he began to attend the progressive Francis W. Parker school, while pursuing an incipient career in the theatre.

The father-son relationship would remain competitive and fractious with long periods of alienation and occasional moments of pleasure. The father's remarriage and the presence of two stepbrothers, Tony (to become an actor with parts in the films *Homicide* and *Lakeboat*), and Bobby (a serious jazz trumpeter), did not occasion a rapprochement. However, when Mamet spent a year in New York at acting school and worked in the evenings at the Off-Broadway hit *The Fantasticks*, his father came to visit. One evening, Mamet recalled, they enjoyed jazz at the Top of the Gate. But such moments were rare. On one return visit to Chicago from college, he decided to see his father at his office but stood outside his door for nearly half an hour without knocking. After deliberating, he turned and walked away.

Only at the end of the father's life did Mamet reconcile with him, and his death in 1991 from cancer at sixty-eight was cause for heartbreak. At his funeral, after the other mourners ritually threw dirt on the coffin, Mamet emotionally grabbed the shovel from the gravedigger to finish the job. He worked furiously for forty minutes in the hot sun. This, his friends understood, was an act of concluding the job, and fulfilling the Jewish practice of the living burying the dead to acknowledge the universal return to the earth. Mamet shoveled relentlessly, until his friend Jonathan Katz signaled "enough already." But afterward, Mamet would always preface any reference to his father with the Hebrew phrase *Olav'sholem*, "of blessed memory," an expression of honor.

At the time of his move to the North Side, Mamet began to pursue an interest in the theatre as a child actor. His uncle, Henry H. Mamet, was chair of the Broadcast Committee of the Chicago Board of Rabbis, responsible for instructional radio and TV shows.[19] With his sister Lynn, Mamet began to play Jewish children on radio and TV broadcasts, an early opportunity for dramatic presentation.

Yiddish theatre provided another early if indirect introduction to Chicago drama for Mamet. Long an entertainment tradition in the city, the first Yiddish theatre company in Chicago formed in 1887, led by the young Boris Thomashefsky. Yiddish theatres grew ostensibly in the Maxwell Street area, and just before World War I, there were ten Yiddish vaudeville houses. Most plays they performed were based on the writings of Yiddish literary giants like Sholem Aleichem or Sholem Asch, but other productions showcased translations of plays by Chekhov, Schiller, Molière, Wilde, and even Shakespeare. *Der Yiddisher Kainag Lear* was a popular hit.[20]

Mamet himself knows Yiddish and would incorporate its inflections and speech patterns in *The Duck Variations* and in the Yiddish expressions used by the producer in his film *State and Main*. He'll also occasionally use Yiddish expressions in interviews. Discussing his film *The Winslow Boy*, he told an interviewer that if he were staging the play, he would likely make cuts as "they used to say in the Yiddish theatre 'fartaytsht un farbesert' which means 'as translated and improved by.'" In 1991 he narrated a documentary entitled *Yiddish Cinema*. At dinner with Saul Bellow in 2002, he and Bellow and Rebecca Pidgeon exchanged verses of various Yiddish songs, Mamet later recounting the evening through every Yiddish nuance. Indirect but nevertheless present, Yiddish and the Yiddish theatre in Chicago has had a presence in Mamet's theatre and film world.[21]

Another powerful element of Chicago for Mamet was its self-image as a city of invention and innovation. The Century of Progress World's Fair held in 1933–34 was the expression of the inventive and the modern for Chicago and the country, symbolizing the nation's power and potential. His own collection of memorabilia from the exposition—a commemorative button from the fair sits on a corkboard in his Vermont writing cabin—recreates an engagement with the event, duplicated in the "chop" or stamp he uses on his correspondence (CA 48). It reproduces the Century of Progress symbol, the earth embraced by a swirling modernist band of stars that reaches out to the universe, a futuristic ribbon of light with "DAVID MAMET / Chicago" printed below. It expresses a streamlined modernity with a futuristic tinge.

Mamet explains the importance of the Century of Progress exposition in an essay from *The Cabin*. Referring to the employee badge he has over his desk, he writes that the fair was "the most recent elaboration of the final subjugation of the material world. This was the apotheosis of the notion of technology as grace" (CA 155). Progress replaced duty as the new goal, which the fair and Chicago represented, repeating a view originally proposed about the World's Columbian Exposition of 1893, which introduced a series of new products—from early moving pictures to an automatic dishwasher, the first zipper, and a new organizational tool, the vertical file.[22]

Mamet's Chicago is a city of work. It is a city of districts and jobs: "factories out in Cicero or down in Blue Island—the Inland Steel plant in East Chicago." Driving a cab, selling carpets, cleaning offices, working as a busboy—Mamet worked all of them (see CA 31). Reading Dreiser, Frank Norris, and Sherwood Anderson made him realize that the bourgeoisie was "not the first subject of literature" (CA 31). He wanted to escape what he felt was literarily an unworthy (or at least unliterary) middle-class life. He wanted to shed the Nice Jewish Boy label (CA 31). When he would take the train into town from the South Shore, he and his buddies would hang out in the city crawling over girders of the unfinished Prudential building or head over to Jackson Park to walk among the caryatids, thirty feet off the ground, at the Museum of Science and Industry at fifty-seventh and Lake Shore Drive. They would haunt the downtown public library with its floor of glass bricks. When he was by himself, he'd spend the day in the city shoplifting. As an older adolescent living in the city with his father on the North Side, he would sometimes dress in a sport coat and tie and walk down in the evening to the hotels, find an empty ballroom and sit in the dark playing the piano (JJH 6–7).

The underside of Chicago also appealed to Mamet: Wabash Avenue under the El rather than flashy Michigan Avenue. Wabash, always in the shadow of the El and always noisy, was strictly business (CA 109). From the vantage point of the fourth floor of Marshall Fields, where there was a stuffed Kodiak bear and the gun department, he loved to watch the EL (CA 110). He also remembered it thundering outside the practice studios at Lyon and Healy's where he used to while away hours in a small piano room always on the Wabash side. (CA 111). He loved not only Lyon and Healy's music store but Abercrombie and Fitch, where he made his first major sporting purchase: a #5 Randall bird and trout knife for $55, the kind that Francis Gary Powers was carrying when his U2 spy plane was shot down over the Soviet Union. Wabash Avenue "had the weight of serious romantic endeavors—hunting, music, dress, reading" (CA 112). In the area, he also got his first credit card—from Kroch's and Brentano's bookstore. He was seventeen and discovered literature in their basement paperback section and the contemporary writing section on the first floor (CA 112). He was also schooled in tobacco at Iwan Ries tobacco store. Merchants on Wabash were "glad to see you smoke, glad to see you enjoy yourself" (CA113).

Nelson Algren in his prose poem *Chicago, City on the Make* (1951) clearly expresses the city's pull for Mamet. Contrasting the cocktail lounge culture of New York or the culture of supplication in Hollywood, Chicago was where literature was "bred by hard times on the river, hard times on the range and hard times in the town." It's a place where the tough little guys make "verbal music out of abuse and loss," which Mamet would duplicate in *American Buffalo* (Stern 103). The city is robust and less academic, precious or mandarin than New York. Chicago is an attitude, not just a place, expressed by Oak Park's Hemingway, when he said that being from Chicago meant having "a good crap-detector."[23]

The Chicago style mixes a survivor's cynicism and a streak of sentimentality without obliterating honest feelings. A writer in Chicago is not in the center of a national literary culture but is on its margins "not by absorbing the national tradition but by pretending to know nothing of it." Mamet, as he repeatedly states, feels like an outsider, the result of being a Jew, a writer, and a Chicago author: "But the question," he emphasizes, "is not how to get into the country club. The question is 'what's going on here?'"[24]

When Mamet moved to the North Side to be with his father, he also began hanging out and working in the theatre, starting at Bob Sickinger's Hull House Theatre on Broadway. This was becoming an important part of the community or resident theatre tradition of Chicago that later, when Mamet developed the St. Nicholas Theatre Company, became part of the storefront theatre movement, which reused commercial space as theatrical space. Replacing the touring companies that appeared and disappeared in the city, resident companies emerged in the sixties. In Chicago producer Bernard Sahlins and the Studebaker Theatre Company tried it, as did the earlier Chicago Little Theatre founded in 1912. For a number of political, financial, and artistic reasons, Chicago rejected the large arts center idea supported by imported theatre companies. Instead, it chose to grow its theatre culture organically in spaces converted from bowling alleys, laundries, warehouses, and, in the case of Mamet's St. Nicholas Theatre Company of the early seventies, a bakery/print shop. Such enterprises would spring up in centers away from downtown and without big budgets, stars, or facilities.

The opening of Hull House Theatre in 1963 kick-started this revival. The energetic Sickinger, who had already made a name for himself in Philadelphia doing engaging, often new work by young playwrights such as Edward Albee, led this movement. He had no formal training; once, to a choreographer in a Hull House production who asked what he wanted in one scene, he replied, "'if I knew what I wanted, I wouldn't need myself'" (TOO 124). He soon moved into 3212 N. Broadway, the home of Hull House Theatre, a former American Legion post and converted a bowling alley in the building into a 110-seat open stage theatre. A successful fundraiser, he soon held breakfast club meetings, auditions for community theatre actors, and began a series of chamber theatre programs, performing in the homes of the well-to-do.

Performances at Hull House Theatre were held on weekends only, partly because the actor pool was nonprofessional. They had day jobs and could only rehearse at night. Mike Nussbaum, who went on to a more than fifty-year career in the theatre and at 82 is still going strong, was nourished at Hull House but owned and operated a pest extermination business. He, in fact, recalled meeting Mamet, then fourteen years old, at the Belmont and Broadway location. The boy was helping out behind the scenes of Murray Schisgal's comedy *The Typist and the Tiger*, in which Nussbaum was acting. Robert Kidder, another stalwart of the company, was an English teacher in Highland Park.

Word soon got around that this was more than community theatre, as Nussbaum recalled: "We knew something was going on when we didn't know anybody in the audience" (TOO 126). Sickinger's energy was displayed everywhere: from directing to rehearsing, to promoting and greeting the audience at the entrance. He was in the audience almost every night and constantly, no matter what stage of the run, would come backstage after performances with notes. One time an actor, in the last week of a run, asked Sickinger, "why are you still giving notes?" Sickinger replied: "'This is nothing. Once, I gave notes on closing night'" (TOO 127). In encouraging others to see theatre in action, he allowed a young student named David Mamet to work backstage.

Mamet was just discovering theatre, learning its modern history at the back of Carol Stoll's Oak Street Bookshop at 54 E. Oak Street next to the Esquire Theatre between State and Michigan. There, he read mostly Pinter and Beckett in Grove Press paperbacks. Stoll's small, narrow shop, stacked to the ceiling, contained new titles and classics. Stoll oversaw the daily activities and knew most of her clients by name. She and a co-partner managed the shop for twenty-three years, which was, Mamet said, a "shrine to intellectual life."[25] Watching productions at Hull House Theatre supplemented his reading.

This was the center of Mamet's genuine theatrical education. He watched productions of Pinter, Ionesco, Beckett and many others. He saw a director at work, one who would send a props manager to forage through Chicago junk shops to find the right kind of milk bottles used in English homes for a production of Pinter's *The Lover*. And through Sickinger's activities, he grasped what was necessary to make a theatre company thrive: hard work, energy, and commitment. In turn, Sickinger remembered Mamet as "'very bright . . . like a sponge. He absorbed everything. But he wasn't a very good actor'" (TOO 131).

One of Sickinger's most successful productions was *Who'll Save the Plowboy?* by Frank D. Gilroy. This Off-Broadway hit about an embittered urban young man opened the small theatre in 1963 and, according to Richard Christiansen, then a young reporter who went on to become the chief drama critic of the *Chicago Tribune*, it was "a defining moment in Chicago theatre life." The acting was superb, the direction expert, and the performance stunning (TOO 127). Beckett's *Happy Days*, Albee's *Tiny Alice*, and a large production of *The Threepenny Opera* were among the many plays presented. One production was noted for its violence: Venable Herndon's *Until the Monkey Comes*, which centered on a chaotic party in which the apartment setting was destroyed at every performance—anticipating the action in the final scene of Mamet's *American Buffalo*.

By the mid 1960s, Hull House had four branches in Chicago, including, on the North Side, the Leo Lerner Theatre/Uptown Center Hull House at 4520 N. Beacon Street, a home for musicals. Later, the Organic Theatre would use this space as the locale for the June 1974 performance of *Sexual Perversity in Chicago*, Mamet's first hit. A playwrights' unit of Hull House Theatre sought to develop new scripts by local authors, while a children's theatre program came up with polished shows. However, conflicts with the board saw the dismissal of Sickinger in 1969: he was producing too many avant-garde theatre pieces, not what the board thought a social service agency should be doing. Nevertheless, the slightly enlarged space—140 seats—became the venue for a variety of itinerant Off-Loop groups including the St. Nicholas Theatre Company, Steppenwolf, and About Face.

The Second City was Mamet's second theatre school. Friendly with Bernard Sahlins and his family, a youthful Mamet was allowed to hang around the place; later, he worked as a soda jerk and bus boy. He also occasionally played piano for the kids' shows held on weekends (CA 97). Preceding Second City was the Playwrights Theatre Cub operating on LaSalle Street and it was not uncommon for some of the actors to live in the building. Ed Asner, Elaine May, and Mike Nichols were early cast members. Alan Arkin, and Bill Murray, joined later, after second city opened in 1959. Everyone pitched in with scenery, programs, costumes, makeup, clean-up, or box office. There was a dedicated communal spirit, although all were divas of one sort or another, claimed Joyce Piven, actor (TOO 103). In its first incarnation in the early fifties, the troupe performed works commercial theatre would not: dramas by Brecht, Beckett, Schnitzler, T. S. Eliot, and Strindberg. However, it closed in 1955 because it violated a host of Chicago Fire Department regulations.

David Sheperd, an actor/director/playwright who joined the group in 1952, envisioned a new version, however: a cabaret-style theatre that would draw from news events of the day, where a comedian would juice up a basic scenario with a clear plot but without the use of scripted, printed dialogue. After a news segment, there would be a "play," actually eight or ten scenes lasting up to an hour with the actors fleshing out the situation as they went along. The goal was to fashion a new scenario every week with the stories grounded in actual events in the news. After the scenario play, the cast took a break and came back with an improvised scene or sketch based on a character and topic suggested by the audience.

The format proved popular: there were shows five nights a week, three on Saturdays. By the spring of 1956, the company moved to a 250-seat theatre at the Argo Off-Beat Room at 6344 North Broadway on Chicago's North Side. The "Living News" segment ceased and the longer scenario plays were replaced by shorter scenes. By January 1957, however, the Compass, as the ensemble was called, had ceased performing. It was not pulling in enough customers. In October 1956, Sahlins leased the 1250-seat Studebaker Theatre in the Fine Arts Building at 450 S. Michigan Avenue and launched the Studebaker Theatre Company. The hope was to establish a genuine resident theatre in Chicago. Sahlins and several partners secured start-up money and a theatre was underway with a series of noble plays including André Gide's *The Immoralist* and Shaw's *Androcles and the Lion*, as well as Arthur Miller's *The View from the Bridge*. But a series of flops followed, ending with *Waiting for Godot*. Then Bernard Sahlins joined Paul Sills for yet another venture, a cabaret theatre featuring satirical reviews. They converted a former Chinese laundry on Wells Street into their space and opened on December 16, 1959. It was an immediate hit. They named it The Second City and did no advertising. Word of mouth and reviews drove their success. Mamet, too, heard of the enterprise and met Sahlins through some friends of his father and was allowed to drop in and eventually work there.

Improvisation, what today is called theatre sports, was the key. Watching and listening to each other carefully on stage was critical to the actors, something Mamet would witness again when he spent a year at Sanford Meisner's Neighborhood Theatre Playhouse in New York. Several scenes—they were never called sketches or skits—became classic: "Football at the U. of C.," about University of Chicago nerds forming a football team; or the encounter between a giddily repressed young woman and a guitar- strumming beatnik at the Chicago Art Institute, in this instance played by Barbara Harris and Alan Arkin (Patinkin 35). "Peep Show," in which two conventioneers looking for action find it in a bizarre world of fantasy presented to them by a mysterious stranger, was especially comic. The broad format was not unlike that of *Sexual Perversity in Chicago*. These serial comedic sketches, Mamet has said, taught him that life couldn't be quantified; it was funny and sad at the same time, in the manner of Chekhov (Kogan CPL).

The original location of Second City at 1842 N. Wells Street (it relocated to 1616 N. Wells Street in 1967), permitted waitresses to squeeze between small tables to sell drinks before and after the show. Mamet worked there as a teenager, preparing ice cream sodas and bussing in the beer garden one summer. He also ran the projector for the old movie screenings occasionally shown during the day, while watching the talents of such comics as Peter Boyle, David Steinberg, Joan Rivers, and Robert Klein. On occasion, he played piano for children's reviews on the weekends. He also took improv workshops, which later influenced his earliest work, notably *Camel*, written and performed at Goddard, and then *Lakeboat* and *The Duck Variations. Sexual Perversity in Chicago* also incorporates this "cut-up" style of the blackout. The six or seven actors of Second City worked in a small, plain space with a pianist on one side. Shifting around bentwood chairs became the chief form of scene changes. Props were minimal and often imaginary. John Belushi, Fred Willard, and Harold Ramis soon joined the cast.

Mamet learned about theatre from the Second City sketches and improvisations. In 1963, when he was working backstage and heard Fred Willard introduce a scene by saying "Let's take a sleigh ride through the snow-covered forests of Entertainment," he knew he had encountered greatness and at that moment realized that he would not follow his father into law (SF103). And he especially remembered Sahlins warning Belushi not to use the word "fuck" in a skit. Belushi paid no attention to him. A year after it opened, a Second City Revue appeared on live TV and in 1961, the troupe was on Broadway. Stuart Gordon, the director whose Organic Theatre Company would put on the first production of Mamet's *Sexual Perversity in Chicago*, when asked about the essential qualities needed for a Chicago actor, instantly answered, "A sense of humor and a skill in improvisation" (TOO 117). At one point, Second City put on "Sexual Perversity Among the Buffalo," a Mamet satire starring James Belushi, Larry Coven, and Miriam Flynn. Richard Christiansen, writing in the *Chicago Tribune* in 1994, declared that all dates in recent Chicago theatre history can be traced from the birth of Second City. The reason? Second City "thumpingly proved that a resident company, bred in Chicago and an essential part of the local scene could be unique, sleek . . . and a commercially viable form of living theatre" (Patinkin 108).

If he spent his nights at Second City, between 1963 and 1965, Mamet spent his days as a student at the Francis W. Parker School on Chicago's North Side. It was not far from his father's apartment on North Lake Shore Drive. A progressive school founded in 1901 by Anita McCormick Blaine, it embodied the ideas of the educator Francis W. Parker, who believed in an emphasis on character, citizenship, and social motive. The social focus and community development of the school remained, as did student-centered learning. Unlike the traditional curriculum of the Chicago Latin School with its concentration on structured learning with set courses and grades, the Parker had no grades, nor did it follow a prescribed curriculum. It encouraged learning by doing in an effort to instill habits of life-long study. Students learned math, for example, in a grocery store on the "campus"; the Grade 4 students traditionally put on a Greek play attended by the entire school, while the *Odyssey* would be read three times during a student's career at the school.

By the time Mamet enrolled at Francis Parker, it had nearly five hundred students, yet maintained small classes. Flora Cooke, the first principal, outlined several of the basic tenets, the most fundamental being that "a child's play is a child's work."[26] Activity-centered learning, dominated by children's projects, defined the approach. The classrooms did not have fixed desks in rows, but round tables and movable sets of chairs. Her approach to education was democratic. She made the children active participants in their own education, which concentrated on unifying subjects and interrelated topics. Traditional education, by contrast, presented subjects in isolation. Encouraging the experimental and making education relate to life were explicit goals. Mamet sustained this pragmatic approach in his own theories of acting and directing. Learning by doing meant that drama was not just writing but acting, directing, producing or banging together a set. Make education relate to life, make it practical, as Mamet would emphasize in his own theories of acting and directing.

The diverse student body (the Parker school admitted black students as early as 1944), interpersonal learning (students teaching each other), deliberate experimentation, and emphasis on learning as pleasure meant an encouraging, individualistic atmosphere. Mamet flourished. The separation between his classroom work and his after-school work diminished. As one student remarked, school life for students is like "a double-shift work day": after the last class, you don't have to be students any longer; "we can be athletes or actors, socialites or authors" (in Stone 302). The school held daily assemblies, called the Morning Exercise (or Morning Ex), with occasional guest speakers: in 1921, it was Albert Einstein on relativity; Tolstoy's daughter, Carl Sandburg, and even Mamet were later visitors. Drama was an important part of the school program, from the mandatory Grade 4 Greek play, where every student had a part and was costumed appropriately, to the senior class's full productions.

At Francis Parker, Mamet was known for his piano playing and had a starring role in Brecht's *The Threepenny Opera*. There, he also met Alaric Jans, later known as Rokko, soon to become a theatre and film composer who would score many of Mamet's films and who would become involved with Mamet's St. Nicholas Theatre. Mamet also participated in sports, notably wrestling and football (once breaking his nose). He also chaired the Committee of Four, the student disciplinary committee. He was sports editor of the school paper (although he once claimed he'd been full editor [DMC 139]). Under his yearbook picture of a studious young man in tie, v-neck sweater, and tweed jacket with dark glasses in the *Record* of 1965 is a quote from the Nineteenth century novelist Charles Kingsley: "And so make life and that vast forever one grand, sweet song." His achievements and idiosyncrasies were then listed: head of the Committee of Four, "turquoise football helmet . . . the hick . . . *Threepenny Opera* star . . . swingin' piano player . . . turtle necks and a beret . . . Superdoo-keen . . . gymnast . . . Weltschmertz!" Next to these remarks is a smiling self-portrait drawing of Mamet as a teddy bear.

Mamet wrote the yearbook report for the Committee of Four, noting an extensive debate on the issue of free time for independent study, the full committee recommending that there be no "specifically assigned homework" over the holidays.

The motion was passed by the committee and accepted by the faculty, he proudly wrote. Other accomplishments include an "outrageously verbose resolution that homework over election night be suspended (said motion involving A. Lincoln, Francis Parker, and God)" (*Record* 88). Beneath the group photo of the Committee of Four is one of Mamet in sweater and slacks studiously playing the piano. In a comment celebrating the one hundredth anniversary of the school, Mamet remarked that the Parker School "in the early 60's had the finest teachers I have ever encountered" (in Stone [i]).[27]

Drama instruction at the school was particularly important because it taught Mamet that acting must concentrate on the audience, not the actor. To have a socializing effect, drama must depersonalize the actor to focus on the actions of the character. The impact of such movement was to demonstrate the consequence of moral choice. What a character did was the only thing that mattered. The acting methods of Sanford Meisner at the Neighborhood Playhouse, which Marnet would later attend, confirmed this approach which he would further outline in *A Practical Handbook for the Actor* and *True and False.*

Mamet attended another school at this time as well: the 1,550-seat Clark Theatre, a Chicago institution at 11 North Clark at the corner of Clark and Madison. This was an unusual Chicago movie house because it played a different double bill every day. Mamet and friends would attend at various hours throughout the day and night (the theatre opened at 7.30 A.M. and the last feature would begin at 4 A.M.). Parker students were there, it seemed, continuously. The film-obsessed manager, Bruce Trinz, would send out a monthly listing of his double bills under the heading "Hark! The Voice of the Clark!" with his own two-line, often rhyming summaries such as "Marx Brothers at college/ Make farce out of knowledge" for *Horse Feathers.* His double bills were like impromptu seminars on the arcane elements of film. which one day might be two westerns, the next, two dramas, and the next, two foreign thrillers. The neighborhood was one of culture with. the original Blue Note jazz club only a few doors away.

After graduation from Francis Parker, though, Mamet substituted rural life for the city, taking off, like Huck Finn, for the country: Goddard College tucked away in tiny Plainfield, Vermont.

2

SOUTH OF THE NORTHEAST KINGDOM

The Stoics, I believe, would nod in recognition of the Vermont ethic.

Mamet, *South of the Northeast Kingdom*

The Northeast Kingdom refers to the northeast corner of Vermont made up of Caledonia, Essex, and Orleans counties, all of which border Québec. Cabot, Vermont, which Mamet has made his home since the late seventies, is just south of the Northeast Kingdom, which location Mamet used as the title of his 2002 celebration of Vermont. The Green Mountain State has held a special place for Mamet ever since he arrived to attend Goddard College in 1965. His attraction to the independent rural life, combining the taciturn and the direct, immediately appealed to him as an embodiment of the values partially hidden by the tough, urban life of Chicago. "Freedom and Unity" is the state's motto. His attachment to Cabot, a community of about 1,000 founded in 1781 by former members of the Continental Army and now renowned for its cheese, became a fixture in his life after he bought a farm house there in 1978 adjacent to the South Woodbury Cemetery, replete with buried Civil War veterans.

His sketch "In Old Vermont" captures the natural qualities of Vermont that most appeal to him: the sky, the cold, the elemental exposure to the changes in nature. Maud, explaining the virtues of Vermont to Roger, says

All the snow is bright.
The cold protects us.
It can warm us.
In the winter. (GS 181)

In this monologue history and nature are united, something Mamet frequently experienced during his stays in Vermont.

Vermont for Mamet first meant Goddard in Plainfield. Founded in 1863 as Goddard Seminary and reorganized as Goddard College in 1938, it was progressive in the same way as Chicago's Parker School, applying the theories of the Vermont-born educational philosopher John Dewey. Goddard believed that learning by doing was central and initiated student-centered programs led by a participatory government made up of students, faculty, and staff. This body made the major administrative and academic decisions. Crucial to the program was independent study and a lack of emphasis on grades. The focus was on constructing a program of study with a commentary rather than grades for feedback (SNK 98).

The Goddard program culminated in a Senior Study, equivalent to a graduating essay. Most students submitted a journal, although Mamet wrote a play. The principles included the idea that learning is individual, developmental, experimental, experiential, and life-long. Importantly, it is also collaborative, something that the theatre constantly required and that Mamet found, and finds, so satisfying. The idea of a company of actors, begun by Mamet when he returned to teach at Goddard in 1971 and then carried back to Chicago when he started the St. Nicholas Theatre Company, found affirmation at Goddard. The rural campus, set on a former farm, generated a sense of community as students walked on gravel paths amid the dark-shingled buildings from The Manor, the administration building, to the large, Haybarn Theater or classroom building, all wooden, clapboard structures.

In the sixties, Goddard was a loosely run academic experience: students frequently attended class barefoot. Mamet would record his experiences at this "Eden of indulgence" in an essay he titled "Sex Camp" (MBT 25). A narrative of one's academic progress was the extent of an official record. Of course, students reveled in the school's laissez-faire attitude, expressed in a constant focus on self-development. Printed on its 2000 *Alumnae Directory* is the slogan "At the heart of your mind"; "Come to Goddard as you are, leave the way you want to be" is the current (2006) phrase.

Goddard refers to itself on its website as a "small college in rural Vermont for plain living and hard thinking." Mamet remembered it differently, recalling only the hippie freedom, calling it "a counter culture institution, a year-round camp" (CA 31). In a 1989 *Observer* (UK) article, he sarcastically identified it as a "'hippie, radical, drug-infested school for fuck-ups like myself. I didn't study anything there. That sounds like a gross overstatement, but it's not.'"[1] On graduation, he and others felt they were prepared "for no society more exclusive than the criminally bohemian" (MBT 27). But Goddard offered more to Mamet: a chance to explore his theatrical talents.

What became important for Mamet at Goddard was its theatre program under the direction of Goddard's French professor, Pablo Vela. Through his exposure to drama classes and theatrical practice, Mamet discovered a form to contain his imaginative impulses. The program encouraged Mamet to write and direct—and he discovered a series of like-minded individuals who sought similar creative outlets.

At Goddard, his most important influences were the teachers. Will Hamlin taught literature, "English" too limiting a phrase. He taught writing, great books, and criticism. He also ran the literature program and during Mamet's stay there (1965–1969) made sure the principles of progressive education were maintained. The successful fantasy/science fiction writer Piers Anthony recalled writing seminars with Hamlin, who, after twelve minutes or so, would let the students lead. Through Hamlin and others, Goddard attracted several important literary visitors during the sixties, notably Robert Creeley and Charles Olson who read from his *Maximus Poems* and lectured on *Moby Dick*.

Vela was another figure of note for Mamet. Of Mexican descent, the lively and athletic Vela had studied at the Yale Drama School and the National Theatre School of Canada in Montreal, as well as mime and mask techniques in Paris with Jacques Lecoq and improv with Viola Spolin from Chicago, creator of theatre games and author of the important work *Improvisation for the Theatre* (1963). Vela would later go on to collaborate and direct with Meredith Monk. Arriving at Goddard in 1965, Vela brought to the campus and to Mamet an international theatre perspective and a background in movement and improv. He was also the advisor of Mamet's Senior Study, a revue play entitled "The Camel Document," and he acted in Mamet's *Duck Variations* when it was produced at Goddard in 1972.

Another decisive figure for Mamet at Goddard was the dance instructor Mark Ryder, who had studied with Martha Graham and at the Neighborhood Playhouse in New York, where Mamet would spend his junior year. In 1976 Mamet told the *New York Times* that he had done a lot of dance at Goddard and got to know Ryder well. He showed Ryder several plays he had written: "I'd say they don't look like plays to me. He'd say, 'that's not your responsibility, you teach your self to write, write it down and then it's a play. Let your critics worry about that.'"[2] Ryder also believed strongly in the educational philosophy of John Dewey, which involved people in the process as part of educating them to learn by doing.

Mamet's summers were varied. He would return to Chicago to visit, although one summer he worked on an ore boat on the Great Lakes as a steward, a job arranged through his father—and the source of what would become his early play *Lakeboat*. Mamet also looked north to Québec, working and acting in Montreal. In 1965, for example, the seventeen-year-old Mamet worked for several months at a roadside diner in Trois-Rivières, Québec, on the autoroute between Montreal and Québec City. His essay "P.Q." in *The Cabin* describes his experiences and his visit to Montreal for Yom Kippur services. His rejection from a synagogue because he did not have a ticket struck him as one of the more egregious insults of his religion.

His 1967 summer at Expo '67 in Montreal was more successful. At the international exposition, he was an "acro-dancer," a member of the Tibor Rudas Australian Living Screen, part of the Maurice Chevalier extravaganza at the Expo, *Toutes voiles dehors!!!* With others, Mamet would run through strips of a giant screen to bring the projected images alive to the audience. Among his roles, he was an Apache thug emerging from a Parisian street scene. At the conclusion of the show, Mamet and hundreds of others joined Chevalier on stage to sing a finale (CA 27). He loved Expo because it encouraged his sense of imagination and love of acting. Montreal also fascinated him—he rode the new Montreal Metro on its inaugural day and shared an apartment with friends on St. Catherine Street.

During the late sixties Mamet began to read a great deal of drama, noting in a 1987 interview for example, the importance of the Chicago dramatist Lanford Wilson (later co-founder of the Circle Repertory Company in Greenwich Village) and collections of his early plays like *Rimers of Eldritch* and *The Madness of Lady Bright*. A Dell paperback entitled *New Theatre in America* published in 1965 was also important. It included William Hanley's *Mrs. Dally Has a Lover* and Harvey Perr's *Upstairs Sleeping*. He also read work by Murray Schisgal, notably the popular double bill *The Tiger and the Typist* and *Luv*.[3] *Waiting for Godot* was a big influence, as was Pinter's *A Night Out* and *Revue Sketches* and Ionesco's *Rhinoceros* (IOW 135). All were significant plays in the sixties. Tennessee Williams and Arthur Miller would later become touchstones for him as well.

Brecht was also instrumental for Mamet's development, his influence later made clear in Mamet's fable *The Water Engine* and in *Edmond*. Mamet would soon teach his work at Marlboro College and "was fascinated by him," although by 1987 he believed that Brecht's writings about theatre were "balderdash, a direct contradiction of the writing itself," which is entirely involving and absorbing. In some ways Brecht, the theorist, wanted to deny what Brecht, the playwright, was doing. "All of the comics like me always want to be tragedians. I think the same was true of Brecht. . . . His stuff is brilliant," Mamet once stated (IOW 136).

Mamet actually spent only three years at Goddard. For his junior year (1967–68) he went to New York to study at the Neighborhood Playhouse acting school, and working backstage at *The Fantasticks*, produced at the Sullivan Street Playhouse in Greenwich Village.[4] Mamet's year in New York was in many ways revolutionary as he sought the practical experience of acting and theatre life. Through the school and Village theatre scene, he found both. Originally founded as the Neighborhood Theatre in 1915 by Alice and Irene Lewisohn on Grand Street as part of the Henry Street Settlement House on the Lower East Side, the Neighborhood Theatre was an early "off-Broadway" venue offering nonrealistic drama ranging from Hindu and Chassidic classics to works by Shaw, Joyce, and Yeats.

In 1927 it closed but in 1928 the two sisters and Rita Wallach Morgenthau opened the Neighborhood Playhouse School of Theatre with a broadly based mandate to provide professional theatre training. Its building at 340 East Fifty Fourth Street became its home in 1947 and attracted a series of important teachers: Martha Graham, Louis Horst and Laura Elliot—and over the years important graduates: Diane Keaton, Jeff Goldblum, Joanne Woodward, Jo Van Fleet, James Broderick, Robert Duvall, James Caan, Richard Conte, Lorne Greene, Tammy Grimes, Anne Jackson, André Gregory, Steve McQueen, Leslie Nielsen, Gregory Peck, Suzanne Pleshette, Mary Steenburgen, Tony Randall, Eli Wallach, and David Mamet, although in fact he did not complete the program.

Theatre as "an organic expression of life interpreted through the fusion of the arts" was the goal of what became the two year program, shortened to "professional actor training," as outlined in their seventy-fifth anniversary brochure (6). Sanford Meisner, who joined the faculty in 1935 from the Group Theatre, became a catalytic figure. From his studies in classical piano at what became the Julliard School to his training in the Stanislavsky system at the Group Theatre of the 1930s, Meisner brought unusual skills to the Neighborhood Theater. He first taught there from 1934 to 1959 and then from 1964 until his retirement in 1990, with a period in-between as head of talent development at Twentieth Century Fox studios in Hollywood (1959–62). His presence, however, was instrumental in forming the philosophy, approach, and teaching method of the Neighborhood Playhouse. Meisner died in 1997. Most of the staff at the Neighborhood Playhouse at the time were his former students.

The Meisner approach originated in his dissatisfaction with the internalized Stanislavsky method and an expansion of Stella Adler's revision of that method. In the spring of 1934, Stella Adler and Harold Clurman met with Stanislavsky in Paris and spent more than five weeks clarifying elements of his system in the version taught to her by Lee Strasberg. Essentially, Stanislavsky deemphasized the "affective memory" element in this theory, the attempt by the actor to remember the circumstance surrounding an emotion-filled event from his real past in order to stimulate an emotion that he could use on the stage. Adler reported that Stanislavsky now thought the key to true emotion was to be found in a full understanding of the "given circumstances" of the human problems contained in the play itself. This meant dealing with the moment in the text as the new reality, not as a past lived experience.

By 1931, Adler, Harold Clurman, Cheryl Crawford, and Meisner broke from the Theatre Guild to establish the Group Theatre which would influence American acting for the next decade. The twenty-five-year-old Adler was a founding member; Clifford Odets was a less talented actor who would become their in-house playwright. Elia Kazan was another actor in the troupe. In 1938 when the Group Theater took its celebrated production of Odets' *Golden Boy* to London, Meisner had a featured role. The *Times of London* praised the acting, noting that it was at a level not seen in England at the time (in SMA 8). Through a series of listening and repetition exercises, Meisner was beginning to teach students how to live truthfully "under imaginary circumstances" (SMA 136).

The Meisner method began with actors learning how to work off each other in order to establish the honesty that makes the lines convincing and believable. "The text is your greatest enemy" Meisner would tell his students. He did not want them to react to it but to respond to each other (SMA 136). Be yourself, Meisner reiterated. "The foundation of acting is the reality of doing" he would announce in the first moment of the first acting class—and then work with the small group of students to clarify their focus (SMA 24, 16). Mamet studied these techniques and found that the acting exercises paralleled exactly what he had seen at Second City:

eight-minute scenes of definite dramatic quality. His earliest writing—seven-or-eight-minute scenes—imitated this process.

Observation exercises—learning to hear and see—were the first step. However, the observing had to be done by the individual, not the character. Repetition exercises followed to get the actors used to hearing the same lines over and over. "Are you repeating what you hear" and are you repeating it "from your point of view?" Meisner would ask (SMA 22). This word repetition game would be instrumental in defining Mamet's early style in which fractured cadences and overlapping dialogue would become his trademark.

The "as if" technique of particularization—act as if an action were occurring—learned from Stanislavsky was another method Meisner stressed. It brought the actor "*personally* to the emotional place you need to be in for the sake of the scene'" (SMA 138). Particularization aids the actor in finding that action "makes the acting have a point," and renders performance an act of "self-revelation" (SMA 145). However, only after one has achieved the basic reality of a scene should one explore what the scene means personally to the actor. Avoid phoniness: "no bullshit. That's the highest criticism" (SMA 146–47).

Another influence on both Mamet's acting style and on his later teaching was Richard Boleslavsky, a student of Stanislavsky's at the Moscow Art Theatre who, with Maria Ouspenskaya, emigrated to New York and in 1924 founded the American Laboratory Theatre. In the six years of its existence, it trained such actors as Stella Adler, Harold Clurman, and Lee Strasberg, before they formed the Group Theatre. Boleslavsky's *Acting, The First Six Lessons* (1933) was a book Mamet admired. It was a constant companion of his in the late sixties and seventies, even turning up in his Lincoln Hotel room when he lived in Chicago in the early seventies (CA 95). In it, Boleslavsky refines his master's ideas in a book structured as a set of interviews between a neophyte student and an instructor who develops six lessons on how to act: concentration, memory of emotion, dramatic action, characterization, observation, and rhythm. Through discussions of various roles the young actor is to play, the instructor outlines his philosophy on the education of an actor, which consists of three essential parts: education of his body, intellect, and soul.

The first element—body—requires exercises of physical movement, the second—intellect—a broadly based cultural and psychological background able to discuss Shakespeare, painting, or emotional expression. By soul, Boleslavsky means being capable of "living through any situation demanded by the author" (ACT 26). Focus is on the craft of acting, not on the abstract and indefinite art of acting. Emphasis is on the reality of creation on the stage: "to imitate is wrong. To create is right" (ACT 41). Boleslavsky focuses on the structure of action, action again becoming the key element of dramatic behavior. No scene can be acted, Boleslavsky argues, without action, and a sense of its goal "in accordance with the character of the part that opposes him," adjusted to include "the individuality of the actor who plays the part" (ACT 63). Characterization emerges from the rhythm of thought established by the playwright (ACT 81).

A repetition exercise originating in a German school exercise expanded by Meisner is next as a key to learning observation, which will define an actor's actions. But organizing all is work and practice and perseverance. Rhythm follows, the sense of orderly and progressive change aimed at stimulating audience attention For the actor, a developed sense of rhythm is the source of spontaneity essential for an honest performance (ACT 112, 116–17). To "command and create your own Rhythm and that of others . . . is perfection" (ACT 120). Mamet intuitively responded to this statement: his mastery of dialogue is the mastery of rhythm, whether of hoods, salesmen, or Hollywood producers.

Boleslavsky emphasizes that it takes years to develop one's acting skills (Meisner would famously tell his students twenty) (SMA xv). *Acting, The First Six Lessons* is a practical book that appealed immensely to Mamet, who in *True and False* would echo many of its ideas, from the responsibility of the author in finding the meaning of what's being said to the clearly stated job of the actor: "learn the lines, find a simple objective . . . speak the lines clearly in an attempt to achieve that objective" (TF 57). The Moscow Art Theatre and its ideas, Mamet wrote, was "my youthful Camelot" (CA 96).[5] A theatrical line then emerges from Stanislavsky and the Moscow Art Theatre to Boleslavsky, to the Group Theatre, to the Neighborhood Playhouse, to Mamet, to a young actor who received Mamet's copy of *Acting* (CA 99).

In New York, Mamet took to the Meisner/Boleslavsky approach immediately. Its bluntness, pragmatism, and directness made sense to him. "Get the work done" had a direct, concrete aspect that he could understand and measure by action. Theory was minimal. There was no talking about a part as much as *doing* it. It wasn't simple, but it was clear, and a method he would later elaborate in texts like *True and False*. One of the strengths of the Meisner method was its honesty, rejecting the use of emotional or other deception. An actor had to be truthful to his or her emotions; otherwise, the scene would be false and the audience would be deceived. They would detect the fraud. The action, crucial to the emotion in the scene and part, had to be direct and unvarnished. There is no room for the fake or the false in the Meisner or Mamet method. "The best way to act well is to live truthfully" Meisner often repeated to his students (SMA 123). "The actor, in learning to be true and simple . . . creates his *own* character; he forges character in himself. Onstage. And it is this character which he brings to the audience, and by which the audience is truly moved" Mamet would write (TF 22). Restated, the principle appears in a passage from *A Practical Handbook for the Actor* written by a number of Mamet's students: "the actor's job is not to bring the truth of his personal life to the stage, but rather to bring the truth of himself to the specific needs of the play" (PHA 32).

"Training to listen," the first step of the Meisner method, was something that made sense to Mamet, whose family life had seemed premised on it. Bernie Mamet hectored his children to listen with "an inner ear" and played games with them to build up their powers of observation and memory. The problem, however, was that "what was correct changed on a daily basis" (FM 73). At home, Mamet listened for danger: the family would "while away the evenings by making ourselves miserable, solely based on our ability to speak the language viciously" he has said (FM 73). So at the Neighborhood Playhouse, listening came naturally for him.

The school was not cheap. It cost $1,200 in 1967–68. The curriculum consisted of Acting, Speech, and Movement—duplicating the curriculum of the Moscow Art Theatre under Stanislavsky—and culminating in performances, usually a program of scenes or dramatic episodes from the first-year students and actual plays from the second-year students.[6] The program began with the basics: repetition and other improvisational exercises occupied students for three months. Only then would they receive their first text, a vehicle to continue the exercises. Most important, in the words of Harold Baldridge, current director of the Neighborhood Playhouse, the students in the first year "never play another character . . . it's always themselves on the line, investigating themselves." "Getting rid of the bullshit is . . . a lot of what this training is about" Baldridge added. He then elaborated: if you have little time to think about yourself, you don't have time "to edit or direct your response. . . . [S]omething may emerge that's really you."[7] This became central to Mamet's ideas on acting.

Meisner headed the acting section with assistance from Ed Moore, William Esper, and John Ulmer. Second year consisted of "advanced technique, interpretation, characterization applied in scenes and plays," according to the 1967–68 school brochure (12). The required movement class, based on Martha Graham's idea "to prepare the body as a dramatic instrument" (13), was taught by Pearl Lang and Jane Dudley. Voice and Speech, an additional first-year course, had an important impact on Mamet; throughout his career he has stressed voice and articulation. The word is an act, he writes in "Against Amplification," and it must always be stated clearly (WR 136; cf TF 55, 57). Karen Kohlhaaus emphasizes this in her Mamet-inspired *The Monologue Audition* when she writes, "good speech can be a make-or-break skill in an audition" (MA xxii). Voice projection, diction, phonetics, and oral interpretation were a constant focus at the Neighborhood Playhouse. Fencing, make-up, theater history, and stage techniques comprised the rest of the program.

Mamet never took the second-year program at the Neighborhood Playhouse because he was not asked back following his first year performance of two-person scenes. Nevertheless, he undertook various acting jobs during his time in New York, including a summer stock job at the tip of Long Island, one of the few times he was hired as an actor (JAF 10).

While Mamet was absorbing Meisner's principles and attending classes at the Neighborhood Playhouse, he was working in the Village at the hit show *The Fantasticks*. His routine at this time began with a walk from his Upper West Side apartment, through Central Park, stopping at a café at the Zoo to have breakfast.

After a day at the Neighborhood Playhouse school, he went to the Village, working first as a temporary usher at a variety of theatres. He saw Irene Pappas and Christopher Walken in *Iphegenia in Aulis* and Geoffrey Holder in *House of Flowers.* He was then hired as a permanent usher at *The Fantasticks* and rose to become assistant stage manger with a stint as house manager (MBT 31–2). He was, however, violating the rules of the Neighborhood Playhouse, which forbade students to work in the theatre during their studies. He had thought that the rule related only to acting. Since he was sure no one would ever hire him as an actor ("I was a terrible acting student"), he was especially proud of circumventing the ban (MBT 32).

He enjoyed himself immensely as he worked out a new schedule: after school on East Fifty-Fourth Street, he would head downtown and go to either the Waverly or the Empire theatres and smoke and watch films until dinner. He would then go to one of the Village cafes, the Dante or the Reggio, for a meal, enjoy an after-dinner cigarette, and then head to the show, where he performed a series of mundane tasks: clean the house and lobby, check and prepare props and costumes (when he was stage manager), sweep the confetti from the previous show and prepare it to be thrown again. He opened the theatre and showed people to their seats, and during intermissions sold souvenir programs and recordings of the cast. He learned various stage manager techniques including how to remember the tasks during a scene change: start with the number of tasks rather than what they are.

At the *Fantasticks*, he also learned an important piece of stage wisdom about the life of a playwright. While watching the play one night from just inside the door to the lobby, Mamet heard a sigh behind him. Tom Jones, who wrote the book and the lyrics for the play, was looking at the stage and shaking his head. "If only they would just Say the Words . . ." he said (MBT 33). Mamet never forgot this remark and turned it into an acting principle. When the evening ended, he often caught Kenny Rankin at the Bitter End or Bill Evans, Horace Silver, or Billy Taylor at the Top of the Gate.

Mamet had what he called "his first true milestone in the Professional Theatre" at *The Fantasticks.* One day in 1967 when the assistant stage manager got sick, he was pressed into running the lightboard. Several lighting changes required much turning, plugging, and adjusting of dials and knobs and sticks. At the climactic moment of the show with a final reprise of "Try to Remember," there was to be an elaborate and dazzling lighting change. However, Mamet accidentally elbowed the master switch and plunged the stage, the house, and the light booth into total darkness for an extended period of time (SF 103). He never forgot it, or the need for precise and rehearsed movements from the technical crew as well as the actors and staff.

The play is no more than a romantic fable, but with music that works. Its breezy songs suggest escape, although always with a sense of danger. It opened with the actors rushing to get ready for the show in front of the audience, leaping into costumes and placing their props (Mamet would duplicate this "process" opening in his adaptation of Chekhov's *Uncle Vanya*). When they were ready they threw clouds of colored paper into the air. The play has a kind of mise-en-scène quality that immediately engages the audience. But from the opening song, "Try to Remember," the theme is "follow," as the narrator introduces the characters and a wall. The sixteen-year-old Girl introduces the ingénue who will suffer the challenges of a romance. "Metaphor," an appropriately literary song, outlines the Boy's feelings for her, although later in Act One "The Rape Ballet" will balance this innocence with experience.

For Mamet, working at *The Fantasticks* introduced him not only to the practical matters of putting a show on every night, but to the well-structured musical in which emotions are played out in an almost Aristotelian form and unity of action. Aristotle's principle of having a beginning, middle, and end, or situation, complication, and denouement, are neatly (and comically) presented by Jones and Harvey Schmidt, who wrote the music. The sense of closure must have also appealed to Mamet, obtainable even through its episodic structure. Here, the blackouts of the Second City join with Aristotle through a set of musical styles that blend story and action.

Not surprisingly, perhaps, Aristotle would soon become one of Mamet's critical touchstones as he progressed as a dramatist. He would often refer to Aristotle, who believed that "while character determines men's qualities . . . it is by their actions that they are happy or the reverse" (AP 62), when commenting on the structure of *American Buffalo* or *Glengarry Glenn Ross*. In 1981 he proclaimed, "I'm of the Aristotelian school: characters are nothing but habitual action. You don't create a character; you describe what he does" (DMC 40; also see 24). Three years later, he elaborated on the importance of Aristotle, declaring that an understanding of "the theory of true action . . . is the essential understanding of drama" (IDM 93).

At *The Fantastiks*, Mamet furthermore experienced how the process of putting on a play could be addressed from the stage and yet engage the audience, from the actors arriving and donning costumes as they do at the opening, to the remarks and asides as the action gets underway in the "Rape Ballet." "Everybody get your swords" says Henry, an elderly Shakespearean actor who shortly corrects the entry of the Indians: "No, no. Indians are off left, damn it!" This appealed to Mamet's preference for nonillusionary theatre in the tradition of Brecht. And in the words of the song that opens Act Two, "This Plum is Too Ripe," Mamet heard something that would stick with him, again echoing Aristotle: the need for an ending.

The play's not done. Oh, no
—not quite,
For life never ends in the moonlit night;
And despite what pretty poets say,
The night is only half the day.
So we would like to truly finish

What we foolishly begun.
For the story is not ended
And the play is never done
Until we've all of us been burned a
Bit and burnished by—the sun.

Importantly, theatre offering a sense of closure is something Mamet—in this way a traditionalist—prized and achieved in his most successful works.

The unity of the cast and crew, a harmony achieved by a small, well-organized production, was another attraction for Mamet. This, too, became one of his goals as he developed his own acting company, first at Goddard with the St. Nicholas Theater Company and then reconstituted in Chicago and then the Atlantic Theater Company in New York. Throughout his career Mamet has also relied on a group of actors he would know and trust, including William H. Macy, Joe Mantegna, J. J. Johnston, Mike Nussbaum, Felicity Huffman, and Rebecca Pidgeon. *The Fantasticks*, which would become the longest-running musical in history, marking 17,162 performances before it closed in January 2002, became a practical laboratory for Mamet, expanding what he was learning at the Neighborhood Playhouse—and confirming what he already knew: that he loved the theatre but would not make it as an actor. "I decided I'd better learn to do something else. I started teaching and directing . . ."[8]

Writing came later.

Mamet was not invited back for a second year of training at the Neighborhood Playhouse. But by this time even he acknowledged his limitations as an actor. In a February 1977 interview with David Witz for *Chicago Theater*, he elaborated on his shortcomings. In answer to the question, "would you do any acting in the future?" he replied, "I don't have the mentality for it":

> You have to be so strict. You have to be like a hunter and look at just one thing at a time and know what's happening, one thing at a time, one thing followed by the next thing. I'm a good teacher, but I'm too ambivalent about everything to be able to be a fine actor. An actor has to . . . every moment, moment to moment, you're putting your life on the line and saying this is how it is. It doesn't matter if it *could* be eight different ways, *this* is the way it is. One moment after the next. It takes an amount of concentration . . . I have a small amount of technique but mentally I haven't the disposition to learn anymore which is why I quit; because I was developing as a director and a teacher, my perceptions about what an actor must be so far have distanced my ability to teach myself that. And that's my desire, to teach myself that.[9]

Fellow actors confirmed this view. Mike Nussbaum, when he first met Mamet in a Chicago production of *The Night they Shot Harry Lindsey with a 155mm Howitzer and Blamed it on Zebras* at the Body Politic, noted his awkwardness and discomfort.

Nussbaum teased him about his distress and in response, a few nights later, Mamet handed him a script. It was *The Duck Variations* and Nussbaum could tell at once Mamet was a better playwright than actor. Mamet has commented little on his failures as an actor, but William H. Macy remarked that Mamet disliked acting because "he wasn't in charge" (Freedman 64). In a later interview, Mamet admitted that he hated acting because he couldn't do it (Kogan CPL). On the photo of Mamet that hangs in the lobby of the Neighborhood Playhouse Theatre School, he wrote these encouraging words: "Take heart, they didn't ask me back either."

But Mamet did learn from his experience at the Neighborhood Playhouse. The idea of a "through-line,"—the "single overriding action that all the individual actions serve" and that unites "the individual beats" of a scene (PHA 33–34)—was paramount. This was Aristotle (character is action) filtered through Stanislavsky and Boleslavsky. Further, the idea of subjugating all aspects of the production—"not just the script, but the acting and the plastic elements—to the through-line of the play" was also crucial. It would help him greatly on stage and in film directing (IOW 136–37). Acting, he also came to realize, was "about two people who want something different." What we try to do, he believes, is "*achieve* our wishes *from* each other" and awareness of this becomes the difference between good and bad playwriting (IOW 137).

Mamet returned to Goddard more determined than ever to pursue a life in the theatre. Acting was a fading possibility, but directing was a likely alternate. Playwriting became a new focus. For his required Senior Study, necessary for graduation, he asked if writing a play was acceptable. He was told yes and began "SEALS," about two lovers in New York who fall into and out of love and then hate each other. He felt it was terrible and after two months of rewriting, the play still remained unfinished. He suddenly found himself at the beginning of the spring semester with no text and "graduation time coming on like an acid rush." With irony he wrote, "never one to panic, I decided to give the situation a month or two to jell."[10] He turned to a journal he kept while at Goddard containing scenes, sketches, one-liners, and anecdotes—the beginning of a habit he would continue throughout his life. (William H. Macy in 1985 commented that wherever Mamet went, he had a notebook to jot down ideas, snatches of conversation, details he observed.) Mamet began to compose a work, or, more accurately, string together a set of scenes, to be called "The Camel Document," shortened to "Camel," congratulating himself at his own invention: "well, I thought, that Southside gypsy mojo has come through again, Dave. Here was my play" (CD 1).

The work combines Chicago with Vermont, in both influence and inflection. Drawing on the blackouts of Second City and the Vermont setting of Goddard, he fashioned thirty-four separate scenes that ranged from mime to the Marines, with a spoof on Swedish movies and a take-off on Pirandello. Mamet's first play even comes with its own critical commentary: a prose introduction, "Preparing Camel," followed by a "Scene Analysis" and then "In Memoriam." Mamet essentially decided to refine "the more potent pieces in my journal into a revue," as he writes in "Preparing Camel" (CD 1). The influence of Second City, of improv at New York's Bitter End, and of Pablo Vela, his drama teacher, lent energy to his plan. The performers, three men and one woman, included Jonathan Katz (who remained a lifelong friend) cast because Mamet owed him money and thought that a part might appease him. Pablo Vela had a role, as did Lynn Klamkin, who won the female part because she lacked the "sicky staginess that poisoned the audiences." At the time he called the review *Divertimentos from Real Life* (CD 1–2). When he went to see about a poster, he hit on a new title with Kaf Warman, *Coke and Camel*, but shortened it to *Camel* because he could not decide what element of the title should be singular or plural.

Another important aspect of the production was Mamet's direction. As he repeated in 2006, he had always wanted to be a director, not a playwright (Kogan CPL). Necessity forced him to become a writer. The need to complete his Senior Study and the absence of appropriate (and short) material for his early acting companies prompted the beginning of his writing career.

He began rehearsals on May 1, 1969, in the basement of D Dormitory on the Northwood campus of Goddard, a ten-minute walk from the main buildings. The stage was makeshift, a six-by-nine-foot riser platform pushed against a wall. He cites Brecht in his commentary to defend the exposure of the lighting apparatus to limit the unwanted element of illusion. His determination to eliminate illusion became one of the "dialectic points of 'Camel' both in writing and in the style of production," Mamet writes, indicating his debt to direct, open productions and performances (CD 3). The lighting, completely visible to the audience, achieved Brecht's alienation effect. Brecht's influence was present also in the exposure of actors who not only casually placed props and costumes on the stage but sat next to the audience when not on stage. Additionally, the reading out of cues and prompts by the stage manager were done in full voice so that the audience heard them after each blackout scene. This approach, drawn not only from Brecht, but also from Pirandello, whom Mamet had studied, and *The Fantasticks*, had a liberating effect for Mamet because he felt that when one commits to "a theatre of *illusion* . . . you must insure the concealment of all elements detracting from the illusion . . . this process is a drag as it creates a totally uninteresting theatre" (CD 6).

Mamet then explained that although he had never directed before, he did not panic. He remembered

> . . . the advice of the Francis Parker School and John Dewey and the Neighborhood Playhouse School of the Theater and most of all, I remember that Acting is Doing. So I just started doing.
>
> I tried to stage each scene for truth rather than for funniness; the more I worked at it the more appropriate this seemed. . . . I found that directing, given a certain background of stage experience, is just common sense combined with an overview of each scene. (CD 6)

This early statement, uncorrupted by theory or even theatre history, remains a viable guide to Mamet's later directorial practice. The most important attribute for a director, adds the twenty-two-year-old, is a "*disposition to action.*" And the director must tell the actors "only things which tend toward action and which do not confuse them" (CD 7). The statement both summarizes what he learned at the Neighborhood Playhouse and anticipates what he repeats in *True and False, Heresy and Common Sense for the Actor* and later texts: "Acting *must* be doing" (CD 8).

Mamet also notes a fault of his own as an actor: that he worried too much about everything but the action. Would others know their lines? Was the costume right? Is there a big audience? Is anyone important in the audience? These concerns divide an actor's attention, and a director must work to remove them. He then provides a detailed account of what should be accomplished in rehearsal and how an actor can overcome these diversions, reminding actors that a rehearsal is not a finished performance. The common effort of striving for a theatrical goal is the key, and making the actor feel he or she is able to establish the task set out is also important. In this way the actor "will be less inclined to push and phony his way through the rehearsal period" but instead will grapple with real issues (CD 10). For a director, Mamet adds, a knowledge of acting makes it easier to detect the bunk.

While preparations for his show were going well, Mamet learned that posters advertising the performances were being torn down around campus. Pablo Vela told him it was a protest against Mamet's wanting to charge admission. But Mamet thought that an audience would pay more respect to a play if they paid to see it and that those involved in the production would have more self-respect. The fifty cent admission, however, outraged the campus and at one point he was stopped by a group of students and told to explain himself: "I did it in a cheerful fuck you tone and this, of course, created a measure of opposition to my project" (CD 11). He was feeling righteous about his charging, but went around campus saying he was ill-used but enjoyed every moment of flaunting his artistic abuse.

May 14 was the dress rehearsal, the night before opening. Among his notes for the actors and crew:

House manger: get the fucking door fixed.
Pre-show: all actors smoke in hall only, not in D Basement.
Opening: Stage manager: don't say stage managed by.
Too much backstage noise.
Kathy: shut the fuck up. This show is not an in-joke. If something funny happens don't go all ape shit. (CD 13–14)

The show opened, was well-received, and Mamet "was happy with it," although ironically at the last minute he had an urge to disassociate himself from it. He enjoyed writing it, staging it, and directing it, but realized it was up to the actors to finish it. But he recalled the advice of an actor friend who explained that some parts are like old lovers remembered with tenderness, while some you remember with scorn, and some you can't even remember, but "when one is finished, you go on, happily or reluctantly, to something new." He stuck with the production (CD 16).

"CAMEL/A revue by David Mamet," ran from May 15–18, 1969. Thirty-four separate scenes make up the work, which began with a man kneeling stage center revising a saying from the Koran: "It is said destiny is a blind camel. Today we know this is to be a mistranslation. In the Koran it is truly written destiny is a humped Venetian. It is so obvious" (CD 18). Following a blackout, the stage manager and a cast member appear, holding foot-long cards on which were printed the show's credits. The cast member turns the cards as the humming of the "Star-Spangled Banner" is heard. The first five scenes consist of a bus ride ("two men on a bus sitting side by side. An exercise in violating theatrical convention"); face masks; mime; Marines; and cages. These are followed by a nude scene, although the stage is empty and just voices are heard; Babel (a bricklayer for the tower of Babel converses with a visitor and cements a brick out of line); Pirandello; Swedish movies; Prokofiev; obscenity; bedtime; Broadway. The range is as varied as the purpose.

Some scenes have commentary. Of "Icebox" Mamet writes that he long believed that the Hunger Strike in Kafka's parable is one of the wisest things he had ever read. "So, in attempt to bring culture to the masses, I staged it" (CD 96). "Pirandello" is meta-theatre: two men speak on a bus again. They argue and in the midst of some physical business there is a call for lights and they come up. One man says, "there's an audience out there man, that awareness improvisation shit is a no go here!" (CD 52). The stage manager then appears and yells for the lights to come on and hustles the actors off stage. A girl then comes on and mimes getting on to the bus, closes the door, and starts to speak while she rides along. She outlines two basic theatrical styles, illusion and convention, concluding her mini-lecture with, "since no illusion can be perfect, the direction of the illusive drama must always rely on convention." She stops the bus, blows a kiss to the audience, and waves. Blackout.

Later scenes mix humor with a certain risqué quality. "Swedish Movies" opens with a woman speaking Swedish to a man on a bed and then beginning fellatio. An off-stage voice says "Cut. Are you kidding? This shit is filthy. It'll never get past the censors. Tell you what. Rewind it and we'll see it again." Woman starts again with "but Tex, I can't stay and let you bleed to death" (CD 66–7). In "Obscenity," a speaker addresses a civic-minded group, explaining that he knows some of them are upset because certain children have received pornographic material in the mail. "I believe this concern is unwarranted. I feel that if those little kids can't take a joke, fuck 'em" (CD 78).

Mamet's commentary relates to almost every scene. He notes repeated themes of blindness, destiny, and smoking. He was reading Borges at the time and found the parable whose center was the epigram, "destiny is a blind camel. Destiny, blindness and Camel cigarettes. Voila opening bit. The addition of the transformation of humped Venetian was pure self-indulgence on my part, I did it, and I'm glad"

(CD 89). For "Mime" (perhaps influenced by Pablo Vela, who studied the subject in Paris), Mamet writes that it is another exercise in convention, although he admits that he never succeeded in establishing that a theatrical mime was taking place but that it worked on stage, although he can't explain why. The actors saved it.

Of the Samson scene (about his marriage to a *shiksa*), Mamet writes that he feels it works because of its Yiddish humor, "the humor I was raised with and that which is supremely funny to me" (CD 94). It is the story of the henpecked man whose wife is a *kvetch* and trying to sell him out to the enemy. The dramatic conflict arises because he can't help but love her. "Samson" works because it is a conventional "stand-up comic Jewish routine. It is Classical American-Yiddische, 1950. Pure South Side Chicago" (CD 94). What is funny is a question he ponders in numerous sketches.

Further Mamet commentary notes how the "Babel" scene is a "pure imitation of Kafka," a serious scene in the midst of frivolity and "a cheap trick to hide second-class writing" (CD 96) and that the laugh that ends the skit Samson II and topped three times is a gesture toward Kaufman and Hart, who top every line from the first curtain to the final curtain with a laugh. "It was good for me to have done it, to see the effect of *playwriting* not just good or funny writing on a play" (CD 98). "Blind," he writes, was originally written in 1966 and presented by the Suitcase Theatre Company of Jeff Glasser and is perhaps by his own admission "the best piece of theatrical writing in the revue." He calls the work "a dark dialectic" because of the interplay between script, actor, and audience. "'Blind' violates the comfortable lines between script and reality. Between things talked of and things left alone" (CD 100). He notes that the opening lines of "Airport" incorporate lines from his incomplete play, "SEALS." He also praises "Pirandello": "This is what theatre should be. Theatre should be: experience, not words." "Too much of 'Camel,'" he adds, "is not experience but *indication* of experience. But by God, I'm learning. Through doing, believe it or not" (CD 101). The lessons of Sanford Meisner and the Neighborhood Theatre are clear, blended here with Brechtian ideas of theatre as an event sustained by "alienation" that dismantles illusion for the audience.

Mamet's concluding remarks emphasize the ephemeral nature of the theatre at the same time beautiful and tragic. A painter can show you last year's work, a writer his manuscript, but an actor can only offer his fleeting performance. "Camel" "was my first theatrical work, and "The Camel Document" is a manifest not of product but of process. Because theater is drama and drama is process" (CD 110). Mamet is also conscious of the transformation of his words to action on the stage. The metamorphosis fascinates him.

"The Camel Document's" commentary is as valuable as the actual scenes. Its twofold importance consists of, first, showing the wide range and reference of Mamet's writing, from Brecht, Borges, and Kafka to Kaufman and Hart and Yiddish theatre. The second element about "Camel" is its self-commentary, an early record of Mamet's theatrical self-evaluation. This reveals the consistency of his theatrical ideas: what they were in the spring of 1969 changed very little decades later when he published *True and False, Heresy and Common Sense for the Actor*, or *A Practical Handbook for the Actor*, and *3 Uses of the Knife*. In *True and False* for example, he writes that great drama on stage is "the performance of great deeds with no emotion whatever" and that the actor is on stage only "to communicate the play to the audience" (TF 13, 9). In his instructions to his young actors at Goddard he makes the same point. "The Camel Document" is an early product of Mamet's evolving sense of theatre and playwriting.

Goddard introduced Mamet to Vermont and he began to explore the surrounding communities. He first saw Cabot, Vermont, in 1965 when he was a student-teacher of French at the Cabot School, part of a college education course. He commuted the twelve miles on a borrowed motorcycle, finding the small community and surrounding landscape irresistible. Mamet revisited Vermont during the next decade in between work in Chicago and New York and found the rural life so appealing (in 1930 cows outnumbered people in Vermont: 421,000 vs. 359,000) that in 1978 he purchased a farm house and 100 acres for $50,000. It had been uninhabited for some thirty years. The home, since expanded, is at the site of the old town of South Woodbury and stands crosswise to a partly paved road. In the late nineteenth century, the town moved five miles away down the hill to the west. The graveyard, however, remains and is easily visible from Mamet's kitchen (SNK 69). It grew to have special resonance for Mamet, a connection with an American past of heroes so much so that he purchased a plot there, writing in 2002 how "terrible it would be that, in that afterlife we all imagine as death, not to rest in Vermont" (SNK 152).

Reconditioning the farmhouse meant replacing windows, building an addition, a barn, and a cabin. The cabin a gift from his first wife Lindsay Crouse, is his workspace, some distance from the home down a sugaring lane and furnished with his 1860 walnut roll-top desk, a safe, a couch, kerosene lamps and a Glenwood parlor stove lifted ten inches off the floor resting on "chubby, foliated bombé legs" (CA 46). In this he duplicated Chekhov who had a small writing lodge built on his estate Melikhovo—fifty miles north of Moscow—on the edge of a cherry orchard.

Importantly, over the years Vermont began to enter Mamet's writing practice, not only through long secluded hours in his cabin, some three hundred yards from his house, but in the setting, use, and stories that form his plays. "Vermont Sketches," seven short works with titles like "Deer Dogs" and "Maple Sugaring," is representative. "Dowsing" from the collection is perhaps the most "Vermontian": set in a Vermont country store, two older men talk about the process of inferring water via geological lines and a stick and how the stick can sometimes locate other items, like a lost watch. This causes one to remark, "Well, you know, the things that you *see* it makes you think that maybe there's something to *everything*." The other replies, "Now, by God, that's the truth" (GS 76). What emerges in his presentation of Vermont is the clarity of action through laconic speech, directness of movement, and what he would later call "acts of reserve, of self-respect, of circumspection," "the Vermont ethic" (SNK 141, 140). A long, low slate wall Mamet built piece by piece on his land embodies this practical ethic rooted in the use of natural materials. The individualism and eccentricity of Vermonters also appealed to Mamet, who long possessed a streak of rebellion and cherished the "go it your own way" philosophy.

Aspects of Vermont appear throughout his prose. "Memorial Day, Cabot, Vt." in *Some Freaks*, and "Sex Camp" and "Deer Hunting" in *Make-Believe Town* reemphasize the rural life that appeals to him so strongly. It is the bedrock value of American crafts and artisans that matter: the potters, woodworkers, glassblowers, cabinetmakers, and blacksmiths. But he recognizes the paradox that even though people seem to seek isolation in this country life, they socialize intensely. This occurs at places like the River Run Café in Plainfield or the Village Restaurant in Hardwick or at the local hardware store. Another appealing aspect of country living for Mamet is the literal acquisition of the past. For Mamet it is his Civil War-era walnut rolltop desk that he bought in the early eighties. It was stunning in its workmanship and just the tool for a writer. It was expensive and he suffered buyer's remorse and tried to cancel the deal the next morning. The storeowner refused: "I'm going to deliver the desk tomorrow, and for years to come *you're* going to thank me." "He did and I do," Mamet wrote (SNK 84).

Mamet initially considered his time in Vermont something of an assimilationist's holiday and did things nice Jewish boys weren't supposed to do, like serious outdoor activities. It pleased him "to think that I was putting something over in myself," acting in a way that was unusual for a Jewish kid from Chicago "whose family has always had the gene for liberalism—spending lots of time gambling, hunting fishing" (DMC 172). But he soon realized he was indeed "a nice Jewish boy" and that in his attempt to escape Midwestern, middle-class life, he was simply recreating it. Ironically, as he admits in *South of the Northeast Kingdom*, most of his Vermont friends are Jewish. His assimilationist move was not a total success.

Vermont inspired a short and unsuccessful venture in the clothing business as Mamet and two of his friends (Chris Kaldor, former hardware store owner and currently Cabot town clerk and Richard Friedman, a Cambridge, Massachusetts, developer) formed the Joseph Morse Company of Cabot, Vermont, specializing in outdoor wear of cotton and wool. Mamet wanted to duplicate what he saw in the old Abercrombie and Fitch and L. L. Bean catalogues offering "colors [that] sound like those in the woods" (SNK 40). The company lasted four years and its clothing was available through selected Banana Republic stores. Sales of its red plaid shirts and suede-collared leather outdoor coats, however, were not strong and the company folded.

Hunting was another aspect of the Vermont ethos Mamet enjoyed. It allowed him free reign to indulge in his passion for guns, which he celebrates not only in a script for an episode of *Hill Street Blues* entitled "A Wasted Weekend," but in essays like "Practical Pistol Competition" and parts of his 1994 novel set in an isolated New England town, *The Village* (see 5TP 127–171; SF 144–153). In the second section of this mostly male novel, the yet unnamed character Henry thinks exclusively of hunting, associating it with a focus on guns and the order of the natural world.

Mamet writes well about guns, finding their precision and detail reflect his own concern with exactness and accuracy. A passage from "The Shooting Auction" illustrates the style he brings to his dialogue and film scripts:

> I opened the bolt of the rifle and laid the stock in the sandbag groove. . . . I got down behind the rifle and looked through the scope. The eye relief was good for me, and it brought the target right up close. I got myself into a good shooting position, my left arm across my chest and the hand hugging the right shoulder; I closed the bolt and took aim at the target. I took a deep breath. In and slowly out; then in and half out, until the crosshairs rested exactly on the bottom center of the bull's eyes, and I squeezed the trigger, which broke clean at what felt like around three and a half pounds. (CA 105)

Gunsmiths, collectors, and dealers are people Mamet relates to: they are professional, committed, and knowledgeable about their wares. They are also disciplined, a quality Mamet himself brings to the theatre.

Mamet's fascination with guns—and knives—is everywhere. In films like *Homicide, Heist, Spartan*, and in his TV series *The Unit*, guns figure importantly in the action. When Bobby Gold loses his gun when unexpectedly jumped by a criminal in *Homicide* and his holster tears, it is a symbolic wound that remains with him throughout the film. Similarly, in an episode of *The Unit*, when one of the special ops team is wounded on the rifle range, it is a symbol of the lack of professionalism and discipline that defines the team. Teach explains the power of a gun when he tells Don that having one would be a good idea when they make their move to steal a coin collection. It's not necessary but it feels good. Don objects:

> Don: We don't need a gun, Teach.
> Teach: I pray that we don't, Don.
> Don: We don't, tell me why we need a gun.
> Teach: It's not a question do we *need* it. . . . *Need* . . . Only that it makes me comfortable, okay? It helps me to relax. (AB 84)

Mamet was initially a collector, gathering up guns at auctions, estate sales and gunsmiths. In his cabin, he had a Colt model 1878 .45-caliber revolver and a Winchester loading tool, both of which function as paperweights. His innate admiration for the military plays into this interest: "anyone who's ever carried a gun is happy to have a gun" he remarked in an interview about *The Unit*.[11] Mamet also reported that his cure for writer's block was to shoot at poker chips—outside. A cartoon he recently drew, entitled "Hunting Handbook," and a headline from September 4, 2002, somewhat archly encapsulates his absorption with weapons: "Mamet Guns Down Dillinger Script Deal." He had signed on to adapt a script about the gangster John Dillinger for Warner Bros. produced by Stephen Soderberg.

Mamet's employment of what in the theatre has been known as "Chekhov's gun" in *3 Uses of the Knife*, a set of lectures on the nature of drama, blends his interest in guns with dramatic structure. Essentially, the term refers to the introduction of an object that is then forgotten but before the end of the play has a role in the drama. Mamet found it an instructive technique. As Chekhov wrote in a letter, "one must not put a loaded rifle on the stage if no one is thinking of firing it."[12] Mamet follows this principle in his theatre works and essays. *House of Games* illustrates this forcefully when Margaret Ford uses a gun she has taken from one of her patients to shoot the con-man Mike not once but three times.

Knives are equally powerful to Mamet. In his novel *The Village*, sharpening knives becomes a dedicated act, as much as caring for one's rifles. And for Mamet they are equally tools of creation as well as destruction. Talk of the knife to be given to the boy John in *The Cryptogram* defines the loss and danger of the past. In *Edmond*, the knife the protagonist uses to turn on a pimp is alternately a means of liberation and entrapment. In his essay "Knives," Mamet analyzes the decline in the manufacture of knives and criticizes the use of stainless steel blades while praising those craftsmen who still hand-forge a blade (JJH 48–50). He admires honesty in the making of knives and with pride refers to his Russell belt knife and his Russell Daddy Barlow. As he writes, "the beauty and the utility of any instrument depends on the single-mindedness and talent of the designer in fitting the tool to the task" (JJH 53).

Guns and knives mark for Mamet an entry into a world of men, and he is unabashed in his pleasure in their presence, especially those who shoot, hunt, gamble, or box. Importantly, in the company of men "you will be greeted on the basis of your actions: no one will inquire into your sincerity, your history, or your views" (SF 89). Masculinity is reaffirmed, identity reinforced. No one will be judged except by what they do.

Mamet's Vermont interests culminate in three prose works, his essay collection *The Cabin* (1992), his novel *The Village* (1994), and his mix of memoir and appreciation, *South of the Northeast Kingdom* (2002). *State and Main*, his 2000 comedy starring Alec Baldwin, Philip Seymour Hoffman, and W. H. Macy, visually represents his appreciation of the state. And in settling in Vermont, Mamet joined a long list of writers, including Rudyard Kipling, Robert Frost, the Spanish poet Lorca, Sinclair Lewis, and Dorothy Thompson, as well as Pearl S. Buck, Alexander Solzhenitsyn, Louise Gluck, Galway Kinnell, and Jamaica Kincaid. Others drawn to the state include Rudolf Serkin, pianist and founder of the Marlboro Music Festival; Carl Ruggles, composer; Norman Rockwell and Rockwell Kent, painters. But as to confirm his identity with the core of Vermont, on the bookshelf near his desk in the cabin are two telling titles: *The Parker Gun Shooter's Bible* and *Black Powder Gun Digest*.

~

After Goddard, Mamet tried to establish a life in the theatre. In Montreal in the summer of 1969, he joined a theatre company at McGill University where he played Lenny in Pinter's *The Homecoming* and the Doormouse in *Alice in*

Wonderland. The theatre company then fell apart and "I wandered back to Chicago where I wandered around looking for work" (CA 29, 30). He found minor parts at the Mill Run Playhouse doing children's shows and at the Pheasant Run Playhouse as an actor. He also began to drive a yellow cab out of Unit 13 on Belmont and Halsted, and once got a fare to a deserted area and had a knife put to his throat and had his money stolen (CA 128). In 1970–71 he had a short stint as a photo model with a pre-cut seersucker three-piece suit, plus boater, bow tie, and walking stick.

He experimented with a new hairstyle, an Italian look, and he liked it. Friends ridiculed him, however, and that very evening he went back to the barber for his favored crew cut: "for the crew cut, you see, is an *honest* haircut. It is the haircut of an honest, two pair of jeans working man—a man from Chicago, a man without vanity whose being stands without need of either introduction or apology. That blue-jeans sort of guy is me" (MBT 45). The image was Brechtian: hard-working, with short hair, clear glasses, and beard. Brecht, too, had a brush cut, round glasses, and workman's outfit, especially during his early years in Berlin (1924–1933). Mamet and Brecht effected the public persona of a literary enfant terrible. Both sought to be understood as workers, rejecting the idea of the playwright as an isolated, Romantic figure removed from everyday life.

Affinities between Mamet and Brecht are broad, from their enjoyment of boxing to their valuation of Chicago. Both favor unorthodox characters and share an enthusiasm for Kipling. Sport for Brecht was a protest against the effete world of intellectuals, and he sought out the company of boxers and racing cyclists. His friendship with Paul Samson-Korner, German light-heavyweight champion, cemented his attachment to the world of the ring and led to an unfinished biography of the fighter to have been called "The Human Fighting Machine." Theatre, wrote Brecht, must acquire "the same fascinating reality as a sporting arena during a boxing match" (BOT 233). Mamet favored boxing as an analogy in his screenplays, Capone lecturing men about gangland survival in *The Untouchables* by explaining that "When you got an all-out prizefight, you wait until the fight is over one guy is left standing 'N' that's how you know who won."

Although they differed in their staging techniques, Mamet and Brecht both recognized drama as confrontation. Both were theorists, directors, teachers, screenwriters, and artistic directors. And both went to Hollywood. Chicago is even a tighter connection. Brecht used the city in such work as *In the Jungle of Cities*, *St. Joan of the Stockyards*, and *The Resistible World of Arturo Ui*. *Happy End*, another work, is a Chicago gangster play. For Mamet, Chicago is the setting of *Sexual Perversity*, *American Buffalo*, and *The Untouchables*. The city of iron and dirt, myth and power, fascinated both writers.

During the fall of 1969, a period of confusion and thwarted ambition, Mamet suffered from depression and was treated by a psychoanalyst. A return to the theatre seemed unlikely and he was indecisive about what to do.[13] Temporary work was the answer and he had a list of Chicago jobs with which he regularly regaled interviewers:

> I worked in so many parts of the city. I sold real estate. I worked with carpets, I washed windows. I was a busboy and a waiter, a short order cook. I did retail sales, inventory. I worked in a truck factory, a canning factory. Beginning at age 13, I worked at something. I did it out of necessity and the curiosity of finding out what it would be like to have some money.[14]

But he needed to escape Chicago, and his desire to return to the theatre prompted him to write to some friends in the summer of 1970 at Marlboro College in Brattleboro, Vermont, asking if they wanted an actor for their summer theater. They said no, but the head of the drama department was going on leave for a year and wondered if Mamet wanted to teach. But did he have anything specific to recommend him? With chutzpah, he said he had just written a new play. "'I hadn't but they said that was great and that I could come to Marlboro to produce it.'" In the interim, he worked on a bunch of notes concerning a job on an ore boat and fashioned them into his second play, *Lakeboat* (DMC 17).

A few years earlier, Mamet had gotten a summer job through his father as a steward on a Great Lakes boat. He kept notes in a journal he started in 1966. It contained jottings, false starts, poems, random thoughts, and formal journal entries.[15] He then transformed the material from his Great Lakes experience into the first version of the play, written on his father's typewriter in his office on 327 South La Salle. A manuscript journal dated September 12, 1970, containing a diary, notes, attempted starts, poems, drawings, and random thoughts also has an entry headed "working on Lakeboat."

Lakeboat was first performed at the Theatre Workshop at Marlboro College during his 1970 appointment.[16] The play is a series of twenty-eight titled scenes, ranging from the concrete, "Fire and Evacuation Drills," to the abstract, "The Illusion of Motion." Essentially brief encounters between various crew members of the boat responding to the mugging of the steward and the reactions to his replacement, the young college student, Dale, the play introduces typical Mamet topics: women, gambling, guns, and drinking. It also follows one of his key acting principles: get into the scene late, get out early (ODF 64). Scene 19, "Arcana," has Stan and Joe walking across the fantail with Stan declaring, "There are many things in this world, Joe, the true meaning of which we will never know." "I knew a Mason," he continues and asks, "You know what he told me?" "No," Joe replies. Would you like to know?" "Yes," Joe answers and "as Stan starts to speak, they continue around the fantail and out of sight" (LB 78). The audience is left literally in the dark.

Like *The Duck Variations*, the play contains an inordinate—for Mamet—number of stage directions, beginning with a description of the set for the ship. At one point, we are told that a character "contemplates the lake," at another, a character "philosophizes" (LB 76, 79). Positions are noted, postures cued. Mamet also develops his love of paradox and contradiction, often expressed in halting, unsure language. Told there will be a nightman for the trip, a steward to run the galley, Joe responds with: "That's good. I don't want to make these sandwiches all the way to Canada. If you know what I mean. Not that I mind it. I just fucking hate making sandwiches. For other people to eat" (LB 36). It's the last, tagged-on sentence that brings some order to the syntax.

Gambling, or more specifically horse racing, is also an important part of the play. Fred, in particular, is a victim of the track, which, however, he sees analytically and in typical Mamet terms of black or white. We get into the scene late:

Fred: Because it's clean. The track is clean. It's like life without all the complicating people. At the track there are no two ways. There is win, place, show, and out-of-the-money. You decide, you're set. I mean, how clean can you get? Your bet is down and it's DOWN. And the winners always pay. . . . you don't even have to look at the fucking things. It's up on the board and it's final and there are two types of people in the world. (LB 61)

Before he can explain the meaning of the last statement, he's out of the scene. Tied up with the gambling are guns, and several scenes have the title "Personal Sidearms," "Sidearms Continued," or "The .38." They are part of the macho grammar of the boat and play.

Language is the largest and most effective sign of the male world in the work. And it is harsh and profane for the audience and for the nightman, the eighteen-year-old second year college student, Dale. Asking the Fireman on the ship what he studies when he watches the engine gauges, the Fireman answers: "I mean if that main goes, if she goes redline, you're fucking fucked. . . . You don't have a standby and the main goes, you're fucking *fucked*. You know what I mean." "Oh yeah," Dale weakly responds (LB 49–50). Throughout *Lakeboat*, the stature of the men seems measured by the degree of their profanity, although Fred tells the young Dale that the men "say 'fuck' in direct proportion to how bored they are." "Yeah," Dale says, seeming to understand (LB 52).

There are also the typical Mamet misunderstandings, features of later works like *American Buffalo* and *Glengarry Glen Ross*. Discussing the cook and his status, for example, Joe remarks that since he's been divorced, he "probably forgot what it is to be married." There is a pause, followed by

Joe: Two cars.

Fred: What the fuck? He worked for them.

Joe: I'm not saying he didn't work for them.

Fred: Oh no.

Joe: I never said that, I mean, it's obvious he worked for them. He's got 'em, right?

Fred: As far as I know. . . .
Joe: Probably only got a couple of Chevys.
Fred: Yeah. (LB 66)

Language here is statement without clarity and meaning without substance. But the wish to be understood persists. A later remark by Joe gets to the point, blending profanity with linguistic desire: "I mean, what the fuck? If you're going to talk to somebody, why fuck around the bush, right?" (LB 105). It's a question all of Mamet's characters ask.

In the play Dale is a second-year student at a school near Boston (LB 83). Mamet was also most likely about to begin (or had just completed) his second year at Goddard at the time he spent a summer working on an ore boat, which would place the time as the summer 1966 or 1967. Also, Mamet favors the name Litko, the first of three usages: Joe Litko is a character in *Lakeboat*; the name of the actor in the curtain-raiser of 1972, *Litko*; and Bernie's last name in *Sexual Perversity in Chicago*. This popular Chicago name had a rhythmic presence that appealed to Mamet.

Following the successful production of *Lakeboat* at Marlboro College and the end of his appointment, Mamet returned to Chicago and worked in a North Side real estate office in the Lincolnwood area, selling real estate over the phone to unsuspecting elderly couples. The "boiler room" was at the intersection of Lincoln and Peterson Avenues. He churned out leads to arrange appointments for salesmen selling non-existent land to retirees. To get to work, he road the length of Lincoln Avenue twice a day on a Chicago Transit Authority bus, reading the entire time (CA 98). This experience in the real estate business would become the source for perhaps his best-known work, the Pulitzer Prize winning *Glengarry Glen Ross*.

He also began working on a third play and then wrote to Goddard (likely to his old drama teacher and head of the drama program, Pablo Vela) to ask if they would like to produce it. This was *The Duck Variations*, inspired "from listening to a lot of old Jewish men all my life, particularly my grandfather."[17] After seeing a draft of the work, again composed of a number of separate scenes, Goddard (again, in all likelihood Vela), hired him for a term and he began to teach acting in the fall of 1971. Two of his students were William H. Macy and Steven Schachter.

The new instructor made a quick impression on his students. Macy and Schachter would recall Mamet's intensity and determination to run his classes punctually, something new for Goddard. Mamet, they remembered, was confident, assured, and convincing. He persuaded others that he knew what he was doing and knew what he wanted from his actor/students. In turn, he gave them the confidence to act, drawn from the principles and practices of Stanislavsky filtered through Meisner and Boleslavsky. Macy remembered how Mamet announced unequivocally that "if you want to learn to act, I'm the guy who can teach you. If you're not here for that, leave. The class just looked at each other going 'Who *is* this fucking guy?'" (FM 76). But he won them over even if his tactics required discipline, respect, and order. "There were no rules whatsoever, but if you were one second late he threw you out of class," Macy recalled. "Six months into the class, he walked in with a script and said 'I just wrote this play and we're going to do it.'" It was an early version of *Sexual Perversity in Chicago*, at that time called *Clark Street or Perversity in Chicago*.[18]

One time, however, Macy and Schachter arrived late to class and Mamet charged them fines. They had to pay him approximately $45 to be in the play that night. Mamet, however, didn't know what to do with the money and decided to burn it on stage before the performance. He did but soon felt remorse, refunded them the money and that night the three went out to drink it.[19] On other occasions, however, he did burn money before the class, the penalty for arriving late.

The situation at Goddard in 1971 encouraged Mamet to become a playwright. Essentially an actor who began to teach other actors and direct students, he started to write, "really to illustrate the points that I was talking about as a teacher." Another reason was that the St. Nicholas Company at Goddard, his first theatrical company, had no money to pay royalties, so it was cheaper and easier for him to write the plays himself (IOW 134).

Mamet was now living in Montpelier, the capital of Vermont, and driving to campus in his Karmann Ghia. He shared a large, corner apartment in a three-story former road house with Pierce Bounds and Jim Lartin-Drake, both of them involved with running the Haybarn Theatre at Goddard. Bounds was there as a technical assistant dealing with stagecraft and lighting. Lartin-Drake dealt with everything else concerning the operation of the theatre including design. William H. Macy and his girlfriend lived in an apartment below them.

Life among the three alternated between Haybarn productions and action in the apartment. Of unending amusement to Mamet was that both Bounds and Lartin-Drake were members of the Goddard College Volunteer Fire Department and had a red phone installed in their apartment to respond to the occasional call. The college had a 2,000 gallon ex-Navy Pumper truck but it required instruction before any volunteer could drive it. With no power steering or power brakes, it was a challenge. Pierce Bounds gained proficiency through an instructor so intriguing that they began to date and eventually married. Mamet found it all very comical and a photo of Mamet in long hair wearing a fireman's hat sitting near the barn door where the Pumper was stationed shows his less than serious commitment to the enterprise.

Known as "Uncle Dave" to his roommates and students, Mamet affected a serious, grown-up air derived in part from his self-confidence and determination. He was also brutally frank and foul-mouthed, outspoken and direct. Robert Falls, Artistic Director of the Goodman Theatre, similarly recalled that when he first met Mamet in 1975 at a poker game in Chicago, he possessed "this incredible confidence and presence." Perhaps the cigar, unfashionable crew cut and odd manner of speaking that alternated between profanities and florid nineteenth-century locutions lent themselves to this image.[20] But Mamet was committed to his work and his friends, and enjoyed nothing more than looking down on State Street, the main drag of Montpelier, from the large third-floor windows while enjoying one of his crooked cigars and contemplating his writing and productions. The title for Mamet's 2000 film *State and Main* derives from the intersection of the two streets visible from the apartment windows.

The Duck Variations was the first effort of the newly formed St. Nicholas Theatre Company and produced in 1972. It consisted of fourteen variations of an extended conversation between two old men on a park bench on the edge of a city. The actors in the original production were Pablo Vela and his friend Peter Vincent. Mamet directed. Unlike his later plays, Mamet provided a set of surprisingly expansive stage directions:

> This is a very simple play.
>
> The set should consist only of a park bench and perhaps a wire garbage can.
>
> The actors can be discovered seated on the bench at rise, or they can come on together, or separately and meet.
>
> Any blocking or business is at the discretion of individual actors and directors.
>
> There should be, though, an interval between each variation—it doesn't need to be a long one—to allow the actors to rest and prepare for the new variation. This interval is analogous to the space between movements in a musical presentation. (DV 73).

The adjective in the last phrase is important because it shows how musical referencing remains important for Mamet's conception of his work. The origin of the play, he told a reporter in 1976 when it opened in New York, was his listening to a number of older, often Jewish, men around Chicago, especially on the Lakefront. He comically dismissed the work in 1977 when he said "you can count the playwrights who haven't written about two men sitting in a park on one hand. This is just another one." (FOM 15)

The play opens with a characteristically Mametian interplay of doubt, clarification, repetition and action:

> Emil: It's Nice.
> George: The Park is nice.
> Emil: You forget.
> George: . . . you remember.
> Emil: I don't know . . .
> George: What's to know? There's a boat! (DV 75).

Digression, not discourse, describes their conversation, which continues throughout the fourteen scenes. Ducks seem at first insignificant but they, too, have problems and will battle day and night for their survival (again, a Mamet theme) (DV 83). The seemingly idle conversation, however, has purpose and reason. "Even those we, at this time, do not clearly understand" Emil states. "There's nothing you could possible name that doesn't have a purpose. Don't even bother to try. Don't waste your time" he adds, evoking Mamet's own sense of rationality and idea of life as a set of objectives (DV 86). George skeptically agrees: "You can't get away with *nothing*." Emil responds with, "And if you *could* it would have a purpose," causing George to answer with, "Nobody knows that better than me." " . . . Well put" Emil responds (DV 87).

The linguistic short circuits of *The Duck Variations* allow Mamet to offer views on nature, the weather, life, death, and friendship. With a Beckett-like simplicity, his conversation masks fundamental concepts. His two characters address broad questions indirectly, only sensing the need to skirt the deeper issues.

Emil: Speak for yourself.
George: I am speaking for myself.
Emil: Then speak to yourself.
George: Who asked you to listen?
Emil: Who asked you to talk?
George: Why are you getting upset?
Emil: You upset me.
George: Yeah? (DV 96)

Language and thought remain Mamet's concern throughout the text. The eleventh variation, "You Know, I Remember," one of the longest, anticipates the rapid dialogue between the characters in *American Buffalo* (DV 109–13). Sitting on the edge of the lake, Emil and George find in it a reflection of their own internal concerns with the work expressing many of Mamet's future worries and obsessions that sometimes show the futility of life. Emil: "What a waste in the life of a duck. To be shot. And not even eaten. Shot. Shot down like some animal" (DV 117). The play ends with a short exchange on mankind's long-term fascination watching birds to learn the secrets of flight.

Sexual Perversity in Chicago was in an early stage of development, and would later be refined in Chicago in preparation for its premier at the Organic Theatre. In its Goddard form, it was a rough set of blackouts, one of them involving William H. Macy as a construction worker tamping down some fresh asphalt. Pierce Bounds and Jim Lartin-Drake had poured some actual asphalt-like substance on the floor in front of the stage. By show time, however, it had not dried very well so that when actors walked on it, the material stuck to their shoes. When Macy had his scene, bare-chested and in a hard hat, he was actually tamping down the gooey substance. And when an off-stage voice shouted, "Lunch!" Macy ad-libbed with, "About fucking time!"

Another spring 1972 production at the Haybarn was called, in its shortened form, *Lone Canoe* (not to be confused with a 1979 production of the same name at the Goodman Theatre in Chicago). The full title of the Goddard production was *Old Chief Hoopjaw's Lone Canoe after the Potlatch Balm and Elixir*. It was a parody of a nineteenth-century Medicine Show, although one that had gone dramatically wrong. More a satire or lampoon, it starred Pablo Vela as the Old Chief, Macy in a bowler hat as the Medicine Man urging the audience to try the all-purpose remedy (a liquid poured into redesigned A-1 Steak Sauce bottles with the Chief's profile in front of a rising sun, all floating over a canoe on the label), and Steve Schachter as a Native American who occasionally shot across the stage on a wheeled tree stump crashing into the scenery. A good deal of the script was improv, worked up by Mamet with the actors. But everything that could go wrong with a production did go wrong—and that was the point. Odd juxtapositions of movement and speech defined the comedy, which was supported by selling advertisements that appeared in nineteenth-century type painted on the pseudo fire curtain.

Slapstick was the operative term for the production devised by Mamet. Wrong items fell from the flies, including, at one point, a stagehand dangling above the stage from ropes. Sets would collapse and the curtain would rise on stagehands trying to repair them. Students would wander onto the stage bewildered, trying to figure out what was going on as various off-stage doors slammed. Asking for his canoe at one point, the Chief would see a large binocular stand fall from above. A six-foot high squaw (modeled on the advertising image for Land-O-Lakes butter) would be wheeled across. At these frequent mishaps, Macy would rush to the stage to try and hawk his elixir, which would not only insure your youth but prevent colds, remove paint, and clean windows. His role would shift, however, from huckster to a toiling desperado determined to sell.

At the end, an actual canoe fell from the flies while a group of student "enforcers," flanking Macy, Vela, and Schachter, would dare anything else to go wrong, all the while trying to insure that the actors said their lines correctly. The stage was in shambles, anticipating the junk shop at the end of *American Buffalo*. With no intermission—although the premise was the attempt of the show to get to an intermission to sell the magic elixir—the play flew along in its madcap manner, a risible presentation of the American Confidence Man, forecasting Mamet's future absorption with the figure and theme. Perhaps unconsciously, Mamet was visualizing what Meisner said repeatedly to his acting classes: "the text is like a canoe and the river on which it sits is the emotion" (SM 115).

Mamet stayed two years at Goddard (1971–72). In his first year he was acting instructor; in his second, writer-in-residence. At the time he also had his first car, a 1967 Karmann Ghia, beige with a black top, which he drove speedily to campus and to New Haven, where he was dating a woman. At one point, seeking a small raise, partly because a new bar opened in Montpelier, increasing his cost of living, as he explained it, he was called into a meeting of the college board to justify the request. "But you have a luxury sports car," they noted. Despite his claim that he paid only nine hundred dollars for it, the raise was denied. He sold the convertible the day he left Vermont, but eight years later bought it in the same color again when he saw one for sale on Sunset Boulevard in Hollywood.

The first season of the St. Nicholas Theatre Company at Goddard included *The Duck Variations*, Chekhov's *The Marriage Proposal*, and O'Neill's *Anna Christie*. All involved limited casts, which meant minimalized costs and transportation. *The Duck Variations* required two actors, *The Marriage Proposal* three. *Anna Christie*, however, with its four acts, needed a cast of thirteen for the story of a daughter who reveals herself as a prostitute after reuniting with her father, a barge captain, and falling in love with a stoker. A poster from the *Anna Christie* production—painted on a dark brown wooden board—advertises performances in the Goddard College Haybarn on July 26–28, 1972. The lettering surrounding a romantically drawn female face announces the title, location, and dates but has no mention of the playwright. The St. Nicholas Theater Company appears at the top left-hand corner.

A review from *The Times-Argus* of Barre-Montpelier, Vermont, of May 4, 1972, comments favorably on the presentation of *The Duck Variations* at Vermont College. Two actors, Steve Schachter and Peter Vincent, also receive praise for their performance in Chekhov's *The Marriage Proposal*. The reviewer ends by citing the St. Nicholas' view that acting is "living truthfully and fully under imaginary circumstances"—a Meisner statement drawn from Stanislavsky—and the remark that "David Mamet and his troupe are serious artists. They deserve our applause and support. Central Vermont is lucky to have them."[21]

Mamet had studied Chekhov earlier, but his engagement with *The Marriage Proposal* initiated a series of productions of this critical playwright that have continued throughout his career. This includes productions of *The Cherry Orchard* and *Uncle Vanya*, which he transformed into the imaginative *Vanya on 42nd Street*. In notes to his adaptation of *The Cherry Orchard*, he expresses his admiration for Chekhov and the play *not* because it is about the struggle between the old values of the Russian aristocracy and the loss of power, but because it is about, as every play is about, "the actions of its characters" or rather "the action the characters are trying to accomplish." His analogy is to a poker game and the strategies involved in determining the cards held by your opponent (CO xv, vii).

After an initial run at Goddard, the St. Nicholas company toured New England with the aid of a grant from the Vermont Council on the Arts, culminating in performances at Boston's Center for the Arts of *The Duck Variations* and the early version of *Sexual Perversity in Chicago* in July 1972.[22] A review in *Boston after Dark*, (July 25, 1972) by Bonnie Jacob and headlined "Of ducks and sex in Chicago," stressed that "Mamet understands conversation well; his use of language is powerfully accurate and at times almost musical." She also notes his origin in the work of Pinter and Beckett.

The Duck Variations, the paper continues, while a good piece of playwriting is too long and repetitious. It needs pruning and a clearer delineation of the two characters. Good acting is evident but the energy level is low; nevertheless, the reviewer praises the St. Nicholas group as offering one of the most interesting and entertaining stage events in the summer.[23] But following the modest success of the summer of '72, there was little more for Mamet to do. He left Vermont for the urban edge of Chicago—not just a place but an attitude.

3

OFF-LOOP

Emil: You know, it is a good thing to be perceptive, but you shouldn't let it get in the way.
George: And that is the point I was trying to make.

Mamet, *The Duck Variations*

St. Nicholas, the patron saint of mountebanks, never visited Clark Street on Chicago's North Side, although for some time the Mamet-inspired theater company of the same name inhabited a Clark Street apartment. A neighborhood of small restaurants, clubs, and a few Off-Loop theatres (outside of the downtown core known as the Loop), Clark Street ran northwest through Lincoln Park, the locale of the singles bars Mamet would use in *Sexual Perversity in Chicago*, which, after its transfer to New York, became a breakout hit. Among his early plays, only *American Buffalo* would be bigger, easily making the journey from the Goodman Theatre to Broadway. Chicago to New York and back again: between 1972 and 1977, Mamet's work in the two cities was explosive, threatening, and unforgettable.

The period did not start out that way. When Mamet returned to Chicago, he had nothing concrete lined up. He had come back because he "didn't have any money [and] because I always believed in the old saying that if you can't make it in Chicago, you can't make it anywhere" (YLC 12). His goal was success in the theatre, but how to achieve it remained a mystery. He had some modest (although not always critical) success with *The Duck Variations* and *Litko* (1972) but returned in the fall of 1972 to a series of nontheatrical jobs, while working on several scripts and taking a few acting parts. The success of *Sexual Perversity in Chicago* at the Organic Theatre, however, encouraged him to risk establishing his own company—to give him control over material, actors, productions, and venues. He invited his two former students, Macy and Schachter, then trying to start their own theater in California, to join him, and they came. With newcomers Linda Kimbrough and musician Alaric 'Rokko" Jans, plus Patricia Cox, the St. Nicholas Theatre Company was reborn—this time with plans for a theatre school as well as an acting company. The timing was right: an experimental, Off-Loop theatre scene was just emerging as a series of new venues were offering original productions that appealed to the idealism and energy of a set of young directors and actors.

Chicago theatre in the sixties, before the Off-Loop scene, largely meant the Ivanhoe, the Harper, and the Candlelight Dinner Playhouse, all fallouts from the Studebaker Theatre of an earlier period that mixed well-known, serious plays with the occasional musical comedy. The 150-seat Candlelight in the southwest suburb of Summit had a hydraulic lift for quick scenery changes and soon *Fiddler on the Roof* and *Man of La Mancha* competed with *Phantom* (the Arthur Kopit-Maury Yeston version). Large musicals played to the dinner theatre crowd, although the producer William Pullinsi often threw in a surprise such as the farce *MacBird!*, Barbara Garson's vision of Lyndon B. Johnson as Macbeth. The adjacent Forum Theater opened in 1972 and staged the musical *Company*. *Boss*, a musical based on Mike Royko's book on mayor Richard J. Daley, also opened there. According to Richard Christiansen, former drama critic of the *Chicago Tribune*, the productions kept "a high downtown level," professional and perfected (TOO 137). On the fringe was Second City, which had opened in 1959 developing a small cadre devoted to its satirical revues and then blackouts that were equally intense and outrageous.

The Harper was a South Side attempt to have a serious theatre in the Hyde Park area. The 300-seat house, opening with Pirandello's *Henry IV*, was not summer theatre, or dinner theatre, or community theatre. It had higher goals but it was tough to find audiences and the Harper soon turned to contemporary dance, although for a short time it tried a repertory program featuring Chekhov's *The Cherry Orchard* directed by Paul Sills and Mailer's *The Deer Park*. The Ivanhoe on the North Side attempted new work by established writers. The director George Keathley in 1971, for example, premiered Tennessee Williams's *Out Cry*, an uneven work made more difficult by Williams's erratic backstage behavior (TOO 141). The Ivanhoe's biggest hit was *Status Quo Vadis*, a satire. Only stars like Sandy Dennis in *A Street Car Named Desire* kept the theatre afloat until it closed in 1975. What these large houses did accomplish, however, was the establishment of a cadre of resident artists and a conscious effort to raise the level of performance for Chicago audiences.

But an activist arts movement led by the Free Street Theatre, founded by Patrick Henry in 1968, and the Body Politic, established by Reverend Jim Shiflett in 1969, initiated genuine theatre innovation in the city. Free Street Theatre formed a series of revues, some improvisational, that performed in inner neighborhoods around the city and focused on urban issues and local musical sounds. The Body Politic, located at 2257–61 N. Lincoln Avenue on the North Side, became a multidisciplinary arts center with a resident theatre company, Paul Sills' Story Theatre. The activist Reverend James Shiflett, a Presbyterian minister, was the moving force who, after the need for a Community Arts Foundation was identified in 1966, began to set up theatre, writing, film, dance, photography, and art workshops in Chicago schools. By 1969, with the aide of a private donor, he acquired a Lincoln Avenue storefront renovated for use as a center. The name Body Politic originated in a statement by the nineteenth-century actor/manager Harley Granville-Barker, who said theater was an expression of the "body politic." The building, which included the rent-paying Oxford Pub, became home to a host of visual and performing arts projects but lacked a theatre group.

Shiflett turned to Paul Sills, a former member of Second City who, after a stint in New York, returned to Chicago to start his Story Theatre. They focused on innovative, experimental work. At the same time June Pyskacek, a part of the Chicago City Players and of the original Community Arts Foundation project, broke away and established the Kingston Mines theatre group, focusing on avant-garde material and the occasional musical satire, in this case the 1971 hit *Grease*, set in a fictional Chicago high school of 1959. Of course, it went on to Broadway and then Hollywood. Sills moved Story Theatre into the Body Politic space in 1969, establishing a 150-seat theatre on the first floor of what had previously been the home of the U.S. Slicing Machine Company. They began with a production of stories from Ovid's *Metamorphoses*. Everyone had the theatre bug, James Shiflett no exception: for a while he had his own theatre company, the improvisatory Dream Theatre, a resident and touring group but, lacking funds and energy, by 1979 Shiflett retreated from Body Politic. However, in 1970, when Paul Sill's Story Theatre left the Body Politic to tour, another young director and troupe filled the space: Stuart Gordon's Organic Theatre.

Chicago-born Gordon had been a student with his own theatre company at the University of Wisconsin at Madison but found the administration unsympathetic to his widely satiric *Game Show* about audience members abused on stage by the host for prizes (the greater the abuse the grander the prize). Neither did they appreciate his original production of Peter Pan with a nude scene that coincided with a hallucinogenic visit to Never Land. He needed a new venue and went to see the Story Theatre at the Body Politic, met Paul Sills and asked if he could bring his company to town. Of course, Sills replied, and with Body Politic and Kingston Mines just up the street they'd be "a scene. And no one will bother you because no one cares" (TOO 162).

Gordon came with a few holdovers from Madison and found a group of new young actors and the Organic Theatre was established with an adaptation of Orwell's *Animal Farm*. Occasionally thought of as hippies, "the Organics" quickly established themselves as an important experimental group who not only shared all the tasks, from cooking to building sets and acting, but the risks. When Sills and the Story Theatre left to go on the road, the Organic Theatre Company took over their space for the next three years at the Body Politic. Their production of *Warp!* (1971–72), a wildly inventive science fiction fantasy, was a hit. The large stage curtain, for example, rose and spread itself precariously over the heads of the audience, where it remained during the performance. The comic-strip, fast-paced show transferred to New York in February 1973, although it had only a short run and the company, after a few months to recover, regrouped in Chicago.

By September 1973, they had new space, the Leo Lerner Theatre of the Uptown Center of Hull House on North Beacon Street. A youthful group of unknowns gathered, including Dennis Franz, Bruce Taylor, and Joe Mantegna. A play by Ray Bradbury, *The Wonderful Ice Cream Suit*, was a hit and for the next eight years, the Organic flourished at the Lerner. One of the successes was *Cops* (1976) by Terry Curtis Fox with Mantegna and Franz as two plainclothes policemen caught late one night in a shoot-out in a diner. Mamet worked on the script with Fox for a while. *Bleacher Bums* (1977) was their last hit, a comedy in nine innings set in the right-field bleachers of Wrigley Field, home of the Cubs. Off-Loop ensemble theatre had been born.

All of this was taking place against the backdrop of a more established theatrical institution, the Goodman Theatre, affiliated with the Art Institute of Chicago. Unlike the community or neighborhood or storefront theatre movement (in some ways these terms are synonymous), the Goodman seemed more formal and perhaps moribund, although it, too, would play a major part in establishing Mamet's reputation. But the Goodman had a very different profile. In 1957, the Goodman hired the Viennese producer, director, and teacher John Reich, who sought a new, professional level of performance. He slowly reinvigorated the Goodman Theatre School, established a new subscription series and imported professional actors to build a solid resident theatre for the city. In 1969 Reich and Douglas Seale, English actor and director, became co-directors of a resident professional company on the Goodman's main stage; student productions occurred in a smaller, 135-seat studio theatre. It was hoped Patrick Henry would become one of its new producer/directors, but he focused on his interracial cast of students and young actors who trucked about the city to parks, empty lots, and neighborhoods as part of his Free Street Theatre. But in fits and starts, the Goodman would move into the vital theatrical orbit that was forming in Chicago, finding its place there only with the arrival from New York of a young assistant director, and later artistic director, Gregory Mosher.

~

Mamet first returned to Chicago in the early fall of 1972, taking time off his teaching job at Goddard College, to oversee production of his first Chicago effort, the curtain-raiser *Litko*, followed by *The Duck Variations*. It took place at the tiny New Room of the Body Politic Theatre on North Lincoln Avenue, the storefront space holding roughly sixty people who suffered inadequate sight lines (YLC 11; TOO 175). Fritzie Sahlins, former wife of Bernard Sahlins, producer of Second City, took a chance on the young playwright Mamet, producing and directing the fourteen variations with little fuss, as the *Chicago Tribune* noted. At opening night, however, Mamet was in the lobby nervously standing off in a corner with a backpack filled with notebooks and pens, dressed in thrift shop clothes and wearing a large grin. He was intense and anxious (YLC 11; TOO 176). Linda Winer, writing in the *Chicago Tribune*, liked the touching "Jewish Estragon and Vladimir" and Mamet's humor in *The Duck Variations* but felt he stretched himself when he treated death as a subtext.[1] Mamet found animals appealing in his early work, moving from his graduating work "The Camel Document" to *The Duck Variations*, then *Squirrels* (1974), *American Buffalo* (1975), *Dark Pony* (1977), *The Revenge of the Space Pandas* (1977), *The Frog Prince* (1982), and *The Dog* (1983).

Litko (1972), on the bill with *The Duck Variations*, was Mamet's early and self-conscious one-hander about theatre, showing the actor doing everything from directing to barking out stage directions, running the light board, setting up props, and creating sound effects. With the stage directions performed as Litko delivers the soliloquy, the audience becomes deeply and comically involved in the process of performance:

Unbutton coat. Litko speaks: Let us dispense with formality, and get down to theatrical clichés.
The audience smiles appreciatively at his candid behavior.
Thanks, gang. Pause (GS 175).

The play embodies Mamet's own multiple efforts in establishing the St. Nicholas Theatre Company, assisting in administration, while directing, writing plays, and auditioning cast members and occasionally aiding in building sets, the stage, or chairs. *Litko* is a metaphor of Mamet's multiple careers in and out and around the theatre. It functions as an introduction to all that Mamet wanted to do in the theatre—but from a Beckettian perspective:

Why, then, does Litko not reply?
Has he been 'struck dumb'?
Shall he lapse into song? Or dance? Or mixed-media? Or some more purely visual form of art? Has he the training? Has he the inclination? Has he the time? Is God dead? (GS 176)

The Duck Variations, his second 1972 production, was less than an hour. It originated at Goddard College when Mamet taught there. Directed by Fritzie Sahlins, it was a set of fourteen short dialogues, revealing in its rhythms of everyday speech a talented writer. The title evokes a musical score or a parody of one, as two elderly men share various stories on a park bench, including several about ducks. Aging, power, competition, nature, loneliness, and death are other themes. A poster for the production shows a photo of the backs of two elderly men, one short and one tall, walking along the Chicago lakeshore. It reads:

In the new room at the Body Politic Theater 2259 N. Lincoln, Chicago
THE DUCK VARIATIONS
A PLAY BY David Mamet—Directed by Fritzie Sahlins

The rhythm of the conversations is as important as the content, Mamet in the habit even then of beating out the iambs of spoken English as he directed. The two speakers are not, however, always in tune with each other, although a lyrical line runs through the language. The understated duet, with its rhythms and repetitions, found audiences willing to listen, sympathetic even when, like the characters, they did not want to hear what was being said. Told that cacti thrive by living alone, Emil responds with, "I don't want to hear it. If it's false, don't waste my time and if it is true I don't want to know" (DV 99). This is a typical Mamet situation, which he later elaborated on in *American Buffalo* and *Glengarry Glen Ross*: a moment when characters face certain truths they would prefer to avoid.

"Yes, the play is close to Beckett" Mamet later told an interviewer. Its theme is the lack of communication, but Mamet and his characters "intensify their relationships into something present on the stage and that is worth seeing" according to a critic in the *New York Times* commenting on a later production.[2] But the obsessive, speculative talk of *The Duck Variations* resonated with Chicago and New York theatre-goers. Mamet was twenty-four when it opened in Chicago in October 1972.

Mamet's return to Chicago, while it meant taking a series of odd jobs, also meant constant script work, rehearsals, and never losing his confidence that he belonged in the theatre. According to Bernard Sahlins, Mamet acted like a 1930s author—playing pool, smoking cigars, and talking about himself as a theatre person immersed in the craft. He even tried out as an actor for Second City but didn't make it. Yet wherever he could, he participated in theatre life (YLC 11). Home became the Hotel Lincoln, where for $130 a month you got maid service, TV, an answering service, an all-night restaurant (Jeff's Laugh Inn), and a view of the lake. He worked daily on his writing but to earn a living he played a dentist in an industrial film, taught acting at Columbia College and helped in the prison program of the Free Street Theatre, which took him to the Pontiac Correctional Facility (a maximum-security, adult male prison with a population of over 1,000). The experience would earn him the nickname "Teach" among his poker-playing pals at a North Side junk store, which would become the featured locale of *American Buffalo*. He also taught at the Dwight Correctional Center, a prison for women. He also sold Walton carpets over the telephone.

Mamet also bought his first typewriter, an Olympia, for $200 (which some twenty year later he still had and used) and began to travel about the city with a spiral notebook in his pocket available to jot down overheard conversation or phrases. (CA 97). Chekhov did the same and, not surprisingly, many of Chekhov's characters are composite figures from those he knew or met. He also re-crafted what people said, as Mamet would do.

At this time, Mamet worked as a waiter at a gay club just up Clark Street and also as a bus boy in the final days of the London House, a restaurant and jazz club. He sat in Jeff's Laugh-Inn in the Hotel Lincoln, amused by its ungrammatical sign, "Where Your Always at Home," and in the park across the street he wrote plays in his notebook. "I had just a few clothes and several theatre books," including Boleslavsky's *Acting: The First Six Lessons.* Years later, when recounting his early theatre life to a young actor visiting Mamet in his Boston home, he generously passed on the volume (CA 98–99).

In October 1973, Mamet found an acting job, a bit part in a revue farce by Dick Cusack, *The Night They Shot Harry Lindsey with a 155 mm Howitzer and Blamed it on Zebras,* directed by Del Close. It played briefly at the Body Politic with a local professional cast that included Mina Kolb, a favorite of the early days of Second City. Mamet played the part of Father Cassattari, a priest involved in a gun-running trade. Though it was a small part, Mamet wrote a long biography of the character; it was fantastic, the actor Byrne Piven recalled, but it had nothing whatsoever to do with the character as written. Piven also remembered an "informed energy and imagination about David even then . . . but he was a terrible actor" (YLC 12). Mike Nussbaum, later to become one of Mamet's favorite actors, agreed. He played Harry Lindsey in the production and teased Mamet about his lack of acting skills. One day after a ribbing, Mamet walked in and thrust a script into Nussbaum's hand without comment: it was *The Duck Variations* and it was astonishing. "I could tell at once he was a better playwright than actor" Nussbaum recalled.[3]

While busy working on the fringes of the theatre, Mamet developed his script for *Sexual Perversity in Chicago,* which he shared, at first reluctantly, with Stuart Gordon, director of the Organic Theatre. Gordon said it needed work. When he first read it, the play was a jumble of disconnected sketches. Working with Mamet in preparation for a June 1974 premiere, they fashioned a structure that set the rise and fall of a love affair against a disturbing sexist atmosphere of modern urban Chicago life.

The language of the play was fast, repetitive, and often, for its time, offensive: "A lot of these broads, you know, you just don't know. You know? I mean what with where they've been and all" (SPC 39). The complex dialogue, however, challenged the actors at the Organic accustomed to improvisational style. When the actor portraying Deborah asked Mamet "What is this?" in rehearsal concerning a particularly difficult passage, Mamet paused, took out the cigar in his mouth and said, without missing a beat, "It's good writing" (TOO 176). In a curious bit of Chicago theatre history, the actor who played Bernie in the original production, Warren Casey, went on to co-write the Broadway hit, *Grease,* which was first a success in Chicago.

The story of *Sexual Perversity* is of the experienced Bernie Litko leading his innocent buddy, Danny, and of the latter's love affair with Deborah, whose cynical, feminist roommate Joan disapproves of Debbie moving in with Danny. The play pits sex in two forms against power. The sex is both sin and salvation in the play, a double role that has difficulty surviving in a world where Vice, in the shape of Bernie, corrupts Goodness in the colorless character of Danny. Spellbinding Danny with a sado-masochistic tale in the first scene prepares the audience for Bernie's philosophy, which echoes that expressed by Fred in *Lakeboat*: "THE WAY TO GET LAID IS TO TREAT THEM LIKE SHIT," the capitalized letters and tone almost echoing the form of sermons found in medieval morality plays (SPC 22; LB 55).

The play with its pessimistic ending—Deborah and Danny split, marking the end of romance—is the result of another theme in the work, power. Bernie again lectures Danny "that when she's on her back, her legs are in the air, she's coming like a choo-choo. . . . I want you to remember. . . . That power . . . (*Pause*) . . . that *power* means *responsibility. (Pause)* Remember that." "I will" Danny meekly answers (SPC 31).

The candid language masks Bernie's anger and intensifies as Bernie becomes more verbally violent and destructive not only toward women but himself. At the end, he achieves satisfaction only by ogling women on the beach with Danny, who has returned to be his cohort. But the voyeur's paradise remains unfulfilled, a kind of punishment for the failure to treat women as anything but objects:

Danny:. . . I gotta say . . .
Bernie: . . . *Oh*, yeah . . .
Danny: . . . that you can *pick* 'em.
Bernie I know I can. And will you look at the chick in the two-piece wet-look jobbie?
Danny Where?
Bernie Where I'm looking. (*Pause.*) *Those* legs . . .
Danny Oh *no*!
Bernie:. . . all the way up to her *ass*!
Danny Jesus.
Bernie And *beyond* for all we know.
Danny: You said it. (SPC 64)

Danny's acquiescence to Bernie's language and perspective confirms his "fall" and acceptance of an unredemptive world. This, however, was not the original ending. In the first version, it was a wordless scene of separation between Danny and Deborah. The two lovers retreat to separate sides of the stage. In the center is a television which they both watch as the "Star Spangled Banner" plays, signaling the end of the broadcast day. The anthem ends and a whining sound of the station signal comes on, followed by a blank screen and a blur of snow. Deborah slowly crosses to center stage to turn it off and the theatre goes silent and dark, ending both love and romance (TOO 176).

Mamet set the play on the North Side of Chicago, referring to singles bars and restaurants in the area he knew well. According to William H. Macy, he also included some of his own pick-up lines, notably, "Is someone taking up a lot of your time these days?" Danny's question to Deborah when he first meets her at the library (SPC 23). At the casting call, Gordon wanted Joe Mantegna, an Organic regular, to play Bernie. Mantegna chose the financially more secure understudy part of *Lenny* downtown at $300 a week (TOO 164).

Reaction to the play in Chicago where it debuted and then New York where it played in an Off-Off Broadway production at the Theatre at St. Clement's, was at first negative. The work seemed too caustic and offensive, lacerating the behavior of single men and women. The *New York Times* praised the authentic dialogue, even if some of the exchanges sounded "as if they came straight off the wall of a public men's toilet."[4] Audiences, however, provided less resistance to recognizing their own social behavior, as Mamet unhesitatingly addressed sexual liberation, feminism, and misguided males, topics to reappear in later works like *American Buffalo* and *Oleanna*. Linda Winer in the *Chicago Tribune* of June 21, 1974, wrote that "clichés get courted around as if the words are printed on the singles bar's fake Bauhaus chrome." In this production, she trumpets, "the bed rolls right out from the bar" to symbolize the crassness between sex and social behavior, which some loved and others hated (Sauer 264). Nevertheless, the play was a hit, although the Organic never shared in its financial success, because Mamet did not divide royalties with the company, something that Gordon resented.

One result of *Sexual Perversity* was an offer by a studio for Mamet to go to Hollywood to write screen dialogue at $1,000 a week. It appealed to the young playwright, who discussed the opportunity with his peers at the St. Nicholas. They discouraged him and he concluded they were right. He was twenty-six and had recently directed his first play, *Squirrels*. Chicago worked for him: "if you dress right and aren't pushy, Chicago's a good town" he said in the 1974 interview explaining his rejection of the Hollywood job. He added that as early as 1968 he began writing seriously and took up the Chicago singles scene: "I was hanging out on Diversey [street], shooting pool at Bensinger's, and I was gonna call the play 'Commonwealth Hot,' for the way the hotel sign read [the Commonwealth Hotel with the e missing]." Lanford Wilson beat Mamet to it with "Hot l Baltimore."[5]

Mamet's acceptance by Chicago audiences was not immediate nor was it easy, although the public agreed that his work was startling and groundbreaking. In 1974, he won the Joseph Jefferson Award for the Best New Chicago Play, *Sexual Perversity*, his first full-length work presented in his hometown, which he acknowledged through its title.

When the Organic Theatre went off on a European tour, Mamet took over the Leo Lerner Theater for the rest of the summer and relaunched his own St. Nicholas Theatre Company. Joined by Macy and Schachter, plus Jans, Patricia Cox, and Linda Kimbrough, he was underway. Although the group had to borrow twenty dollars to obtain a certificate of incorporation, it had early financial supporters, including Byrne and Joyce Piven and then Dick Cusack. Cusack owned an advertising agency and would help company members by hiring them for voiceovers and other jobs.

Kimbrough's first meeting with Mamet was memorable. She met him at Steve Schachter's Clark Street apartment, which at the time was used as the St. Nicholas headquarters. Mamet discussed her theatre experience and then asked her to come back for an audition after another actor dropped out of his new production,

Squirrels. At the audition, he had her repeat certain lines over and over until he was able to sense how she might discover her own emotional center by eliminating any embellishment or interpretation in her acting style. At one point during rehearsal, he had her repeat her entrance thirty times. However, she quickly absorbed the Meisner method combined with Mamet's evolving ideas about an unadorned style of acting. She satisfied his demands, although he always retained an edgy attitude. Years later, when Kimbrough arrived to play a small part in his film *Homicide*, Mamet's greeting card read "Don't embarrass me."

Mamet at this time was expanding his own ideas on acting as he worked up *Squirrels*. Essentially drawing from radio drama, he was learning that great theatre works by "leaving the *endowment* of characters, place and especially action up to the audience." "Good drama," he writes "has no stage directions" (WR 14). We increase our enjoyment and involvement by the absence of the descriptive. The best productions occur in the mind of the audience; consequently, the best acting is straight up, emotionless, and clipped.

A statement from the 1974 St. Nicholas program for *Squirrels* contains a brief history of the St. Nicholas company:

> St. Nich formed in Plainfield, Vermont in 1972 by actors and actresses then associated with Goddard and Marlboro Colleges.
>
> The group had been investigating aspects of the Stanislavsky System in workshops and classes and felt the need of a production organization which would permit the employment and the extension of their training.
>
> The aim of the group is work—in workshops, rehearsal, and production—based on a shared understanding of the technique of creation on stage.
>
> Using Stanislavsky's definition that "acting is living truthfully under imaginary circumstances," we have worked to est. a common vocabulary, and a common method which will permit us to bring to the stage (not through our insights, but through our craft) this truth in the form of *action*.
>
> We are in Chicago with the intention of making it our permanent home, and are currently looking for theatrical space which would permit the year-round performance of plays in repertory and the conducting of classes and workshop with and for both the professional and amateur communities.

The St. Nicholas, a nonprofit corporation approved by the state of Illinois, "is named for Nicholas of Maya, Patron of mountebanks, prostitutes and the *demimonde*." The first season of the St. Nicholas, 1974–75, listed *Squirrels*, Eugene O'Neill's *Beyond the Horizon* and Mamet's play for children, *The Poet and the Rent*. Among the patrons noted in the 1974 program were Mr. and Mrs. Bernard Mamet, Mr. and Mrs. William Macy, Sr., and Mr. Saul Schachter.

Squirrels, a work that satirized the writing process, was their first production in October 1974, and anticipated 1988's *Speed-the-Plow*. In preparation for its reception and as an early form of self-promotion, Mamet published an article in the *Chicago Sun-Times* entitled "Stanislavsky and Squirrels" in which he explains that the work deals with "nut-tropism," a perverse element of human "mentality" that causes one to acquire mental baggage rather than "learning how to live in the moment." The young writer, named Edmond, discovers that Arthur, the older writer, has been working on the same one-paragraph story for some fifteen years. Only an ambitious cleaning woman whose early literary efforts had been plagiarized by Arthur seems to cut through the nonsense of literary delay, rewriting, and revision.

Linda Kimbrough played the cleaning woman and she recalled how Mamet composed lines during rehearsal. Insisting on a simple, unadorned acting style, he urged her to "stop performing." To overcome her frustration at having to repeat lines, he then suggested she take a break and go into a nearby dance studio. After fifteen minutes, she returned and did it exactly as he wanted—as a reflection of her self.[6]

Reviews of *Squirrels* complained of its obscurity, narcissistic story, and turgid dialogue, possibly reflecting the spontaneous writing of the play. Mamet composed it as he went along, according to Kimbrough, to whom he dedicated the play. But a critic from the *Chicago Tribune* complained that "Sartre or Burroughs is more wakening to read than Mamet is to listen to."[7] The *Chicago Reader*, however, loved it, summarized by the headline of Meredith Anthony's review: "Nuts over Squirrels." Unhesitatingly, she compared the play to Peter Handke's avant-gardism, noting at one point how the character Arthur, the older writer, repeats the word "meaning" nine times before admitting "you ask me about meaning and I respond with gibberish. What kind of friend am I" (SQ 23)? "There's more to life than a facility with modifiers," he later announces to the Cleaning Lady (SQ 41). Anthony also praises Mamet's irrepressible if somewhat self-indulgent sense of humor and odd tidbits like the Metaphysical Restaurant where the menu reads "Idea of Ham, $8.50; Conception of Veal, $6.85 . . . Pre-conception of Veal, $12.00" (SQ 7).

Tanya Akason in "Squirrels and St. Nick" in the *Triad Guide* remarks that *Squirrels* has four episodes and three interludes and that music is an important part of the drama. For St. Nicholas actors, she observes, action comes first, feelings later, catching the central tenet of Mamet's acting method: "The words of the script are read to establish the idea of what is happening. Then, they go to work on the sub-text that lies below the written word."[8] This going below sets the company process apart from the traditional approach to dramatic creation—easier, of course, if your playwright is present and directing.

She then quotes Macy who played Arthur, the older writer. Macy offers an acute statement on Mamet's technique:

> We divide the play into small sequences. We decide on the personal objectives which usually conflict. We forget about the play. Then we go through outrageous improvisations on the objectives of each page. We name the objective from our own personal point of

view. Sometimes they change. Like getting the beat to the music. We try to get the beat of what is happening between the characters involved on the stage. The same thing that makes people tick makes actors and actresses tick. All we have to draw on is ourselves. We put the beat in our own terms. It takes it from being truthful to being very beautiful (80).

This passage condenses what Mamet would later elaborate in *True and False, Heresy and Common Sense for the Actor* (1997).

Michael ver Meulen's radio review noted that Mamet structures his work in the "scene upon scene style of his Organic theatre hit, *Sexual Perversity in Chicago*"and that most of the lines in *Squirrels* are droll throwaways. But he loved the work: "the pace is so rapid and the action so absurdly funny that there are moments when the scene fade-out is a welcome reprieve if only to sooth throbbing ribs." However, the problem is that Mamet's appeal to comedy and his concentration on humor detracts from relationships between each of the play's characters as they feed incestuously off each others' ideas. Nonetheless, it is a funny play containing "the best elements of Marx brothers' humor with a healthy dose of Eugene Ionesco word games thrown in. It captures the feeling of the writer who sees a blank page and is driven with an almost sexual delight to define its purity."[9]

By mid-February 1975, the St. Nicholas Theatre Company had grown and was offering classes in "Acting Technique" and "Voice & Speech for the Theatre." Located at the Grace Lutheran Church at 555 West Belden Street, Chicago, it was expanding, even if it ran a deficit of $98.74. Mamet was its artistic director, although it was Schachter who signed a six-week lease for the space, giving 2110 N. Clark Street as his home address.

Beyond the Horizon by O'Neill was their next production and had a mid-February opening in the 130-seat church theatre. A long and difficult work, O'Neill's first on Broadway, it nevertheless won a Pulitzer Prize in 1921, but rebuffed Chicago theater-goers. In 1975, Richard Christiansen's review highlighted the problems, beginning with its awkward, two-stage set—one to represent the closed world of a farmhouse, the other the open road. In the St. Nicholas production, the cast whisked through the text at breakneck speed making the plot of the two competing brothers—one who opts for a life of hardship on the family farm out of a mistaken romantic impulse and the other forced to leave to make his fortune abroad—difficult to follow. Complicating matters, both have fallen in love with the same girl. Byrne Piven as the father received good notices, Macy, "cursed here by a persistently boyish face," got adequate reviews. But the cast was considered too inexperienced to carry the work and Mamet's direction deemed too rapid. The flat and at times banal dialogue of the original, however, may have satisfied Mamet's need for the unadorned acting style he was promoting. Audiences stayed away, forcing the company to cancel two of its performances.

Nonetheless, Mamet defended his production as an example of the fallacy of romanticism. Against their instincts and inclinations, the brothers make a romantic choice and ruin their lives. O'Neill, Mamet explained to an interviewer, "is a lot more negative than he would like to admit. It's an inherently existential view he takes of life." It should be attacked boldly, vividly, he stressed, so that the "life forces are avowed one hundred per cent." He then explained that he had cut some of the rhetorical dialogue and that in rehearsal used the Stanislavsky method. Dressed in a long coat and even longer scarf while puffing on a cigar during his interview, Mamet seemed as if he just stepped off the 20th Century Limited from New York with a voice "that is of the counter man at Ashkenaz Delicatessen, his general aura that of a North Side Duddy Kravitz."[10]

The Poet and the Rent "a play for kids from 7 to 77,000" was the third production of the St. Nicholas. It's a children's play written by Mamet (who received a fee of $150.00) and was directed by Macy. It is about a day in the life of a working poet who faces a nasty landlord, falls in love, gets a job, goes to jail, almost makes a million dollars and almost lives happily ever after. Sgt. Preston of the Yukon and his dog King join him, as do the girlfriend, a band of thieves, and others. Music alone seems to hold the madcap plot together.

For about a year after *Squirrels*, the St. Nicholas operated from Schachter's second-floor apartment above the Luv Boutique on North Clark. Early on, however, the group had ideas of establishing a theatre school that would help to defray production costs. In a short while, that idea would grow to include classes in dance, directing, speech, and, of course, acting when in 1975 they found their permanent home at 2851 North Halsted Street.

A former bakery (although some believe it was also a print shop at one time), the converted space at North Halsted—soon to have a 211-seat theatre with a broad but shallow open stage—became the home of the St. Nicholas Theatre School, which used the building as a mix of rehearsal space, dance studio, offices, and even, when necessary, sleeping quarters. Within a year there would be fourteen classes offered in theatre and dance, starting with beginning acting techniques and including direction, mime, tap dance, and theatre management. Each eight-week class would be taught by a theatre professional such as William Woodman, John Economos, George Keathely, and David Mamet.[11] A midnight series of plays was launched early in 1976 with Mamet's *Reunion* directed by Cecil O'Neal.

Years later when the St. Nicholas finally left, the building retained its theatre heritage, becoming, successively, home to Steppenwolf, the Organic/ Touchstone Theatre, and ComedySportz, as well as the center for the early careers not only of Mamet and Macy, but also of John Malkovich, Laurie Metcalf, John Mahoney, and Gary Sinise. Lily Tomlin, Patti LuPone, and Peter Weller also performed there. Robert Falls and Gerald Gutierrez both directed in the space.[12]

Mamet was still at the Hotel Lincoln at 1816 North Clark across from Lincoln Park and close to the zoo. The location and space was a kind of "paradise," he wrote, with only Clark Street separating him from the park. Facing east, he watched remarkable sunrises, and he reveled in the "shelter and solitude" (CA 96–97). The twelve-story hotel also had color, from the groups that gathered for the chartered buses to the race track to the prostitutes and supposed crap game in the men's room. He also enjoyed the sounds of the animals at night from the zoo. One evening when Gregory Mosher visited him shortly after arriving from New York, he heard the sound of seals barking outside Mamet's window. "I had no idea there were seals in Lake Michigan" he remarked. "They're not," Mamet replied, pointing to the zoo across the street.

When not working with the St. Nicholas, Mamet continued to travel about Chicago, notebook in hand, to capture dialogue, expressions, and phrases. He would constantly scribble ideas, conversation, and specialized language as he visited junk shops, bars, pool halls, gyms, coffee shops, and old Jewish bathhouses partly for recreation and partly for material. Mamet was always "looking for characters" said the actor J. J. Johnston. He was always comfortable around the "regular guys, the blue-collar guys, even the hustlers, the burglars."[13]

The second season of the St. Nicholas was frantic, especially in the summer of 1975 with everyone playing a triple bill on weekends. It would begin at midday with a Renaissance Faire in Gurnee, Illinois, where they performed both their version of *The Canterbury Tales* and enacted a strolling mind-reading act principally between Mamet and Macy. They would then rush south to a Lake Street shopping mall in suburban Oak Park where they did a madcap *A Midsummer Night's Dream* featuring Mamet in the double role of Theseus and Oberon. Linda Kimbrough played Hippolyta and Titania and Macy was Puck. At midnight on the same day, they would appear at Hull House Theatre on North Broadway performing Mamet's children's play *The Poet and the Rent*, directed by Macy.

The Shakespeare received much press, a good deal of it criticizing Mamet's acting. He was directed by Schachter, whose director's notes include this passage: "David come all the way down stage. for 'Because it hath no bottom' (private moment w/ audience). Take to and Hot ice. David go for chink, stop; look & go again. David Mamet—don't say 'Wobble Beast' till he comes out."

Linda Winer in her review for the *Tribune* includes a photo of a young-looking Mamet wearing an ascot, white shirt, and jacket as Oberon. The play is abridged and telescoped, she notes; it's all a bit of a shoestring production, while a "scruffy variety of costumes defines the characters. David Mamet changes from a Zero Mostel kind of Forum Theseus to a debonairly maladroit Oberon. Linda K is his tough dolly of a Hippolyta and a Bo Peep Southern belle Titania. . . . W. H. Macy's brat face revitalizes Puck." The real complaint is not enough chairs and poor sight lines. "Many of us had to sit on curbs or stand at the sides." But then again, the nine performances took place at the Tudor shopping mall at Oak Park Village at Lake and Marion.

Richard Christiansen was more lighthearted in his comments headlined "Bard meets the Marx Brothers." This is an "engagingly knockout and endearingly nutsy little production of *A Midsummer Night's Dream*"—with free July evening performances. "Stratford-on-Avon it's not. Shakespeare it's almost not." But it's a lot of fun, rather like a "zany talent show put on by the brightest kids in summer camp."

The shortened, two-hour version, with a total costume budget of $35, is unquestionably a romp:

> Theseus, the king of Athens (portrayed with mush-mouthed versifying by David Mamet) comes on as a Grecian Groucho, leering at his Queen Hippolyta (LK), a chorus girl cutie who wears purple platform shoes and bops along listening to her transistor radio. Oberon, king of the fairies (Mamet again) is cast as a somewhat bumbling Fred Astaire (who also loves to embroider) and Titania (Ms. Kimbrough) is costumed and accented as Scarlett O'Hara, a slapstick Southern belle. Macy gives a frisky performance as Puck. Zaps around in socks, shorts suspenders and a bow tie. Schachter has loaded the work with lots of old vaudeville bits and contemporary counterculture humor.

The evening has "a giddy, affectionate and wonderfully refreshing Fellini-esque touch." Love-smitten Lysander, for example, wears a Greek letter fraternity T-shirt and runs into the woods lugging a backpack and Hermia's four suitcases.

The *Chicago Reader* review made no bones about it: Mamet was a better playwright than actor. While Schachter developed the circus aspect of the play, imagining Theseus as a cigar-chomping philistine and Oberon as an urban cosmopolitan, Mamet provides the comic vehicle:

> Mamet regales in the physical schtick and vaudeville bits that go with his parts. Rather than play his roles, he comments upon them. The last act is a trial to see if Mamet will crack up before he can get off stage. Apparently he takes to heart his line: "Our sport will be to take what they mistake." At least he's having fun up there.[14]

Mamet was also working on another play at this time for which he received a $1,000 commission from the Skokie, Illinois, Jewish Community Center: *Marranos*, a drama about "passing." This was the act of Jews during the Inquisition who claimed they had converted to Christianity, a kind of Jewish "con" set in a historicized context. Such behavior was dangerous, deceptive, dishonest, and immensely appealing to Mamet because he could unite a Jewish past with practices of the present.

The unpublished historical play was written concurrently with *American Buffalo*. It ran for ten performances in November 1975 at the Bernard Horwich Jewish Community Center in Skokie where Mamet also produced *Mackinac*, a children's play about life on Mackinac Island, in November 1974. Douglas J. Lieberman, who directed *Marranos*, recalled that Mamet told him he was also working "on another play about a nickel." In the fall of 1975, Mamet disappeared for several weeks, leaving the director to complete revisions to the third draft of *Marranos*, a corrupted production version.[15]

Marannos begins with a nun rolling out a blackboard and describing her work in South America. She describes the unexpected discovery of a menorah and several pieces of silver in the tent of some natives. The play proper then begins as a flashback, initially a series of questions asked by twelve-year old Joao of his grandfather, Dom H., about the absence of his parents. The grandfather explains their hidden Jewish identity. The teaching of ethnic identity begins for the young boy as the grandfather even tells him his Hebrew name, Moshe (Moses). The boy then exclaims, "How could I be a Jew if I did not know!" Suddenly, a con is revealed. The boy has been raised as a Catholic. Fearful that the grandson could now give them away, the grandfather tells him, "You must act naturally. You're going to have to learn to be an actor, and you don't get a rehearsal . . . curtain's up, son." The con is for real.

Tonio, the brother of Diogo, Joao's father, arrives to confirm the family's exposure. Tonio accuses their servant of the betrayal. Fearful of imminent death, the elderly men face opposition from Joao, who suddenly shifts his attitude as the grandfather offers a traditional blessing to his departing son, Tonio, "Shalom Avram." This is code-switching, revealing the family's ability to speak differently given altered social and linguistic contexts. Father and uncle depart and Joao is left asking his grandfather again why the Jews are being persecuted—"You are asking as a Jew yourself?" asks the grandfather to clarify the moral position.

An "aggadic" narrative tradition of storytelling, originating in the imaginative elements of the Talmud expressed as fables, takes over. Mamet employs instructional stories and parables in *Marranos* to establish a thematic link between Jewish history, persecution, and revelation of the Law. At one point, Dom H. opens a secret panel in the fireplace to retrieve religious articles including a tallit and Torah. He then tells the story of Moses, drawing a parallel with the Jews in Portugal. The worry is that as Moses failed to see the Promised Land, the family may never escape persecution.

Memories flood the scene in Act Two as heirlooms are gathered in an area where Joao and his grandfather await a boat. Suddenly, an armed guard with Fra Benedetto (blessed one) arrive and question Dom H. He assumes a series of defensive postures, improvising a series of different roles and is by turns helpful, indignant, obsequious, and histrionic. Complications follow including an attack on Fra Benedetto by a servant. A predatory nurse reenters and we learn it is she who has betrayed the family. Accompanied by armed guards, she foils the family's planned departure. Only the young Joao, sent to search for his sister's doll, escapes, although he witnesses the family's arrest. He departs wearing his father's traveling cloak with the Sabbath lamp and Torah, and is the only survivor. He carries a Jewish identity, heritage, and history, as well as the responsibility for the protection of the sacred ceremonial objects.

In the epilogue to *Marranos*, the modern nun reappears and concludes her lesson of the lost tribe. But a strange gap appears: upstage, a young boy goes out the window in Portugal and four hundred years later we find a menorah in the Amazon. At this moment, we are left to imagine the rest of the boy's life and how he fled to South America. The play shows Mamet's quest to rediscover and resolve

Jewish history, while reaffirming its teachings threatened by both assimilation and anti-Semitism. The play is less a eulogy to a fading heritage than a demonstration of survival.

Marranos is Mamet's first play of any length after *Sexual Perversity*, written just before he began *American Buffalo*. Both are about the con, one historical, the other modern and both are about being caught or exposed by a world that seems arbitrary and capricious. As Teach in *American Buffalo* explains, "All the preparation in the world does not mean *shit*, the path of some crazed lunatic sees you as an invasion of his personal domain. Guy goes nuts. . . . All I'm saying, look out for your own" (AB 85). Few knew that at the time he was revising *Marranos*, Mamet was writing *American Buffalo*, a work of concentrated structural and linguistic brilliance. Macy remembers that after an absence of several weeks, Mamet reappeared with the script. One morning at breakfast, Mamet pulled out from his leather satchel pages he had not shown to anyone and asked Linda Kimbrough to read it—immediately. "So I read it, and when I finished, he asked me what I thought of it. 'It's an American classic.' I said. And he said, 'God bless you.'" It was the play about the nickel (TOO 178).

4

SOUTH SIDE GYPSY

"You still using cards?"
Bernard Mamet

"Yes" was David Mamet's straight answer to his father's question. For years in the early seventies, Mamet played cards every day in an old junk store on Waveland Avenue on the North Side, the place apparently a front for a fence. The game ran daily from noon until eight. On the day his father asked him, Mamet had gone downtown on an errand and stopped in to see his father but as noon approached he said he had to leave. "Where're you going?" "Poker" was the answer (MBT 10). A year or so later, the locale would become the source of his first major hit, *American Buffalo*, an expression of his affection for the world of Chicago's petty criminals: "I've always been fascinated by the picaresque. That's part of the Chicago tradition: to love our gangsters and con men, the bunko artists and so forth" (AOT 59).

This South Side gypsy attitude of Mamet's found further expression in his truculent, ironic, and aggressive manner, capped by his masking his intellectual interests and middle-class life. The allure of the underworld was strong. Chicago was a tough town and he was proud he was part of it. "Dave got hit with the gangster bug early" said his acting friend and the original Donny in *American Buffalo*, J. J. Johnston (FM 76). This partly explains Mamet's mix of South Side patois and educated diction. Attracted to one, he couldn't leave the other. Chicago also provided him with the confidence that he could succeed in whatever he wanted to do, something learned from his father, who felt any problem could be solved if you attacked it (DMC 167). But the gypsy style was more than a restless, devil-may-care attitude that put security and comfort behind adventure and experience; it was also the rebelliousness and determination to be an individual who came by his work and achievements honestly. Hence, the pull to a no-frills acting style originating in Stanislavsky and Meisner: "it is *your* character which you take onstage." Acting is honesty: "invent nothing" (TF 39, 24).

Mamet was not, at first, invited to join the poker game. The group was distrustful of the young, college-educated drop-in. Then one day he wasn't there and when he returned they asked him what had happened. He said he was teaching drama at the Pontiac Correctional Center where it turned out several of them had spent time (he had also taught at the Dwight Correctional Center, a woman's prison). With this pedigree, he was invited to sit in. His nickname: "Teach."

In the "Foreword" to the Arion Press edition of *American Buffalo* (1992), Mamet offered more detail about the sources of his characters: a woman named Rose, who played poker with Mamet, ran a gang of photography hustlers at Comisky Park and Wrigley Field. She and her crew would snap photos of people as they left the ball game, would give them an envelope to sign and return with two dollars on the promise that the photo would then be mailed. But there was never any film in the camera. Fanny was her girlfriend and she hovered over Rose throughout the poker game and got her smokes and coffee. Fanny didn't play cards and looked worried all the time. And then there was Kenny, who ran the game. He owned the junk store where the game took place seven days a week. The junk store, Mamet writes, was not quite a "front" but was "a half-legit, half-criminal emporium." Everything from toys to hubcaps, guns, jewelry, and "various strata of stolen merchandise was there."[1]

Woody was a regular and a roofer. He and Kenny often burglarized after the game, frequently using Woody's information from jobs he had cased. Fletcher was a truck driver "or something." Fat Jeff worked with Mamet at the time and Mamet introduced him to poker. Earl was also there but one night, when the game temporarily moved to Rosie's, he pulled a gun on Mamet. Someone bet and Mamet said "straight call." Earl whipped out a revolver and stuck it in Mamet's face thinking there was some form of underhanded trick in using the phrase "straight call" instead of the accepted but unadorned "call" (F 7). Mamet was unfazed: "I played in the game every day I could for, I think, several years; and one day I began to write about it. The writings formed themselves into this play, a tragedy in free verse about my days in that poker game" (F. 7).

What other elements pulled *American Buffalo* into existence? Mamet explained that when he and Macy were in Chicago in the first year of the reconstituted St. Nicholas and Mamet was living in a tiny room at the Hotel Lincoln, there was an incident. Mamet came over to Macy's place (likely 1210 N. Clark, where he and Schachter were living) to talk about some equipment for a play and opened the refrigerator. He stared at a large piece of cheese and, not having eaten for some time, cut off a chunk and began to chew. Macy blurted out, "'Hey, *help yourself*.'" Mamet was hurt and fumed about it for several days. "Then I just started writing, and out of that came this scene which was the start of the play: Ruthie comes in furious because someone had just said to him . . . 'Help yourself.'" (AOT 71; Mamet's reference changes to Teach in the actual text). Mamet altered the opening structure for the Broadway production, however, beginning with a conversation between Bobbie and Donny that quickly turns into a summary of the previous night's poker game in which both Fletch and Ruthie won, Fletch taking $400. This opening also contains the first of several definitions of business: "people taking *care* of themselves" (AB 7). Then Teach bursts in on the "lesson" and his diatribe against Ruthie begins, the famous "Fuckin' Ruthie" speech (AB 9). What caused it? He had sat down in the diner with Grace and Ruthie and took a piece of toast off of Ruthie's breakfast plate " . . . and she goes 'Help yourself'" (AB 10). His anger at her sarcastic statement provides the explosive opening to the play:

> Teach: Only (and I tell you this, Don). Only, and I'm not, I don't think, casting anything on anyone: from the mouth of a Southern bulldyke asshole ingrate of a vicious nowhere cunt can this trash come. (*To* Bob) And I take nothing back, and I know you're close with them. (AB 10–11)

The formality of his syntax contradicts with the profanity and intensity of his outburst.

The significance of *American Buffalo* was not only its impact on American theatre and its effect on Mamet's reputation but its starting a twenty-year relationship with Gregory Mosher, then associate director of the Goodman Theatre.

Gregory Mosher arrived in Chicago in 1974, appointed assistant to William Woodman, artistic director of the Goodman then located across from the Art Institute. Mamet had by then written his first play for children, *Mackinac*, about the Natives in North Michigan, saw the Organic Theatre's production of *Sexual Perversity* win a Jefferson Award as Best New Chicago play, directed the premiere of *Squirrels* at the St. Nicholas and became part of the new, "Off-Loop" theatre movement with the establishment of the Wisdom Bridge, Victory Gardens, and Northlight Repertory theatres.

Gregory Mosher had studied at Oberlin, Ithaca College, and Julliard, where he was one of their first directing students. He had performed in the New York Shakespeare Festival and directed at the Williamstown Summer Theatre before coming to Chicago. Woodman hired him to assist with the expanding Goodman program and Mosher soon became the Goodman's literary manager, casting director, assistant to the Mainstage directors, and assistant to the artistic director. At the start of his second year, he became coordinator of Stage 2, an attempt to broaden offerings with a focus on experimental works, although the largely conservative board of the Goodman often had difficulty in accepting its programming.

Mosher's appearance roughly coincided with Mamet's reassembling the St. Nicholas Theatre Company. And as the St. Nicholas began to attract attention with *Squirrels* and then their production of O'Neill's *Beyond the Horizon*, Mosher knew Mamet was one of the three or four people he had to meet. He had heard of Stuart Gordon's successful production of *Sexual Perversity in Chicago* in June 1974 and that Mamet was challenging Chicago's theatre practice with some unorthodox ideas about acting. They first met, however, because Mosher wanted Mamet to direct a show for the new Stage 2. After receiving a script, he returned a few days later to tell Mosher and Woodman that what they gave him to review was terrible. "Why don't you do one of *my* plays?" he asked. Mosher was surprised but impressed by the question.

Shortly after, the twenty-six-year-old playwright cornered the twenty-five-year-old director in his office with a play under his arm, self-confidently announcing, "Something for your next season." Mosher told him he would read it over the weekend. "You don't need to read it. Just do it" Mamet replied, his confidence overreaching itself when he added, "tell you what. I'll put five grand in escrow, and if the play doesn't win the Pulitzer, keep the money."[2] Mosher later explained that there really wasn't a "bet" but they both accepted the mythology of the moment and never contradicted it.[3] Mosher recalled that "we still barely knew each other at that point. I said I would read it and think about it," but it did not take Mosher long to realize the play was important.[4]

Mamet had already held an informal first reading of the work. One evening at Stuart Gordon's Organic Theatre, he had appeared with the script of *American Buffalo* while Joe Mantegna was doing *Huckleberry Finn*. Mamet asked if two other actors in the show and Mantegna would mind reading through his new script. Soon after a performance, they sat around—Jack Wallace, Brian Hicky and Mantegna—and read the work. Mantegna read Teach, likely the first time Mamet heard the work read out loud. It was for Mamet's benefit so he could figure out how to change it. Everyone debated the ending, which remained unclear.[5]

Convinced that *American Buffalo* was a significant and original play, Mosher agreed to direct it for the Goodman Stage 2. Auditions quickly followed, with J. J. Johnston, a former gambler turned actor, who knew the world of Teach and Donny intimately, signing on as Donny. William H. Macy got the part of Bobby and a fellow who came in covered in blood sought the role of Teach. He said he fell out of a car and muttered, "Let's just do the fucking audition." He got the part. It was New York actor Bernard Erhard. At the first rehearsal Mamet kept tearing out pages and throwing them away. There were only nineteen rehearsals before the premiere on October 23, 1975, at the Goodman's Stage 2, but a walk-through at the midway point showed the shortcomings and problems with the script. Mamet left the theatre for the China Door up the street and after several drinks told Mosher perhaps they should cancel.

They did not and the opening was a hit, breaking all box office records for Stage 2 although it premiered to largely negative reviews. Nevertheless, audiences loved it and the work transferred to the new St. Nicholas Theatre space in December, but only for weekend performances, and was referred to as a "work in progress" in the program. Mosher recalled that the budget was about \$100 for the set and \$25 for costumes. The surviving working scripts contain changes, rewrites, blocking, character notes, and the original opening. The set at Goodman Stage 2 also took advantage of the many chairs in the rehearsal space; in fact, hundreds of metal chairs formed the set's back wall, abstract and conceptual with the chairs more or less hanging in the air. Mosher did not want it to be realistic but when the play opened at the St. Clement's Theatre in New York in January 1976, he found that Akira Yoshimura had designed a realistic set with actual walls and a doorway. Mosher was upset because it limited the metaphysical dimension of the play (Mosher, "Interview" 234).

In its original form, *American Buffalo* began with Donny opening a grate in front of the shop with Bobby helping, the lines anticipating the focus on the nickel:

Don: Some guys are gonn'a flip a coin, always calling "heads." You ever notice this?

Bob: Yes.

Don: I call tails. Nine out of ten guys (maybe eight), somebody says "call it" what do they say?

Bob: Heads.

Don: Any given minute. All over the world. Heads. Huuh?

The odds are the same, however, fifty-fifty, so why do most call heads, Don wonders. They then move into the store and Don begins a long speech praising Fletcher and his talent: "what I'm saying is he'll know his way *around* in any situation."[6] The printed version of the play opens with Don and Bobby seated inside the junk shop and the question, "So? *Pause.* So what, Bob?" An apology follows because Bobby has lost his "tail," the coin collector who bought the American Buffalo nickel for $90.00. This isn't good enough, Donny explains, "If you want to do business . . . if we got a business deal, it isn't good enough" (AB ORD 3; AB 3).

Other changes and cuts to the Goodman Stage 2 version include eliminating a long, self-conscious speech by Teach about why he blew up at the poker game that Ruthie won, a section on dwarfs (Teach: "Uh, did I tell you I keep seeing dwarfs?") and a lengthy section on crimes and a later passage on trust (Act I. AB ORD: 14, 17–18).

Each night the set had to be reassembled because space at the Ruth Page Auditorium was used to rehearse another play during the day. But as the first play of the second season of Goodman's Stage 2, *American Buffalo* received much publicity, although Mamet was not well-known at the time and was just getting minor notice from *Sexual Perversity*, which had opened in New York at the St. Clement's Theatre in September 1975.

The three grifters who make up the world of *American Buffalo* represent, in Mamet's view, a family. Linear acts replaced the short scenes that defined *The Duck Variations* and *Sexual Perversity*. Mamet refers to it as "a tragedy about life in the family," a kind of parodic Oedipal triangle with Walter Cole, aka "Teach," and Donny competing over Bobby as the object-child of contrasting dynamics. Teach's angry entrance presages his later objections to Fletch's involvement, Bobby's incompetence and Donny's seeming indecisiveness. Humiliated by Ruthie's sarcasm about his eating Grace's toast, Teach relegates women to insulting categories of demeanor concluding (and foreshadowing) later violence with "the only way to teach these people is to kill them" (AB 11).

Cards and the scam, two of the most fundamental features of the con, mark the beginning of the play and run throughout. The con tried on Bobby, after it was tried on Donny by the purchaser of the nickel, becomes the operative form of relationship: Teach soon cons Donny that he can do the job without needing Fletch, Donny cons Teach that Bobby can really do the job of tailing the mark and Bobby cons both Donny and Teach into thinking he recovered the buffalo nickel when in fact he bought one. Counterfeiting action and even feelings, a form of the con, describes the behavior of the protagonists.

"No one ever talks except to accomplish an objective" Mamet said in a 1995 *Playboy* interview (DMC 126). *American Buffalo* shows this in spades. Every comment, with or without direct meaning, is a push or pull toward action that is shown to be self-serving and amoral, as Don tries to explain to Bobby:

Don: 'Cause there's business and there's friendship, Bobby . . . there are many things, and when you walk around you *hear* a lot of things, and what you got to do is keep clear who your friends are, and who treated you like what. Or else the rest is garbage, Bob, because I want to tell you something.

Bob: Okay.

Don: Things are not always what they seem to be.

Bob: I know.

Pause.

Don: There's lotsa of people on this street, Bob, they want this and they want that. Do anything to get it. You don't have *friends* this life . . . (AB 7–8).

Greed and selfishness dominate behavior and confirm the underlying lack of ethics in American business.

Economic lessons are sprinkled through the text. One of the most memorable is Teach's description of free enterprise. Reworking America's founding principles, he explains the system to Donny:

Teach: You know what is free enterprise?

Don: No. What?

Teach: The freedom . . .

Don:. . . yeah?

Teach: Of the *Individual* . . .

Don:. . . yeah?

Teach: To Embark on Any Fucking Course that he sees fit.

Don: Uh-huh . . .

Teach: In order to secure his honest chance to make a profit. Am I so out of line on this?

Don: No.
Teach: Does this make me a Commie?
Don: No.
Teach: The country's *founded* on this, Don. You know this. . . .
Without this we're just savage shitheads in the wilderness. . . .
Sitting around some vicious campfire. That's why *Ruthie* burns me up (AB 72–3)

Mamet, Mosher wrote, "worked the iambic pentameter out of the vernacular of the underclass, he made it sound like people talking, and he made it funny" (Introd. AB xi). But it was still a challenge for actors. Dustin Hoffman playing Teach in the 1996 movie version of the play one day stood watching the video replay of his part and said "Wait, stop the tape a second. I *had* this. Christine, is it 'Fuck you. Pause. Fuck. Pause. Fuck you'? or 'Fuck you. Fuck. Pause. Fuck . . . ' Aaagh fuck *me*, what's the line?" (Intro. x). For Mamet, language determines action: "Words cause specific behavior. . . . it is impossible to perform a nonmoral action. And type of language determines the type of action."[7]

William H. Macy, the original Bobby and who later played Teach, explained what he felt the play was about: a man whose character is defined by his action. But the big question is, "how can I live in a world where . . . nobody does what they say they're going to do, where everybody is capable of anything, where everybody will screw you over and most people do" (in W&W 26)? Mamet himself said the play is about Donny Dubrow and how to live like a man but that there "are no extenuating circumstances for supporting the betrayal of a friend" (in W&W 27).

Critics offered mixed reactions to the play. Bury St. Edmund in the *Reader* (Chicago) admired the "comically bitter emotional core" of the characters and their chemistry. Although there is little physical action—"in the Mametian universe no one knows what the hell they're doing, and very rarely attempts to do it anyway"—there is plot. But Mosher seems to direct each line individually without a sense of how the whole scene or script functions. Much of the humor in the script is lost and twenty minutes could easily be cut. The final verdict? Paraphrasing a phrase Mamet himself had used in the *Reader*, *American Buffalo* "is just like a play, only longer." With some fat trimmed and "hustle" added, it will better show what it is: "an exciting piece of theatre by someone who's got something to say and a god damn original way of saying it."[8]

Moving the play to the newly opened but not completed St. Nicholas Theatre at 2851 N. Halsted after its weekend performances at the Ruth Page Auditorium brought more attention and change. Mosher and Mamet altered the script, mostly making cuts. Richard Christiansen in the *Chicago Tribune* noted improvements and called it "the best work yet to come from the best playwright Chicago has produced in this decade." He had seen the work three times and each time felt it possessed a deeper meaning.

Christiansen especially notes how some speeches have been embellished to improve plot and how the ending was reworked. There is now a "horrible awareness" that dawns at the end in the mind of Bobby. He felt, too, that the expansion of some of the speeches also made the plot development stronger, though the play remained a revelation of character "shot through with buffoonish humor that makes its casual violence all the more horrible." The play, Christiansen concluded, "makes its own beautiful music from the ugly and often obscene sounds of this city." Linda Winer in the *Chicago Sun* praised the work for its depiction of the "self-hustle, emphatic ramblings and the obsessive lip service to simple American truths." Character language is Mamet's gift, "almost poetic in its patter profanity, the dry stylized rhythms and rich reality of the sounds." It's a hit.[9]

American Buffalo, however, brought some sneers along with cheers. Claudia Cassidy, reviewing the play for WFMT radio, called the play "a foul-mouthed episode" that might be subtitled "waiting for Fletch." Fletch never comes and "raises the hackles and tensions as a couple of gutter types and a corrupted boy talk about—you could hardly call it plan—the heist of a coin collector." Donny is the "moose-like owner," "Teach, the reptilian visitor with the fanged smile loaded with poison," and Bobby, "the laconic boy with the disarming smile," she continues. The problem is the play: Mamet does have a talent for characterization, a strong sense of suddenly shifting moods and hazardous imbalances that occur in the vicious undercurrents of the rootless, shiftless, and unstable who are momentarily lured by the glam of something for nothing. But "in this triangle, the moose-like one is the manipulated, the snakelike one is the manipulator, the boy is the unknown quality. It finally reaches a savage climax and the release of anticlimax. But it takes a very long, very dull time." She closes with this question: "Does the Goodman's Stage Two really believe that filthy language is a substitute for drama?"

Glenna Syse, in "American Buffalo Needs More Work" in the *Chicago Sun Times*, praises the idea of Stage 2 and notes that the ranks of Chicago playwrights are not legion but that when the subject comes up, the name of David Mamet is at the top. *American Buffalo*, however, is still a work in progress. Her criticism is clear: "Sometimes it has a sinister lure, a spasm of suspense and an undercurrent of dark comedy that comes from his keen ear for the burdensome cliché, the ignorant bully talk and the aimless desperate life of these men who lie behind the tawdry neon signs and barred windows of the shady and seedy side of the street." But "at this point, it is just a dreary slice of life that needs tightening, focusing and clarifying. Shortening? Yes, but if they took out all the four-letter words, it would last ten minutes and somewhere along the line it needs an ending." The direction and acting remain solid, however.[10]

Mamet offered few rebuttals but at one point provided this satiric remark: "a critic in Chicago says I write plays where a character wakes up in Act I and finally gets around to putting on his bathrobe in Act II." He didn't entirely disagree with the comment, which initiated a long series of good-natured parodies and skits that take off from Mamet's work. [11]

What *is* significant about *American Buffalo*, beyond its blunt language, strong characterizations, and street-fighting attitude, is Mamet's shift in structure. The play marks his move from the episodic to an extended and sustained play in two continuous acts. The Aristotelian arrangement of premise/conflict/resolution finds finished form in the work. A 1977 interview, given when *Buffalo* was about to appear in New York staring Robert Duvall, clarifies this shift which seems to have occurred in the mid-70s.

CT: Does it take longer to write your plays now?

DM: Having discarded episodic form to write an extended action takes a lot more time. It's like making a series of sketches is so much easier than doing an oil. You take one sketch out and replace it with something else, disposable parts, but every line on the oil can change the entire picture. So learning to work with an extended form—'*Buffalo*'—was my first play with an extended action. That takes time. And this new play is killing me. *The Woods*. It's supposed to be in rehearsal now, supposed to open next week.[12]

Working with Mosher every night of rehearsal influenced the structure of *Buffalo*, which became even more polished when it moved to the St. Nicholas, after which it was nominated for three Jefferson awards and won for Outstanding Play of 1975. Extended until February 15, 1976, the production overlapped with a New York version at the St. Clement's Theatre that opened January 23rd and ran through February 7, 1976, and that Mosher also directed. New York critics generally liked it. Mel Gussow in the *New York Times*, for example, praised Mamet's calibration of how "tempers flare and words fail." The seediness of these pretenders seems authentic in the performances, although the violence at the end "seems to have strayed from a different work."[13]

When it played in New York at the Ethel Barrymore Theatre in 1977 with Duvall, *American Buffalo* was an even greater success. But during the actual premiere, as Richard Christiansen reported, Mamet was anxiously pacing around at the back of the theatre. After the audience's cheers had ended, he went out to play a few games of pool to unwind before he joined the traditional opening night party at Sardi's. Applause greeted him when he entered as friends, relatives and backers from Chicago cheered. Mamet's father was there and announced to all, "I'm sure we have a hit." Mamet laughed and reported that his favorite congratulatory telegram came from Bernard Sahlins, producer of Second City. It read "'Good luck on the road.'"

The Broadway production budget, Christiansen adds as an afterthought, was $240,000, a very large sum for a three-person work. However, he felt the trip to Broadway boosted the play's power. Santo Loquasto created a superbly cluttered setting that amplified Michael Merritt's small design for the Chicago productions. It was directed by Ulu Grosbard, who directed the 1965 Pulitzer Prize winning play *The Subject was Roses*, produced by Edgar Lansbury, one of *Buffalo's* producers. The producers were especially aware that *Buffalo* was a risk but they gave it the best of what a Broadway production should have: the commercial theatre's top craftsmanship and artistry. [14]

Mamet revised the script again and substantially strengthened the ending, clarifying and deepening its dirge for the lives of the play's three lost human beings. He even added a new scene after the burglary scheme had ended in a bloody bungle. The three men, sick and exhausted at the crumbling of their grand plan, stare silently at each other and Teach, the hood, blurts out, "there is nothing out there. . . I fuck myself" (AB 104).

In an interview in *Time* magazine in February 1977 in relation to the show, the reporter noted that the most conspicuous piece of furniture in Mamet's New York apartment was a large filing cabinet "crammed with pages of dialogue overheard in pool halls, bars, elevators, Ping Pong parlors, gambling halls and every other stopping place in a brief, varied career." Mamet has a good ear and knows "the cadences of loneliness and fear behind their bluntness and he also knows how to make bluntness very funny." He does like to ornament his own speech, he continued with quotes from Tolstoy, Marx, Voltaire, Jesus, and Stanislavsky. Mamet told the interviewer that the first thing he learned was that "the exigent speak poetry. They do not speak the language of newspapers." He currently lives alone and is working on a film of *Sexual Perversity* and an adaptation of an old Alec Guinness film, *Last Holiday*, he wrote. In the end, though, Mamet doesn't think of Hollywood in a serious way: "I don't want to break into the movies. Who's got the time?"[15]

~

Mosher, who saw the potential of *American Buffalo* and oversaw its production in Chicago and New York, would go on to direct or produce nearly twenty plays by Mamet including either world or North American premieres of *American Buffalo* (1975), *A Life in the Theatre* (1977), *Lone Canoe* (1979), *Lakeboat* (1982), *Edmond* (1982), *The Disappearance of the Jews* (1983), *Glengarry Glen Ross* (1984), *The Shawl* (1985), Mamet's adaptation of Chekhov's *The Cherry Orchard* (1985), *Speed-the-Plow* (1988), *Bobby Gould in Hell* (1989), and *The Cryptogram* (1994). Additionally, they worked together on the 1978 production of Richard Wright's *Native Son* for the Goodman. No other director has worked so extensively and consistently with Mamet. Why? What explains their synergy—and Mamet dedicating *The Woods*, *A Life in the Theatre*, and *The Cryptogram* to Mosher?

Mosher preferred "minimalist" direction and believed that a play should be uncluttered by visual metaphors or elaborate designs. This paralleled exactly Mamet's own ideas on acting. Mosher understood clearly that "You can't stage the text; you can only stage the action. . . . [R]ehearsal is always to find the action underneath . . . [and] "*what* the guy wants, that's what the action is" (Mosher, "Interview" 238, 239). "Acting is action" was a placarded slogan found on walls and bulletin boards backstage at the Goodman in Mosher's years.[16] In Mosher, Mamet found a sympathetic director who translated *his* unadorned style (with virtually no voice inflections or stage directions) into convincing action. Even rehearsals were collegial. Mosher frequently turned them over to Mamet. Each gave what the other needed: Mamet gave Mosher the excitement of the discovery of a major Chicago playwright; Mosher gave Mamet a venue that was established and yet seeking a wider, subscription-based audience, which the St. Nicholas had not yet achieved. They would work together for more than twenty years.

Financing a theatre career was still a tenuous proposition and Mamet took a job as a writer at *Oui* men's magazine for $20,000 in 1975–76. He'd been approached by someone at a Chicago party who said he knew Mamet's work and wanted him to work as a contributing editor at the magazine. Mamet made it clear he was not a "company man" and disliked conformity but he soon had a cubicle at the office located in the Playboy Building (*Playboy* owned *Oui*) (MBT 50). He wrote letters to the editor, cartoon captions, "service features"—surveys of particular gadgets mostly items advertised in the magazine—as well as puns, gags, and photo captions. His favorite photo caption was "Upwardly mobile homes" for a house trailer turned into a helicopter. He even invented a social craze that supposedly swept the swinging North Side of Chicago: strip darts (MBT 51). The goal was always entertainment.

The energy for such efforts derived in part from his frustration with writing "Girl Copy." These were fantasy passages accompanying the sexy photos of the naked women that were the centerpiece of the magazine and which lined the corkboard walls of his cubicle. This was hard work but he felt his personal best was "Katya with her pants down" (MBT 52). One considerable change at the magazine was "going Pink," or presenting the labia, something which the magazine first opposed but then, because of the competition, had to accept. Hopes of uniting a life of sexual escapades with his fantasy writing, however, never materialized. Although his rented hotel room on Lake Shore Dive allowed him to see the sun "pop out of the lake most mornings," he soon found an offer to teach at Yale too tempting to resist. After reporting his good fortune to his editor, *Oui* made him a counter offer: three days a week at *Oui*, four at Yale, and roundtrip airfare. He turned them down and headed to Yale "to discover that teaching writing was yet one more thing that I could not do" (MBT 56).

While writing for *Oui*, Mamet's own work was still being performed, *Squirrels* revived by the St. Nicholas in January 1976 and *Reunion* (written in 1973) presented in a Midnight Showcase. In late January, *Buffalo* opened in New York at the St. Clement's Theater. But he resigned as artistic director of the St. Nicholas in the spring just as *Sexual Perversity* and *The Duck Variations* opened in New York.

The reasons for Mamet's spring resignation of 1976 included his busy schedule, objections to producing Julian Barry's technically complicated and uninspiring play, *Sitcom*, and an eagerness to try New York. It also initiated a period of attention, exposure, and new work—as well as marriage, a decision to move to Vermont, and the pursuit of a new field: film. "Whore that I am—I came to New York" is his disingenuous summary of his move (AOT 65). But his view was ambivalent: he looked at New York as either the Big Apple or "the world's biggest hick town" because much of what is spoken there is "the equivalent of the Royal Nonesuch—you know, a bunch of people crawling around, barking and calling it theatre" (AOT 65).

Mamet left Chicago and the St. Nicholas Theatre Company in the spring of 1976 with a one-sentence letter dated May 12, 1976. Importantly, copies of his resignation letter went to the four principal drama critics in Chicago: Richard Christiansen, Glenna Syse, Michael ver Meulen, and Linda Winer. What his note does not convey is the vehemence of his opposition to Julian Barry's *Sitcom*, which he felt posed technical problems, high costs, and was overwritten. And while his disagreement with the board over its decision to produce *Sitcom* prompted his resignation, he was also too busy with new productions to focus on the St. Nicholas. The letter reads:

> Friends:
>
> It is with imaginable regret that I inform you that I find that the irreconcilable artistic differences currently between us force me to resign my position as artistic director of the company.
>
> Sincerely,
> David Mamet

By the time of the letter, Mamet had won an Obie Award in New York for the 1976 St. Clement's production of *American Buffalo* directed by Mosher and understood the potential and importance of producing plays in the city. He moved to Chelsea, an area that reminded him of Chicago. He had one floor of an old row house but spent many evenings at The Athens Diner at Twenty-third and Ninth, often reading, mostly Willa Cather. For the first time in his life, he was making his living as a writer and he felt good about the independence and income (CA 13–4). A bearskin rug (once a prop in a Chicago production of his) lay in front of the fireplace. He would exercise at the Chelsea YMCA, directly across from the legendary Chelsea Hotel, former home to Thomas Wolfe, Dylan Thomas, Brendan Behan, Virgil Thomson, and, for a while, Leonard Cohen. Mamet himself had spent a few nights there on his first visit to New York, somewhat "terrified by the squalor and violence and noise" (CA 17). He would also jog on the West Side Highway, which was closed to traffic because of its collapse in 1973, sometimes racing oceanliners heading out to sea on the Hudson. Chelsea had been a shipping neighborhood and there were deserted piers just two blocks from his apartment. Madison's Men's Shop on Eleventh Avenue became a hangout: he found the atmosphere of work and nostalgia intriguing since it sold work clothes and items for the marine trades. North of his apartment was Chelsea Stationers, where he would buy report covers, pens, and "legal-looking blank books in which to write" (CA 16).

Mamet befriended Louis Herrmann, brother to Bernard, who had been involved with Orson Welles' Mercury Theatre. Both brothers had been in the radio studio for the 1938 broadcast of Welles' "War of the Worlds." Kenny Fish was a furniture man in the neighborhood and Mamet spent hours playing gin with him, as well as the picture framer Joe Rosenberg. Clement Clark Moore, composer of "'Twas the Night Before Christmas" at one time lived nearby, as did Anthony Perkins.

His apartment, at 410 W. 23rd on the south side of the street between 9th and 10th Avenues, had a view of the Empire State Building from the living room, but little in the way of furniture: a pair of silver candlesticks, the only things his grandparents brought with them from Poland; a Barnum and Bailey Circus poster; and the bearskin rug were his prize possessions. He would often sit by his rear window at an oak-and-steel café table and smoke and look at the gardens running behind the houses. He had no television and for a long time no telephone: nonetheless, "I had a lot of books, and for the first time in my life, a little money. It was a romantic time" (CA 23).

Early in his residence, Mamet oversaw the Off-Broadway production of *Sexual Perversity in Chicago* and *The Duck Variations* at the Cherry Lane Theatre. The double-bill opened on Bloomsday, June 16, 1976, and ran until April 17, 1977, a remarkable 273 performances. At the same time, *Buffalo* had won a Jefferson Award in Chicago for its production. Mamet was winning more awards in 1976: a New York State Council of the Arts Grant (for the children's play *Revenge of the Space Pandas: or, Binky Rudich and the Two-Speed Clock*, which he created on his way to complete the application forms just before the deadline), a Rockefeller Award, and a CBS Fellowship in Creative Writing, which involved part-time lecturing at Yale. He chose to take the Rockefeller at the St. Nicholas, allowing him to return to the company. The writing fellowship meant frequent trips to Yale.

Early in 1977, Mamet gave an important interview to David Witz for *Chicago Theater* magazine, one that assessed his work and career to that date. Witz knew Mamet was a difficult interviewee which another critic expressed in this manner: "One doesn't talk with David Mamet. One jockeys for position. His side of the conversation is like his dialog: tense words and quick conclusions, epigrams in blue-collar language, metaphysic expressed in four letter words."[17]

During his year of personal accomplishment in New York (1976), Mamet maintained ties with Chicago, as his interview with *Chicago Theatre* magazine underscored. Held the day after winning a special Jefferson Award in Chicago for *American Buffalo*, Mamet and Witz squeezed into his *Oui* office for the discussion. Mamet noted that he had returned to Chicago and spoke of the importance of his work there. He commented on his 1976 break with the St. Nicholas, explaining that he was no longer able to spend a large portion of his time running the theatre artistically. Also Schachter and Macy "started to develop along different aesthetic lines and we got into many, many squabbles." "Eventually," he continues, "it became that if I were going to write and they were going to freely develop, they were going to have to develop their own theatre. I went through a couple of climactic moments in this disengagement, but basically it was pretty organic."

Mamet added that he planned to work on a musical in 1978 with Rokko Jans. "I've been relying on Rokko's theatrical advice since I was fourteen, literally. . . . I'm sort of a duffer musician, so I can talk in musical terms and he's got a great sense of poetry, as anyone who's ever heard his music knows." He then celebrated the "nuclear theatrical community" of Chicago while "all of the members are tied to individual theaters," they still work with each other whether part of Victory Gardens, the Organic, the St. Nicholas, or the Goodman.

The wide-ranging interview is important for framing Mamet's bi-city views: that New York is difficult and driven by commercial theatre, while Chicago is not, and still operates successfully in its "Off-Loop" mode. But success in both cities remained important. A sign of Mamet's continuing commitment to Chicago was the premiere of *A Life in the Theatre* in Chicago at the Goodman. Dedicated to Gregory Mosher, it was originally a set of scenes with two actors set throughout Chicago—a Chinese restaurant, a gym, an office. Mosher read them in the fall of 1976 after *Buffalo* and suggested structural changes, but he did not leap to produce the work. When he realized he did not have enough funding for the remainder of the Stage 2 season and needed a play with a smaller cast, he asked Mamet if he could produce it with scene changes. Mamet made the changes and finished a corrected typescript on December 9, 1976. The play opened on February 3, 1977.

The subject of the play is the changing of the guard in the theatre. An older actor cannot quite face his fading power, while a younger actor is on his way up. The theme is ironic, particularly for Mamet, who was drawing on his own experiences of theatre life and wrote a good deal of it while trying to succeed in the theatrical world of New York. The premiere took place as part of Chicago's Goodman Stage 2 series before productions in New York (October 20, 1977), London (July 18, 1979) and then again in a revised form in the West End of London (October 31, 1979; a few extra scenes added, some Americanisms removed). It was staged at the Goodman again as part of its 2006 Mamet Festival (March-April). In 1979, PBS taped it for broadcast with slight modifications; and in 1993 Mosher directed a film of the play starring Matthew Broderick as John and Jack Lemmon as the older Robert. Mamet wrote several new scenes and speeches for this version.

In an essay about *A Life in the Theatre*, Mamet wrote that "excellence in the theatre is the art of giving things away" (WR 104). The actor, he continued, "strives not to *fix* . . . but to *create* for the moment, freely" (104). Its rewards and pains are paramount, and stage lore, repeated among actors, directors, producers, and managers is essential to maintain the theatre since its history and accomplishments are temporal. He cites Sanford Meisner's comment to Mamet when he attended the Neighborhood Playhouse Theatre School in New York that a young actor will always encounter an older one who will offer stories, direction, and advice, but will always ignore them. Listen, but act for yourself. Let the text guide you: "the good play does not *need* the support of the actor." Great drama is "the performance of great deeds with no emotion whatever" he writes in *True and False* (TF 12, 13). The audience, furthermore, is your best guide and will "teach you how to act and . . . how to write and to direct" (TF 19). This is as difficult as it is necessary. *A Life in the Theatre* summarizes Mamet's love affair with the theatre and language, which in later years has spread to fiction, poetry, journalism, children's stories, essays, and film.

Mamet is a theatrical pragmatist concerned as much with how to produce a show as how to act in it. Hence, he complains that critics know so little. If only they would spend two to three weeks in a theater, they would understand what is involved in producing a work and acting. "Fucking leeches" is Robert's harsh comment about them in *A Life in the Theatre*. "They'll praise you for the things you never did and pan you for a split second of godliness. What do they know? They create nothing. They come in the front door. They don't even buy a ticket" (ALT 77).

The twenty-six scenes in the original performance text of *A Life in the Theatre* concentrate on the frustrations of the older actor and the supposed advice he provides for the younger. Set against their roles in a repertory company, a good deal of humor emerges, backstage and downstage. Six of the scenes are of clichéd plays or films, set in, among other places, a hospital, a war, a lawyer's office and a lifeboat. Robert, in Scene 16 for example, storms the barricades during the French Revolution but in the midst of the action forgets some of his lines, creating unintended but hilarious comedy:

Robert: A new day rises . . . those who must connect themselves to yesterday for succor will be left behind . . . their souls are in the histories, their heads on pikes . . . now we must look ahead . . . Our heads between the breasts of women, plight our troth to that security far greater than protection of mere rank or fortune. (ALT 64)

Increasingly, Robert's attempt to pass on his knowledge to John meets with resistance, if not distain:

Robert: When one's been in the theatre as long as I . . .
John: Can we do this later?
Robert: I feel that there is something here of worth to you.
John: You do?
Robert: Yes.
John: (*sighs*): Let us hear it then. (ALT 66)

The play alternates between backstage, dressing room exchanges and scenes where the two act improbable and exaggerated moments from a set of hackneyed productions, ranging from a lifeboat scene to Shakespeare. Comments on acting run throughout, as well as barbs at critics, although the play satirizes actors with equal malice. Robert may tell John that it is important they support each other, but then asks an unexpected favor:

John: What?

Pause.

Robert: In our scene tonight . . .

John: Yes?

Robert: Mmmm . . .

John: What?

Robert: Could you . . . perhaps . . . *do* less?. . . .

John: Do less *what???*

Robert: You know.

John: You mean . . . what do you mean?

Pause.

Robert: You know.

John: Do you mean I'm walking on your scene? (*Pause.*) What do you mean?

Robert: Nothing. It's a thought I had. An aesthetic consideration. (ALT 41–2)

The *New York Times* came to the Goodman opening, the first time in anyone's memory the paper appeared to cover a premiere. The attention the play received, along with the Broadway *Buffalo* two weeks later, made David Mamet famous, or at least well-known. *A Life in the Theatre* was also the last "innocent" production done by Mosher. The set cost a few hundred dollars, with Mosher acting as house manager as well as director. *A Life in the Theatre* was also the last show Mosher did at the Goodman before being named artistic director at age twenty-seven. The work was a triumph and a turning point for both the playwright and director and brought accolades to the original cast, both Mamet veterans: Mike Nussbaum and Joe Mantegna.

Reviews of the original production, however, were initially mixed, some criticizing the way the onstage scenes were played to an invisible audience upstage, while the off-stage scenes were played facing front. Christiansen, again, stresses that this is an early Mamet work: the writing was seemingly abrupt and mannered, while the onstage scenes reached too hard for laughs. He liked the ending, however, in which Robert, alone in a darkened theatre, stands in front of a single worklight and rehearses a thank you speech for an audience tribute that we know will never happen. Mel Gussow of the *New York Times* found the play accomplished. The production is like being backstage at "a magic show in which all the tricks fail."[18] The dependencies and jealousies of the actors never bore us, the older Robert masking his insecurity through a condescending authority and pretentious turn of phrase that, by the end, is reversed.

In the 2006 Goodman Mamet Festival production directed by Robert Falls, the play ran a breakneck eighty minutes with no intermission with, on average, a scene change every three minutes. The accelerated speed intensified the work's satiric power, a cold-eyed dissection of the mercurial games played by those trapped by theatrical life, in contrast to the more comic pictures of upstage life depicted in Michael Frayn's *Noises Off* or Ronald Harwood's *The Dresser*. The challenge of the play, however, is to show how the young and inexperienced usurp those with craft and seniority.

The Water Engine, An American Fable, directed by Steven Schachter and starring Macy, opened at the St. Nicholas in May 1977. Anticipating the theme of the power and moral failure of business in America (eventually to dominate *Glengarry Glen Ross*), the play exposes how a potential American hero, the inventor of an engine that runs on water, must die. Mamet's favored Century of Progress Exhibition, a mythic moment in Chicago and American history, was featured in the production, which became a new box office hit at the relocated St. Nicholas.

At first a radio play and then expanded to two acts for the theatre, the work is multilayered and multivoiced. Cast members sing as well as act. It opens with an announcer setting the scene of The Century of Progress Exhibition and then presenting a drama within a drama: an inventor visiting a patent lawyer asks him to meet a businessman who wants to buy the invention, although, we believe, only with intentions to destroy it. Threats and the police intervene but the inventor escapes only to discover that his sister has been kidnapped because he called a reporter to arrange to tell his story. Charles, the inventor, agrees not to do this and to exchange his plans for his sister. Instead, he mails the plans to the son of a friend. At the end, the announcer reveals that two tortured bodes were found in a lake. Throughout the play voices are heard, especially the continuing voice of a chain letter that speaks of consequences and rewards. The betrayal of trust, first presented in *American Buffalo*, is the theme melodramatically and violently presented here.

The unconventional production surprised reviewers who found the programmed opposition to advertising clichés, technological advances and gossip about the Roosevelts, as well as the Lindbergh kidnapping and the efficacy of chain letters, distracting. Unfortunately, the translation to the stage was half-hearted. Schachter had originally visualized the work as a radio play, with most of the cast sitting most of the time behind a long table whispering into microphones. Mel Gussow in the *New York Times* found that the radio framework for social commentary worked well, although the work still seemed in the blueprint stage.[19] The play contains themes that future Mamet work would explore, notably ethics, violence, and an American tendency to destroy the imagination.

Despite Chicago successes, New Haven called. Mamet first went to Yale with Kevin Kline and Patti LuPone for a performance of *All Men Are Whores* at the Yale Cabaret Theatre in February 1977. At the time, he was a CBS Fellow in Playwriting at the School of Drama, sharing the honor with Arthur Kopit and Eric Bentley.

Derek Walcott was also at Yale at the time. One evening, Mamet left the theatre unhappy with his work and walked up and down in front of the Yale Rep. A woman came up to him and said " 'God Bless you: You are the Savior of the American Theatre. I have been to see your play six times.' I cheered up and thanked her," Mamet writes, and told her "she had given me hope and that, yes, I was going to go home and write. I thanked her again. 'Not at all, Mr. Durang.' she replied" (SF 103).

Walt Jones, who would direct *Reunion* and *Dark Pony* at Yale in October 1977, first met Mamet at that time. That summer Robert Brustein, at the time head of the Yale School of Drama and founding director of the Yale Repertory Theatre, contacted Jones, who was running theatre workshops in Sun Valley, Idaho, about directing two Mamet plays. He agreed after he read them and spoke to Mamet, discovering, for example, that both favored minimal stage blocking. But he worked on the plays without meeting him, Mamet occupied with a production of his children's play *Revenge of the Space Pandas* at the St. Clemens Theatre in New York. In the summer of 1977, when he was directing Sam Shepard's *Suicide in B Flat* at Yale, Jones was told Mamet would appear after an evening's performance. Following the Shepard play, there was a discussion with the actors and audience but throughout, someone in the sixth row kept cutting people off and asking if this wasn't a schizophrenic writer who was writing only to be produced and that all the pieces do not connect. The aggressive manner of the speaker offended the actors and Jones; this guy seemed to be redirecting their production. When it was over, the figure approached him: it was Mamet, affable and pleased with his own aggressiveness.

Mamet then threw himself into the production of *Reunion* and *Dark Pony*, although he was at first miffed that Brustein had picked Lindsay Crouse for the female part without his consultation. But he had wanted to meet her, ever since seeing her in *Slap Shot*, a 1977 hockey movie with Paul Newman. In fact, he reportedly told Gregory Mosher that he would someday marry her. She had been dating Robert Duvall, who was in the *American Buffalo* production on Broadway, but was otherwise unattached. Mamet pursued her and, halfway through rehearsal, they moved into a hotel together.

Crouse was making her debut with the Yale Rep. She had been in *All the President's Men* with Robert Redford, and *Slap Shot*. At the Kennedy Center, she had acted in Jason Robard's production of *Long Days Journey into Night* and a production of Noel Coward's *Present Laughter* working with Douglas Fairbanks, Jr.

Mamet not only fell in love with her but found that her acting style suited his approach perfectly. She always let the text do the work and never embellished her acting. This was the essential Mamet style, allowing the text to go forward without stopping for emotion. "Let the text carry you" was Mamet's direction according to Walt Jones. "Everything that you need to communicate is in the text; everything else is in the casting" said Jones, paraphrasing Mamet. "Play it, don't perform it" is Mamet's own succinct summary of his style.[20] Mamet participated in every aspect of the production and was present at rehearsals and afterward. According to Jones,

Mamet was the least neurotic playwright he had encountered, although he did think some of Mamet's acting ideas extreme. The view that the actor is just the embodiment of the text discounted any talent the actor might bring to the part, which Jones felt was important.

But Mamet is an actor's director, Jones believes, and was always there for the actor, although changes to the script were difficult for him to make. "He splits syllables" and once the rhythm is fixed, it stays. His preference for an unadorned, minimalist acting style, Jones believes, originates in his wish for actors *not* to judge their characters, which is at the root of why he doesn't want the actors to embroider their style. Any judgment is the job of the audience. This, in turn, explains the directness and immediacy of his acting style, which actors praise. They find his work similar to Chekhov's in his effort to eliminate the traps actors get into from routine. He lets them discover why there is a pause or a beat in the script; he doesn't tell them. Mamet intuitively knows the value of such discoveries from his own training as an actor, but, ironically, writes what he cannot do himself.

By that December, in the midst of his courtship of Crouse, Mamet gave an interview to Terry Curtis Fox in *New Times* in which he expressed disappointment with producers and New York. Fifteen years ago you could bring your work to a producer or agent "neither of whom could *read* or you could go to an amateur community theatre." The producers who read *American Buffalo* said "'nothing happens. People won't sit through it.'" They preferred to fly to England and pick up a package in the West End which was cheaper to bring over than do a production of their own. Fox concludes that Mamet is a regional writer who attends to the details of language: "he hears the way Chicagoans talk," reproducing their vocal patterns on stage. But he uses Chicago to talk about things that relate to the entire country. To discuss the myths of America he focuses on precise dialogue, regional detail, and a vibrant subculture.[21] His models are musical rather than narrative. Mamet is an aural not visual dramatist.

Mamet continued to pursue Crouse and by the end of the year, they married. Crouse came from a gold-plated theatrical family: she was the daughter of famed playwright Russell Crouse, who named her for his longtime partner, Howard Lindsay. Together, they wrote hits like *Life with Father, State of the Union, Call Me Madam*, and *The Sound of Music*. Crouse grew up with Ethel Merman singing in her home, Irving Berlin playing piano, and Rogers and Hammerstein dropping by. She went to the Chapin School and Radcliffe, graduating in 1971. She returned to New York as a dancer (she was a choreographer of the Cambridge Dance Theatre Company) and had studied dance with Ina Hahn but began acting in theatrical showcases and eventually regional theatre, where she eventually played Stella in *Streetcar Named Desire* at the Arena Stage in Washington.

The wedding, on December 21, 1977, following an intense three-month courtship, took place in the Park Avenue apartment of Crouse's mother and was performed by a judge. At the time, *The Water Engine* was in performance at the New York Shakespeare Festival Public Theatre on Lafayette Street, while *A Life in the Theatre* was continuing its run at the Theatre de Lys in Greenwich Village (there would be a record 288 performances). And on December 1 *Sexual Perversity* and *The Duck Variations* opened at the Regent Theatre in London. the first performance of his work abroad.

A month before his marriage, Mamet directed his own production of *The Woods* at the St. Nicholas opening November 17, 1977. In advance of the premier, he gave three talks on theatre, an early summary of his well-formed ideas about theatre practice and influences. The three lectures were drawn mostly from his journal/notebooks. Marilyn Preston, a reporter for the *Chicago Tribune*, attended all three and provided a thorough account of Mamet's idea of drama and the stage.

Mamet began by noting the intellectual veneer of his work in the theatre and during the talks incorporated Aristotle ("The *Poetics* is the greatest book on playwriting ever written"), Stanislavsky, Tolstoy, Freud, Dreiser, Marx, and Jung. Mamet implied that he might be in such a tradition of teacher/thinker/playwright/philosopher.

Lecture one focused on theatre as myth and dream. Theatre is the mechanism in society that is equal to dreams in an individual life. We explain ourselves to ourselves through dreams and myth, which take the form of the theatre. "'We create myths (theatre) then for the same reason we create dreams. . . . [B]oth dreams and drama make us happier by helping us solve problems we can't deal with rationally.'"

The second talk concentrated on the techniques of acting. His passion and knowledge of the craft was evident, Peterson writes. His detailed analysis stripped away the magic of being in the theatre. Mamet believes that, with hard work, anyone can learn how to act, although it takes discipline and the ability to know the bitter truth and face it. But "the best theatre is painful."

The third lecture was actually a read-through of *The Woods* with the director, playwright, and both actors, Patti LuPone and Peter Weller. The accompanying commentary addressed technique, meaning, and scenic truths.[22]

The Woods, dedicated to Gregory Mosher, is actually a two-hander in three scenes about a couple at a summer house in early September. The character Ruth has most of the speeches, which are spoken as poetry. She encourages her partner Nick to open up and by the end of the first scene he awkwardly tells his father's war story. Later scenes lead to a failed attempt to make love, rejection, anger, and then violence as Ruth swings an oar at Nick and he hits her in the mouth. He then breaks down and admits that he's alone and begs her to stay. "Down in the City everything is vicious. I need time to be up here," he says, but he cannot speak truthfully to her (W 96, 97–9). As the lights fade, she holds him and begins a story of two children in the woods, as Nick appears to subdue his fears.

Mamet directed LuPone and Weller, who received generally strong notices. Critics were less generous about the play, however. Richard Christiansen pointed out that the production undercut the text, a mix of the mythic and prosaic.

Richard Eder, reviewing for the *New York Times*—Mamet was by now regularly reviewed by the paper—found it broadened Mamet's emotional currency, giving the limited cast a broader emotional range. Sherman Kaplan on WBBM radio, however, felt the language and style was too self-conscious; it seemed clipped and pasted into the script from a printed page.[23] Nevertheless, a New York production went forward, directed by Ulu Grosbard and opened in April 1979. One curious reaction was that the *Village Voice* ran reviews by three different critics to address the question of whether or not Mamet was a misogynist, anticipating later debates about his work.

~

Two years after they married, Crouse ventured her opinion of Mamet as a writer, praising his ability to edit: "He's a very fine cutter. He knows what to cut, and where" but acknowledged that some times there is disagreement. In a scene in *Reunion* in rehearsal for the Yale Rep production, Mamet decided to make a cut. Crouse was angry about losing the lines:

> She was my character and I defended her. We did it again, with the cut and David said afterward that it was much better—not because of the cut but because I was *feeling* hurt and cheated and betrayed. But he wasn't playing some kind of game with me. He made the cut as a writer and I reacted to my emotions as an actor.

She also acknowledged their mutual approach to the theatre: "We have to work together, we have to rely on each other. It's a family experience. You'd sew your own costume if it came down to it." That same year, 1979, in an essay titled "The Actor's Job," Crouse repeats the Mamet approach, emphasizing that action alone brings character alive on the stage, separate from the events of the play. "The events are like milestones in the course of a journey; the actions move the characters along the way." To clarify her point, she tells a story from Meisner's acting class in which a student had to ask a girl to marry him. The actor was having problems and confessed to Meisner that he wasn't feeling anything emotional. "'Never mind what you feel,' answered Meisner. 'Just *really* ask her to marry you.'" "If the commitment to action is complete," Crouse continues, "there will be consequences. This is a hard-and-fast law of the theatre and a lesson for our lives." [24] Mamet's ideas on acting found full expression in Crouse's theatrical practice.

Uncertainty over whether New York or Chicago was Mamet's home, however, continued. An October 1977 interview tried to pin him down but he proved elusive: he preferred the food and pool in Chicago, especially at the Twin Anchors and Bensinger's (the original location of "The Hustler") at Diversey and Clark Streets, but he liked the action in New York. The interviewer adds that, like his dialogue, Mamet appears hard and tough but underneath he is warm and generous. Mamet brings to New York a certain South Side Chicago cynicism. For example, walking into the Grill Room at the Four Seasons in New York and responding to book editor Michael Korda's description of it as the place where New York powerbrokers eat, Mamet asked, more directly, "can a guy get laid here?"[25]

The interviewer, however, learns that when Mamet is in rehearsal, he listens for lines the actors have trouble remembering—the fault he feels lies not with the actors but with the text, which must be "a-rhythmic." He cites a Danish production of *American Buffalo* in which the translation, by a poet, got all the meters right and the gags came at the right places. "After seeing it in Danish for the third time, I forgot I didn't understand the language" (Kiss). He concentrates on language and the ear, not the eye—and "that's why the theatre speaks with moral authority—if the actor believes the words you believe him."

He expressed his divided attitude toward Chicago and New York a year before when he commented on the difficulty in locating his style, partly reflected in the ambivalent reception and quality of his work. There is, he admits, "schizophrenia in my writing. On the one hand, I like to write very esoteric stuff. Some of it makes Tom Stoppard look like Paddy Chayefsky." But he also likes to write "neo-realist plays like *American Buffalo*. My true *métier* lies somewhere in between," although he is "really into language as poetry" (DMC 21). He was not ready to forsake Chicago, however. One paper reported that in May he would speak at the Morning Exercise (a school address) at his alma mater, the Francis Parker School. He said he was deeply grateful to the school: "They so acculturated me that when I graduated I thought the word garish referred to a French railway station."[26]

But another Chicago project was emerging that would occupy both Mamet and Mosher: a production of Richard Wright's *Native Son*, Mosher's first production as artistic director of the Goodman. Appointed in 1978, one of his first acts was to make Mamet associate artistic director and playwright-in-residence. For Mamet, this meant a continued association with Chicago and possible adoption by the Goodman of any new work by him.. For Mosher, it meant benefiting from Mamet's critical sense, "a general aesthetic conscience." He was also there to signal to "the Chicago community that this was going to be a writer's theatre, a Chicago theatre and a contemporary theatre."[27] By the fall of 1978, Mamet's appointment also implied assistance with a number of productions, notably Mosher's effort to put Wright's searing Chicago novel, *Native Son* (1940) on the stage.

The novel had been dramatized before: in 1941 Wright and the North Carolina playwright Paul Green adapted it for a production by the Mercury Theatre, directed by Orson Wells and produced by John Houseman. Difficulties with the text, however, meant that Houseman had to rework it with Wright to adjust it for the stage. Green's version altered Wright's ending, diluting Bigger Thomas' confession and morally threatening stance that until he killed, he had not lived. Green reduced Bigger's brutality and the violence of his emotions. Green made Bigger seem mad whereas in the novel he has dignity and self-understanding despite his act of violence.[28]

Mosher wished to cast Meshach Taylor in the lead. This Chicago actor had great success in his role in the Goodman's *Sizwe Bansi is Dead* by Athol Fugard, the production winning three Jefferson Awards. Mosher knew the Wright novel, although not the Paul Green script. Nonetheless, they announced the Green adaptation (partly for copyright reasons) in the newly printed subscription brochures. But when he read this version, he immediately saw its limitations.

Mosher then had someone underline all the dialogue in the novel which he started to string together so that if anyone raised copyright questions about this new version, he could claim the words were Wright's. Once a draft was done, he took it to New York to show Mamet, thinking it would be the basis of a new draft. Mamet liked it and "went to sit on the terrace." Mosher then spent two days at Mamet's desk rewriting, mostly combining similar scenes into one and cutting. Mamet reviewed it again and made additional cuts. In rehearsal, he added a few lines in the very last scene.

Mamet always felt strongly about the book. In a 2003 column in the *Guardian* just before *Edmond* was to open at the National Theatre in London, he wrote that *Native Son* gets his "vote for the Great American Novel." He calls the book "a tragedy of race," emphasizing that it is not "a paean to violence," but "a soul-deep cry for reason." Its interpretation of racism is similar to Mamet's views of anti-Semitism: both arise out of society's need to hate. But Jews, and by extension blacks, cannot cure it by "only defending ourselves against it." Both must become assertive if not aggressive. Explanation, reason, and tolerance are disastrous. "The least appearance of race hatred is a questioning wedge whose end is murder"—which Bigger Thomas feared and understood. The victims of racism and anti-Semitism are not its instigators.[29]

Mosher made several additions to the script when he returned to Chicago, notably using archived passages from the *Chicago Tribune* for scene changes. At the time Mosher was reviewing the Robert Nixon trial, a young Chicago black accused of murder and executed in 1939. This was a partial source of the novel. Mosher was shocked at the inflammatory, tabloid language used by the paper, but saw its dramatic potential. Originally, he thought it might be used in the program but decided it would work better in the text. Colin Stinton read the material live each night at an offstage microphone.

A typed memo likely from Mosher offers further suggestions to the cast and crew: there should be no blackouts but dissolves in the manner of *A Life in the Theatre*. Sounds should be human, not an "impressionistic sound montage." The only exception should be clocks, "which Wright uses continuously through the novel," although Mosher is not crazy about this device. Other suggestions are to use direct quotation in the script and greater incorporation of radio. The parallel is again with Mamet: note, Mosher writes, how Wright talks about tantalization in his introduction: "perhaps the radio can serve this function a la *Water Engine* refrain, 'the fair is closing.'" The memo ends with "I *think* dialogue can be lifted straight from the book and it will tell the story. We will have to act out certain parts, of course."[30]

Beginning with a white set which as performance space captured the imprisoning color barrier and racial tone of the novel, Mosher returned Bigger's crucial point of view to the play, although the audience seemed diverted at the end by the long moralizing speech by Max, Bigger's lawyer, which precedes Bigger's final scene in both the novel and the play. Mosher's changes clearly brought the script more in line with the novel, a work, in Wright's words, where "no one would weep over it, that it would be so hard and deep that they would face it without consolation of tears."

The riveting production of *Native Son* opened on the Goodman Main Stage on October 12, 1978. The set alone drew gasps. The play began with the audience unable to see: they were blinded by a set of powerful searchlights aimed directly at them to give the feeling of entrapment and danger. When the lights dimmed, they saw twenty-one white cells on three levels constructed out of white pipes in which various actors entered and left. It was to suggest a labyrinth or tenement or set of jail cells emphasizing segregation, oppression, imprisonment, and psychological enclosure. Cyclone fences would also appear to surround Bigger Thomas, the accused. But the floodlights were not as sensational, perhaps, as the blank cartridges fired into the audience in the original 1941 Mercury Theatre production, which also had a posse hollering from the rear of the theatre.

Unlike Orson Welles' ten blackout scenes of equal length without an intermission, Mosher preferred a two-act version, presenting the action with a kind of Brechtian epic detachment. Twenty-eight actors, almost entirely from Chicago, performed and, in the trial scene at the end, the entire cast sat in judgment on Bigger in cells above the stage. However, since theatre limits the presentation of consciousness (the core of the captivating but gritty urban novel), Mosher relied on Brechtian alienation to make the play objective and didactic. Bigger's statement that "I killed for what I am" and Max's defense that "it made him free. It was an act of creation" are at odds with the audience's emotions; they may not be detached enough to question such special pleading. In the 1941 Broadway production, Bigger's violence diminished; not so in Mosher's presentation, which presents Bigger more as a victim of society. Nonetheless, the play was popular with Chicago theatre audiences because it was dramatic, powerful, and splashy. Mosher began his reign at the Goodman with a hit.[31]

Mamet, however, was displeased. He, in fact, left during the tech rehearsal because he hated the set. He had an argument with Mosher one morning at the Drake and he and Crouse suddenly left for New York. Both may have reacted against the Brechtian elements, which virtually eliminated any liberal sentiments. It was also an "in your face," sensationalized production that both Mamet and Crouse may have found untheatrical. Nevertheless, in *Make-Believe Town*, Mamet writes approvingly of the production, especially the strength of Mosher in constructing a powerful new script where Bigger Thomas "told off the white race" and what "they were doing to the Blacks" (MBT 63). "I think Richard Wright would have appreciated it. It was brave and it was vicious and it was no-kidding," he adds (MBT 63).

Mamet spent the balance of 1978 overseeing productions, directing, and working on a new play. In June, *American Buffalo* had its European premiere at the National Theatre in London and received good notices. Michael Billington in the *Guardian* admired the unexpected reversals of tone (friendship one moment, violence the next), while Michael Coveney in the *Financial Times* praised the way language distilled hard meaning and veiled threats.[32] But the real focus for Mamet that year was a new work to conclude the 1978–79 subscription series at the Goodman: *Lone Canoe*.

In 1979 he began to visit Chicago frequently and for a term taught at the University of Chicago—unsuccessfully. The course was an English department seminar on playwriting and acting, but the students were neither playwrights nor actors. Nor were they sure what they were getting in for when they first had to write an entrance essay about what they would like to see in theatre before they would be accepted into the seminar. When they walked into the seminar room and found a young instructor wearing blue denim overalls and red horn-rimmed glasses, they were surprised. His first class, according to a former student, consisted of a rambling talk about a science fiction novel he had read, *The Demolished Man* by Alfred Bester, about a world where people could communicate telepathically.

Mamet grew increasingly frustrated with the class as the inexperience of the students with theatre history, let alone theatre practice, became unbearable. One afternoon finding only silence and stares, he rolled his eyes—"then his voice turned from its usual sardonic tone to a more bullying tone—and then to one that was shrill and exasperated." His major complaint was that all anyone did was read.[33] He regained their interest, however, by telling tales about the theatre and writing and how one had to observe the world and note what was going on around one. He seemed especially fascinated by the rituals salesmen went through when they met. Most of the students agreed that his digressions were more educational than his teaching. He refused to appear at office hours as his impatience each week increased.

At the same time, he was working on *Lone Canoe*, his first musical. The students sensed it was not going well according to a few comments he made early in the quarter. The final class and the opening of *Lone Canoe* almost coincided, and halfway through the class, in an attempt at an acting exercise, Mamet moved the group outside. It didn't help; the acting exercise "bombed" and Mamet exploded, sparked perhaps by the stress of the play's opening. He chewed out individual students, then the class as a whole and then he started shouting and gesturing "crazily—a walking screaming caricature of one of his own characters"

(Helbig 38). Finals were a week later: he never showed up but gave everyone in the class an "A."

Lone Canoe was a new play under an old title—the original St. Nicholas Company did a kind of farce using this title in its earliest, *Vermont Days*—but one that contradicted much of Mamet's theory about Aristotelian structure and character as action. The new work was a historical musical, based on Jack London's short story "In the Forests of the North" from his 1902 collection *Children of the Frost*. Music became part of Mamet's narrative concerning a lost British explorer in the wilds of northern Michigan. Its premiere on May 24, 1979, before the American Theatre Critics Association assembled in Chicago for a convention, almost assured its failure. Critics from *The Wall Street Journal* and *Village Voice* to the *Toledo Blade*, *St. Louis Post-Dispatch*, and the *Kalamazoo Gazette* united in their dislike of a work defined by turgid prose and an outlandish plot. The previous year, Mamet had given a scathing address to the group in Minneapolis and in a later interview suggested that the hostile reception of *Lone Canoe* was payback.

Mamet had begun his Minneapolis talk by explaining the use of criticism for the actor and the need to replace egocentric goals with those of a technical and philosophic nature. Sterile actors are self-satisfied actors who lack the ability to criticize themselves and are always "looking for someone either to kiss their ass or to hold their hand" (WR 140). So, too, are critics, he argued. "If you do not learn your craft, the Theatre, and its moral and practical precepts . . . if you do not learn to judge yourself against a standard of artistic perfection . . . you *must* be unhappy" (WR 140). Don't disparage or exploit the theatre unless you are a part of it, he admonished his audience. If you are not part of it, you are only a "hack and a plaything of our advertisers" (WR 141). Study acting and learn to write "for *yourself*, and be an artist" he exclaims (WR 141). His audience was as surprised as it was displeased by this attitude and may have delighted in Mamet's theatrical disaster a year later.

Lone Canoe was Mamet's second attempt at a historical drama. *Marranos* was his first. Pulled toward history and the historical, he would later express his attraction to the past through film adaptations of works like *The Winslow Boy* (1999) or his staging of *Boston Marriage* (1999) or adaptations of Chekhov or Harley Granville-Barker's *The Voysey Inheritance* (2005). For *Lone Canoe*, however, he was unable to integrate successfully the story of a Victorian explorer with ideas of Imperialism and nation. But Mamet clearly did not want to write another *American Buffalo*—"three guys talking dirty"—but a fable, one about the price of fame, which he himself was beginning to experience.[34] The inspiration for the set was Vakhtangov, a Russian director and protégé of Stanislavsky's. In the work, Mamet sought to blend narrative drama with song expressed through stilted, pseudo-Nineteenth century language.

Another parallel is with Vsevolod Meyerhold and Constructivism and even Brecht in his larger plays. Mamet, himself, offered the comparison to Meyerhold during a March 27, 2006, discussion at the Goodman Theatre, referring to

Meyerhold's attempt to achieve an accord between the designer, composer, playwright, and director in an effort to have the lines spoken to music with distinct voices and pure sound to create an "inner thrill." Stylized movements and gestures in the manner of a fresco were also important. Meyerhold described this kind of acting as "plastic" and it characterizes how the actors moved in the Goodman production of *Lone Canoe*. The result was an abstracted style typical of symbolist productions and the opposite of realistic theatre.

Mamet wrote the play in a manner different than his usual style. Instead of beginning with one or two interesting characters and then finding out what they're talking about, he began with plot, with each scene leading up to a revelation: "I'm taken up with the whole notion of theatricality" he explained, trying something new. An adventure story, it's about an English explorer "who gets lost in the mythological North of North America." But it was anti-naturalistic and contained no comedy, nor cynicism (May 25, 1979 in FOM 44).

The plot of *Lone Canoe or The Explorer* concentrates on the disappearance of Sir John Fairfax in the far north and the task of Frederick van Brandt to locate him and bring him back. Enlarging the two acts of three scenes each are eight musical numbers including an overture. Alaric (Rokko) Jans composed the music. Colin Stinton played van Brandt, while Norman Snow played Sir John Fairfax. Stinton had been in *Native Son* and won an award for his role in the Broadway production of *The Water Engine*. The teaser used to promote the play was the line, "What I am for you frightens me—what I am with you comforts me." A banner hanging in the theatre asked, "Where are our heroes in the North?"

The original script had many more characters than the staged version, including a Voyageur guide, a keen brave of the Athabascan Tribe, and various tribal people. The first version begins with van Brandt and his guide preparing to return after five years of searching for Sir John Fairfax. Unexpectedly, they meet several Athabasca natives and discover that Fairfax has adapted to the wild and married Thom, daughter of a chief. They suddenly meet him and question his adjustment to native life. He explains to van Brandt that "it's been hard, and it's been good. In short, it has been simple"—and he will *not* return. He has a new life as a "militarist," teaching Western warfare to the Natives. "This is life, Man! Here. Out in the world. Alone. Time. Time to think. A clean life. Unambiguous. You hunt and kill, you eat. You meet a man in battle, one lives one dies. Woman likes you and she tells you so and takes you, that is that."[35]

A corrected script dated May 27,1979, three days after the opening, reduced the number of characters and began with van Brandt alone in his canoe writing in his journal, "I am lost." His Voyageur is gone and as Scene 2 shows, so is Thom's husband, Fairfax. A shaman comforts her. A famine has occurred and Fairfax has gone to find food and returns before the scene ends in a display of loyalty. A vision of deer occurred to him and he prepares to hunt the next day with friends, bursting out in song: "Only love made me leave you/apart, my yearning was constant for thee" (10 Rev).

Van Brandt then discovers Fairfax, who tells him how his men died in a freak storm some years earlier and how he was saved by Natives and does not want to have anything to do with England. Van Brandt then cons him into believing he must return to correct the charge in a newly discovered journal that Fairfax's pride drove his men on and caused their deaths. Fairfax claims it's a forgery, a hoax, but van Brandt says the reputation of himself and his men has been ruined—unless he returns to correct it. Fairfax decides to return to right the wrong as Act One ends.

Act Two opens with a Ulysses-like song in the tradition of Tennyson praising the open road and loyalty of the men who have served him (Fairfax). A jingoistic chorus sings, "We are Englishmen/and we know no fear, /to the world's uncharted regions/we will bear the Union Jack" (32 Rev.). Fairfax restates his desire to return to England to his wife. The sudden appearance of a Shaman, who wounds van Brandt with an arrow to prevent him from stealing Fairfax, leads Fairfax to shoot the Shaman, who dies—or at least appears to until he is resurrected in a final scene.

Fairfax now escapes with the wounded van Brandt but reads his journals to learn that it is van Brandt who is in disgrace, not himself. He sought out Fairfax so that van Brandt would appear a hero if he brought him back. Betrayal and the con come into play, while van Brandt appears to expire. A humiliated Fairfax returns to Thom, prepared to pay the price of a murderer only to find that the Shaman has been restored to life seconds before Fairfax is to kill himself. Thom still loves him and both she and the Shaman welcome him. This final trio then sings the maudlin "all will come round/in its turn" (49 Rev.). Sentiment and platitude compete to complete the work, although a nine-year-old attending the performance stood up at the end and announced that it was the best play he had ever seen.[36]

The solemnity of the explorer finding his life among the Natives in the Goodman production brought nothing but derision, which angered Mamet. Linda Winer in *The Chicago Tribune* wrote that "Chicago has had many worse evenings in the theatre, but rarely one this anguished." The play, she writes, is about testing, exploring and "really getting lost. And so, for the moment, is Mamet." The review then calls the work a "serious failure," a "didactic myth" about a nineteenth-century British explorer who must choose between English glory and a simple life among the "noble savages" of the north.

The leaden dialogue, combined with a static plot and over-emphatic expressions, caused uneasy laughter in the audience. The first public collaboration of Mosher and Mamet (Mamet's work on *Native Son* was minor and uncredited), they faced an almost unworkable combination in the two-act production, trying to mix Nineteenth-century melodrama, doctrinaire moralizing, and too many simple declarative sentences.

The songs were especially disconcerting, wrote Roger Ellis in *Theatre Journal*, a cross between Gilbert and Sullivan and a Bob Hope-Bing Crosby road movie, especially in the "Heroes of the Empire" duet. As well, *Lone Canoe* seemed to further Mamet's interest in the mystical idea of the forest expressed in *The Woods*, "but he seems to have lost his poetic rhythm in the quest for simpler, more direct action." The work is less an adventure story or fable than an "oratorio," not helped by the use of bleachers upon which the four actors stood and emoted. At one point, Fairfax and van Brandt sit on them, rather like a pause on the playing field of an English school quipped one viewer. Among more pedestrian problems were that the four characters have no English accents, no one appears weak from the famine that has beset the Natives, figures do not die when shot. Moreover, a dangling overhead canoe which looked more like a museum display from Chicago's Field Museum, distracted viewers. A confession toward the end is more like a Maoist self-criticism session, while the realistic costumes contrasted with the mythic hopes of the work, said another critic. In short, the work falls short.[37]

The acting was not much better, possessing a "bullied simplicity" as the actors moved in a wooden manner, facing the audience and declaiming their lines in front of a large set consisting of a backdrop painted with Native motifs and the suspended canoe. Costumes were also out of sync: Susan Dafoe, for example, who played Thom, Fairfax's wife, looked more "like an executive trainee dressed by a Native handicrafts shop." The characters, however, sing throatily to each other, much like "Nelson Eddy and Jeannette Macdonald doing 'Indian Love Call.'" Phrases in the dialogue and singing, however, seem as if they were "lifted verbatim from a 19th century opera libretto. "You are my whole life; fore'er I cleave to thee," Fairfax tells his wife. "And I cleave to thee," she replies. Van Brandt, at one point, admonishes Fairfax with these words: "Quit this savage idyll and take up your yoke again . . . Come home, Johnny." "A lot of this goes a short way," Richard Eder concluded, conceding that Mamet has succeeded in the past in "stripping down speech to bring out the force and tension that underlie the banal phrase that most people utter." But here, he has fallen off his tightrope and "plunged right into the middle of the awkwardness and banality he was to hover above."[38]

Not all the critics, however, were so downbeat, and some tried to find virtue. Roger Ellis in *Theatre Journal* was partly sympathetic: "this attempt at serious musical theatre" failed only because of the staging, marked by hasty preparation and an inconsistent production style. Fairfax, he acknowledges, is "something of a Victorian drop-out," but emerges as the great explorer who discovered a simple life with the Natives. In contrast to the drives for fame and power in so-called civilized society are the natural rhythms of simpler societies. The greatest error in the production, he writes, is that Mamet's characters must sing about all this. The night the critics attended, "a sort of riot broke out." But in defense of Mamet's writing, Mosher later stated that the "thee and thou" side of David "is just as important as the motherfucker side of David—the two [are] strains in him" (Mosher, Interview 235).

Mosher's attempt to mix nineteenth-century melodrama with an English music hall-style, and combining it with fairytale moralizing, undermined the production. The scenic elements were similarly inadequate: the stage was totally enclosed by curtains and a backdrop bearing Native motifs of hunting and totems, but the tribal atmosphere, aided by realistic costumes, seemed inappropriate to a drama that, in Mamet's words, "deals abstractly with 'a wild place' and 'an England of the mind.'"

Mamet treated history as myth. But he was disgruntled, despite his own view that "playwrights can grow immensely from poor rejection of their new plays" and Ellis saying that through revision *Lone Canoe* may "represent a significant new step in the development of historical drama." He never published the text, nor approved another production and remained highly displeased with the critics, whom he accused of being drunk (they attended the performance after a reception). The critics in turn were outraged at the accusation.[39]

Another nautical drama soon followed the disappointment of *Lone Canoe*. *Lakeboat* is set somewhat closer to home, on the ore carriers of the Great Lakes. It was a 1980 reworking of one of his earliest efforts written for the St. Nicholas Company at Marlboro and then Goddard. Directed by John Dillon, the revision for the Milwaukee Repertory Company has twenty-eight short scenes opening with a report of violence: a drunken night cook was mugged in East Chicago and lost his money and identification. His attempt to return to the ship is rebuffed and he's thrown off. But violence exists at two levels, the physical and mental, while Mamet's signature, staccato language runs throughout.

The twenty-eight scenes aboard the steel-carrying Great Lakes ship describes the life of eight sailors, one of whom is a college student, Dale, to whom the others confide their fears and dreams. The play becomes Mamet's *Life on the Mississippi*, substituting a lake-boat steward for the river pilot in Twain's book. The episodic play is a chain of monologues and dialogues rather than an integrated play, and lacks any dramatic arc. The text is reminiscent of *Camel* in its structure, although there is a single, general setting. The "macho maritime milieu," as one reviewer wrote of a 1994 production, dominates the work. Again, blackouts and inter-cutting define the form. When Joe Mantegna decided to film the work in 2000, he added several flashback scenes to background the tales. Tony Mamet, David Mamet's stepbrother and an actor, played the role of Dale Katzman.

Interestingly, Mamet's work at this time continued to focus on "off-shore," marginalized figures and situations. From the petty thieves and junk dealer of *American Buffalo* to the "lost" Fairfax and van Brandt in *Lone Canoe* and the isolated crew of *Lakeboat*, soon to be extended to *Edmond* and *Glengarry Glen Ross*, Mamet's characters remained outsiders. They even seem to choose to be so, as Edmond illustrates when he consciously renounces his bland, middle-class world for one of danger and death that ends in prison.

But Mamet's reputation by 1979 was no longer ironclad. Critics were finding his plays repetitive, with a surfeit of profane language delivered in a staccato manner. He seemed to have almost nothing new to say. *Reunion* was meeting with harsh criticism, while Mel Gussow of the *New York Times* quipped that his short play "The Sanctity of Marriage," triple-billed with *Reunion*, "adds nothing to the evening except 10 minutes."

Clive Barnes, offering another negative opinion, titled his review of "Reunion," "Dark Pony," and "The Sanctity of Marriage," "Mamet falls short." Other critics began to note that Mamet had an up-and-down affair with audiences: "when he is bad, we are easily mystified. Where is the talent that seemed so true?" Barnes laments. In turn Mamet was finding critics less appealing. In one interview he mused that he would like his own theatre with a subscription audience who would be advised in advance that no attention to reviews will be paid. Critics in this theatre would be obliged to stay through curtain calls and, Mamet amusingly said, the "epitaph of Walter Kerr's grave would read 'at last, he did something for the theatre.'"[40]

But then, likely encouraged by his wife's success, Mamet thought of the movies. By the late 1970s, Crouse had an active movie career underway. She had appeared in *All the President's Men* (1976), *Eleanor and Franklin* (TV, 1976), *Between the Lines* (1977), and *Prince of the City* (1981). In 1981, with Mamet and Crouse living in New York and he directing her as Viola in *Twelfth Night*, Crouse went to test for a part in Bob Rafelson's remake of James M. Cain's noir thriller, *The Postman Always Rings Twice*. Mamet kiddingly (although perhaps he meant it) told her to tell Rafelson that he would be a fool if he didn't get Mamet to do the screenplay. Mamet had recently been re-reading Cain's novels. Crouse did not get the part—it went to Jessica Lange—but Rafelson called unexpectedly and asked why he should hire the playwright. "I'll either give you a really good screenplay or a sincere apology" was Mamet's smart-ass reply, also telling him, "I'm flattered but you're nuts. I've never written a movie and I can't [even] get arrested in Hollywood."[41] They came to an agreement, even though Mamet was a novice. Rafelson decided he might be able to do the job if he gave Mamet a crash course in screenwriting. He flew Mamet to California to study movies, and offered a tutorial on what made sound scripts, reviewing films and successful screenplays. Mamet learned quickly. It was an important apprenticeship as he began to work on *Postman*, partly on the west coast and partly in Vermont. He was also soon offering *his* view of Hollywood: "There isn't any life there. Just climate." With joking reference to a neo-Marxist view, he said "instead of everything being determined by economics, it's determined by the climate. It's a land where it's always afternoon" (NYT 20 March 1981). Crouse, it might be said, brought Mamet into the movies and he has never left. It also brought his work to a new level of development as he began to move from the stage to the screen.

Until Rafelson invited Mamet to work on *Postman*, Mamet had only done a few adaptations of his own work, notably *Sexual Perversity in Chicago*, which had not yet been made, and *A Life in the Theatre*, which was adapted for TV and shown on PBS on October 3, 1979. In an interview about writing the *Postman* screenplay, Mamet quotes Ulu Grosbard (who directed *American Buffalo* on Broadway with Duvall in 1977) that "'the better the play, the worse the movie it's going to make.' That may be true."[42] Rafelson instilled confidence in Mamet, who, after several months of discussion with him, went off and wrote several drafts. He was on the set almost half the shooting time and did a fair amount of work there, although he remarked that "the actual film was very close to the first draft." He also sat in on pre-and-post-production, while learning the elements of direction and was treated almost as an equal by Rafelson and his star (and friend) Jack Nicholson (Ea 260). Additionally, Mamet found indirect help through Rafelson's uncle, the legendary Hollywood screenwriter Samson Raphaelson, author of several notable Ernst Lubitsch movies and the dramatist of *The Day of Atonement*, which became the first talking movie, *The Jazz Singer*. Raphaelson read Mamet's script and offered notes through his nephew.

Despite earlier resistance, Mamet found working in film seductive. The money was good and it aided his playwriting, especially his sense of structure. In a movie, he said, "you're trying to show what the characters did and in a play they're trying to convey what they want. The only tool they have in a play is what they're trying to say. What might be wretched playwriting . . . may be good screenwriting" (Ea 260). Stage dialogue could also be more lyrical than film dialogue.

Drawing on his talent for short, broken dialogue, Mamet kept the scenes of *Postman* brief and choppy. Rafelson, he remembers, told him, "if you see a lot of dialogue, then it's a bad screenplay" (Ea 260). In the theatre, the director serves the play and the playwright is king; in film, you work for the director. "The closest thing to playwright is film editing, because the real art is in the cutting room. . . . it's all in the juxtaposition of cutting" (Ea 261). Furthermore, Mamet adds that "the best way to teach playwriting is to teach acting, to make writers really understand what can happen onstage" (Ea 261). But Rafelson's basic principle was to not talk about the needs of the camera but to "describe what the audience should see. There should be great clarity and simplicity. In a way it's very much like writing jokes. . . . It's keeping only those things you absolutely must know in order for you to get the punch line" (Ea 261).

An interview in *Film Comment* just after the release of *Postman* has Mamet again differentiating between film and drama. Film is a narrative medium, the stage a dramatic one, where characters interact and friction emerges "because they want things that contradict each other's desires. The drama is in this interaction of opposites."[43] Writing a play, the author starts from the inside out, beginning with scenes and characters but with little sense of who the characters are. With a movie, it's the other way, beginning with structure and working backward into character (Yakir 21). The first draft of *Postman* was without adverbs, the way Mamet wrote plays, because the dialogue should be self-explanatory. But the studio felt it lacked something and he added terms like "savagely" or "feelingly" after each character's name. The studio then said it was a great screenplay.

The story for the film, Mamet further explains, is 4,000 years old: that of an aging man with a young wife who takes on a younger, more virile stranger. He cites the American playwright Sidney Howard's *They Knew What They Wanted*, a work about an Italian immigrant who becomes rich and owns a vineyard in California.

His mail order bride falls in love with a drifter and disruption follows (he would later cite Howard and his "group" dramas when discussing *Glengarry Glen Ross*). Cain's original 1933 novel presents a wonderful picture of the country at that time, but it's really about "killing and screwing and betraying each other—and under all this very cynical vision is a crying need for human contact in a bad, bad world" (Yakir 21). The book, Mamet said, is striking in its plot because where others would have ended, this one begins: "'It's what happens *after* the murder that's the interesting part'" (Yakir 22).

Working from the book meant dramatizing the narrative sequences. Mamet restates his basic aesthetic: "I'm of the Aristotelian school: characters are nothing but habitual action. You don't create a character; you describe what he does" (Yakir 21). This meant putting the audience in the same position as the protagonists—"led forth by events, by the inevitability of the previous actions. They don't know what they're going to do next either. They find out after they've done it" (Yakir 22). However, Mamet consciously avoided reproducing the "hard-boiled" tone of the novel because, he felt, it is "not actable" (Yakir 22). The essence of dialogue is "always to make a point. To go on and on is to betray your objective'" (Yakir 23). One of his favorite characters in the film which he created is the crooked lawyer Katz, keen to convince the insurance investigator to drop his charges against the couple.

What influenced him strongly in working on the film was *Double Indemnity*, the film of Cain's novel, the screenplay of which was written by Raymond Chandler. In fact, he found that his own dialogue was closer to Chandler than Cain: punchy, funny, catchy. Chandler worked, Mamet felt, because his dialogue is meant to be spoken: "You read him and you hear it and you understand the people from what they say to each other, while in Cain you understand them [the characters] from what they say about themselves" (Yakir 24). Much like himself, he understands that Chandler is a dramatist because rather than giving actors the answers, he "incites them—by leaving out steps—to act" (Yakir 24). Rafelson and Mamet spent nearly a year on the script, even rewriting on the set. Mamet also admired the classical style of the film, referring to Rafelson's manner as "the motivated camera; it doesn't move gratuitously" (Yakir 24). Reviews were divided over the brooding and brutally erotic vision of the 1934 novel. Mamet's script, however, did receive good notice.[44] However, Cain's emphasis in the novel on the "killing and screwing and betraying" as a cynical expression of the need for human contact, anticipated precisely the themes of Mamet's next dark, dramatic work, *Edmond*.

The effect of screenwriting for Mamet meant removing the onus of working on a plot, which he had always found difficult, preferring the episodic to the fully plotted. But the challenge, he admitted, was to "write a play structured along traditional Aristotelian lines" (Ea 261). Ironically, his next major work would precisely embody those features, although he also claims that his children's plays represent such an approach. "'What happens next' is crucial to kids. And that's the question in movies. The minute the audience stops wondering, forget it'" (Ea 262). The result of his screenwriting was new self-confidence: "After nine openings of new plays in five years I began to feel a physical revulsion every time I entered a theatre. I feel very refreshed now" (Ea 262). The result of that refreshment would be a new energy focused on American morality and ethics.

5

THE AMERICAN WAY

Ford: You were going to con me out of my money.
Mike: It was only business.
Ford: It was only business, huh?
Joey: It's the American Way.

Mamet, *House of Games*

This exchange from Mamet's 1987 film highlights the combination of bravado, deception, and morality his work was elaborating. The expression of these notions in Mamet's drama, film and even prose underscores his suspicious view of human behavior. Another line in the film short-handedly states: "Don't Trust Nobody" (HG 37). For Mamet, that meant don't even trust language.

A Mamet joke epitomizes his repudiation of politeness and preference for provocation: "A passerby on a windy Chicago street pauses in front of a homeless man looking for a handout. After fishing for some change, he gives him fifty cents adding 'Neither a borrower nor a lender be. Shakespeare.' Glancing at the coins, the beggar replies, 'Fuck you. David Mamet.' *American Buffalo* set the tone; *Edmond* intensified the darkness; *Glengarry Glen Ross* enlarged the scope. In the two latter works, Mamet provided bitter plays that indicted the hopes and dreams of American life, nailing the fury, anger, deceptiveness, and con that is inimical to the enterprise, as Mamet might phrase it.

Capitalizing on issues suggested by *The Postman*, Mamet addressed sex, racism, and urban violence in his account of Edmond Burke, a middle-class white man who chooses to renounce his placid life for one of danger and destruction. In many ways, it inverts Richard Wright's *Native Son* as a white rejects the very world Bigger Thomas seeks but cannot possess. Both Bigger and Edmond, however, share a world of anger, prejudice, violence, death, and imprisonment. Mamet's play takes audiences into a dark underworld reminiscent of Dante or perhaps Georg Büchner's *Woyzeck* or Maxim Gorki's *The Lower Depths*. Pimps, prostitutes, and petty criminals populate the work, one of Mamet's most disturbing plays.

In an essay entitled "Misguided, excessive and true," Mamet identified racism as the single most oppressive and abusive element in American life. *Native Son* is for him the "Great American Novel" because of its violent presentation of the "tragedy of race."[1] Mamet does not condone violence but admits that we are all capable of it and that drama, especially tragedy, has the power "to release the repressed in a safe—indeed, in a sanctified—setting and, so, restore balance to the individual." The "dark, dark secret of America is and always has been race," code-named many things by white America, the favorite, "sex." Sadly, the lynching of black men by whites for even the suggestion of sex with their women was, in actuality, defending "the white male's insecurity, not his female's chastity."

Offering comment on the sexless marriages of much of white America, Mamet asks, "Where is this sexual energy cathected?" In *Edmond*, it is in the tradition of race. Edmond's sexless marriage is the symbol of his meaningless life, which he rejects. The sexual encounters along his journey from respectability to depravity are all empty signs of "the American way" and no more than barter and business. Only through violence, killing first a pimp and then a waitress, does Edmond feel free and empowered, much the same as Bigger Thomas, who admits to himself that "he had murdered and had created a new life for himself." Mamet says of his "harsh play," which the critics originally called misguided and excessive, "I didn't mind. I thought it was accurate. I still do." Reviewers of its most recent major production, at the National Theatre in London (2003) starring Kenneth Branagh, agreed.[2]

Edmond's voyage of sensation involves a dark odyssey that sees him murder two people, as Bigger Thomas did. Robbed, beaten, humiliated, Edmond becomes a killer in a desperate effort to reclaim some dignity. Ironically, he finds love with a black man in the final, chilling scene of the work. In his cell and after he has been raped, Edmond exchanges thoughts on the condition of society with his fellow prisoner and then "*gets up, goes over and exchanges a goodnight kiss with the* PRISONER" (E 106). The startling act is one, however, of final and eager union.

The nightmare of New York is the catalyst for Mamet's modern morality play, which begins with the ironically named Edmond Burke (alluding to the Eighteenth-century English conservative philosopher, Edmund Burke), a thirty-four-year-old businessman, listening to a fortune teller say to him, "you are not where you belong" (E 16). He then leaves his wife, harshly telling her that he never loved her spiritually or sexually (E 20). In a bar, he's told the "niggers" have it easy but that one has to get out of the rat race, his barmate explaining that life's simply "*Pussy . . . Power . . . Money . . .* adventure [and] self-*destruction*" (E 23–4). A peep show emphasizes the barriers between Edmond and sexuality that he thinks money can bridge. A con game (the classic "Three Card Monte") presents further chicanery.

Soon at a brothel, money is again thought to be the means of sexual pleasure but in a reversal, physical pleasure takes a back seat to financial negotiations. An attempt, then, to win some cash at a card game ends with a beating. The violence continues as he exchanges his wedding ring for an ironically named "*survival* knife" at a pawn shop (E 57). An unprovoked outburst at a woman in a subway station reveals his anger and out-of-control language. Attacked by a pimp, he beats him violently as he screams obscenities, but, like Bigger Thomas, such violence makes him feel alive and free as he tells a waitress in Scene Fifteen, "The Coffeehouse:" without it, "we've bred the life out of ourselves. . . . we're dead" (E 64–5, 67).

Edmond believes his previous, middle-class life has been wasted, but through his violence and then brief affair with Glenna, the waitress, he tries to regenerate a radicalized energy. Of the pimp, for example, he says "I wanted to KILL him. (*Pause.*) In that *moment* thirty years of prejudice came out of me. *(Pause.)* Thirty *years* (E 69). Glenna then tells him she hates gays and he agrees. Anarchy in society means individual morality: "There is NO *LAW* . . . there is no *history* . . . there is just *now*" (E 71). Ironically, Glenna reveals that she is trying for a career in the theatre and Edmond asks that she act something for him. But the scene turns ugly as Edmond threatens her and she orders him to leave. Her anxious, frantic state incites his anger and he attacks her. She won't "shut up" so he stabs her with his knife: "You stupid fucking *bitch* . . . you stupid fucking . . . *now* look what you've done" (E 78). Mary Dalton in *Native Son* would also not keep quite when her mother entered her bedroom; Bigger Thomas had to smother her with her pillow to be sure she (and he) would not be detected.

Found by a policeman who discovers Edmond's "survival knife," he's arrested, interrogated, and caught in his lies, despite his pleas, that now he wants to return home. Instead, he goes to jail for murdering Glenna. His wife visits but he can't explain what he's done. He expresses a longing to be close to her but cannot. All she can ask is if he's got the newspapers, another echo of *Native Son*: only through the papers does Bigger Thomas learn (a) what is happening to his own case and (b) how society has distorted its picture of him. In Scene Twenty of *Edmond*, "The New Cell," Edmond is with a black prisoner explaining to him that "when we *fear* things I think that we *wish* for them," adding that "I always knew that I would end up here" (E 89). White people should be in jail—to be with blacks, he explains.

Surprisingly, in jail for the first time, he doesn't feel afraid. And then the prisoner orders him to perform fellatio: "You going to try or you goin' to die." Edmond, unwilling, is then beaten and raped by the prisoner (E 93). In Scene Twenty-two, Edmond nostalgically writes to a Mrs. Brown, saying he's Eddie Burke "who lived on Euclid," actually the street where Mamet grew up in Chicago. The final scene has Edmond philosophizing with his cellmate again, now about destiny, quoting Shakespeare and the possibility of someone knowing "what's happening" (E 102). The play ends with a wandering discussion about heaven and its possible existence. And then, as a sign of completeness and peace, Edmond kisses his cellmate good night (E 106).

Although Chicago was the location of the premiere, New York was the immediate catalyst for the play, the city where Mamet and Crouse had been living. A

Chelsea duplex with a spacious living room and baby grand piano was their home, the area allowing both of them access to the theatre and movie world. But Mamet felt that the city was getting out of control: "The city's nuts. It's a society that's lost its flywheel, and its spinning itself apart. That's my vision of New York. It's a kind of vision of hell."[3] Hell is the constant backdrop for *Edmond*, presented through darkness, fires, and violence. At one point, a distraught Glenna even calls Edmond "the *devil*" (E 78). Ironically, he is both the victim and perpetrator of violence in a city that seems populated by figures who struggle to survive.

Other influences on the work, according to Mamet, were Büchner's *Woyzeck* and Dreiser's *An American Tragedy*. Like Büchner, whose play charts the fall of an uneducated soldier who commits murder, Mamet identifies his minor characters only by their profession or descriptions, not by names. And like *Woyzeck*, the play is about the descent of a man to into animal-like behavior, leading from sexual desire to murder. Stripped of his humanity Woyzeck transforms himself into, and is treated as, an animal, as is Edmond. Debasement is common to both characters. "Stab the bitch to death" is a hallucinatory voice Woyzeck hears repeatedly, not unlike some of the statements Edmond makes (*Woyzeck*, Scene XII). Arrested and jailed like Edmond, Woyzeck's world becomes one in which a Court Clerk admires "a good murder, a real murder, a beautiful murder" (*Woyzeck*, Scene XXVI). Of *An American Tragedy*, Mamet told an interviewer that he read the novel some ten times "and it always struck me what a great achievement it would be if I could, one day, write a scene to make people understand why somebody killed" (in Shewey NYT). Ironically, when a Chaplain does ask why he did kill, Edmond is inarticulate: "I . . . I don't. . . . I don't . . . I don't think . . . " before being led away (E 97).

Mosher's production of *Edmond*, opening at the Goodman in June 1982 with Colin Stinton as Edmond and Linda Kimbrough as the wife, emphasized the brutality in the work. Critics, in turn, found the play harrowing and remorseless, but praised it precisely because of its power. Christiansen called it a "play of shattering yet exhilarating ferocity," while Syse sensed an element of redemption at the end with the possibility of catharsis. The night of the premiere, Mamet appeared on stage before the 100 or so members of the audience and enigmatically answered questions. But to each query that suggested a problem with the play, he replied, "How would you have done it?" The audience was mystified and disturbed by his reluctance to be clear. Later productions, such as a 1996 revival at the Atlantic Theatre and a remarkable 2003 production at the National Theatre in London, rediscovered the dark intensity of the work. In 2006 William H. Macy as Edmond and Joe Mantegna as the Man appeared in a film version of the play directed by Stuart Gordon.[4]

Mamet completed *Edmond* while finishing *The Postman Always Rings Twice* and writing *The Verdict*, in which Paul Newman plays a down-and-out lawyer who makes a bid for personal and professional redemption, for Sidney Lumet. *Edmond* and the film tell the same story but from different angles. *The Verdict* is a more realistic drama about loss and regaining faith, Mamet told Don Shewey. Newman in the film "is desperate and depressed because he's denying the life of the soul. . . . *Edmond* presents the tragic view of a man who doesn't think faith exists." He commits the "modern New York heresy of denying the life of the soul" (Shewey NYT). Mamet further added that *Edmond* deals with people who are "divided by sex, by sexual preference, by monetary position, by race." Because Edmond allows himself to express his hatred of blacks and gays, he thinks he's free, but only at the end of the play, having destroyed himself, does he realize how destructive and hateful such an attitude is. Ironically, he ends up in a gay alliance with a black fellow prisoner but "because of that alliance, because he resolves those basic dichotomies, I think it's a very, very hopeful play" Mamet concludes (Shewey *NYT*).

Critics disagreed. From the first, the violence, obscenities and emotional intensity of the play disturbed them (and the public), who, while perhaps accustomed to Mamet's profanities, were less prepared for the bleakness of his vision. When it opened in New York in 1982 at the Provincetown Playhouse, reviewers were similarly hostile, finding it annoyingly mannered and pretentious. Few understood that it was a fable, a morality play of an aimless man driven to murder to discover himself. At its 1996 remounting at New York's Atlantic Theatre, a number of surreal "city-on-the-verge-of-collapse" plays reflected similar situations, notably Howard Korder's *Lights* and Caryl Churchill's *Skriker*. Although the critical reaction was mixed and only seventy-seven performances of the New York production took place, the play won two *Village Voice* Off-Broadway awards (Obie's) and was named best new American play. Mosher received an Obie for best direction.

Violence and deception were inimical to all three works Mamet was writing at this time: *Postman, The Verdict*, and *Edmond*. From *Postman*, however, he learned the importance of structuring plot so that the audience knew what happened next. He was also learning to refine his talent for dialogue.

Both Edmond and the city decay at a rapid rate, and Mamet's trademark pauses, clipped sentences, half-stated themes, and strong ideas intensify the breakdown. Mamet encouraged a political reading of the play, emphasizing the urban destruction of the individual and an inability to deal with the frustrations of modern life, which eradicates the human. (DMC 74). He also acknowledged Brecht's influence, adding that he was once fascinated by his work but found his writings about theatre nonsense. However, he admires the plays, which he calls "quintessentially dramatic writing" (DMC 74). But when an interviewer remarks that Brecht the theorist wanted to deny what Brecht the playwright was doing, Mamet agrees. He experiences the same, adding that comics like him always want to be tragedians (DMC 74). The disparity between theory and practice even reaches the performance, for, as Mamet acknowledges, the through-line is so strong that the characters can be saying things that are very different from what is really being communicated in the subtext. "That's why theatre's like life," Mamet adds, "No one really says what they mean, but they always mean what they mean" (DMC 74).

"Few playwrights accept criticism well; David Mamet accepts it not at all" *The Wall Street Journal* opined when *Edmond* opened in New York. Mamet had been on the attack, relentlessly berating critics for not understanding his play. In the early eighties, for example, he submitted the following to *New York Magazine's* "the Best of Anything" contest. He offered the "Best Review:" "I never understood the theatre until this night. Please excuse every thing I've ever written. When you read this I'll be dead. Signed Clive Barnes." Barnes was the influential drama critic of the *New York Post*, occasionally unreceptive toward Mamet's work and yet still a fan. But for Mamet, all critics were a kind of thought-police, "and the effect is to limit those ideas which are being discussed."[5] However, he still cons the press into thinking they play a critical role, agreeing to interviews and articles, although he often offers only enigmatic and incomplete responses. But practical Mamet knows the press is important in getting audiences to see his plays.

Ironically, while brief staccato exchanges mark his plays, Mamet enjoys expounding at length on a variety of ideas regarding the theatre. As *Edmond* was to open in New York at the Provincetown Playhouse, for example, he told a reporter that "The American Dream has gone bad." The American predilection for abuse, physically and economically, might have the capacity for one to become rich but the capitalist dream turned people against each other: "They fight each other to get something for nothing."

Mamet explained that he set the play in New York because it is "the world capital of speculation," the city a spiritually barren landscape where things are traded rather than created.[6] Whites, in particular, feel disassociated because they have no tragedy: "in effect that *is* their tragedy." As a consequence, they try to steal or co-opt the lives and identities of others. That is what Edmond seeks. Empathy disappears in a world where the belief and fear is "that if I go up, you go down" (Ibid). Furthermore, *Edmond* is a "morality play about modern society . . . about a man trying to discover himself and what he views as a sick society" (DMC 68).

The theatrical creator is to "bring the life of the human soul to the stage," Mamet grandiosely states. We seek the theatre "by our need to express and hear the truth." Can this happen in a soap opera? No, because that is only gossip, although everyone loves it. Mamet also admits to Mimi Leahey that when he first came to New York, he tried to get a job writing soaps. The money was great but no one would hire him. (Leahey 3). He also explains that his early interest in playwriting was something almost physical: "If I wrote for an hour a day I felt good. If I didn't write, I felt bad." And from his training as an actor, he learned how to construct scenes:

> I was trained . . . to look at the progression of a scene as a progression of moments. A play is like a syllogism or a lesson in ethics. If we do this, then we get that. You put in a number of variables and you look for the logical reduction of these variables.
>
> For many of my characters, those variables can only be expunged by violence. (Leahey 3)

According to Mamet, the conventional view is that anyone can write a good first act, which may be true, but, "the problem in writing a play is in writing the last act. . . . the challenge is in correctly understanding, embodying an expression of what the *true* outcome of the actions in the play will be" (Leahey 3). Only by following the conflict to its logical extension can a commitment to characters occur. However, Mamet reasserts that character must resonate with the audience: we must see ourselves in them, as we do in Chekhov, and that, yes, in these terms, Brecht did have merit. For all Brecht's essays about alienating the audience, Mamet believes that "he remains the most charming of playwrights because everything he wrote was deeply felt" (Leahey 3).

While this debate was taking place, Mamet found himself in a new role, that of a father. His daughter Willa Ives Mamet, named after Willa Cather and the American composer, Chares Ives, was born in 1982. Anticipating his new responsibilities, movie work, with its greater remuneration, suddenly looked attractive.

Success with *Postman* made Mamet a hot property. Richard Zanuck and David Brown, the producers of *Jaws*, hired Mamet to write the screenplay of a 1980 novel entitled *Verdict* by a Boston lawyer, Barry Reed. Mamet did, but they didn't like it. They paid him and made a better offer: "If you'd like to write it again, we'll pay you again." "That's very flattering but I couldn't write anything differently" he replied (DMC 194). New writers were brought in while a somewhat morose Mamet sent the script to Sidney Lumet, an acquaintance. Meanwhile, it turned out that Robert Redford, who was supposed to direct and star in the film, was uncomfortable with the main character and hired another writer to do a draft, and then another, until he decided he didn't want to do the film. He was unhappy playing an alcoholic. The producers then contracted with Lumet to direct and sent him all the scripts they had except Mamet's. Lumet read them and told the producers that he definitely wanted to do the movie but only with Mamet's script, which he had already seen: "if I'd ever read the book first, before I read the script, I never would have done it. It's fascinating to me that David drew that story from it." By accident, Mamet was in (DMC 194).

Lumet, who had already directed *12 Angry Men, The Pawnbroker, Serpico, Dog Day Afternoon, Network*, and *Prince of the City*, accepted. Paul Newman then agreed to star and the film was underway. Mamet even agreed to put the outcome of the verdict in the script. In the earlier version, he kept it out to the distress of Zanuck and Brown, who supposedly threw him out when he refused to make this change. Lumet, however, convinced him to include it.[7]

But even in a script about the redemption of an alcoholic Boston lawyer, Frank Galvin, who takes on and wins a malpractice suit against a Roman Catholic hospital in Boston, Mamet could not resist including a con. In preparation for a meeting with his client, the sister of a now comatose victim injured during childbirth, Galvin tidies up his grimy office, then locks it and leaves a note from his non-existent secretary about a non-existent lunch date with a judge. When he rushes back for his appointment, he does his best to look busy. Of course, he hasn't had a case or client for months. The script, however, also displays integrity: offered a large out-of-court settlement from the church's prestigious law firm, Galvin realizes that "if I take the money, I'm lost." He won't be bought off, but he does commit a few misdemeanors along the way to win.

The screenplay is terse but full of surprises. It's a maze because, although the audience knows from the outset where Galvin should end up, it has no idea of how he might get there, overcoming such obstacles as a biased, Catholic judge who in court says, "It seems to me, a fellow's trying to come back, he'd take the settlement. I myself would take it and run like a thief." Galvin: "I'm sure you would." Another feature that appealed to Mamet was the film's sense of history: because it is about people trapped in the past, Lumet decided that there would be nothing new in it—no modern buildings or furniture. "Everything is old, from another time, as if time stopped for them a long while ago."[8]

Critics noted parallels to Chekhov, especially in structure. The reference is not unusual: Lumet admired Chekhov and filmed *The Seagull*, Lumet's favorite play. The presence in the film of a cold girlfriend, Laura Fischer (Charlotte Rampling), shows how in Mamet's world desperate men often make the wrong choices, doing the right thing at the worst moment. She betrays him on many levels, and, when Galvin decks her in a crowded restaurant, the audience almost cheers this Mamet moment.

The trial scenes, the courthouse exterior, and the corridors shot in the Tweed Building in Lower Manhattan, are all carefully structured. In his final address to the jury, Galvin challenges their ability to act morally. We might think that the law is a sham but "today you are the law. You are the law . . . not some book and not the lawyer or the marble statues and the trappings of the court." One must act as though they had "faith in justice," and "act with justice. (*Beat.*) And I believe that there is justice in our hearts. (*Beat.*) Thank you." Not every speech is so rhetorical or religious, however. When Galvin concedes that his opposing attorney is "a good man," his mentor (Jack Warden) snaps back with "Good? He's the prince of fuckin' darkness."

Nominated for Academy Awards for best picture, director, actor, supporting actor, and best screenplay adapted from another medium, the picture received much attention—but lost to *Gandhi* in most categories. Mamet, nominated in the adapted screenplay category, lost to Costa Garvas for his screenplay *Missing*. Nevertheless, *The Verdict* afforded Mamet a higher profile and a rapport with Lumet, who asked him to do the screenplay of *Malcolm X*, which he hoped to direct for Warner Bros. starring Richard Pryor.[9] But the film had trouble with financing and was never made as Lumet and Mamet envisioned it. Lumet, however, continued to admire Mamet's style, praising his ability to leave things out or unsaid, allowing the actors to flesh out their roles through action. Lumet's esteem for Mamet may have originated in his early theatrical experiences: as a child actor. Lumet was a member of the legendary Group Theatre, where Sanford Meisner had studied before establishing his own theatre school.

A consequence of this was Lumet's normal practice of rehearsing his actors for two weeks before shooting. For *The Verdict*, he assigned three because of the complex characters and the need to blend the actors' presentational styles: Newman's Method Acting, James Mason's classical training, and Charlotte Rampling's "no method" needed to meld. From *his* experience with Lumet, Mamet learned the value of table readings (the first read-through with the actors before filming) to discover if rewrites are necessary.

After the success of *The Verdict* and its Academy Award nominations, Mamet was a desirable Hollywood writer but after the release of the movie and the controversy surrounding *Edmond*, he retreated to a series of short works to recharge his artistic batteries. He wrote *Five Unrelated Pieces* ("Two Conversations," "Two Scenes," and "Yes, But So What") and then an adaptation of another work about revolution and change: Pierre Laville's *Red River* (*Le Fleuve Rouge*). Laville, a contemporary French dramatist, focused on Twentieth-century Russia and the impact of Communism. Mamet also worked on *The Disappearance of the Jews* and both premiered at the Goodman in May and June 1983. That same year, Mamet's *Glengarry Glen Ross* premiered at the National Theatre in London.

Mamet worked on *Glengarry* not long after *Edmond*. His Laville adaptation, based on a literal translation by Tilde Sankovitch, coincided with the writing of *Glengarry*. All three works—*Edmond*, *Red River*, and *Glengarry*—focus on ethics, political/social corruption, and moral decay. They may all be thought of on the same continuum, although *Red River* is more consciously historical, dealing with Russia between 1925 and 1940. But all three plays deal with the individual's relation to society and the cost and benefits, if any, involved in trying to step outside its boundaries.

Pierre Laville, born in France in 1937, earned a Doctor of Laws and was sent by the UN to Africa. He later became an assistant to the Parisian theatre director Jean Marie Serreau and translated *American Buffalo* into French. The original French production of *Red River* took place in Marseille in 1980 and the American premiere opened at the Goodman on May 2, 1983, with Robert Woodruff replacing Andre Gregory, who had been originally scheduled to direct. The play, set in post-revolutionary Russia, combines history and fantasy to explore the lives of Mayakofsky and Bulgakov, the first the futurist poet who, censured for his writing after a life of dedication to the new Communist world, committed suicide in 1930. Bulgakov, author of *The Master and Margarita*, was a controversial writer who had his works banned during his lifetime (1891–1940). The play explores how totalitarianism crushes the creative spirit.

A good deal of the play is about the theatre, specifically Stanislavsky which appealed to Mamet. Here was a chance to stage Stanislavsky's ideas and his approach to theatre. However, in the text, Stanislavsky is imperious and authoritarian, ruling the Moscow Art Theatre completely. When he objects to an assassination scene in Bulgakov's play, and the author refuses changes, the play is withdrawn, although its remounting is forced. The director then elaborates his ideas on performance, which Mamet himself had incorporated into his theatre practice: "Say the text as it is written (PAUSE). I'm perfectly capable of deciphering it. That's how we'll play it, as its written. Nearly as we can. We're going to *take* those words you've sold us which exist as silly black marks on a page dead as *sand* and breath some into *life*. Now, that's what *we're* doing here" (II. 86–7).

Lenin died on January 21, 1924, marking the end of the birth of Soviet Russia and the beginning of its adolescence. *Red River* explores the condition of the artist in post-revolutionary Russia and the link between politics and art based on Bulgakov's *The Master and Margarita* and *Black Snow*. The issue in the play is the conflict between two men—one who wants to work outside the system and demands freedom, the other who commits himself actively and completely to the system.

The final sequence of the play is set in 1940 and outlines the way Bulgakov was shunned by both the authorities and the public. The marginalized playwright/author becomes impotent and ineffective. Silence greets his death, which eventually occurred two years after Stanislavsky's. At one point the disbelieving Bulgakov receives a phone call from Stalin telling him he has granted permission for his work to appear. The end is set off by lines from *Uncle Vanya*. Sonia's speech begins with "there is another life, a radiant life." Ermalinsky, playing Vanya, says, "We will rest," then breaks off with "What have they done to us? The World is moving . . ."

Helena: These are New Times. . . .
Erm: Oh. We need another life. We must hope.

The play ends with Helena's equally Chekhovian, "Listen to the silence" (168). Importantly, Laville's use of Chekhov, plus the presentation of Stanislavksy's ideas, revivified the importance of the playwright for Mamet, who within two years would offer his version of *The Cherry Orchard* at the Goodman.

Russia as a subject had not previously appealed to Mamet, although Stanislavsky and Chekhov remained the major influences on his theatrical ideas. The chance to dramatize Stanislavsky and scenes at the Moscow Art Theatre were irresistible. But the sweep, subject matter, and Brechtian, epic scale of the play (which anticipates Tom Stoppard's Russian trilogy, *The Coast of Utopia* [2002]) was both a departure and a challenge for Mamet. Critics, however, found *Red River* an uncharacteristic project, more in the mold of *Lone Canoe* with its historical elements than the concentrated structure and language of *American Buffalo* or even *Edmond*. But *Red River* allowed Mamet to work with an ensemble cast and to contextualize historical themes. The "gang play," as Mamet would call it, was making sense.

Before the excitement of the explosive *Glengarry*, Mamet wrote *The Disappearance of the Jews* as part of a triple bill at the Goodman Studio with Elaine May's *Hotline* and Shel Silverstein's *Gorilla* in June 1983. *Disappearance*, directed by Mosher, was a one-acter about Bobby Gould and his childhood friend Joey reminiscing about their Jewish past but facing for the first time some troubling questions about that past. Contradictions and doubts identify their Jewish world, which faces new threats.

Shel Silverstein, Chicago cartoonist, children's writer, illustrator, songwriter, satiric dramatist, and bon vivant was a hero to Mamet. He was a figure who maintained his artistic independence and originality, while finding a steady income via his cartoons for *Playboy* and his other work, which allowed him to live in Key West, California and Chicago. As their friendship deepened, the two would call each other to trade jokes, with Silverstein assisting if Mamet needed a new joke or plot twist. Silverstein also showed Mamet that limiting himself to one genre was unnecessary; Silverstein's eclecticism was infectious. Silverstein's full beard, bald head, and combination of a gravelly and squeaky voice presented a unique figure, who likely influenced the way Mamet was developing his own image.

Silverstein confirmed the comic properties of Mamet's street talk, even when applied to a classic work. Silverstein's *Hamlet as told on the Street*, originally a 1990 play, anticipated Mamet's approach to his own original works. It took the hard-edged language of Mamet's *American Buffalo* and turned it into sheer pleasure:

"Enough," says Polonius, "That Prince has ruined my day.
Now we gotta see his fuckin' play within a play.
Hell, the place will be drafty, the seats won't be com'fa'ble
I wouldn't go at all but these tickets ain't refundable."

Silverstein loved to dismantle plays and had reduced *Hamlet* to a country and western ballad, "The Crate," and had transposed *Faust* into a contemporary TV game show, "The Lady or the Tiger."

Soon, the two Chicago figures began to collaborate. In 1988 they worked on the film *Things Change*, a satire on the mafia that Mamet termed "a mobster fairytale." An elderly Chicago shoeshine man, Gino, is mistaken, first, for a Mafia hit man and then agrees to take the rap and go to jail in return for money, which will allow him to buy his lifelong desire: a fishing boat in Sicily. His minder is a not-so-bright younger mafioso who takes him to Lake Tahoe for a final fling where Gino is, for the second time, mistakenly identified as a major Mafia capo and honored. On their return, they find they have been double-crossed and call on their Lake Tahoe host to act. The losers, *poseurs*, become winners. Don Ameche, then eighty, and Joe Mantegna starred. The gangster film was a natural for both Mamet and Silverstein because, as Mamet told Michael Billington of the *Guardian*, they both shared a common heritage as Jewish Chicagoans for whom "the idea of organized crime is part of the Chicago myth."[10]

Mamet wrote the screenplay at the same time he was directing his first film, *House of Games*, a darker psychological thriller involving the con. For this first effort at writing and directing, he followed the advice of both Mike Nichols and Sidney Lumet and story-boarded 98 percent of the film. This careful pre-planning left less room for error and presented a seamless construction in the final film, which became one of the year's ten best in the *New York Times*. But preceding this first effort to get his own work on the screen was a cinematic disaster.

It began when two producers from Chicago bought the rights to *Sexual Perversity* for little money and approached Mamet to do the script. He became a partner in the enterprise. Once he finished the screenplay, however, the producers were advised that no one would understand it. Mamet was fired and a new script, by Tim Kazurinsky and Denise DeClue, was written. Directed by Edward Zwick, the film imposed a conventional, completely unthreatening narrative on the original work and gave the protagonists new surnames that removed all ethnic associations: Shapiro becomes Martin and Soloman shifts to Sullivan, although Litko remained. Only snippets of the original Mamet dialogue appear, and in odd places, such as behind the opening credits. Released with the title *About Last Night*, Mamet claims to have never seen it, but as a result of the debacle, he decided that in the future he would control everything concerning adaptations of his work.

His early films, however, had difficulty finding distribution because they seemed too complex and difficult for general audiences. *House of Games*, for example, was never fully released in the U. S. and played in only approximately twenty theatres. *Things Change* played in one hundred theatres—perhaps because the subject was similar to *House of Games*: mistaken identity, false information, and the power of sustained illusions. Mistaken identity, in fact, is one of the themes in Mamet's third film *We're No Angels*: it is about two escaped convicts who are mistaken for priests.

In 1989, Mosher produced Silverstein's *The Devil and Billy Markham* along with Mamet's *Bobby Gould in Hell* at Lincoln Center in an evening billed as "Oh, Hell." Silverstein's contribution is about a rock singer narrating in blues verses, an attempt to beat the devil in craps, pool, and love. Mamet's play pursues Bobby Gould, later to become the erstwhile movie producer in *Speed-the-Plow*, in a men's club interrogated by a devil who "sounds like David Letterman and looks like a walking advertisement for the entire L. L. Bean catalogue of fishing gear."[11] They are interrupted by Glenna arriving in the underworld with a copy of *TV Guide* and a remote control. That same year, Silverstein and Mamet wrote "Live from the Empire Room," acted by Macy on WBAI radio. Mamet published an important appreciation of Silverstein, who died in 1999 in the *New York Times*. "In short, I suppose he was my hero," Mamet wrote.[12] Mamet's own recent turn to cartooning—a book of them appeared in 2007—echoes Silverstein's example.

~

Mamet's major work of the early eighties was the one he was at first most unsure of: *Glengarry Glen Ross*. A read-through of the play in the New York apartment of

Ulu Grosbard left it unclear what he had and, in a moment of uncharacteristic doubt, he sent the play to Harold Pinter asking what should be done to make it work. The only thing to be done, Pinter replied, was to produce it at the National. He passed it on to Peter Hall, artistic director who, in turn, chose Bill Bryden, who had done the original British *American Buffalo* at the Cottesloe (the small theatre at the National) in June 1978, to direct. On September 21, 1983, *Glengarry Glen Ross* had its world premiere, like *Buffalo*, at the Cottesloe.

Mamet's developing concept of acting set the scene for *Glengarry Glen Ross*. Acting, he believed, was about two people who want something different: "If the two people don't want something different, what the hell is the scene about? Stay home. The same is true for writing. If two people don't want something from each other then why are you having the scene? Throw the goddam scene out. . . . If two people don't want something different, the audience is going to go to sleep. Power, that's another way of putting it" (DMC 75).

These ideas are germane for *Glengarry Glen Ross*. Shelly Levene's plea to the office manager John Williamson for the leads in order to prove himself and earn some money at the opening is painful but honest. Defending his current lack of success against his proven past record, Levene desperately fights for a chance: "Do I want charity? Do I want *pity*? . . . Give me a chance. That's all I want. I'm going to *get* up on that fucking board and all I want is a chance" (GGR 22). Williamson resists—until Levene offers him 10 percent of his end of a deal. Williamson again resists, asking for 20 percent and fifty dollars a lead. Levene agrees but he doesn't have the money needed at that moment to get the premium leads. Defeated, he resigns himself to a lead from the B list of less likely buyers.

"Any business will eventually degenerate into a con game," Mamet stated in a 1995 *Playboy* interview. Not only the opening scene of *Glengarry Glen Ross* but the entire play confirms that, the work a devastating indictment of American business practice (DMC 128). This is a world without principles, an ensemble work about men deceiving each other and competing to get ahead, painfully exposing the betrayal and mistrust that drives one to crime. Based on Mamet's experience in 1969–70 working in a real estate office on Peterson Avenue on the North Side of Chicago where he made cold calls to sell questionable property in Florida, the play is loosely autobiographical. From his year's work there, he drew portraits of a series of characters equally self-serving and desperate. For structure, he explicitly followed his "what happens next" principle, first separating his drama into sets of characters and then uniting them in a petty act of crime—the theft of the leads—which has serious consequences.

The actual writing of the play was inspired by Mamet's fascination with overheard street talk and conversations in the next restaurant booth: "So I worked a bunch of these scenes with people using extremely arcane language—kind of the canting language of the real-estate crowd . . . and I thought, well, if it fascinates me, it will probably fascinate them too" (AOT 57). Mamet here identifies the first act of *Glengarry*, which involves three scenes in restaurant booths.

Scene two reveals a fragmented conversation that illustrates Mamet's method. A frustrated Dave Moss and George Aaronow, under pressure to sell "the whole fuckin' thing," begin to consider alternatives. Moss begins: "The pressure's just too great. You're ab . . . you're absolu . . . they're too important. All of them. You go in the door. I . . . 'I got to *close* this fucker, or I don't eat lunch,' or 'I don't win the *Cadillac*.' . . . We fuckin' work too hard. You work too hard" (GGR 30). The thought of working for the competition, Jerry Graff, looks better and better to both men. Moss then encourages Aaronow to strike back at Murray and Mitch, who run the downtown office, by breaking in and stealing the leads and selling them to Graff. Aaronow, realizing Moss means it, gets cold feet. But Moss explains that while "it is a crime. It's also very safe," a marvelous conundrum, echoing those in *American Buffalo* (GGR 40).

Characteristically brief, incomplete, and staccato statements identify their plan. The money tempts Aaronow: a quick twenty-five hundred for one night's work, *and* a job with Graff. Moss then finesses the crime so that Aaronow is the one to go in and steal the leads, and says it must be done that same night because the leads are being moved downtown in the morning: "I took you in on this, you have to go. That's your thing. I've made the deal with Graff. I can't go. . . . I've spoken on this too much" (GGR 43). Moss then explains to Aaronow that he is already an accessory merely because they talked about it, even if Aaronow didn't ask to be part of it. He's an accessory because Moss told him about it. He has to take the consequences. "Why?" Aaronow asks. "Because you listened," Moss answers (GGR 46).

Richard Roma's two-and-a-half page sales pitch to James Lingk is the substance of the third scene of *Glengarry* and, according to reviewers and critics is one of Mamet's best dramatic pieces because it gives voice—urgent and dramatic—to both the chicanery and the appeal of the salesman working at his highest pitch. Roma tries to get Lingk to live in the moment: "What I'm saying, what is our life? (*Pause.*) It's looking forward or it's looking back. And that's our life. That's *it*. Where is the *moment*? (*Pause.*) And what is it that we're afraid of? Loss. What else? (*Pause.*)." How, then, should we act? Roma has an answer: "I say *this* is how we must act. I do those things which seem correct to me *today*. I trust myself" (GGR 48–9). In this way, Roma says, security builds and wealth comes. The philosophy of opportunity is what Roma promotes as he cons his listener: things that happen to you can be opportunities, but since we are all different, we must decide what we want to do.

Mamet has skillfully organized three plots in the opening three scenes of *Glengarry*: Levene and his desperation for leads to put himself back on the board; Moss and Aaronow, plotting to better themselves by stealing the leads and sell them to Graff; and Roma setting up Lingk to buy with the dangerous words, "look *here*: what is this? This is a piece of land. Listen to what I'm going to tell you now" (GGR 51). In Act Two the plot lines coalesce.

The play continues, driven by the consequences of the talk witnessed in Act One: the office has been ransacked, the leads stolen, some contracts taken, and the police are investigating. Roma, concerned only with his status, finds that the Lingk contract he closed was filed and he crows with happiness, disregarding any of the problems of the break-in. To Williamson he shouts, "then I'm over the fucking top and you owe me a Cadillac . . . and I don't want any fucking shit and I don't give a shit" (GGR 54–5). Amid the destruction of the office there is the appearance of success, curtailed, however, by Aaronow's lack of success and Roma's shock at the work he will have to do in the wake of the break-in. But Roma, without the leads and even the phones—the phones were stolen—will still go out to chase clients even with only last year's leads. Talking to the cop will be just a waste of time, he announces. And when Aaronow gets nervous about talking to the police, Roma ironically advises him just to tell the truth: "Always tell the truth. It's the easiest thing to remember" (GGR 61).

At this moment, Shelly Levene triumphantly enters: "Get the *chalk*. Get the *chalk*. . . . I closed 'em . . . get the chalk and put me on the *board*. I'm going to Hawaii! Put me on the Cadillac board": eight units at Mountain View for eighty-two thousand dollars from the Nyborgs, he announces (GGR 63). He then realizes there was a robbery and antagonisms among the sales group erupt, partly because they are envious of both Roma and now Levene. Moss, in particular, is angry, humiliated by the police interrogation and then insulted by Roma and Levene's success. After insulting both, he leaves.

Roma disregards these remarks and celebrates Levene's success, asking him to recount his triumph. Levene cannot resist and gives a full account of how he signed the Nyborgs using the old methods of closing, even holding the pen and waiting with his words "now is the time" hanging in the air (GGR 73–4). But then Williamson casts doubt on the Nyborgs, who are notorious for pulling out. Levene's optimism, that things change and that his skill made the sale, allows his hubris to take flight as he tells Williamson off. Contrasted with his abject and groveling behavior in Scene One, he exclaims, "Fuck you and kiss my ass. . . . Put me on the board. And I want three worthwhile leads today and I don't want any bullshit about them" (GGR 77).

At that moment, Lingk returns to invalidate his contract. Roma senses this and urges Levene to impersonate a client (GGR 78). The con is on as Levene, now "Ray Morton," "director of all European sales and services for American Ex," acts like a big purchaser (GGR 79). But the law again interferes. A consumer has three days to revoke a signed contract. This stops Roma as he tries to calm the increasingly agitated Lingk, who clearly wants to cancel. Levene's cover is then almost undone as the policeman calls out his real name to be interrogated, while Aaronow seems to unravel under the police questioning. Williamson tries to get him out of the office; Roma tries to save his deal.

It's now Roma's turn to talk to the detective, and Lingk leaves to call the state's attorney general's office. Worried, Roma uses his best tactic on Lingk, beginning with "*Forget* the deal" and "let's talk about *you*." As they head for the door, the detective calls out Roma's name again and Williamson reveals that Lingk's check was cashed, the deal done. He leaves in anger and Roma turns his venom on Williamson with the insulting "whoever told you you could work with *men*?" (GGR 96). The chorus of the detective's interruptions continue, as Levene then admonishes Williamson to keep his mouth shut because your "partner *depends* on it" (GGR 97). Again, it's the honor among men that matters, conveniently leaving out any one on the other side of the deal.

Levene then defends Roma and laments his lost deal and bonus because "you didn't know the *shot*" (GGR 98). Williamson then shocks him by saying he made it up: he didn't take the contracts to the bank. Only Levene knew that, which meant *he* was the one that robbed the office. Even at this crisis point, however, Williamson tries to make a deal: tell me where the leads are and I won't turn you in (GGR 100). Levene, under pressure, admits he sold them to Jerry Graff for $5,000, giving half to Moss. In a fruitless confession, he explains that he almost hoped to get caught and that he was made to get out there and sell, not to be a thief. Now that he's got his "*balls* back," following the Nyborg sale, he'll make it right. Williamson starts to go to the detective while Levene desperately tries to offer him $2,500 not to tell the police the truth. Frightened, he offers Williamson 20 per cent and then 50 per cent of his future sales, making him a partner. Williamson refuses and tells him the Nyborgs are entirely unreliable and have no money to back their check. He has failed again. In fact, he's been conned.

Leaving his interrogation, Roma tells Baylen, the detective, that "it's not a world of men . . . it's not a world of men . . . it's a world of clock watchers, bureaucrats, officeholders . . . what it is, it's a fucked-up world . . . there's no adventure *to* it (*Pause.*) Dying breed. Yes it is (*Pause.*)." He then turns to Levene to compliment him and his great success by using the "old stuff": "There's things that I could learn from you" and invites him to eat at the nearby Chinese restaurant after his police interview (GGR 105). He has no idea that Levene robbed the office and sold the leads as the detective manhandles Levene into the room and Roma exclaims, "Hey, hey, hey, *easy* friend, That's the 'Machine.' That is Shelly 'The Machine' Lev . . . " (GGR 106). Finally, he tells Williamson that he wants to share half of Levene's commissions, another form of betrayal. "My stuff is mine, his stuff is ours. I'm taking half of his commissions" (GGR 107). The play ironically ends as if nothing has changed, Aaronow continues to gripe and Roma waits for new leads while at the restaurant.

Unlike his earlier plays, *Glengarry Glen Ross* is an ensemble piece, what Mamet calls a gang drama or "gang comedy." He defines this as a play about "revealing the specific natures and the unifying natures of a bunch of people who happen to be involved in one enterprise" (DMC 64). He learned this structure in part through American plays like *Front Page* and *Men in White*, the former by the Chicago writer Ben Hecht, the latter by the popular but now forgotten dramatist Sidney Kingsley. In his controversial Pulitzer Prize winning medical drama of 1933, *Men in White* (produced by the Group Theatre and starring Luther Adler, Morris Carnovsky, Elia Kazan, Clifford Odets, and Sanford Meisner as Dr. Wren and Mr. Smith),

Kingsley chronicled the life of medical interns and proselytized in favor of legalized abortion. His later works, including *Dead End* and *Detective Story*, were similarly "gang dramas." The latter especially appealed to Mamet: it focused on the squad room of a New York police precinct in August 1940. As the cases unfold, the multiple narratives of crime in the city emerge and the mix of detectives and policemen interact. Yet, despite the ensemble character of *Glengarry*, Mamet explained that he wanted to stress the opposite: "the conflicting impulses in the individual. That is what *all* drama is about" (DMC 65). *Glengarry* might even be thought of as a comedy, he says, because it presents many "somewhat dissimilar renditions of the same attitude. Which I think is true in all gang comedies and it is certainly true of *Glengarry*" (DMC 65).

A week before the opening of *Glengarry* at the Goodman on February 6, 1984, Mamet was upbeat, partly because the production at the National had just won the Society of West End Theatres' Award as the best play, although it didn't allow him to forget the difficulties he had in writing the play the preceding spring and how he sent it to Pinter for comment; he, in turn, forwarded it to Peter Hall, director of the National Theatre, who relayed to him one word: "September," referring to a planned production of the work. It went on to great acclaim. Al Pacino was also just ending his run on Broadway with *American Buffalo*, so, with a future Broadway production of *Glengarry* planned, Mamet might anticipate earning some money. But playfully, he tells the press his plays don't actually earn money—or at least not a lot.

He makes money, he told the Chicago critic Glenna Syse, as an amateur dealer of antique pocket knives, haunting junk shops, flea markets, and auctions. He subscribes to *American Blade*, *Knife Collector*, and *Edges*: "I buy low and sell high. It's the American way." Additionally, he explained that he makes money "by letting people in the television industry insult me." They come to him admiring his work and asking if he would write a show for them. He does and feels they are good but when the TV people read them, they come back and say "Who the hell do you think you are? This is a piece of garbage." He also reported that he was just fired from the "The Autobiography of Malcolm X," a film project he had been working on for months. The cause? A change of studio personnel, which regularly occurs: "someone with a background in cost accounting telling me how to write a play. All it does is send my price up" He suggested, however, that in the spring of 1984, he would be working on a new piece with Elaine May.[13]

Two months after the success of the London opening of *Glengarry*, *American Buffalo* hit Broadway on October 27, 1983. This was a revival of the Long Wharf production starring Pacino, and it, too, was a hit, Benedict Nightingale beginning his review with, "It was Edward Albee, I believe, who said he [Mamet] showed little evidence of a mind as fine as his ear." Mamet contradicts that in *American Buffalo*, a play "about the American ethic of business. About how we excuse all sorts of great and small betrayals and ethical compromises called business."

The shadowy, elusive frontier between business and friendship is the concern of *American Buffalo*, greed overtaking altruism. The despair of Teach transforms him into one of the richest characters in the contemporary repertory; but he's stuck in the urban ashcan. The powerful, nervous energy of Pacino in the production reminded Nightingale of the advice Peter Ustinov once gave a young Method actor: "Don't just do something—stand there!" What Mamet addresses at the end is the question, do values exist? Quietly and unsentimentally, he answers in the affirmative as Donny tells Bobby, "you done good."[14]

Glengarry opened at the Goodman Theatre Studio on February 6, 1984, directed by Mosher and staring Mike Nussbaum as Aaronow, Robert Prosky as Levene, and Joe Mantegna as Roma. In the lobby at intermission during the opening, the Chicago journalist Mike Royko stood about asking who was this "Mameeeet, Mameeeet? I could've written this thing." Suddenly, someone tapped him on the shoulder. It was Bernie Mamet, who said, "Mamet—as in dammit!" The two talked and later went out together. Bernie Mamet called his son to report the news. The son was impressed.

Mamet was becoming a presence at the Goodman, but not always a successful one. When he arrived one day on a visit to the press office, he entered wearing a hat, smoking a cigar, and wearing a wool lumberjack-style shirt. On his belt hung a large hunting knife, which accidentally caught the back of the chair he was sitting in. When he got up, the chair swung around with him, knocking over everything in its path. "That's okay," he told the two startled young press representatives staring in disbelief: "you can come over any time and fuck up my place too" (TOO 186).

The Chicago production of *Glengarry*, however, was a challenge. The roles were difficult and tested the actors, especially those with several twisting, long speeches such as Mantegna. On opening night, at the end of the first act when Roma unrolls his seductive sales pitch to Lingk whom he just met over drinks in the Chinese restaurant, the knotted speech threw the veteran actor. Until that moment, Mantegna had been sailing through the play. Then he dried up, blanked out. He could see that the actor playing Lingk was upset and Mantegna wanted to tell him it wasn't his fault. The stage manager threw lines at him in a voice so loud the audience could hear but it did no good. With a few mumbled words, Mantegna ended the act. As he stepped off stage, Mosher, Mamet, and Lindsay Crouse were there to hug him and say they loved him. Their support made it possible for him to go on and he tore into the role in the Second Act and received a standing ovation. "I learned [then] you can't be vague in learning David's lines. They're poetry and you have to know every moment" Mantegna said (TOO 184). It was, he added, his worst moment in the theatre but one that led to his best: he won the Tony Award for best supporting actor when the play went to Broadway.

From the first, it appeared as if *Glengarry* would be a hit, and after its brief run in Chicago (at the small Studio Theatre of the Goodman, just as the London production took place in the small Cottesloe at the National), it transferred to the Golden

Theatre on Broadway where it would run for a record 378 performances. But Mamet wasn't happy with the Chicago production and, after attending a matinee before its transfer, wrote Mosher about the difficulties. The letter is a penetrating critique beginning with the production's lack of drive, what he thought was missing from the work from the first. This defuses the lacerating dialogue. Perhaps, he suggests, Mosher is too close to this production: it's not a question of what the actors do; it is a question "of HOW, and that lack of PUSH is sorely felt throughout."[15]

Mamet observes that *Glengarry* is a different kind of play for "*both* you and me: it is a play about viciousness . . . it is a play about *ambition*." The important thing is not Mamet's techniques or Mosher's "BUT THE *PLAY*. THE PLAY IS THE IMPORTANT THING, and what I see is this: . . . .

> The reason everybody seems to like this play is that it is UNABASHEDLY DRIVEN—the play is about people with the WRAPS OFF, VICIOUSLY PURSUING THEIR OBJECTIVES . . . and the STAGED PLAY must be that, also. . . . not to bring that VIOLENT PURSUIT to the stage, is to betray the play and the audience." (3–4)

By contrast, he continues, "BUFFALOS was really a play about the NEED FOR TENDERNESS, which is why nobody but you ever got it right. GGR is a play about VICIOUS AMBITION, which, I think is why you are missing it." When Levene says get the chalk, he has "got to be REALLY proclaiming it, not 'fake' announcing it. It is a great dramatic moment, and if he is not doing it HUGE you are cheating the play and cheating the public." Prosky can't be lazy with the scene; he has to be pushed. In fact, Mamet continues, the entire cast has to be pushed: "I know this is not your way, but *IT IS WHAT THE PLAY NEEDS*" (4–5).

Mamet then gets tough. If Mosher won't or can't take the play in this direction, one that Mamet feels will definitely improve the work, he will, himself, take over directing the week of rehearsals in New York. It is what the play needs. The cast has to break their relationship with the audience and turn their thoughts to "performing the play *BIG. Driven, HONESTLY* in a big house. They need to be BROKEN LOOSE—and the best way to do that is get them out of the 'studio' out of 'Chicago' and into an atmosphere of NEW HARD WORK in New York" (6).

Mamet concludes by suggesting that there be some violence up on the stage with things broken, things thrown. Get over the politeness, which defined the London version. What's wrong with the entire production is that "all the 'not nice things' that we don't like to think of ourselves as doing, taking advantage of the weak, humiliating those inferior to us, pressing an unfair advantage, driving an undecided person off-balance: THESE THINGS ARE WHAT THE PLAY IS ABOUT—AND THE PLAY'S frankness is dealing with these things is why everybody likes it. . . . "

Mamet ends by telling Mosher these things are simple to do with the actors but, importantly, you do not have to reason with them or convince them or give them time to grow: "you have to FORCE them TODAY to do the play correctly" (10). In short, the play needs work, "direct vicious *work*" that must be done; if it's not, "for the good of the play, for the good of *my* career, and of *your* career . . . I am going to step in and help." (11). Mosher listened and the play opened to strong reviews in New York, capped by winning the 1985 Pulitzer Prize for Drama.

How he found out about the award is vintage Mamet. During one of the later performances of the play on Broadway, when Mamet was bored with seeing the production again, he ducked out to go to a movie, Jane Fonda's 1978 western, *Comes a Horseman* at a revival house. There were few people in the theatre when suddenly, midway in the film, a man began to shower kisses on him. "Whatever" was Mamet's first thought but then he realized it was his agent Howard Rosenstone, who had found him in the dark. With tears running down his face, he told him he had just won the Pulitzer. Mamet was shocked.

A strong box office and even an award, however, do not always mean positive reviews, and some critics were offended by *Glengarry*. But that only pleased Mamet. Several felt it was anti-business and unrealistic in its portrayal of salesmen, while others felt the world of these "sharks" was accurate and extolled the play for its refusal to sympathize with any of the characters. The greatest praise came from those who understood the salesmen as struggling to survive in a corrupt system. Mamet's characters "gallantly endure" their hollow life. Critics frequently compared it to *Death of a Salesman* partly because Dustin Hoffman's production of the play had also just opened on Broadway that March. *Variety*, the entertainment trade paper, provided a summary of the reviews: *Glengarry* opened on March 25, 1984, to eighteen favorable notices, one mixed, and one unfavorable.[16] The lack of pity for the despicable and detestable characters, however, perfectly matched Mamet's approach, which he had outlined in his letter to Mosher.

Many saw *Glengarry* as a step forward, returning Mamet to what he could do best: apply his "Mametspeak" to the lives of individuals creating their own morality. The blank, almost prosy style of *Lone Canoe* and *Edmond* that encouraged so-called Great Mythical Statements was an embarrassing digression in works that too emphatically went after story. The multiple facets of his odyssey structure in such plays seemed to slip out of his control, the title characters forced to behave in accordance, it seemed, with a philosophical dialogue. There were arbitrary, uneven shifts in tone. Not so in *Glengarry*. This work has the same courage in portraying aggression but has a narrative energy that is always controlled through dialogue that most agreed was stunning. Its darting rhythms, hesitations, fragments, and overlapping statements all exist with almost "breathtaking fluency." It gains tension by what it leaves out (reactions, motivations, inflections)—as well as what it includes.[17]

Part of the success of the play originated in Mamet's constant awareness of audience, which he learned from Stanislavsky's disciple Vakhtangov: "if I'm not writing for the audience, if I'm not writing to make it easier for *them*, then who the hell am I doing it for?" And the way you make it easier is by cutting, building to a climax, leaving out expositions, and "always progressing toward the single goal of the protagonist" (AOT 57). The matter is again Aristotelian. Character is action, not thinking: "it's not what they say. It's what they do, what they are physically trying to accomplish on the stage" that counts according to Mamet (AOT 56). But ironically, Mamet did not think *Glengarry* was as good structurally as *American Buffalo*, at least not in Aristotelian terms. The poetry wasn't as strong, he felt, but it spoke to something in the country at a critical time: the difference between business and fraud, "what is permissible in the name of getting a living and what isn't" (DMC 64).

The impact of the play and its effect on Mamet and his career was immense—his success financial as well as professional, which winning the Pulitzer Prize confirmed. He then had choices: movies, another drama, or simply retreat to Vermont. He did all three.

Before *Glengarry*, Mamet taught, running a series of classes with Macy and others at New York University, where he elaborated his ideas on acting that he had been developing from the earliest days of the St. Nicholas. The program originated in October 1982. Mamet was in New York for the premiere of *Edmond* when he was recruited to give several talks entitled "Aesthetics of Theatre." From that series, Mamet and Macy decided they wanted to run an acting program addressing concerns many theatre practitioners had about the direction of mainstream American actor training. To counteract a focus on self-indulgence and the failure of actors to realize a writer's work, Mamet and Macy concentrated on the practical needs of the actor—what happened in rehearsal and what the script required of you. Mamet called this "Practical Aesthetics," understood as the practical application of getting the page onto the stage and how an actor figures into the process: late Stanislavsky blended with elements of the Group Theatre leavened with Meisner and Mamet.

Practical Aesthetics meant acting as a craft through practical training, beginning with theatrical discipline and then moving on to scene analysis and preparation so that one can improvise on stage (PHA 8). Attention to other actors took precedence over attention to one's self. With this approach, an actor analyzes a scene, determines its accomplishable objective, and then goes on stage to achieve it using the words of the playwright as written. The action has to be physically possible, in line with the intentions of the scene. The process is clear: "Juiced with a concretely identifiable task to complete, the actor attempts to accomplish that objective working 'moment to moment' off the other actors in the scene."[18] This is compelling for an audience because they see an actor committed to the single pursuit of an objective scene by scene despite obstacles set before him. Script analysis is the homework the actor does, choosing galvanizing action he then habituates himself to in rehearsal, learning the action he or she will do on stage. One works a bit like a scientist applying intellect to establish the groundwork for the performance to come.

Another feature of Practical Aesthetics was repetition, borrowed from Meisner. The aim was to heighten the actor's awareness of the truth-of-the moment, what's going on at any given instant in a scene, enabling the actor to act on the perception impulsively but in a way that best helps him achieve his objective or action. The through-line is crucial, defined as "the single, overriding action" that all the individual actions serve (PHA 33). The overall goal of the actor, according to Mamet and Practical Aesthetics, is "not to bring the truth of his personal life to the stage, but rather to bring the truth of himself to the specific needs of the play" (PHA 32).

To advance and rehearse these ideas, Mamet and Macy (with help from such visitors as Mike Nussbaum, Colin Stinton, Peter Riegert, Gregory Mosher, Elaine May, and Shel Silverstein) organized a summer acting school at Vermont College in Montpelier in 1983 and 1984. Approximately twenty-five attended the six-week intensive, acting-training workshop made up mostly of NYU undergraduate drama majors, joined by others who in time would become known as FODS, "Friends of David's." Even Lindsay Crouse attended classes and took part in the improvised acting exercises that Mamet dubbed *études*. Most of the group had been dissatisfied with their study of acting elsewhere and were frustrated because their instructors could not always explain clearly what they taught. The students were looking for a more concrete, sensible approach to acting, preferring clarity to intuition. Mamet's practical approach made sense as he drew from the later teachings of Stanislavsky (post *An Actor Prepares*; more useful was *Creating a Role*) and from his work with Meisner and his own experience.

Essentially, what Mamet drew from Stanislavsky and Meisner was an emphasis on the practical matter of playing objectives beat by beat, according to an analysis of the through-line and super-objectives of the play. Meisner, furthermore, trained his students to focus on others on stage in order to respond honestly to the moments created each night between the actors.[19] This parallels Stanislavsky's Physical Actions, finding the action in a scene. Mamet became more anti-Method or anti-emotional than anti-Stanislavsky, although he did downplay Stanislavsky's "emotional memory." But when offering his ideas on acting, Mamet also relies on overstatement, dogmatism, and hyperbole for rhetorical effect. For example, he scorns the authority of acting teachers and believes most are charlatans, yet he practices the craft himself. And he prefers pronouncement to carefully thought-out analyses. He wants to be in charge and loves to provoke debate, the former perhaps the reason why he himself was not a good actor and an explanation why he is a better director and playwright.[20] *True and False*, Mamet's book on acting, would contain many of these overstatements, such as the need to stay out of school, believing that the best teacher is the audience. Doing the play for the audience "is what acting is. The rest is just practice" (TF 4).

Practical Aesthetics combined script analysis and repetition exercises for the actor to prepare and then improvise: not the lines of the play, but the ways in which the actor tries to achieve his objective based on what other actors are doing on any given night and adjusting accordingly. Acting, Mamet believes, is living truthfully in the moment under the imaginary circumstances of the play. Habit was the key, and he assigned William James's essay "Habit" from his *Principles of*

Psychology. Mamet repeated to his students that "what you rehearse is what you'll perform," with the opposite an invitation to disaster: "if you fail to plan, plan to fail" (Lage 41). He reiterated Stanislavsky's idea that the difficult must become easy and the easy habitual before the habitual can become beautiful (JJH 65–6). A work ethic defined by preparation and habit to turn words into action was what Mamet taught, occasionally directing students to the writings of the Stoic philosophers, Epictetus and Marcus Aurelius, as well as to Aristotle, Freud, Joseph Campbell, and Bruno Bettelheim. Mixing the didactic with the charismatic, Mamet nevertheless held himself accountable for what he taught.

A Practical Handbook, written by six of the students, codifies the ideas of Mamet's approach stressing economy in acting, beginning with identifying the action of the character in each scene and formulating the through-line of the work (PHA 33). Memorizing lines without inflection is a basic technique that will avoid the habit of repeating lines in a predetermined manner regardless of what is going on in the scene. The job of the actor is to forget his personal life on stage and respond to "the specific needs of the play" (PHA 32). Character, the authors emphasize, is a myth: it is impossible to become the character you are playing because it is an illusion created by words. Play yourself through the language by your actions. Don't bring your life to the theatre. "That is not a *character* onstage. It is *you* onstage" he would repeat (TF 104).

Further directives: prepare in order to improvise, and learn that acting is "living truthfully under the imaginary circumstances of a play," a distinct echo of Meisner (PHA 8). "Generality is the enemy of all art," a quote from Stanislavsky, underscores the Mamet line that "if your action is in general then everything you do on stage will be in general." Only a specific action will "provide you with a clear, specific path to follow when playing the scene," which will bring authenticity to your performance (PHA 15). "An action," the authors emphasize, must be "*physically capable of being done*. . . . physical action the main building block of an actor's technique" (PHA 14, 13). From the system of "physical action" an emotional condition will rise; there is "no correct emotion" for a given scene. Do not work for an emotional result (PHA 71).

Acting for Mamet is a craft with a definite set of skills and not much talent, a controversial claim (PHA 6). But the value of the book for actors and the appeal of Mamet's Practical Aesthetics is its no-nonsense and "doable" dimension. *A Practical Handbook for the Actor* still remains assigned reading at the Atlantic Theatre School. The work—which Mamet in the foreword unashamedly says is "the best book on acting written in the last twenty years"—plus *True and False* and *3 Uses of the Knife*, expresses Mamet's core acting principles (PHA x).

Mamet re-emphasized the benefits of the practical in Vermont with his acting students, underlining the importance of vocal expression, especially diction, and the physical. Training the body for posture and muscle control to provide the actor with the tools to allow him to do the job was essential. Mamet's enthusiasm and passion were contagious, and the students worked hard in a highly charged atmosphere. His convictions were not to be questioned, but enacted. As one student wrote, "the appeal of the technique was its practicality" and the freedom to concentrate "solely on achieving a concrete physical do-able objective and allow emotion and inflection to come of the difficulty (or ease) of that pursuit. [This] was a very liberating idea" (Lage 42). Mamet's own experience with the repetition exercise made it possible for him to look at a person and know their thoughts and moods. "You can't hide human emotion" he would say and then offer his own comments, which were largely on target (Lage 42). As the actor Linda Kimbrough noted, Mamet could uncannily read people and often see right through them.

Following the 1984 workshop, a number of students decided to organize and publish a book containing the key points they'd learned from Mamet and Macy. This coincided with a group of them going on to the Goodman in Chicago to intern on a production Macy was doing and then back to New York where, in 1985, after Mamet announced he had secured nonprofit status and a name, he told them to form a theatre company: it became The Atlantic. Its principles were those Mamet and Macy promoted in Vermont: "a good actor sticks to his objective. . . . emotion comes, sure, but it's a byproduct of the larger action. It's all about serving the play" as the current artistic director of The Atlantic, Neil Pepe, explained.[21] Twenty-one years later, the company remains a success, with several notable Broadway transfers and premieres.[22]

Macy summarized the philosophy of The Atlantic, now located in New York's Chelsea district in a former church chapter house with a 182-seat theatre, as an extension of Mamet's acting technique: "It doesn't matter what you say, or how your feel; it's what you *do*." You can't act words or emotions: "you can only act actions" which you'll see in Mamet's plays as well, Macy added (Freedman, 64). The company modeled itself on the Moscow Art Theatre and the more recent Steppenwolf company in Chicago: an inventive ensemble group with an active acting school. In a letter to the company dated July 21, 1985, that hangs in the Atlantic acting school, Mamet summarizes and reviews their goals. He begins by complimenting them on their first production performed at Montpelier, praising the company's organization and reiterating that "our company is founded not on *talent*, not on *effect*, but on *discipline*," which is the quality of a good actor who "sticks to the *objective*, rather than the emotion."[23] The strength of character displayed through training shows on stage, but one must avoid the temptations of money and second-rate, easy performances. "Re-dedicate yourselves to the *small, mechanical* first principles we have been discussing over the last couple of years: punctuality, courtesy, common sense" (2). Don't indulge in your feelings in rehearsal but "investigate and practice *certain specific skills*." Always be aware of the specific purpose of each rehearsal as you are of each scene (2).

Mamet also makes clear in his letter that the task of the director is "to help the actor understand the tasks required by the scene and to help him learn to *fully perform* those tasks" (2). And while group discipline is important, Mamet also stresses the importance of time off: "get away from each other," he writes (3). Following his signature is a stamp: a single evergreen tree with the message "An Appeal to Heaven" and below, the words "Crouse & Mamet, Cabot, Vermont."

But Mamet was exploring avenues other than teaching during the mid-eighties. He premiered *The Shawl* in 1985 and his play *The Spanish Prisoner* (originally 1973 and later a movie with the same title but different story). He presented "Goldberg Street" and "Cross Patch" on Northwestern University's radio station and worked on the screenplay of *The Untouchables*, a movie to be released in 1987. He also published his first collection of essays, *Writing in Restaurants*, which ranged from personal narratives on writing and poker, to accounts of life in the theatre. He continued to receive awards, honored by the American Academy and Institute of Arts and Letters with their Award for Literature in 1986.

During this time, he also left New York for Cambridge, Massachusetts, where he set up shop, literally. He chose a set of offices in a yellow clapboard building at 14A Eliot Street above a comic book store across the street from the Charles Hotel. He soon became a regular for breakfast at the hotel, quickly befriending the owner, the real estate developer Dick Friedman, who would have a bit part in Mamet's comedy *State and Main* (2000).

Homes and domestic space for Mamet at this time were becoming important, especially because earlier in his life he associated them with security, or its absence. "The Decoration of Jewish Homes," in *Some Freaks*, details the habits and design in Jewish homes, especially the irony that although the homes speak of "rest, of identity, we have no symbols. We do not know how a Jewish home (finally, we do not know how a *Jew*) is supposed to look" (SF 13). The absence of signs makes the home itself one of an outsider; he feels exiled in his own space, even if it was Euclid Avenue in the Jewish South Side of Chicago. Mamet grew up "surrounded by sofas wrapped in thick clear plastic" (C 123). The situation recalls the old joke (possibly from Jackie Mason) that a gentile's living room is a workshop: "See that, I made it. Sit in it; it's sturdy." A Jew's living room is a cross between an order catalogue and warehouse. "See that? I had it delivered. What? You don't like the color? I'll get rid of it."

Mamet's own private space has varied. In Chicago after Goddard, a room at the Hotel Lincoln provided his sense of home, identity, and place. The hotel gave him "shelter and solitude," while each night the hotel telephone operator would call him about eleven or twelve to ask if he wanted a cup of tea (CA 96).

Following his Chelsea apartment in New York in 1976 and then Chelsea townhouse with Lindsay Crouse, he found a home in Boston. Correspondingly, he became more deeply attached to his Vermont home, the Cabot farmhouse purchased in the late seventies, improved and expanded over the years to include more living space and a writing cabin, celebrated in the title essay of his collection *The Cabin*. It is clear, however, that the cabin is more than a writing space: it is a psychological and physical refuge where simplicity reigns: only a wood- burning stove heats the room, while a winter wind, coming up from the pond below, might pound the west side of the building. Without electricity, he found a natural calm in the heat generated by his Glenwood parlor stove. Next to his desk hang photographs of his four grandparents, handprints of his daughters, detective badges from New York State and Chicago, and notes for projects done, to be done, or never done. And his walnut roll top desk, ca. 1860, is both a realization and metaphor of the past, its pigeonholes containing memorabilia of his life and of others'.

A brass container made of an artillery shell sits next to a loading tool for a .38 Long Cartridge and a Colt model 1878 .45 caliber revolver, all three paperweights. Knowledge and violence for him coexist (C 47). The details he offers of his desk express his world, which he wants readers to know and understand and which orient him in time, echoed in his collection of pin-back buttons commemorating Lindberg, Chicago's Century of Progress, and Eugene Debs. He elaborates his thoughts about them and how they connect him to history in "The Buttons on the Board" in *The Cabin* (especially pages 153–55).

After his marriage to Rebecca Pidgeon in 1991—he had met her in 1989 in London in a production of *Speed-the-Plow* for the National—Boston became their home, in a row house in the Eight Streets area of the South End. He restored much of the detail in the 1870s building, which, unlike others in the area, was not partitioned into a rooming house. He outlines this in his essay "My House" from *The Cabin*. He also offers this thought: "if fashion is an attempt by the middle class to co-opt tragedy, home décor is a claim to history"(CA 123). This he tried to do by incorporating American craftsmanship in the restoration. Several years later, he and Pidgeon moved to a large, three-story, colonial-style home in Newton, Massachusetts, about six miles from Boston, the ostensible reason being the problem with city parking. The imposing corner lot bordered by trees and a white picket fence reaffirmed the New England roots of Mamet's domesticity. More recently, he has left Newton for Santa Monica, where he lives in an equally spacious home.

Moving to Cambridge from New York in the eighties allowed Mamet to develop a working relationship with the American Repertory Theatre then run by Robert Brustein, whom he knew from Yale. There, he adapted and directed new work. In fact, the mid-eighties saw Mamet concentrate on adaptations, which began with Pierre Laville's *Red River* in 1983 but soon shifted to the playwright who intrigued him the most, Chekhov. The playwright, however, posed challenges as one of John Guare's characters in *Rich and Famous* lamented: "I hate people like Chekhov. . . . people like that are so good they don't leave room for the new people."

Mamet felt there was wonderful humor in Chekhov's work, sensed in the short stories, but hardly conveyed in the plays. No translation seemed to reflect the comedy in the minute exchanges between characters (DMC 93, 220). As early as 1977, critics were comparing Mamet's dialogical structure to that of the Russian: it is not only what is said but the manner in which things are left *unsaid* that counts, wrote Mel Gussow. Mamet's plays are about "indirect action," as are Chekhov's.[24]

Two works especially interested Mamet: *The Cherry Orchard* and *Vint*, a short story. Mamet dramatized *Vint* for a 1985 production at the Ensemble Studio Theatre. It then played in repertory with seven other newly adapted Chekhov works in Robert Falls' The Acting Company (the other works included adaptations by Wendy Wasserstein, John Guare, and Spalding Gray). Appropriately for Mamet, Chekhov's story is about a card game, "Vint," surreptitiously played in a government ministry office late one night. Each card is the picture of a different functionary: Treasury officials are hearts, employees of the State Bank are spades, Councilors of State are aces. In a satiric touch, a surprised Commissioner, Persolin, discovers the game, but can't resist and joins his clerks to play throughout the night.

Mamet's 1985 adaptation of *The Cherry Orchard*, based on a literal translation by Peter Nelles, was produced for the New Theatre Company of the Goodman. He then "tried to choose between the alternate word meanings where he [Nelles] supplied them, and to adapt the literal meanings into rhythmic dramatic prose."[25] The last phrase encapsulates Mamet's approach to adaptations, although he also added that he thought his effort was in line with what he believed to be Chekhov's intention.

The production originated in Vermont. At a summer dinner at their farmhouse with Gregory Mosher, Crouse told both her husband and Mosher that one day she would like to play Madam Ranevskaya. "Gregory," she then said after a conference in the kitchen with Mamet, "I want to play Ranevskaya now." Mosher agreed and Mamet began to adapt the text during the 1984 Christmas holidays.

The timing of *The Cherry Orchard* coincided with Mosher's formation of his New Theatre Company, established by the Goodman's parent organization, the Chicago Theatre Group. Ironically, Mosher realized this long-sought-for goal on the eve of his departure for the Beaumont Theatre of Lincoln Center in New York, a departure that was not welcomed in Chicago. The change occurred at a sensitive time in the future of the Goodman. Mosher had brought stability to the Goodman during his tenure, arriving in 1974, creating a startling impression with the premiere of *American Buffalo* on his experimental Stage 2 the following year. But he was never at home as a director in the Goodman's 683-seat main stage, objecting to the acoustics, seating arrangement, and backstage space. *Lakeboat* was his last production there, produced in 1982. *Glengarry* was a success in the smaller Theatre Studio.

Hoping to free himself from the main stage led Mosher to form the New Theatre Company, with *The Cherry Orchard* its first production. In this way, he hoped to be free physically and aesthetically from the mainstage. The idea formed in 1982 during the New York run of *Edmond*, when Mosher and others took stock: running six plays a year on the main stage and five in the studio was becoming "enervating." Renewal might come about by establishing a more challenging program. As he pointed out, the Goodman was created when plays had large casts, not for the kind of work Mamet writes. The answer was to create a company inside a company. The logo of the New Theatre Company was an American buffalo. In addition to the adaptation of *The Cherry Orchard*, Mamet's two new plays, *The Spanish Prisoner* and *The Shawl*, would be NTC productions. Mamet actors made up the principal members of the company, including Lindsay Crouse, William H. Macy, Mike Nussbaum, Peter Riegert, and Linda Kimbrough.

To insure a fresh start, Mosher allowed for plenty of rehearsal and preview time. *The Cherry Orchard* was allotted six weeks of rehearsal and two weeks of previews. Casting, however, was not complete until a few days before the start of rehearsal. Mosher was seeking young actors to play the daughters so that Crouse would look slightly older on stage. New space at the 350-seat Briar Street Theatre on North Halsted would not be ready in time, so the work premiered at the smaller Studio Theatre. Most importantly, the company broke with Goodman tradition and dropped a subscription plan in favor of single ticket sales. Ironically, while Mosher publicly praised the new set of challenges by this new company, he would shortly leave for New York and Lincoln Center. Original plans, however, called for stage sharing, Mosher continuing to be involved with the New Theatre Company while overseeing the revitalization of the Beaumont. The plan did not work. The board of the Goodman faced some critical decisions, not the least the future home of the company and the need to move out of its limited 1920s building at the rear of the Art Institute.[26]

In his "Notes on The Cherry Orchard" published after his production, Mamet links the characterization of Chekhov with action and the search for the revelatory gestures, what in poker Mamet identifies as the "tells." He then examines the choices the characters do *not* make to save the cherry orchard, which, frankly, no one gives a damn about. The play is a series of scenes about sexuality, particularly "frustrated sexuality," as Lopakhin and Varya never express their love or marry (WR 121). In fact, all the characters exist in a state of frustrated love. Mamet adds that the play has no "through-action," only "one scene repeated by various couples" (WR 122). Importantly, Mamet realizes that the obstacle in the play does not even refer to the actions of the characters: "The play works because it is a compilation of brilliant scenes" (WR 123). The structure of the work is to Mamet a series of review sketches with a common theme, close to the "revue-play" or "theme play," giving as examples several works by Sidney Kingsley: *Men in White,* and *Detective Story*. Of course, this is the structure of his own early works, originating in "The Camel Document" and then *Sexual Perversity*. What Chekhov does is come up with a pretext to keep his thirteen characters in the summer house and talking to each other. We cherish the play not because it is about the struggle between the old aristocracy and their loss of power, but because "the play is about—and is *only* about—the actions of its characters" (125).

Reception of the work, however, was critical of the performance more so than the text. It was nearly two hours without an intermission, and the delivery was strained and unemotional. As Richard Christiansen wrote in the *Chicago Tribune*, most of the actors have "worked so hard on polishing each separate syllable that they've become automatons, mouthing words with such flat imperfect mechanics that the speeches are stone dead, the style is painfully mannered and the play is dead in its tracks." The effect is so uninspiring that its "arch style of presentation" played "like a spoof of Mamet spoofing Chekhov." Lindsay Crouse was Madame Ranevskaya; Macy, playing Trofimov, was one of the few actors able to "marry the Mamet cadences with the Chekhovian feelings."

Glenna Syse summarized the production when she wrote that "when playwright David Mamet and director Gregory Mosher collaborate, they provoke." She found the production audacious and yet arresting, avoiding "colloquial pitfalls, arch elaborations, muddled obscurities or vulgar excesses." But, Syse said, Mamet and Mosher remain in conflict with Chekhov: "the phrasing is percussive and the pauses come as if from a firearm equipped with a silencer and conducted from some almighty master metronome." Mamet's preference for unemotional speech seems to have backfired, and the minimalist set, notable for the absence of furniture, made Syse actually relieved when a chair was brought out; watching the actors get up and down off the floor exhausted her.

Mamet was determined to excise from the text anything ornamental, unnatural, or literary from the play's language. This was "an act of deconstruction," wrote Robert Brustein, "designed to exhume the living energies of C's writing from under the heavy topsoil of 'masterpiece'. . . . As a result, the dialogue is a series of interrupted sentences, random hesitations, odd emphases, overlapping lines, simultaneous speeches and above all a colloquial, almost Chicagoized idiom." *The Cherry Orchard* had become a Mamet play.[27]

Critical disappointment over the Goodman production did not, however, weaken Mamet's resolve in how he treated Chekhov. In an interview at the time, he justified what he did to Chekhov as "nothing that Chekhov wouldn't do to me."[28] Mamet had to take Chekhov apart to understand how he (Chekhov) assembled his plays, especially his structure, so that Mamet could improve his own. Mamet's later productions of *Uncle Vanya* (1988) and *The Three Sisters* (1991) demonstrate what he learned. Adaptations were the practical approach to grasping Chekhov's technique.

Nineteen-eighty-five was a stellar year for Crouse and Mamet. He won a Pulitzer for *Glengarry*, while she was nominated for an Oscar for best supporting actress in *Places in The Heart*, starring Sally Field. The couple flew to Los Angeles to attend the Oscars in 1985 on a Monday night and then rushed back to Chicago in time for Crouse to play *Cherry Orchard* on Tuesday. The press noted Mamet's presence accompanying Crouse, but all the TV cameras focused on was his crew cut and cigar.[29] During the Chicago production of Chekhov, however, the top floor of the Ritz-Carlton became their home with their daughter Willa. For Mamet, it was a far cry from the Hotel Lincoln.

But for Mamet another interest competed with Chekhov, one that his outdoor Vermont life and Chicago's mythical past encouraged. This blended the military with the macho, expressed by the phrase "in the company of men" and given purchase through poker, hunting, and guns. When the chance to attend a Soldier of Fortune convention came up, Mamet jumped at it.

1 David Mamet's Yearbook photo for the Francis W. Parker School, class of 1965. Credit: Francis W. Parker School.

2 Mamet playing piano in a photograph from the Yearbook accompanying his report of the "Committee of Four" which actually had nine members. Credit: Francis W. Parker School.

3 Mamet on the doorstep of the workshop at the Haybarn Theatre at Goddard College in 1972. Credit: A. Pierce Bounds.

4 A scene from "Old Chief Hoopjaw's Lone Canoe" (1972) at Goddard with William H. Macy far left and Steven Schachter far right. Credit: A. Pierce Bounds.

5 Founding members of the St. Nicholas Theatre Group in Chicago. From l to r., David Mamet, Steven Schachter, Patricia Cox, William H. Macy. Credit: Goodman Theatre, CPL.

6 Mamet as a cigar-smoking Theseus in the 1975 St. Nicholas production of *A Midsummer Night's Dream*. To his left is Linda Kimbrough as Hippolyta. Credit: Ransom Humanities Research Center, University of Texas, Austin.

7 Scene from the original 1975 Goodman Theater production of *American Buffalo* with, from left to right, J.J. Johnston, Mike Nussbaum and William H. Macy. Credit: James C. Clark, Goodman Theatre, Special Collections, CPL.

8 David Mamet sharing a moment of synchronicity with Gregory Mosher in the 1970's at the Goodman Theatre, Chicago. Credit: Goodman Theatre, Special Collections. CPL.

9 Mamet directing during the Goodman Theatre's unsuccessful production of *Lone Canoe* of May 1979. Credit: Goodman Theatre, Special Collections, CPL.

10 David Mamet's writing cabin on his farm in Cabot, Vermont. To the left it overlooks a small lake. Credit: I.B. Nadel.

11 Mamet on set of *The Postman. Always Rings Twice*, 1981. Credit: Ransom Humanities Research Center, Univ. of Texas, Austin.

12 Mamet revising a script in the eighties. Credit: Ransom Humanities Research Center, University of Texas, Austin.

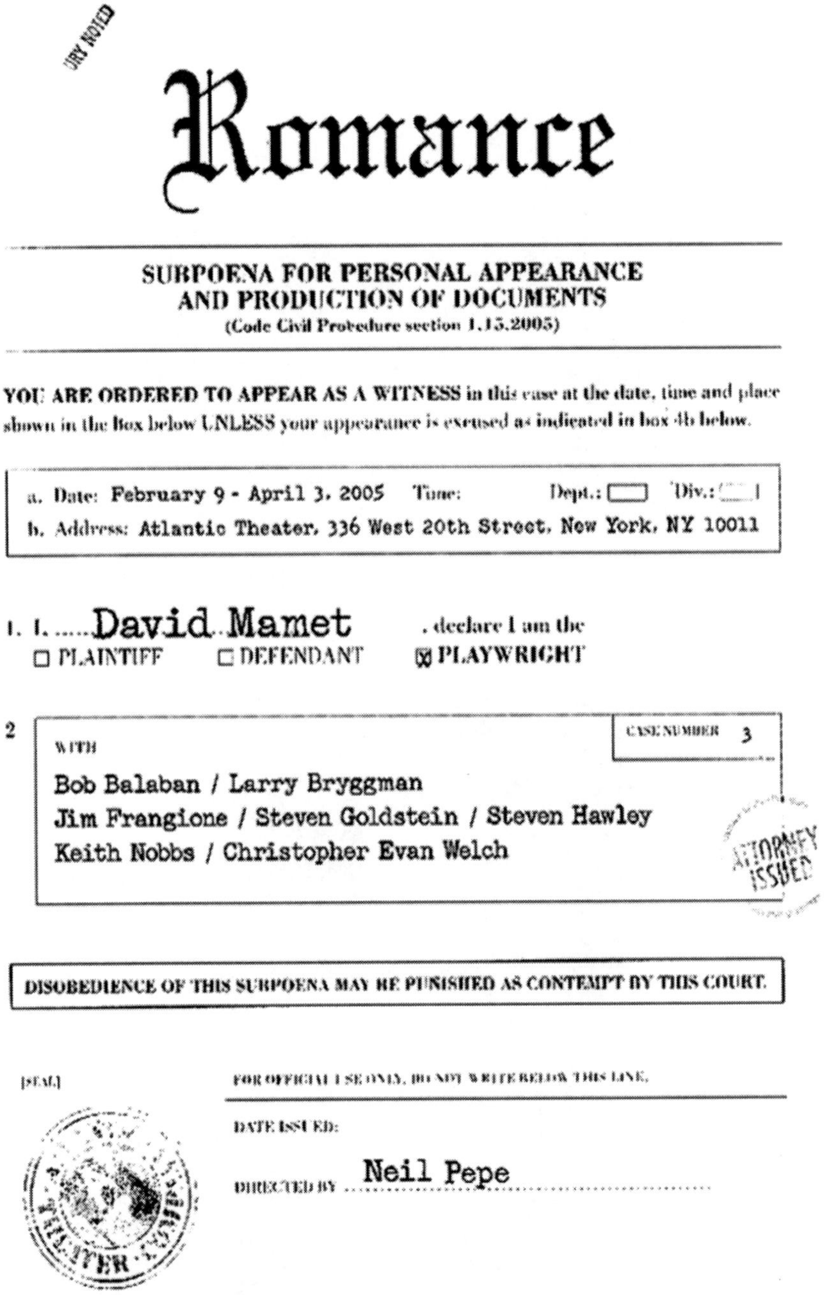
Romance
SUBPOENA FOR PERSONAL APPEARANCE
AND PRODUCTION OF DOCUMENTS
(Code Civil Procedure section 1.15.2005)
YOU ARE ORDERED TO APPEAR AS A WITNESS in this case at the date, time and place shown in the box below UNLESS your appearance is excused as indicated in box 4b below.
a. Date: February 9 - April 3, 2005 Time: Dept.: Div.:
b. Address: Atlantic Theater, 336 West 20th Street, New York, NY 10011
1. I, David Mamet, declare I am the
PLAINTIFF DEFENDANT PLAYWRIGHT
2
WITH
Bob Balaban / Larry Bryggman
Jim Frangione / Steven Goldstein / Steven Hawley
Keith Nobbs / Christopher Evan Welch
CASE NUMBER 3
ATTORNEY ISSUED
DISOBEDIENCE OF THIS SUBPOENA MAY BE PUNISHED AS CONTEMPT BY THIS COURT.
[SEAL]
FOR OFFICIAL USE ONLY. DO NOT WRITE BELOW THIS LINE.
DATE ISSUED:
DIRECTED BY Neil Pepe

13 Advertisement in the form of a subpoena for the world premiere of his courtroom comedy *Romance* at the Atlantic Theater, New York City in February 2005. Credit: Atlantic Theatre Company, New York City.

14 The marquee of the Goodman Theatre, Chicago, advertising Chicago's first ever David Mamet festival in March 2006. Credit: I.B. Nadel.

15 Mamet in conversation at the Chicago Public Library during the Chicago Book Festival, October 2006, the day after he won the Carl Sandburg Award. Credit: Phil Moloitis, Chicago Public Library.

6

SOLDIER OF FORTUNE

By seven P.M. the pool area was filled with conventioneers dressed in camouflage fatigues.

Mamet, "Conventional Warfare"

Suddenly, terrorists appeared on a third-floor balcony holding a group of hostages. Moments later three men in black began to rappel down from the roof of the building, tossing a concussion grenade into the room. When the small-arms fire died down, the hostages were released. At the same time, a woman in a violet ball gown appeared on the balcony beneath, shrugged, and wandered back in. The scene at the Sahara Hotel in Las Vegas was the opening vignette of a Soldier of Fortune convention Mamet attended. This was his chance to observe firsthand the world of tactical weapons, survival knives and SWAT Teams in action. Sponsored by *Soldier of Fortune* magazine, it was a hyper-male paradise.

Mamet loved every minute of it, as his March 1985 article in *Esquire*, "Conventional Warfare," reports. Following his observation of the hostage rescue, he dramatizes a poolside pugil-stick contest, while detailing the events and people at the convention, including a five-mile cross-country obstacle/orienteering/endurance race called Operation Headhunter and a three-gun shooting competition. An interest in warfare, especially guerrilla warfare, drew the conventioneers—as did patriotism, an idea Mamet found tremendously compelling.

His arrival presaged his luck. The cabdriver wanted to flip for the four-dollar fare. Mamet agreed and reached for a coin. "No, we'll use mine," said the cabby. Mamet understood the move at once, but, unexpectedly, he won. "What a great beginning to a Weekend with the Boys" he writes.[1] At the gathering, he knows only Bill Bagwell, a manufacturer of knives from east Texas and knife editor of *Soldier of Fortune* magazine. But Mamet soon meets an air marshal, late of the RAF, and the two tour the arms show, examining holsters, rifles, handguns, and even blowguns. That afternoon he attends a seminar on "Light Machine Guns: History, Evolution, Employment."

A new Beretta pistol, a group of would-be paratroopers, and learning the proper way to load a Bren machine gun enliven his time. Defeat in a pugil-stick competition meant little in comparison to the thrill of competing in it. The next morning at a demonstration of firepower at a pistol range, the only disappointment was the failure of the demolitions expert to blow up part of a mountain because of faulty wiring. A mortar demonstration ended the show, but before returning to town, Mamet *did* try the new Beretta pistol on some unsuspecting tin cans. The Marines presented the Colors at the closing dinner, followed by a set of anti-communist speeches and awards. The next day when the cab driver asked Mamet how long he had been in Las Vegas, he said two days. Asked whether he liked it, he said, "I considered it my second home" (CON 44).

Of course, Mamet's experience represents a life-long interest in male camaraderie, the military, and the machismo associated with it. This took the form of his poker-playing, hunting, knife-collecting, and admiration for well-made guns. Even his dress reflected his male attitude, preferring the appearance of a hunter with a slight military flair to that of an unkempt writer. His ubiquitous cigar placed him more in the mold of General Curtis LeMay than Tennessee Williams. Although Mamet told John Lahr that if he hadn't been a dramatist he might have been a criminal, in actual fact, he would have more likely become a Green Beret (AOT 59).

The appeal of this world and its shorthand, technical language occurs at many levels for Mamet and begins with clarity: it's black or white, strong or weak, hero or coward, action or passivity. Technical language reinforces precision: when the lecturer at the machine gun seminar spoke of the details of the weapon and then named the parts as he field-stripped a MAG in eight seconds, Mamet, like the others in the room, cheered. When he learned that the biggest cause of loading malfunction for a Bren machine gun is Failure to Feed (failure of the gun to chamber a cartridge properly), he was thrilled: "I have made my living all my adult life on my ability to retrieve bizarre and arcane information, and this was a gem . . . I still cherish it" (CON 40).

The pugil-stick competition occurred that evening, and a psychologically prepared Mamet, "dressed in the full suit of camouflage fatigues" he had bought that morning, was ready. He unexpectedly threw his first opponent off the beam and into the swimming pool below but in his own triumph, dropped his weapon in the water. Was his victory valid? He had to jump into the pool, retrieve his stick, and fight again. He won a second time but "in the best tradition of the Eastern Intellectual," immediately started feeling sorry for his opponent (CON 41). He awaited his next challenger, offered his war cry and at a second start, was soundly knocked off the beam. He recalled Kipling's poem "If," about treating victory and defeat the same, as he removed his soggy fatigues in his room and prepared for dinner in the uniform of a journalist: blue oxford shirt, black knit tie, blue jeans, and Bass Weejuns.

Such a macho/military world contradicts the vague language of art and the perceived world of the writer, the person who sits immobile at a desk. The male action-hero acts. Furthermore, the honor, commitment, and *Semper Fidelis* character of the special operations team or the hunting party is unquestioned. Loyalty is assumed, especially among the cadre of actors Mamet has trained over the years. It is no surprise that he named his hit TV series of 2006 with the generic term "The Unit," which is the epitome of the macho, take-no-prisoners world he admires. Not surprisingly, conflicting loyalties create the dilemmas in his plays. For many characters like Donny, or later Bobby Gould in *Speed-the-Plow*, there are no longer right answers—and that's what makes the works so captivating.

In some ways, Mamet's fascination with this behavior is the effort to overcome the idea of the writer/dramatist as a "wussy Eastern Intellectual with a marvelous gift of dialogue," as he writes in his *Esquire* article (CON 35). It is the extension of the Hemingway figure who acts and is always on the frontline, the figure who exhibits bravery, confidence, and control—the figure who takes command, as Mamet does whenever he directs, produces, or writes. In these situations, Mamet performs "man's work."

Mamet's prose and dramatic work at this time anticipate and expand his love of machismo. "In the Company of Men," and "A Community of Groups" in *Some Freaks*, and "Practical Pistol Competition" and "Black as the Ace of Spades" from the same collection, repeat these themes. "Deer Hunting" in *Make-Believe Town* and "Cops and Cars," "Knives," "Race Driving School," and "Late Season Hunt" are examples from *Jafsie and John Henry* (1999). It is the world of male unity and *simultaneously* of combat expressed dramatically in work as diverse as *American Buffalo*, *Glengarry Glen Ross*, and his Hollywood play, *Speed-the-Plow*.

"Goldberg Street," and "Cross Patch," two short works of 1985, echo the macho/military world through reminiscence. "Goldberg Street," written for Mike Nussbaum and his daughter Susan, focuses on a father elliptically recalling his military experience to his daughter about how he hunted the enemy and now hunts deer. He also reveals an element of Jewish self-hatred as he recalls his time in France and the account of Patton slapping a Jewish soldier in a hospital. The eight-minute work—it originally appeared on radio—ends with resignation and irony as the man realizes they sent him to "the Unit" to fight only because he could read a compass, although he was glad to go. But "I . . . have no desire to go to Israel. (*Pause.*) But I went to France" (GS 5, 6).

"Cross Patch" was performed with "Goldberg Street" on WNUR, Northwestern University's radio station, in March 1985, directed by Mamet and with student actors from his Practical Aesthetics workshop at NYU. It was later a part of *Sketches of War*, a Vietnam Veterans benefit in Boston. The scene in "Cross Patch" is a reunion of patriotic, if chauvinistic, fighting men of the Green Division addressed by a set of speakers on patriotism and the entrepreneurial spirit. The line between God, money, and force soon disappears. Delusions of grandeur affect each speaker, the first, a Dr. Pearce, actually a reserve brigadier general and veteran of three wars and the author of *Cross Patch—The View of a Free Man*, which celebrates the idea of being armed, "accountable for our *acts*," as the key source of pride (GS 9). Countering a fatalistic philosophy (we can't control the world) is "the force of arms" confirming our role as the stewards of life and freedom (GS 11). The next speaker analyzes what appears to be illegal but actually entrepreneurial acts, beginning with why the Chicago White Sox threw the World Series to the Cincinnati Reds in 1919 (GS 13). Moral dilemmas exist and one must learn to face them. But now, in a world ruled by war, honor is no longer respected when weapons can wipe out entire cities. The gathering ends with the unified shout of the password, "Answer to the Call." And what is the Call? the chair asks. "Willing to serve" is the resounding reply. Earnestness framed by satire seems Mamet's intent.

Mamet's TV script for *Hill Street Blues*, "A Wasted Weekend" (aired January 13, 1987, number twelve of the seventh season), encompasses all of these macho elements as hunting, sex, cards, and law enforcement unite. There is violence and a whiff of anti-Semitism. The protagonist is a Lieutenant Henry Goldblume who, when we first see him in the squad room addressing the patrolmen, is dressed in hunting clothes. He and others are planning a weekend hunting trip, but he will have difficulty leaving.

Throughout the episode, Mamet maintains a sinister sense of the danger of weapons, masked by a tone of sarcasm and overconfidence. As one officer tells a State Trooper, calmly but authoritatively, "the *thing* of it, you should *never* give up the gun" (5TP 144). Several unexpected events delay Goldblume's departure for the hunting cabin: he has to address a group of visiting Boy Scouts on "Law Enforcement as a Career" and stop at a currency exchange shop to cash a check on his way to the cabin, where he discovers a robbery and is taken hostage.

Forced to drive off, he is then told by the excited robber to pull over and begin digging a grave. Goldblume eventually manages to talk his way free, convincing the robber to take the car loaded with hunting goods, including several rifles. In the woods, his buddies, having first settled in the wrong cabin, go off early in the morning, and discover a buck. But as one is about to shoot, another screams: he's stepped on a spike. Back at the grave, Goldblume has convinced the robber that he will never identify him and that he should be allowed to live. Distraught, he sits on the edge of the grave only to hear the car being driven off. A startled Goldblume, disbelieving his luck, recovers to find that no one will stop to help him as he tries to flag down a car; he is alone.

Mamet turns the moment into an existential cry of the marginalized man, the Jew. Even being a police officer is of no value: "Won't somebody *help* me??? Isn't anybody going to *help* me??? I'm a *police* officer!!!" he cries (5TP 165). Returning to the station, Goldblume retrieves a backup gun (his own has been taken, paralleling the situation at the police station in *Homicide* when Bobby Gold's gun is grabbed by a killer), humiliated by agreeing to a practice session at the range. He then denies ever seeing the robber to the owner of the money exchange who is now at the station looking at mug shots of suspects. Goldblume compromises himself in not telling the truth of what happened but in the final moments of the episode reverses himself, admitting to his captain that he was kidnapped. The final scene shows Officer Renko, as the men leave the cabin, firing three shots with his revolver at a juice can on a stump, the only shooting done by the hunters. He misses.

The *Hill Street Blues* episode "A Wasted Weekend" turns on the company of men and their affinities, which, from the perspective of the single female character, Sergeant Lucy Bates, is no more than "manly nonsense": "It's manly nonsense if it's not your 'thing;' if not, what is this, '*Name* calling' . . . ?"Officer Buntz replies (5TP 170). The episode implicitly critiques and celebrates the unity of men doing male things. Mamet's wife, Lindsay Crouse, had a recurring role in the series as Officer Kate McBride, and she went on to act in a number of other TV shows, from *NYPD* and *Buffy the Vampire Slayer* (Prof. Maggie Walsh) to roles on *Law and Order* and *CSI: Crime Scene Investigation.*

When they aren't deerstalking, gambling is the principle activity of the hunters and is Mamet's favorite sport. The poker game in "A Wasted Weekend" is brief because of the unexpected arrival of a couple eager to jump into bed. The police had broken into the wrong cabin but manage to get out of the situation partly because one of them realizes the married owner is *not* with his wife but with another woman. This gives them some leverage, although the police leave. But the significance of the gambling scene is not to be overlooked.

Since college, Mamet had loved poker, and various essays recount his good and bad hands and, more important, what he learned from the game. "Gems from a Gambler's Bookshelf," the opening essay of *Make-Believe Town*, is representative. It begins with him recounting the daily poker game that became the source for *American Buffalo*. Mamet then cites one of his favorite books, *Super System or How I Made Over $1,000,000 Playing Poker* by Doyle Brunson. In the section on seven card stud by David "Chip" Reese, the author agues that "the mathematically correct play is not always the best play," to which Mamet adds, "you can neither bluff nor can you impress someone who isn't paying attention" (MBT 11). This view is as much about dramatic construction to keep audiences involved as it is about playing better poker.

Titling this chapter "Soldier of Fortune" actually alludes to Melville's *The Confidence-Man, A Masquerade*. The title of chapter nineteen in the novel is "A Soldier of Fortune." It touches on personal fortune rather than on a hired, military fighter, although it does emphasize the easy loss of fortune to swindle and chicanery. It characterizes Mamet's preferred treatment and understanding of relationships: deceptive. The con is the best way he knows to keep audiences absorbed in his drama, and he has developed consummate techniques for doing so. From *American Buffalo*, *Glengarry Glen Ross*, and *The Shawl*, to the films *House of Games, Things Change, The Spanish Prisoner*, and *Heist*, Mamet finesses dishonesty, betrayal and missteps into constant audience curiosity (and sometimes confusion). In *The Spanish Prisoner*, he repeatedly twists the plot so that even the characters do not understand the action. In this film about the inventor Joe Ross (Campbell Scott) whose corporate boss (Ben Gazzara) seeks control over his "process" and who then meets the friendly but tricky international businessman played by Steve Martin, issues of integrity vie with suspicion as an elaborate confidence game unfolds.

Wag the Dog is about conning a nation. Dustin Hoffman plays the producer Stanley Motss, constructing a fake war to distract the nation from the sexual misbehavior of the president up for re-election. Dominating *The Cryptogram* is the unhappy con of the mother concerning the return of the young boy's father. In *Boston Marriage*, the way one of the two women cons a lover is the means of their modest affluence. The con is Mamet's form of suspense, replacing violence, special effects, or even sex.

Mamet learned early that the bluff or con is at the core of poker: deception, betrayal, misdirection were the key moves. Ironically, the most important early mention of poker, in fact the first mention of "poker" in any book, is in an actor's autobiography: *Diary of 20–30 Years Spent in America as an Actor* by Joe Cowells, published in 1829. Almost comically, Mamet was a near victim of the con at the Soldier of Fortune convention he attended, the event perhaps an indirect contributor to the genesis of *The Spanish Prisoner*. After filing his *Esquire* story, a fact checker called him to ask if he (Mamet) loaned any money to the British air vice marshal. "Why?" Mamet asked. The guy's a con artist, he was told, and notorious for taking money. Mamet then recalled that the officer had talked a lot about investments in the Cayman Islands. Suddenly, Mamet remembered details that didn't quite jive and realized in retrospect that the British "officer" was a confidence man. But, he rationalized, "I was really privileged to have met him . . . because the big con is just not being done that much." The short con, often done on the streets of New York, occurs constantly, but not the big one he said. And because Mamet had no money to loan him, the air vice marshal moved on (DMC 103).

The laws of poker might have helped. Mamet lists them as: (1) knowledge of the rules and (2) "when something looks too good to be true, it is not true." There may also be a third, Mamet writes, offered by Thorstein Veblen: "'Every profession is a conspiracy against the Laity'" (MBT 12). And then he adds one more: play "tight but aggressive"; if you have the best hand, make them pay (MBT 15). In a book he calls "stunningly vicious," Frank Wallace's *Advanced Concepts in Poker*, Mamet notes that the purpose of play is to win money and an "educated player should school himself to win *all* the money." You do this by taking every legitimate advantage—which is anything not "patently illegal" (MBT 15, 16). What Mamet learned is that there can be no substitute for the goal: winning the money. In poker as in life, one must call things by their name. And if you are going to be in charge, *be* in charge. "Trust everyone, but cut the cards" is his final warning: keep control (MBT 20).

The Spanish Prisoner, a short 1985 play, presented as a double bill by the New Theatre Company of the Goodman with *The Shawl*, shows how deception again rules. The title refers to an actual con game in which the mark is convinced that a beautiful sister and a fortune, held hostage in Spain, can be freed through an investment of personal funds. Through the one-sided conversation of a man who seems to stutter, skip, and jump about in an unnatural fashion and who, following Mosher's direction, delivers lines without inflection or volume, the play constructs a history of a Spanish galleon sunk in 1542 by the weight of its gold, of a conquered people, and acts of love. Very few profit from happiness, the man explains, but no one will succeed unless they possess "THE WILL TO EXPLOIT" (GS 22). One critic wrote of this truncated work that it appeared as if "Mamet wrote a play and then cut sentences off at the pass." But the remark also offers the reverse: an explanation of why Mosher, who directed, connected so well with Mamet. He understood and encouraged the Mamet style of unadorned, bare acting, which his blocking and sets reflected. Cutting both the text and action is their common goal. In fact, the knife, rather than the pen, might be Mamet's preferred writing tool. Not only is a knife a key Mamet metaphor and object (see *Edmond* or *The Cryptogram*), but it is his preferred tool of composition: cut away, never add. Words are to be taken out, never added.

The more powerful work expanding the idea of the con is *The Shawl*, Mamet's account of a psychic deceiving a woman, or rather giving her what she desires. Produced in 1985 in Chicago, critics described it as a cross between *Antigone* and the TV series *Alfred Hitchcock Presents*.[2] Lindsay Crouse and Mike Nussbaum starred in the premiere, Nussbaum recounting how at a break during rehearsal he and Crouse worked on a scene so that they would at one point move from a table and walk to a window. When they showed it to Mamet, he stared blankly and then blurted out, "fuck it. Get back to the way I did it": stationary and at the table. While Mamet admires the con and *The Shawl* is about exposing a con, he prefers actors who seemingly never con the audience into action that seems forced, awkward, or unnatural.

A note in the program for *The Shawl*, which has as its centerpiece a séance seeking the return of the woman's mother, thanks the sleight-of-hand artist and magician Ricky Jay for his assistance. The reference marks the beginning of a long association between the master of misdirection and Mamet.

"I love deception" Ricky Jay writes in his remarkable volume, *Jay's Journal of Anomalies, Conjurers, Cheats, Hustlers, Hoaxsters, Pranksters, Jokesters, Imposters, Pretenders, Sideshow Men, Armless Calligraphers, Mechanical Marvels, Popular Entertainments* (2001). This conjuror, actor, author, and scholar of the unusual and arcane, as well as founder of the movie consulting company Deceptive Practices ("Arcane knowledge on a need-to-know basis"), a company that advises movies about magic—*Forrest Gump* and *The Illusionist* were two clients—was the youngest magician ever to appear on television. He performed his first magic trick at four and appeared on TV at seven. A career as a magician began in earnest while at Cornell, and during that time, he performed twice on Johnny Carson's *Tonight Show* and worked frequently in Aspen and Lake George, New York, making studies a low priority. In the seventies, he frequently opened for various rock and jazz groups like Ike and Tina Turner, Leon Redbone, Al Jarreau, Emmylou Harris, Herbie Hancock, and the Nitty Gritty Dirt Band. He moved to L. A. at that time and became a regular at the Magic Castle and other venues.

Jay discovered many of his remarkable tricks through research, mostly in his collection of historical books on magic. He would read about a trick in an arcane or rare magic text—he is a knowledgeable and expert collector—and then study how to perfect it. But he is insistent in never sharing his magic tricks with other magicians, and, in fact, he is expert in tricking them. Persi Diaconis, a noted magician, told of how Jay had borrowed his deck and had him pick a card. Then he had Diaconis reach into his left trousers' pocket and there was the card he'd picked: "In order for him to bring that about, he had to take dead aim at me. That's a phrase we use in discussing the big con: taking dead aim—deeply researching somebody's habits."[3] Jay holds *The Guinness Book of World Records* distance throw for a card—195 feet at 90 mph—and is the author of *Cards as Weapons.* Known as the "scholar of subterfuge," his expertise is close-up magic, not stage illusion, although his historical preference is for the sensational.

Jay is also a bibliophile who at one time or another owned Thomas Ady's *A Candle in the Dark: Or a Treatise Concerning the Nature of Witches and Witchcraft*, which includes a Seventeenth-century account of an English magic performance, and Jean Prévost's *La Première Partie des Subtiles et Plaisantes Inventions*, the earliest known important conjuring book (Lyons, 1584). Jay has authored a number of scholarly and amusing accounts of magic and its more unusual performers, presented in *Learned Pigs & Fireproof Women* (1987), *Jay's Journal of Anomalies* (2001), and *Extraordinary Exhibitions* (2005). The first is an account of unusual and eccentric and overlooked entertainers like Harry Kahne, who wrote five different words simultaneously with pieces of chalk held in each hand, each foot, and his mouth—exceeded, perhaps, by Thea Alba, "The Woman with 10 Brains" who wrote different sentences in French, German, and English at the same time and ambidextrously drew a landscape in colored chalks. She soon was able to write with both feet and her mouth, as well as writing ten different figures at the same time using ten pieces of chalk mounted on long pointers attached to each of her fingers.

Matthew Buchinger and Sarah Biffin were equally impressive: born without arms or legs, Buchinger, for example, displayed the ability to play more than half a dozen musical instruments, become a marksmen, calligrapher, portraitist and magician. He never grew taller than 29 inches. Sarah Biffin, a well-known Nineteenth-century performer, had neither hands, feet, nor legs but painted landscapes, portraits, and miniatures, some on fine china. She placed a brush in her mouth and supported it with her shoulder.

Jay's renowned collection of dice resulted in another volume, *Dice, Deception, Fate & Rotten Luck* (2003), a combination picture book and account of their history as well as natural and inexplicable decomposition (dice are made of celluloid). He has lectured police forces on the confidence game and universities on the historical dimensions of magic. For the American Antiquarian Society he has prepared *Many Mysteries Unraveled: Conjuring Literature in America 1786–1874.*

Mamet contacted Ricky Jay for assistance with the séance portions of *The Shawl*. He was the most recognized conjurer and sleight-of-hand artist of the 80s, a man who like Mamet loved the ways in which "the mind is led on step by step to ingeniously defeat its own logic" (JJA 191). For *House of Games*, Jay actually invented a new short-change scam. Asked by Mamet to reveal some of the short-change tricks, Jay demurred, not wanting to betray the confidence of the hustlers he knew who still relied on such methods. Instead, he invented the envelope switch, which appears in the film. It was later reported that an amateur thief who had seen the movie had been caught attempting to use the switch.

For Mamet, Ricky Jay was, and remains, the ultimate confidence man, and cast him in that role in *House of Games* (he was first a technical advisor). In the film he plays George and the Vegas Man. In *The Spanish Prisoner* he is George Lang; in *Heist* (2001) he is Don "Pinky" Pincus.[4] He also appears in *State and Main* (2000) as Jack the short-order cook.

Jay's appeal to Mamet may be his casual demeanor and surprise at his own skill. He seems startled by his own feats. Such an attitude takes in audiences immediately with the belief that what he does seems so simple and that the magician is one of us—and recalls a remark of Orson Welles (who also loved magic): women didn't like magic because they didn't like to be fooled, while men did because they did like to be fooled, and often were.[5] The con-man aspect makes everything seem rational and clear to these two erudite performers. For the last four centuries, however, "confidence man" has been one of our most ironic terms, since it suggests trust but means deception. The manipulation of confidence is its goal. Whether in the Renaissance or mid-nineteenth-century America, the confidence man (and woman) has existed and often flourished, the character type predating the term.[6]

Mamet has actually directed Jay on stage twice, each a success: *Ricky Jay and his 52 Assistants* (1994), a show devoted entirely to cards, and *Ricky Jay: On the Stem* (2002), a one man, rakish vaudevillian tour of New York with its colorful gamblers, con men, and clowns. Hard-working scam artists at the crossroads of "show business, crime and commerce" are Jay's métier.[7]

Mamet and Jay also put on "Two Hussies. No Waiting" at Town Hall in New York in October 2001. A shameless promotion of their latest books (*Jay's Journal of Anomalies* and Mamet's *Wilson: A Consideration of Sources*), the evening became banter on magic and chicanery interspersed with readings or mention of each work. As the two sat in comfortable arm chairs, fanciful ideas floated in the air such as their development of a unified field theory that linked magic, crime, drama, and politics. Mamet, for example, said that *Oedipus Rex* as described in Aristotle's *Poetics* bears a striking resemblance to the performance of a game of three-card monte. In both instances the mark is led to believe that only he can solve the problem at hand. Jay, meanwhile, focused on his interest on the influence of magic on culture.

Once or twice during the evening, Mamet's reductive intellectualism revealed a curious sensitivity. Asked about his use of vulgarity in his work, he strangely, if ironically, compared himself to a presidential assassin: "I thought I was writing poetry. It's like Charles Guiteau: he could have cured cancer, but he's only known for killing a president" (Guiteau shot President James Garfield in the back in July 1881). But Mamet stressed during the evening that Jay "doesn't make anything up. He knows the difference between doing things and not doing things. The magician performs a task and the illusion is created in the mind of the audience. And that's what acting is about." Or as Jay more succinctly stated, "as a breed, magicians suffer from having to conceal their most important work" (in Singer 72; JJA 133).

During the performance of *The Shawl* in Chicago, Lindsay Crouse offered some insights into the play and life with Mamet. "David wrote this play for me," she begins: he wanted to construct an "old fashioned type of play": "it's a little chamber piece. And the way he's led the audience one way and then leads them another is a type of device that was used a long time ago."[8] To do Mamet, however, "you have to be very brave":

> And when he directs you its even scarier because David refuses to orchestrate his plays at all. He won't say that this is the climax of the play, or this is the place where you should be very gentle or whatever. He says "whatever's happening in the other guy, you keep playing with that. *Whatever's* happening." It makes for greatness but you've got to be really brave. . . .
>
> He writes poetry, and he writes things that if you looked at them musically you'd see that they are pieces of chamber music or little operas or whatever. And that to a certain extent you have to know how to sing them before you can drop it and then appear natural. (Adler 46)

Being married to Mamet is no easier, but for different reasons: it's like

> being married to Cassandra. Half of my job is to say "David, look they don't *want* to hear about Troy. Today they don't want to hear about it, so calm down. Let's have dinner. . . ." We have an extremely analytical household. Everything means something. I'm a complete mystic, and David is—I don't know what you would call him. But there are symbols. You can't imagine the symbols that are in our household. The wind blows the curtains and something is being said to us. . . .
>
> Both of us have a strong sense of ethics and we're always considering what it is that we're doing with out lives. To a certain extent we always have to say to each other, "let's restore our sense of humor here and just go out and kick some ass." We get bogged down sometimes with the moral responsibility of what we're doing. (Adler 47)

At this point in his career, Mamet was seeing more possibilities in film, first with the unexpected success of *The Verdict* and then the unsuccessful attempt to write the script for *Sexual Perversity in Chicago*, released as *About Last Night* in 1986. The disappointment over the screenplay of *Sexual Perversity* was short-lived, however. Mamet was on to *The Untouchables*, approached in 1985 by Art Linson, a Chicago-born independent producer noted for his off-beat productions (*Car Wash*, *Scrooged*). Inspired by the violent TV series of the same name with Robert Stack as Eliot Ness, the crime-fighting federal agent who nailed Al Capone, Linson thought there might be a film in the story. The television series, however, featured the struggle for power that followed Capone's conviction and ran for 117 episodes from 1959 to 1963. Linson wanted the backstory, the capture of Capone. He admired Mamet's tough-guy dialogue and knowledge of Chicago's past. When they first met (Linson flew to New York, hosting Mamet at a small Italian restaurant in SoHo), he asked him if it was a good career move for someone who recently won the Pulitzer Prize to adapt an old television series "for a *shitload* of money?" "Yes, I think so," Mamet answered.[9]

A month after the deal closed, Mamet came up with a workable script, although the path to production was rocky and Mamet's presence comically unnerving: "when he climbed into my limo, he reminded me of a Jew with a buzz cut trying to impersonate a biker," Linson recalled (Linson 66). Linson thought that the first draft had problems: the character of Capone, who did not appear in the TV series, needed to be enlarged, and the plot was confused. The invention of the Malone character (Sean Connery) as the reluctant teacher of Ness, was brilliant. But Paramount had doubts because of the elliptical dialogue style it considered both stilted and unintelligible. But Mamet hated to do rewrites, especially if they took more than two days. The script had also been sneaked to a couple of A-list directors who turned it down (Linson 68).

Mamet came to L. A. for a brief set of revisions and in Linson's secretary's office wrote up the baseball bat scene, where Capone, after a dramatic speech on individual achievement and the team, bashes in the head of one of his lieutenants. But studio execs still resisted. Given a set of notes and asked to do more, Mamet resisted, telling Linson that he weighed the notes before he threw them away (Linson 70). But when Brian De Palma agreed to direct, the studio agreed to use Mamet's script. In 1983, De Palma had had a hit with *Scarface*, although it was an expensive production.

A meeting with Mamet, Linson, and De Palma in New York did not go well. De Palma pointed out there were plot points that did not make sense. Mamet, used to sitting in the back of a theatre with his eyes closed to concentrate on the cadence of words spoken by the actors, was not going to be able to do that now. He had to be awake and listen. Capone needed a bigger role to attract a big name; the income tax element to capture Capone was unclear; Capone's relationship with Frank Nitti, a gangland hitman, also needed more detail. Additionally, De Palma wanted more dramatic settings for the climactic moments. The four screenplay's protagonist characters, Eliot Ness (Kevin Costner), the Irish American cop Malone (Connery), the accountant Wallace (Charles Martin Smith), and the Italian

American rookie cop Stone (Andy Garcia) worked well with Robert de Niro (Capone). Interestingly, except for Ness, Capone and Nittti, all the characters were Mamet's invention.[10]

A week later, Mamet offered another version, the last owed under the deal. More revisions would mean more money. Now, there was more Capone, but still no clarification of plot. Asked, however, why the rewrite took a week, Mamet sarcastically replied that it "got delayed in typing" (Linson 73). A third set of revisions would not happen: the studio would not pay any more money and Mamet was about to direct his own movie, *House of Games*. But four weeks before principal shooting, Linson and De Palma were getting desperate. They couldn't do the dialogue but needed two scenes, one that tied Capone to Malone's death, the other a more exciting climactic scene to catch the accountant. Linson actually flew to Seattle to see Mamet for a rewrite (he was on location with *House of Games*). He refused. Back in Chicago before shooting, De Palma came up with the baby carriage rolling down the steps scene, and then with Linson, the operatic sequence where Nitti could tell Capone about Malone's death. The first scene is silent, the second filled with sound of a clown's aria; both avoided the problem of trying to write Mamet-like dialogue, which they knew they couldn't do. Mamet was shocked by the operatic scene and squirmed when he saw it, but Linson, turning to him, said, "be a good sport, you are bought and paid for" (Linson 75).

The film itself is operatic, with costumes by Armani and a score by Ennio Morricone. Games and competitions are alluded to throughout, from Al Capone's analogy between baseball and crime, to the cops-and-robbers routine as a ritualized game of machismo and death. Capone walks around his circular dinner table with the baseball bat in his hand, emphasizing the need for team play before he bludgeons one of his lieutenants to death for disloyalty. Later, after the murders of Wallace and the D.A.'s star witness, Malone asks Ness if they're finished. "You're sayin that we sat down in a game that was above our head?" The poker analogy is right for Ness—"it does appear so. It would appear so to Mr. Wallace," he replies.[11] Capone offers a boxing metaphor to the press for his war with Ness. Game structure, so much a part of Mamet's dramatic structure, fashions a great deal of *The Untouchables*, from opposing players to rules and a clear field of play/battle. Celebrating the company of men is its core theme, supported by the first rule of behavior, which Malone tells Ness: "You can trust *nobody*" which in *House of Games* comes out as "Don't Trust Nobody," the advice of the con man Mike to Margaret Ford (HG 37).

Released in June 1987, the film grossed $76 million (production costs were $25 million). The film was a hit, partly for its celebration and eulogy of an earlier time in America's mythic history and partly for its depiction of its hero, Ness. Part of the reason was also the dialogue. When Malone instructs the neophyte Ness in the tradition of Chicago violence, he rhythmically makes his point: "he pulls a knife, you pull a gun; he sends one of yours to the hospital, you send one of his to the morgue. That's the Chicago way" (in Brewer 110). There is some historical license, however, since the film's murderous Eliot Ness is only fictionally sound; the same applies to the guilty plea made for Al Capone by his attorney against the mobster's will. This could not, of course, happen in any court still observing the Constitution. Mamet, however, felt comfortable in this milieu having long been attracted to criminals and criminal types from his gambling days through his working at the North Side scam real estate office. "I guess I consider myself an outlaw as a writer," he once said. "I'm good at writing criminals because (A) I was born in Chicago and (B) I know a lot of these people."[12]

The film also allowed for a certain cynicism, highlighted by one of Ness' final comments. Told at the end by a reporter that the repeal of Prohibition seems likely and then asked what he will do, the script reads "(*Beat*). *Ness smiles.* NESS: I think I'll have a drink" (in Brewer 117). Drawing on the conventions of the Western and its ambivalences that border on cynicism (although at times coupled with a high-minded tone that verges on sanctimony), the film praises and criticizes America in a way that audiences found, through its blend of violence and heroics, irresistible.

House of Games, released in October 1987, had another type of appeal. The first film Mamet directed, it encapsulated all his central themes, most importantly the confidence game. When the psychiatrist Margaret Ford discovers she has been tricked as she is about to write a check for $6,000, she angrily leaves the House of Games, the name of the betting parlor, surprised that she has uncovered the truth (HG 23–5). She later returns to locate Mike, the con man, with an idea: to study the confidence game to which he introduced her. A demonstration of the short con follows—and then the big, with Ford the victim. Mamet plays games in the film with various cons following one another, the biggest the false businessman acting like a policeman who is shot as $80,000 is stolen. The need to replace the mob money is immediate and Ford, attracted to Mike, offers to provide it to protect him. She gets the money but is told by Mike that he and his pal Joey will have to get out of Chicago for a while. But when she returns to the bar where she first met them, she finds the group reassembled, including the supposedly dead businessman, now recounting how they tricked her. At the airport, where Mike is now about to depart for Las Vegas, she confronts him and takes her revenge. The film, starring Lindsey Crouse and Joe Mantegna, was an absorbing exploration of the title of Ford's book: *Driven: A Guide to Compulsive Behavior.*

Mamet's direction embodied his emerging film aesthetic, beginning with "don't let the protagonist tell the story" (ODF 23). "Withholding information" is another principle that the film exhibits, especially through Mike. Mamet carefully prepared a shot list following the storyboarding of the film, which resulted in the uninflected shot, the camera shot that required no narrative elaboration. "You always want to tell the story in cuts. Which is to say, through a juxtaposition of images that are basically uninflected." The aim is to put the protagonist in the "same position as the *audience*—through the *cut*—by making the viewer create the idea himself, in his own mind, as Eisenstein told us." [13]

The alternate title for the film was *The Tell*, that signal or sign that gives away deceptive behavior, as Mike instructs Ford early in the film (HG 15–16). Yet her flaw is not a tic, but her ready acceptance of his trust, the fundamental principle of confidence men. She, as a psychiatrist, is naturally attracted to role-playing and deception. For her, the con also possesses a sexual intensity. She forgets that "whatever truth a con artist speaks is only at the service of a lie. . . . he gets us to believe in fiction by showing us things that are true. In the end he's a philosophical nihilist."[14]

Mamet developed the idea for *House of Games* with the comedian Jonathan Katz seven years before its release and became its director by default (DMC 83). Peter Yates was originally to direct but had to pull out. Why don't you do it, he asked Mamet? When Mike Hausman agreed to produce, Mamet was on his way and went to see Mike Medavoy, head of Orion Films, for additional funding. Medavoy admired Mamet's "original, idiosyncratic voice" and his dialogue, which was both "electric and menacing."[15] Mamet had never directed a film yet when he went to see Medavoy, the meeting took only ten minutes, the deal taking only "eleven words of low-level Mamet-speak." He showed up, took a Cuban cigar, cut the end off, and lit up. Medavoy:

> "So," I said, clenching my own cigar, "you want to direct a movie?"
>
> Mamet nodded.
>
> "Fine. Let's do it," I told him.
>
> Eleven words and off Mamet went to Panavision to rent the necessary camera equipment (Medavoy 169).

When he finished the first cut, he and Hausman showed up one afternoon unannounced and dumped the canisters of film on Medavoy's desk while Mamet helped himself to a couple of cigars. "Here's your movie" Mamet said as he and Hausman lit up and headed out the door. "That was delivery Mamet style," writes Medavoy (169).

Mamet had problems cutting, however. A great scenarist and playwright whose words in a play text are sacred, "he had to learn how to pace his movies." This can be done in the editing room, especially for a film like *House of Games* that depends on a succession of subplots. Medavoy was honest with Mamet without being hostile, and the result was editing the film down to a tight, film noir thriller of 102 minutes (Medavoy 169–70).

For Mamet, making the actual movie was an exercise in confidence according to Mantegna. From the first, Mamet was sure of what he wanted to do in part because every shot had been outlined and storyboarded (DMC 85). For authenticity and effectiveness, Mamet actually flew three of his Vermont poker buddies out to Seattle, the location. They were backup advisors and operators in an actual poker game taking place during breaks from filming, making it difficult to separate the fictitious game from the real according to one actor (DMC 82).

Just before the release of *House of Games*, Mamet lectured on film at the Columbia University Film School in the fall of 1987. This came about through Michael Hausman, who had connections with the school via his friend Milos Forman. Hausman, to whom Mamet would dedicate his book *On Directing Film*, was a former stockbroker and still photographer who became a movie producer. Equally important to Mamet was his involvement in the movie-making process as a production manager, second unit director, miscellaneous crew member, line producer, or executive producer. For Mamet, meeting Hausman was a breakthrough.

They met when Mamet went to Texas, where Lindsay Crouse was shooting *Places in the Heart* (for which she would be nominated for an Academy Award as Best Supporting Actress). Hausman was executive producer and present on the set. He agreed to read the script of *House of Games* and decided to produce it, taking a chance on Mamet as director. For Mamet, this was a major step in a new genre. Ever interested in being part of the shooting, Hausman became the film's still photographer, which Mamet gleefully pointed out to Art Linson when he visited Mamet on the Seattle set when he sought help with the rewrites of *The Untouchables* (Linson, 74).

Hausman liked the movie-making process, and even on his recent hit *Brokeback Mountain* (2005), he was first assistant director, as well as executive producer. His other hits have included *Silkwood* (1983), *Amadeus* (1984), *The Firm* (1993), *The People vs. Larry Flynt* (1997), and *Eternal Sunshine of the Spotless Mind* (2004). For Mamet, he produced *House of Games, Things Change*, and *Homicide*. But Hausman's importance for Mamet was as much practical as it was financial. Mamet has called Hausman his "mentor in moviemaking" who revealed to him the deep dark secret of filmmaking: that "any film can be made for any budget." Mamet understood the lesson and could do a decent film for $4 million.[16]

Mamet's limited experience as a screenwriter and first-time director, although he had just completed his second film, *Things Change*, did not curb his immoderate confidence, which gave him the credentials, he believed, to offer his views on storytelling, camera angles, and editing. In the preface to his Columbia lectures, however, he does admit that he was much like a pilot with 200 hours flying time: he was the most dangerous thing around, a step beyond neophyte but not experienced enough to recognize his ignorance. Yet he applied his basic principle of dramatic writing to film writing: "Having discovered what is essential, you then know what to cut" (ODF 79). His repeated examples and references in his discussion of film are to drama. For both drama and film, the "scene is the correct unit of study. If you understand the scene, you understand the play or movie." Additionally, "to get into the scene late and to get out early is to demonstrate respect for your audience" (ODF 64).

Throughout *On Directing Film*, Mamet constantly "critiques" producers, the necessary evil without whom one cannot make a film. Without the producer, there is no deal, no money to hire a director or locate a star. But producers are undereducated and know nothing about the task of movie-making. They have never had a "run-in with the demands of a craft" and "see all ideas as basically equal and his own as first among them, for no reason other than that he has thought of it" (ODF 48). Hausman, however, was an exception: he had been involved directly with production.

Mamet's view of producers is consistent: he ridicules them in *Speed-the-Plow*, satirizes them in *State and Main*, and excoriates them in his essay "Bambi v. Godzilla." In a June 2005 article, Mamet calls producers (as well as critics and casting agents) "parasites" (BG 36). The producer, he contends, "struggles for power; the artist, for power and fulfillment. The artist must lose" (BG37). Resorting to extremes to make a point, Mamet writes: "nowhere in film [he means represented in films] do we find a Good Producer. We find Good Nazis but no Good Producers" (BG37). From his experience involving "financial interchange with Hollywood," writers always end with "an accusation by the corporation of theft." This he interprets as the company saying, "you forgot to work for nothing" (BG37). As a consequence, Mamet has striven to make his films independently, earning money from scripting films like *Ronin* or *Hannibal* to finance his own projects. But despite continuously railing against producers, Mamet knows he has to work with them.

In a 1987 interview, Mamet acknowledged his austere production style both on stage and in film. He simplifies his directorial principles to "where does this take place?" and what does it mean to the film, reducing elements to a through-line. He also acknowledges his limited visual sense, which parallels his severe sense of text and the importance he places on cutting (IOW 143). Importantly, he defines the job of the director as telling "*the story through the juxtaposition of uninflected images* . . . because that's the nature of human perception: to perceive two events, determine a progression, and want to know what happens next" (ODF 60). The artistry of a film director is "to learn to do without the exposition; and, so, involve the audience" (ODF 86).

In October 1987, coinciding with the filming of *Things Change*, Jack Kroll visited Mamet at the Cal-Neva lodge on the Lake Tahoe set (the California Nevada border runs through the lobby, with gambling on the Nevada side, no betting on the California side). Noting first that Mamet is hot—not only had *The Untouchables* already grossed high but his first film was chosen as the closing night selection at the New York Film Festival—Kroll admires the "calm intensity" of Mamet's directorial style. Reflecting a certain military precision, Kroll writes, "Mamet is in total command."[17] Mamet, however, displayed a certain irony about Hollywood power, which did not always bow before his theatrical reputation, noting that he was greeted with disappointment after his script for *Postman* was delivered: that Zanuck and Brown rejected his work on *The Verdict* and that his script for *The Untouchables* was thought "*dreck*" by the producers at Paramount until Art Linson convinced them to do it (Kroll 85).

These experiences brought Mamet into contact with Hollywood's basic distrust of writers, which *Speed-the-Plow* would illuminate. "Hollywood people," he said in an *American Theatre* interview, "are very, very cruel and also very, very cunning." One thing they say "'if they don't understand something or it's not bad enough for them is 'it's very theatrical. It's too theatrical.' That is used as a curse word. Also as an irrefutable statement. What are you going to say? 'It's *not* theatrical?'"[18] *Speed-the-Plow* would be entirely devoted to this shark-infested world. "We all know we should stay away from Hollywood but we don't," he confessed, and as a subject, even *he* couldn't resist it (IOW 142). But his experience with producers and directors demanded he confront it. *Speed-the-Plow* opened in New York in May 1988 with Joe Mantegna, Ron Silver, and, in either a piece of casting bravado or disaster, Madonna. It ran for 278 performances and Ron Silver received a Tony for Best Actor.

Filled with cynicism and one-upmanship, *Speed's* critical view of Hollywood may emanate from Mamet's rough experience with *About Last Night*, the adaptation and severely altered script of *Sexual Perversity in Chicago*, which he had drafted and then had rejected. It may also reflect his "education" in Hollywood with his early movies and his experience with Ned Tanen, head of production for Paramount (the brash, Bobby Gould character) who was deeply involved with *The Untouchables*. Art Linson may be the source of the quieter film producer, Charlie Fox. It also reflects Mamet's exposure to the intricacies of financing, distribution, and marketing and why some movies are made and others are not. Regardless of the sources, the play, like *American Buffalo* and *Glengarry*, is about hustlers in business battling for survival and masking their fear of failure with bravado.

Moral posturing replaces integrity, as the "stop-stutter" dialogue exposes the emptiness of the newly promoted Bobby Gould (who has the ear and wallet of the studio) and his long-suffering but hustling studio buddy, Charlie Fox. Fantasizing about their success with the possible "buddy action prison movie" Charlie brings to Bobby, they pridefully "dish" their proposed wealth:

Gould: I piss on money.
Fox: I know that you do. I'll help you.
Gould: *Fuck* money.
Fox: Fuck it. Fuck "things" too . . .
Gould: Uh huh. But don't fuck "people." (SP 21)

This last is precisely the dilemma they face in the plot as Karen, the temp, sent off to do the "courtesy read" of a novel on radiation, returns the next day having convinced Bobby Gould to drop the buddy movie for the more serious work (Karen's having slept with him the night before aids in his change of mind).

Act Three begins with Charlie wondering if he is worthy to be rich, or if he is just greedy, unaware of Gould's change of heart. He also can't believe that he will share producing credits with Bobby. Before he can talk further, Bobby tells him he will not do the action film starring Douglas Brown. Charlie goes on the attack, first by calling the new work "a talky piece of puke" (SP 62). Told that Gould will see *his* boss, Ross, himself, Charlie gets desperate and finally absorbs that his prison buddy film will not be "greenlighted." Charlie mentally regroups by telling Bobby what he should be doing: approving films that *make* money. Bobby won't listen and becomes more devoted to *The Bridge; or, Radiation, Half-Life and Decay of Society*. Understood by Bobby as his chance to do something right rather than just profitable, Charlie then turns vicious: "You're gonna buy a piece of shit" (SP 69). If the film doesn't work out, Charlie shouts, your reputation will be shot; no one will talk to you let alone hire you.

Suddenly, Charlie senses that the secretary has changed Bobby's mind and, as his anger at Bobby increases, he realizes his own chance of success is failing. He hits him:

All this bullshit; you *wimp*, you *coward* . . . now you got the job, and now you're going to *run* all over everything . . . you *fool*—your fucken' sissy film—you squat to pee. You old *woman* . . . all of my life I've been eating your shit and taking your leavings. . . . *Fuck* you, the Head of Production. Job I could of done ten *times* better'n you . . . cost me my, my, my . . . *fortune?* Not In This Life, Pal." (SP 70)

Suddenly, Charlie is in charge and takes over and in *his* "reading" of the situation, tells Bobby that he's been sucked in by the beautiful and ambitious temp.

Gould: I want you to be careful what you say about her.
Fox: It's only words, unless they're true. (SP 71)

Bobby listens to Charlie's analysis: the secretary has come to Hollywood for power. Men get it by work, women by sex. "She's different? Nobody's different. *You* aren't. *I'm* not, why should she? The broad wants power" (SP 71). Like an expert confidence man, "she lured *you* in" (SP 71). You're a whore, Charlie tells Bobby, bought and paid for. Don't ask for sympathy from her or me, he says: "This broad *just took you down*" (SP 72). She wanted something from you. "I wouldn't believe this shit if it was *true*" Charlie tells Bobby after reading to him a passage from the radiation book (SP73). Charlie then starts to ask Karen, who has just come in, one question, but before he can, she explains to him that last night they talked about the possibility of doing a film that would make a difference. And then Charlie's question: did you go to his house "with the preconception, you wanted him to greenlight the book?" (SP 77). "Yes," she answers. And then he asks, if Bobby had said no, would she have gone to bed with him? She truthfully answers, "No." Charlie again explodes: "I know who *he* [Bobby] is, who are *you*? . . . A Tight Pussy wrapped around Ambition. That's who *you* are, Pal" (SP 78).

It gets uglier as the venality gets stronger. Charlie in response to Karen's saying Bobby reached out to her, shouts, "He reached out to you? He fucked you on a bet." "I don't care" is her quick reply (SP 78). Bobby is now lost, and is to meet with his boss in ten minutes. Bobby then makes his choice and Karen is out the door, while Charlie focuses on restoring Bobby to some sense of balance. The two "buddies" then head to Ross' office, ready to pitch the buddy action prison movie, satisfied that they know what they're doing:

Gould: We're here to make a movie.
Fox: Whose name goes above the title?
Gould: Fox and Gould.
Fox: Then how bad can life be? (SP 82).

The expressive inarticulateness of the play reaches numerous levels of intensity as when Charlie Fox offers his analysis of Hollywood: "Life in the movie business is like the, is like the beginning of a new love affair: it's full of surprises, and you're constantly getting fucked" (SP29). This is a world in which lunch reservations at the right place have the highest priority. And "learning . . . to think in a . . . -business fashion" means learning to act treacherously while kissing ass and recognizing that a movie is neither good nor bad but a commodity (SP 40, 41). "We're in business to . . . *Make the thing everyone made last year. Make that image people want to see.* That *is* what they, it's more than what they want. It is what they require" (SP 56). But Karen's dialogue with Fox, while Gould freshens up, suggests that from the first she knew what *she* wanted: power and control for her own movie idea, the radiation book. Her only mistake, Fox tells her, was choosing a book that could never be made into a film.

The brilliance of the play is Mamet's collision of cupidity and idealism to confirm what we already know: art has no place in the movies and in Hollywood one person's moment of venom is another's moment of love. Or as he said in a later interview, "the wonderful thing about Hollywood is that you can't insult anyone. . . . they just might do business with you in the future."[19]

Speed-the-Plow presents a world where "cynicism is a breakfast food" (Linson 195). It's brutal, male-driven, and ego-driven and matches Mamet's definition of a movie producer: "Ivan the Terrible with a car phone!", "Greed untempered by reason!", "whore!" (Linson, 9). It also matches, or at least is the pendant, to *A Life in the Theatre*. Whereas that work revealed the backstage competition and insecurities of the two actors, *Speed-the-Plow* reveals the competition and insecurities of the two studio executives. And in both works, you don't get a great deal of background story: "what you see is what you get. You invent for yourself who these people are," Mantegna explained. But the great thing about Mamet is the way "he can say so much with so little," although this means the actor "has to be able to be precisely on the money in translating that amount of dialogue correctly. . . . as much is said between the lines as with the lines" (in Kane, interview 253–55).

Speed-the Plow, Mamet's first full-length play since *Glengarry*, was a hit. Silver as Charlie Fox earned raves and a Tony for the Broadway production. Madonna, of course, received much press. Several critics found her "crafty innocence" and beauty welcoming, while others found her flat and uncomprehending in her delivery. The *Daily News* headline of the review read "NO, SHE CAN'T ACT." The *Daily Mail* (London) reported that she gave a performance "that would make an empty space look like talent."[20] However, when her name had been announced, advanced sales for the production topped $1 million. Madonna, twenty-eight at the time, auditioned for the part after she wrote to Mamet in September 1987 praising *House of Games*. A few months later she heard about *Speed-the-Plow* through Mike Nichols and contacted Gregory Mosher, for whom she and her then husband Sean Penn had worked in a nonpublic workshop staging of David Rabe's *Goose and Tom-Tom* at Lincoln Center in August 1986.

Madonna auditioned twice. Why he selected her Mamet never made clear, although some thought a play about the moral emptiness of the American entertainment business would benefit from including its greatest symbol, the Material Girl. Mamet made some adjustments to the Karen character, removing the victimized, poor soul quality and providing an element of doubt. As Mosher, who directed, phrased it, "the audience is meant to go out asking one another: Is she an angel or a whore?"[21]

Madonna's departure from the production occurred when her contract expired, although a rumor circulated that she left three months early, supposedly when she forget some lines on stage when she was to read a passage from the radiation book. As she picked it up, she burst into laughter. Mamet was to have demanded a replacement.[22] Felicity Huffman would eventually take her role when the entire cast changed.

The European premiere of the play occurred in July 1988 at the Spoleto festival in Italy and was performed in Italian. One of the two male actors was criticized as "too Byronic and unsleazy looking for the role," but the play was a hit, more for its language than performance.[23] The British production at the National Theatre, which opened in January 1989, had a new cast: Colin Stinton as Bobby Gould, Alfred Molina as Charlie Fox, and a youthful rock singer/actor, Rebecca Pidgeon, as Karen. Mosher again directed his third production of the play (the first two were with the two Broadway casts, which ran for eight months).

Pidgeon was twenty-three and had already acted with Anthony Hopkins, Ian Holm, Miranda Richardson, and Dame Peggy Ashcroft. Born in 1965 to Scottish parents in Cambridge, Massachusetts, while her father was a visiting professor of physics at MIT, she grew up in Scotland. She trained at the Royal Academy of Dramatic Arts but, despite a promising career in film—she was in *The Dawning* with Trevor Howard and Jean Simmons—she diverted to rock music becoming, in the mid 80s, the mainstay of the British folk/pop band Ruby Blue. She left to pursue acting, beginning with the Cambridge Theatre company. She then created some attention in a TV soap opera entitled *Campaign*, performed in the film *The*

Dawning, and joined the National Theatre, London, in 1988, making her debut as Isabella in *The Changeling*.

She snagged the role of Karen in *Speed-the-Plow* and was exceedingly nervous when Mamet appeared at rehearsal: "I was expecting Arthur Miller and there he was, with a little scarf tied nattily around his neck like some Parisian mime artist. I couldn't understand how such a young person had written all this work." [24] One night during performance when Mamet appeared, she felt completely unsure about going on. Low energy and frayed nerves made her not want to even begin with her role. She stood backstage and told Mamet she really didn't feel like doing the play that night. He answered with care and good judgment which she says was the beginning of a love affair. It also began the revision of her artistic philosophy and started her journey toward her Bat Mitzvah: "He looked at me and said, 'You don't gotta feel like it. You just gotta do it. It's your *job*'" (Pidgeon 117).

Mamet was smitten by Pidgeon, who was nineteen years younger than himself. Her straightforward and resourceful manner appealed to him and she didn't bore him. His friend the painter Donald Sultan who had accompanied him to London, suffered from constant Mamet questions about whether she liked him or not. Sultan would assure him she did, partly because for weeks she had been speaking his words and learning his gestures. Pidgeon herself seemed surprised that she liked him, first expecting a "tall, very intellectual, cold, godlike kind of writer, and then I see this young vibrant kind of street urchin" (FM 81). In the meantime, Mamet called his sister in Los Angeles and said "I've found her." After listening, his sister replied, "So you'll marry her." A long-distance relationship continued for two more years before they married.

Reaction to Pidgeon in the role of Karen was generally positive, critics praising her ingénue quality and greater depth in the part than Madonna: "she's all spirituality with a hint of metal." Another, less expected response was to the language, as Tony Dunn noted: "Americans are democrats so, in American speech, the little words, like the little man, get their chance to star," as he began a review that celebrated Mamet as a "brilliant unmoralising recorder of life." As Dunn writes, "yes and no, the tiny language particles we use, cancel each other out the nearer you get to power." But as the buddy movie of Bobby Gould and Charlie resumes after Karen is undone, even the two men are unaware of what they are saying because, as they maneuver for control, even the simplest words are merely positional. As the American performance artist Laurie Anderson remarked, "in my country goodbye looks just like hello."[25] Mamet's phatic repetitions and explicit jokes fit a national linguistic criteria in which language is camouflage, not communication. The spiraling speeches, fast riffs, and spats, backed up by coarseness and a staccato delivery, found responsive English audiences, even if critics were ungenerous with the performances.

One of the most interesting responses to the play was that of Sandy Lieberson, former president of 20th Century Fox. In a 1989 article in the *Evening Standard*, he noted the accuracy of Mamet's portrayal of Hollywood and the dilemma of those caught between conscience and the box office. "I gave the green light to *Chariots of Fire* and a dog movie starring Chevy Chase, *Oh Heavenly Dog*, in the same week. In theory, the dog movie was going to cover any potential losses from *Chariots*. What happened? Exactly the reverse."

Hollywood, says Lieberson, directly felt the impact of *Speed-the-Plow*. How? By causing the most powerful Hollywood executives to rethink their dress code. Bobby Gould does not wear socks. Since the New York opening, said Lieberson, there has been not one sockless executive in Hollywood as no one wants to identify with Gould. Mamet has also pinpointed the most powerful motivator in the film world: fear of failure. It's better to do nothing or remake what was made last year, than to try something new, which is the fastest way to lose your job.[26]

Earlier, in 1987, Mamet and his wife, Lindsay Crouse, completed a children's story, *The Owl*. Dedicated to Willa Mamet, it is the story of how a young boy with the help of a mysterious owl, rescues his ducks sold by his father to a slaughterhouse. Allegorically, it may be akin to Mamet's new sense of responsibility in "saving" the Jews—or his Jewish identity—by reasserting Jewish themes in his work. Courage and standing up for what is right are the distinguishing traits of the young hero in *The Owl*.[27] The co-authorship, however, masked difficulties in Mamet's relationship with Crouse that led to their breakup, the result of his unhappiness and disenchantment with the marriage.

Mamet and Crouse had always had a strong personal and professional attachment then in its tenth year. But "'sometimes I trust him, other times I'm thoroughly pissed'" she said, adding "'we're passionate people, it's natural to have conflict, but there is never pettiness or bitterness'" (in Kroll 85). Half jokingly, in 1981 she referred to him as "the troll that lives upstairs." By the late eighties, however, friction in the marriage had accelerated and led to a separation and then divorce in 1990. The following year, Mamet married Rebecca Pidgeon who would convert to Judaism.

In *The Disappearance of the Jews*, Bobby confronts several anti-Semitic slurs, notably that the Jews were responsible for their own oppression.[28] He had no response but in the play Joey bursts out against the *goyim*, first arguing that non-Jews have such views because they feel left out. We don't descend to their level and have our ideas on higher things, he shouts: "we got something better to do than all day to fuckin' beat the women up and go kill things" (the defendant in Mamet's 2005 play *Romance* makes a similar claim [ROM 45]). Joey's solution is simple: "You're too shut off, Bob. You should come back here" to the old neighborhood (DOJ 15–16). Mamet's alignment with Judaism and Pidgeon's conversion would mark stages of his own "return."

Mamet's adaptation of Chekhov's *Uncle Vanya* during this difficult time reflects many of the tensions he appears to have undergone. Robert Brustein commissioned Mamet to prepare a new version of *Vanya* after seeing his adaptation of *The Cherry Orchard*. The story of a retired professor and his attractive young wife returning to the country estate left to him by his deceased first wife, plunges the characters into a precarious situation of romance and boredom. Working again from a literal translation, Mamet enlivened the language and situations. Lindsay Crouse played the youthful wife, Yelena, Christopher Walken, the disillusioned doctor, Astrov.

The play, however, had broader connotations. Chekhov focuses on the repression of happiness in the work. Life slips away from many of the figures, as Ivan, Uncle Vanya, reminds so many, including himself. And like others, he is infatuated with the beautiful twenty-seven-year-old Yelena. Disenchanted with life, as is Astrov the doctor, Ivan seeks a chance to love Yelena. He repeatedly tells her of his love but she, with equal determination, rejects him, partly because she is intrigued by Astrov.[29] But he, too, is disappointed in life, especially provincial life: only the woods make him happy. He works alone and feels isolated: "There is no one. . . . there is nothing for me. And do you know, I don't *like* people. And, for the longest time, have loved no one," he confides to Sofya, the professor's daughter from his first marriage (UV 34). Affection he has felt, but not love.

To assign such feelings to Mamet at this time, six months before he met Rebecca Pidgeon in London, may or may not be correct. But the play resonates with signs of his own frustration with his marriage and feelings of isolation, as it shows a range of characters confronting the absence of love. Even the apparently devoted Yelena finds that her love for her professor husband has altered, anticipating, perhaps, Mamet's view of his own relationship. Of her love for her older husband, Yelena says, "the love was not real. But I *thought* it was real. At the time I *thought* it was real" (UV 39). That Lindsay Crouse says these lines is doubly ironic. Three pages earlier, Astrov told Sofya, "I have lost capacity for all attachment," becoming blind to love even when it stands in front of him, as it does with her. She loves him, as does Yelena, which she reveals when the two women confide in each other in Act II (UV 37–41).

The question Yelena asks Sofya about her powerful attachment to Astrov is one Mamet may have asked himself: "how long are you to live in uncertainty" (UV 46)? Mamet personally answered it within months. The answer is embodied in Yelena's statement a few lines later, when she agrees to tell Sofya Astrov's truthful response to Sofya's love. "I think the *truth*, no matter how bad, is never so bad as an uncertainty" (UV 47). The statement is core Mamet, not only expressed by his characters but articulated in his theories of acting. The irony, however, is that few have the courage to live up to it. And yet, there is always hope, as Uncle Vanya expresses to Astrov: "If I could live the rest of my life out in some different *way*, if that were possible. . . . How could a man start anew? And begin a new life" (UV 71)? The pragmatic doctor, however, denies that such change is possible, establishing a dilemma that can be solved only by action, another Mamet principle. But sometimes such action can be dangerous, as Astrov suggests to Yelena, explaining that if she had chosen to stay and not go with her husband, something quite terrible would have happened between them (UV 75). In the play, hearts break and guns fire, although the professor poses a remedy: "it's not enough to *think*; one must *work* . . . the greatest joy is to do some real *work* in the work world" (UV 77). Again, pure Mamet.

Uncle Vanya also highlights a shift in Mamet's theatrical focus. After the success of *Speed-the-Plow*, Mamet turned to regional theatre, preferring the freedom and noncommercial pressure of productions in venues like the American Repertory Theatre in Cambridge and the Atlantic in New York, as well as the American Conservatory Theatre and the Magic Theatre, both of San Francisco. Leaving New York also meant leaving Gregory Mosher as his principal director. Living in Cambridge and Vermont, New York seemed less necessary for his work and Hollywood no more than a place to visit rather than reside. The distance gave him the creative and physical independence that, among other things, allowed him to turn to Chekhov and his past. The shift began with an April 1988 production of *Uncle Vanya* restaged in a May 1990 production at the Goodman.

Mamet at this time was also confronting his Jewish past, which may have consolidated his decision to end his relationship with Lindsay Crouse. This past also became more prominent in works like "Bobby Gould in Hell," produced at Lincoln Center with Shel Silverstein's *The Devil and Billy Markham* in the fall of 1989. Mamet's work addresses the issue of taking responsibility for one's actions, adding Christian worry to Jewish guilt. The use of the Bobby Gould character—he appeared in *The Old Neighborhood* and, of course, *Speed-the-Plow*, is as a figure who lies, cheats, and blasphemes his way through life. He's a crook but honest about it, and we accept him. "Everycad" one critic quipped about Gould, a man honest about his being no good.[30] The presence of Glenna (Felicity Huffman) who "attacks" Gould for his misbehavior, generates his exasperating cry, "There was no pleasing her!"

But through all this domestic and literary upheaval, the macho world of Mamet, with its equal parts of bravado and deception, did not recede. Poker, guns, and knives were still prominent. The epitome of deception was, indeed, poker, where deceit, or the bluff, determined the winner. Throughout the eighties, he wrote frequently about the subject in essays devoted to what he learned from the game that he could then apply to activities like playwriting and producing films. He even had a cameo acting role as a gambler in Bob Rafelson's *Black Widow* (1987), typecast at a poker table as a cigar-chomping player billed as Herb.

No less than Thorstein Veblen provided material for Mamet's value theory of poker. In *Theory of the Leisure Class*, Chapter XI, entitled "The Belief in Luck," deals with chance and gambling, suggesting that "the belief in luck is a sense of fortuitous necessity in the sequence of phenomena." Veblen then begins an analysis of its impact on economic structure and function, as well as its relation to "the leisure class." But Veblen also identifies gambling as "another subsidiary trait of the barbarian temperament" and of certain warlike activities.[31] Belief in luck and backing that luck through betting is also a sign of a predatory character, Veblen argues (278). Mamet, who long admired Veblen's book, would not disagree.

Knives, hunting, and martial arts merely extended the macho world that poker embodied. A wrestler in high school, Mamet found camaraderie in fellow sportsmen, whether deer hunters, knife collectors, or simply people who executed their tasks soundly. Indeed, the well-made object has always been a Mamet objective. The language of the outdoorsmen/hunter was also cherished by Mamet, as indicated in his essays "The Shooting Auction" in *The Cabin*, or "Cops and Cars," in *Jasfie and John Henry*. "Bad Boys" from the latter collection sums up in many ways his overall view of the value of the company of men (see "In the Company of Men," SF, 85–91).

Guns held a particular appeal: on his desk is an artillery shell, and a Colt .45 is a paperweight. In *House of Games*, Margaret Ford takes Billy Hahn's nickeled automatic pistol, which will have lethal effect at the end of the movie, while the fake gun (it's a water pistol) that the Vegas man places on the table in the poker game signals the danger and yet deception guns create. At the end of the movie, Mike doesn't believe he is actually going to be shot and tries the language of poker to ward off any bullets: "You can't bluff someone who's not paying attention" he tells Ford. "*Ford shoots him. He falls.* Are you nuts? What are you . . . *nuts* . . . ?" Wounded, he still thinks it's a bluff. Shot again, he says in an extreme state of bravado, imitating Mickey Spillane rather than David Mamet, "Thank you, sir. May I have another?' *Ford shoots him three times*" (HG 69–70).

Loss of one's gun is for Mamet a deadly mistake. At the end of *Homicide*, the murderer Randolph wounds the police officer Gold because Gold has lost his gun. A gun provides psychological (if not moral), as well as physical protection, as Teach understood in *American Buffalo*. As he prepares to go out and "take the shot" (rob the coin collector), he pulls out a revolver. Don is upset. We don't need it, he tells Teach. Tell me why we need it?

Teach: It's not a question do we *need* it. . . . *Need* . . . Only that it makes me comfortable, okay? It helps me to relax. So, God forbid, something inevitable occurs and the choice is (And I'm *saying* "God forbid") it's either him or us.

Still, Don is uncomfortable. Teach answers, "it's a personal thing, Don. A personal thing of mine. A silly personal thing. I just like to have it along. Is this so unreasonable?" Protection is the real reason, but it is still not a good enough reason for Don, who tells him "I don't want it with." Teach answers,

I got to have it with. The light of things as they are.
Don: Why?
Teach: Because of the way *things* are. (AB 84–5)

The coded macho language and self-protection here suggest an ethos of guns which Mamet, a gun collector and shooter understands.

Some Freaks (1989) contains a number of essays about this macho world, and sustains the image as well as reality of Mamet as a Hemingway-esque figure stepping out of the woods to pound out another masterpiece. Happily situated in an isolated cabin far from the entrapments of the city, he gambles late at night with friends, returning in his truck to his farmhouse, braving the winter and loving his family—solid American behavior and values. But the undercurrent of adventure is never far away, expressed in the opening sentence of his essay "Liberty." It begins, "In Hemingway's *A Farewell to Arms*, an American soldier, fleeing from the War, is playing billiards with a European Nobleman" (SF 104). This is a quintessential Mamet scene, uniting machismo with mystery (why is the soldier fleeing?) written in this case by Hemingway. It is the soldier of fortune confirming his place in the American landscape.

7

A JEW IN THE NINETIES

I knew the downside of being Jewish, but I didn't understand the upside until much later.

Mamet, 1997

Rabbi Lawrence Kushner is the energetic author of more than a dozen books, one of them with David Mamet. He has taught at the Hebrew Union College—Jewish Institute of Religion in New York and for twenty-eight years was the rabbi of Congregation Beth El of Sudbury, Massachusetts, where he first met Mamet. They clicked: Mamet's desire to renew his Judaism and his wish to have Rebecca Pidgeon convert converged on the Boston area's "funkiest"—the term is Kushner's—Reform synagogue. Since the late eighties, Mamet had been vigorously confronting both the absence and the needs of his Judaism. Kushner was the man to guide and nurture its redevelopment.

What brought about this change? It had begun years earlier with Mamet's realization at his niece's Bat Mitzvah that he hadn't been in a synagogue for more than thirty years. The reason, he admitted, had something to do with his sense of assimilation and "perhaps self-hatred that was nobody's fault but my own. And that I thought perhaps I could remedy that" (DMC 172). Other factors included his sense of being marginalized, of being an outsider, which Mamet now saw as a challenge. The way to combat anti-Semitism, religious abuse, or his own neglected Judaism was to become *more* Jewish. Only an aggressive, confident, and determined Judaism, which would stand up for itself out of knowledge, not pity, out of confidence, not self-hatred, mattered. Mamet began to express this in a number of controversial essays including "The Jew for Export," in which he complains that "Jewish actors won acceptance at the cost of shedding a Jewish identity" (MBT 139).[1] Mamet would not, and he began to assume a more active stance, determined to live a Jewish life, not only through a Jewish marriage but through the study of Hebrew and the Hebrew Bible. He realized that a divided sensibility paralyzed the outcast Jew. By contrast, he sought spiritual unity. Rebecca Pidgeon didn't have a chance.

Mamet's recovery of his Judaism had been brewing for some time. Throughout his life, he was aware of his Jewish identity, although it was often submerged by his family's determination to assimilate. This was in contrast to his grandmother Calara's practice, whose Orthodox home he and his family would regularly visit. He soon became aware of the loss of Jewish identity and the gap between traditional practice and the behavior of an assimilated Jew, a member of a Reform synagogue that mixed its "rituals" with received secular behavior, preferring, for example, a trumpet to a shofar to announce the new year (MBT 16). He also found the symbols of Judaism absent from his Chicago boyhood home, a semiconscious effort by his parents to deny or cover up the past. Prejudice in various forms also affected him, as his numerous essays recount.[2] Most important, Mamet recovered pride in being Jewish, religiously, historically, and culturally, a theme that would soon emerge as the pendant to the sense of family loss in his work. His 2002 visit to Israel reinforced his Jewish values, which the militarism and independence of the country underscored. He fiercely admired the nation-state, which he had first visited in 1991.

Mamet's resurgence, of course, did not happen suddenly. Under Kushner's direction, Mamet studied, discussed, debated, and challenged received views of Jewish law and practice. He questioned, judged, and contemplated, sometimes even calling Kushner late at night with questions about biblical interpretation. He also played an active role in his synagogue, regularly attending services and providing unrecognized and substantial financial assistance when it was needed. He took courses, including Hebrew of the Bible, and learned how to read it fluently. In his Jewish education with Kushner, Mamet found the opportunity to debate, rediscover and experience a set of spiritual and intellectual values nothing else could equal.

Kushner first met Mamet and Pidgeon in 1990 when they came to his synagogue to discuss conversion. They were referred to him by another rabbi, who realized they would find Kushner's shul more to their taste. It was Reform but "radically egalitarian." For example, the congregation translated, wrote, edited, and published their own gender-neutral prayer book, one of the first in the Reform movement. The synagogue, west of Boston in the suburb of Sudbury, almost an hour's drive from the Mamet South End home, was also small, limited to 450 families, so Mamet quickly came to know many through his regular participation in Shabbat services. They also eagerly attended Kushner's popular course on introductory Hebrew. Mamet, in particular, learned the language quickly and found a certain excitement in the literal discussions of weekly passages that would find later expression in a book he and Kushner wrote based on their dialogue.

In the Introduction to *Five Cities of Refuge* (2003), Mamet explains the premise: Kushner and himself followed: that "the biblical text always knew more than we did. A passage you suspect may be in error, mistaken, corrupt, incomplete or just plain wrong, offers only two real options: either it's stupid or you are" (FCR ix). This is similar to his approach to dramatic texts (just say the words clearly and the meaning will emerge), explaining that you must not place yourself above the text, because you can no longer be instructed or chastened by it. Literalism reigns but only because you recognize that each word has "*infinite* meaning" (FCR x).

The emergence of the cities of refuge, where one could escape vengeance from accidental transgressions, originated with divine instruction to Moses in the Book of Numbers. There were to be six but because the Pentateuch has only five volumes, Kushner and Mamet followed the Torah, limiting their cities to five. Such asylum was founded in the Hebrew Bible's reference to "cities of solace and safety" (FCR xi). Mamet and Kushner's book, containing written commentary on selected passages, was the product of weekly breakfasts at Johnny's Delicatessen in Newton Centre, Massachusetts, where they would regularly meet, discuss, and exchange interpretations on Torah passages. But sharing material with Mamet meant adopting an almost unconscious application of Mametesque cadences to the passages Kushner noted. It was unavoidable.

For Mamet, the idea of the Bible itself as a refuge is a metaphor that he earlier explored in his essay "The Story of Noach." Beginning with the idea of manifest and latent dreams, he understands the Tower of Babel as the sign of God's wish to scramble the world. But this is only his manifest action. The latent is found in the flood, needed because the imagination and thought of man is always directed to evil. Repentance is not possible. But Noach found grace: he was able to rise above the flood and avoid world destruction. Or, as Mamet writes, "the double-encrypted wish-dream in the Noach story is the memory of the desire to renounce/forget murder" (NOA 62).

Mamet relates this to the message of the Torah: "though we conquer our lower nature once, and at the beginning . . . it will reassert itself, for that's what it is to be human. The clean and unclean animals will be on the ark" (NOA 62). "The Torah time and again and continually informs us that there is a story beneath the story and that every fact of its encryption should compel our interest and study" (NOA 62). This is the interpretative scaffold Mamet walks not only in his biblical studies but in his drama. Situations that on the surface seem self-evident (and are expressed in idiomatic, street language) contain depths.

Judaism, through both its complexity and literalism, became an intense object of study for Mamet, experienced in his life and expressed in his art. In the decade of the nineties, he expressed his Jewish concerns in the following works: *Homicide* (1991), *The Cryptogram* (1994), *Passover* (1995), *The Old Neighborhood* (1997), *The Old Religion* (1997; dedicated to Kushner), *Bar Mitzvah* (1999) and *State and Main* (2000; in this film, the appearance of a Jewish movie producer partly leads to an entire New England town eating Matzo). Narrating a documentary on Yiddish cinema for the National Center for Jewish Film in 1991 was another sign of reasserting his identity as a Jew. A trip to Israel in July 2002 was a capstone to the period, while *Five Cities of Refuge* was a coda to the decade. *The Wicked Son* (2006) a discussion of anti-Semitism, was a continuation.

Passover (1995), an illustrated children's book, confirmed his renewal. Initially the story of a grandmother and granddaughter preparing traditional recipes for the holiday, with the grandmother explaining the significance of each dish and retelling the story of the Exodus in the process, it quickly becomes an occasion for the grandmother to recall the pogrom that nearly killed her family in a Polish village. She explains to her granddaughter how deception saved their lives: she broke the windows, killed the chickens, tossed their blood about and ransacked the rooms to make it look like the house had already been attacked. She and her family then hid outside in the dung pile. It worked: the villagers passed by, believing that others had taken up weapons and destroyed the Jewish home. They survived, like the religion, with new energy and awareness of the importance of their values. The story is one of rediscovery through suffering, a Jewish story, and one that Mamet had himself experienced, although for his characters it ends with a sense of anxiety as the grandmother and child hear a key turning in a door and cling to each other as they anticipate an intruder. The dedicatee of *Passover* is Mamet's daughter, Clara, born the year before.

~

Mamet and Pidgeon were married at Stillington Hall, a rented mansion by the sea in America's oldest seaport, Gloucester, Massachusetts, on September 22, 1991. Mamet and Pidgeon, along with Kushner, wrote their own ceremony. It began with the two of them being brought to either ends of a long table, with bagpipes playing in the background. Their Kituba (marriage contract) was then read aloud and they spoke to one another. The hupa or canopy was then erected at the opposite end of the garden and a procession moved to that area, where they stood under the canopy as the ceremony was performed. Howard Rosenstone, Mamet's agent, was best man.

Al Pacino attended, as well as the producer Michael Hausman, actor Mike Nussbaum, lawyer Alan Dershowitz, and more than 200 others. Kushner later reported to his mother that he had met Pacino. "Isn't he a gangster?" she asked. "No, no he's an actor," Kushner answered. "I have a bad feeling about him. You should stay away from him," she replied. Mamet seemed transformed at the ceremony, according to William H. Macy: "He was completely stripped of all defenses. He stood as pure and alone and defenseless as I've ever seen him. There was a completely open channel from his heart to his mouth." Rebecca Pidgeon, he continued, "had a phenomenal calming effect on him"; Lynn Mamet agreed, reporting that Pidgeon has had "a tremendous effect in anchoring him, in calming him down."[3]

Pidgeon has in fact said that studying with Kushner "affected my entire being" and for her second CD, she wrote an upbeat song called "Jerusalem" that drew clear differences between her staid British upbringing and her new, exuberant Judaism: "In the days . . . when I was a West End kind / gray was the only colour./ Now, I'm going for gold," reads one verse.[4]

Her theology is one of action, akin to Mamet's view of acting: "you can't control your beliefs . . . . we can only control what we do, how we act on it. [Judaism] is not about belief, it's about action." Such imperatives helped her refine her acting style. With Mamet's assistance, she's stripped away "any baggage that I might bring to a performance, to analyze a scene and find a simple, easy-to-do, actable thing, and then concentrate on achieving my goal" (Pidgeon 117).

Her performance in numerous Mamet works from *Oleanna* and the New York production of *The Old Neighborhood* to *The Winslow Boy* and *Boston Marriage*, reveal her to be an actor of depth and determination, more enigmatic, perhaps, than startling. Her understated and then powerful performance as the student in *Oleanna*, her independence and determination as an Edwardian woman in *The Winslow Boy* who saves the family from ruin, and her mysterious smile when she is caught out at the end *The Spanish Prisoner* attest to her presence on stage and screen—and Mamet's fascination with her as an actor. In Mamet's production of J. B. Priestley's psychological mystery *Dangerous Corner*, when her character stops short of revealing an important secret, she simply stands up and smiles. It was a wonderfully simple but moving and emotional moment, the actor Mary McCann remembered (Pidgeon, 118).

In her role as Deeny in *The Disappearance of the Jews*, Pidgeon becomes the matrix of Mamet's personal history, religious identity, and personal life. The character considers the past, tries to start anew, and in the end finds that circumstances force her to make changes. The three plays had their collective premiere in 1997 in Cambridge, Massachusetts, Mamet making numerous changes to the manuscript before and during rehearsal. This reencounter with the past, as the three plays that make up *Disappearance* shows, projects issues involved with Mamet's parents, marriage, and religion that seemed a necessary step before he could reclaim his Judaism.

"Deeny," for example, evokes a Chekhovian vacillation between love and loss, hope and disillusionment: the protagonist talks about seeds and a garden and things righting themselves as she searches for the nurture that has escaped her life. Considering rituals and ceremonies of the past, Deeny tells Bob that it's communities that force you to do certain things, but that you must "undergo the pain of, the pain of, the pain of giving birth to yourself. And that *sorrow of years . . .* " (DOJ 63). This coded statement—like Chekhov, it is the unspoken that reveals—is a kind of recognition that it is "ok" for Mamet to embrace his new Judaism and allows him to embark on a new life with Rebecca Pidgeon. It also confirms that the old life and its confusions are over. Deeny confesses to Bob, "I never knew what you wanted. (*pause*) I thought that I knew" (DOJ 65). But Mamet, in writing this work, now knows.

Other plays of the eighties similarly reflect the new bloom of Judaism, including *Russian-Poland*, and *The Luftmensch*. The first is an unproduced screenplay based on several Hasidic tales by Isaac Luria told to Mamet by Larry Kushner, the title taken from Mamet's grandmother's constant reference to the land of her origin. The tales are framed by three Jewish American volunteers commandeering a plane from the British and flying to pre-Mandate Israel. They share the folktales, set in a Nineteenth-century *shtetl*, before the plane runs out of gas. Mamet read the entire screenplay at a special session of the ninth annual Jerusalem Film Festival in July 2002. *The Luftmensch* (1984), originally a radio play, conveys the world of an older European Jew surviving on the South Side of Chicago who connects with numerous ethnic groups from Poland, Ukraine, and Bosnia, summarized as "gypsies" because of their dislocation. As recounted by two old men who narrate the adventures of the Luftmensch, the rootless, casual wheeler-dealer, without a definite occupation, they reveal his success bonding with these people. He would drink with them, sell to them, and, to the surprise of the two narrators, gain their admiration.

The tough men working in the steel mills respected him. And to him they did not speak the language of exiles: "He spoke to all of them, of course. He spoke all of their . . . . they, you know." But sadly, their languages are gone: "they were never written. The dialects. You see. People refer to them in books. He *spoke* them. European . . . he spoke *Gypsy* . . . . He spoke all their languages. He was a bird" (LUF 39).

In Scene Two of the play, reference is made to a possible coin collection he supposedly had locked away, but that was probably of no value. In the final scene, a monologue, the old man is celebrated as the embodiment of tradition, a person whose friends "were the very people who had over the course of a thousand years destroyed his race" (LUF 43). Yet, he was a "last vestige of Europe. On the Far South Side. He loved the Polish. Who at Home . . . but in a Foreign Soil . . . moved West." In the end, what did he leave us? Very little except that he talked to them and he is missed: "We didn't care that he did not come home. Then but not now. I wish that I had gone with him" is the final, wistful comment of the man known only as "A" (LUF 43).[5]

Perhaps the clearest sign of the state of Mamet's Judaism in the nineties, however, is his 1991 movie, *Homicide*. Written and produced in 1989/90, it deals with anti-Semitism, racism, and the extremes of Jewish activism and consolidated his Jewish attitudes as they were reformulating. Any overview of Mamet's Judaism must include his essays about early Jewish family life in Chicago and *The Disappearance of The Jews*, first performed in 1983 (rev. 1997).[6] *Homicide*, however, dramatically presents his reevaluation of tradition and innovation through the career of Detective Bobby Gold.

"If a man is secluded then he feels superior. Or rage. But where's the good in that?" asks the Man in *Goldberg Street* (GS. 3). This is precisely the question Mamet explores in his third film, which focuses on a self-deluding, self-hating Jew, Gold. It was shot in 1990, a year in which Mamet faced tremendous personal challenges involving his divorce, plans to remarry and the illness of his father. The shooting, in fact, was delayed and switched from Chicago to Baltimore because "David had been through a lot recently, professionally and personally" Joe Mantegna explained. The two had actually talked about the work as early as 1988 when Mamet came across *Suspects*, a novel by William Caunitz, the source of the film adaptation (Man 261).

The final screenplay, completed three years after the project began, bears little resemblance to the novel. Orion films rejected it as being "too Jewish" and because it had departed from the formula-action picture outlined in the source.[7] In a later interview, Mamet explained that in Hollywood, "there are no scripts that are Jewish, only scripts that are too Jewish." Describing how difficult it was to get funding for *Homicide*, he reported that a bunch of Japanese investors, who had never seen a Jew, read the script and concluded, "it's too Jewish." Yet he found everyone in Hollywood used Jewish cadences in their speech and Samuel Goldwynisms like "how did you love it?"[8]

Unashamed of the film's "Jewishness," Mamet pressed ahead, the new confidence originating in his enthusiastic recovery of his Jewish identity, replacing the confusion and repression expressed in essays like "The Decoration of Jewish Homes, "A Plain Brown Wrapper," and "Minority Rights." He wanted to tell a similar story through the character of Detective Bobby Gold who, in a conversation in a diner with Chava, part of a Jewish underground, admits that he has always been considered by his fellow officers weak because he was a Jew:

Gold: All my goddamned life, and I listened to it . . . . I was the donkey. I was the "clown."
Chava: You were the Outsider.
Gold: . . . yes . . .
Chava: . . . I understand.
Gold: They made me the hostage negotiator, 'cause I knew how the bad guys felt. (H 103)

Following this, however, he acts, planting a bomb for Chava that will destroy a model train shop that has been printing anti-Semitic leaflets and possibly housing the headquarters of an anti-Semitic, neo-Nazi movement (H 105–07).

The bombing, however, leads to further pressure on Gold, who must supply the Jewish activists with a list of names he discovered at the back of the candy store. These are the names of several prominent Jews, including the dead woman of the candy store, involved in the illegal procurement of arms. Several of these figures participated in the Israeli War of Independence. The list is now police evidence. He faces a moral dilemma, intensified when he is shown photos of himself entering the model train shop to blow it up taken from a surveillance camera. He realizes that the operation was a sting to get him to release the names on the neo-Nazis' list, then seized as evidence.

At that moment, realizing how his judgment has been compromised, he remembers the trap set for the fugitive Randolph and rushes to the scene to find a gunfight underway, his partner Sullivan wounded. Angered, he goes after Randolph with Sullivan's gun and flashlight but in the chase, loses the gun and is shot as he confronts Randolph, who, before he tries to escape, is surprised to find that Gold will not beg for his life because, as Gold says, "it's not worth anything" (H 120). An unarmed Jew is worth nothing, Randolph replies, but Gold then tells Randolph that his mother turned him over. Sarcastically looking at the wounded detective, Randolph remarks of Gold's wiseguy attitude, 'Oh, you know, huh? One Smart Kike. Ain't cha Mr. Gold?'" (H 121). Earlier in the film, a black assistant to the deputy mayor also called Gold a kike; Gold had to restrain his partner from attacking him (11–12). Now, he lets it go, confirming his statement that "he is a piece of shit," a definitive statement of the self-hating Jew (H 122). Gold is then shot again, but at that point, sniper fire hits Randolph and he dies, Gold compassionately cradling his head.

The choices of Gold—does he accept his Jewishness and participate fully with the Jewish extremists or not?—conflate with the death of his partner and the threat to his own life. Such confusions of identity and action had also been Mamet's until a series of events coalesced in his own life, beginning with his decision to reclaim his Judaism and marry Rebecca Pidgeon who converted. The film marks this symbolically in her role as the young and attractive Miss Klein, *soigné* granddaughter of the murdered shop keeper. Replacing a sense of marginalization was Mamet's sense of Jewish pride and anger at Jewish abuse. But Bobby Gold is caught between what he believes to be the actions of a good cop and what he thinks it means to be a good Jew. This is not so much to test as to demonstrate that fulfillment comes from accepting one's identity even if it means a persistent threat to one's well-being.

Gold's repressed Judaism prevents him from recognizing his own Jewishness, although it does not hide his Jewishness from others. "To the non-cops he's a cop, but to the cops, he's a Jew," Mamet said (W&W 279.). The self-hatred expresses itself almost unconsciously because of his non-identity with fellow Jews. At the home of the grown children of the murdered Mrs. Klein, Gold speaks to a fellow officer on the phone and says, "I'm stuck here with my Jews. You should see this fucken room .... Not ... 'my' people, baby ... *Fuck*'em, there's so much anti-Semitism, last four thousand years, they must be doin *something* bring it about" (H 60–61). This, of course, restates the view expressed by Bobby to Joey in "The Disappearance of the Jews" (ON 15–16). Unknown to him, Miss Klein, the granddaughter of the murdered woman, has overheard Gold and she confronts him: "You're a Jew. *Beat.* And you talk that way. In the house of the dead. *Beat.* (*Softly:*) Do you have any shame?" (H 62). Momentarily, he is speechless. "Do you hate yourself that much?" she asks and all he can say is that he will find the grandmother's killer (H 63).

Hebrew in the film is another sign of Mamet's pronounced Judaism. Visual and spoken Hebrew appear repeatedly to reinforce the Jewish element. The Book of Esther is also referred to, an essential narrative of warning. It reminds us that if Jews are going to be killed, it could as easily happen in the palace (where Esther weaves her story to King Asherius) as on the street. "You can be a Jew or not [but] you're kidding yourself if you think you're going to be protected" Mamet has warned (W&W 295). In the film, Gold encounters the Book of Esther when he meets a young Chasidic scholar in a Jewish library while tracking down the acronym GROFAZ. The scholar tells him that "Esther" is from "Sathar," to *conceal*, but what is concealed? The student shows Gold a Hebrew text but he can't read it. "You say you're a Jew and you can't read Hebrew? What *are* you then . . . ?" he asks the embarrassed officer (H 91). As a denouement to the treatment of language in the story, when Gold later returns to the station and is given an evidence folder, he learns that the acronym GROFATZ was no more than a brand of pigeon feed.

Mamet met Kushner just after he finished *Homicide*, a film Kushner, in fact, found possessed a "Jewish chauvinist undertone," not uncharacteristic of many who return to Judaism late in life, he added. This is the arrogant attitude of a newly minted self-confidence Kushner intimated when he said: "wait a minute, I am a Jew so fuck you; anti-Semites, rot in hell." But, Kushner continued, such a view quickly dissolved as Mamet's spirituality matured.[9]

Actively pursuing his Jewishness became for Mamet an important means of reconciliation, not only with his religion but with his past, especially with his father, who ambivalently rejected (but perhaps secretly longed for) his Jewish past in the face of the drive to assimilate. Mamet at this time began to sympathize more with his father's behavior and gave him a small part and one line in *Homicide*. The father, however, became ill on the chilly set, which may have contributed to his death, although cancer was the main cause. But to Mamet, it was a major blow. At the funeral in July 1991, after the others had thrown the ritual shovelful of dirt on the coffin, Mamet grabbed the shovel and vigorously, if not violently, proceeded to fill up the grave in the boiling sun until at one point his friend Jonathan Katz signaled to him as if to say, "enough already." A sign of the importance of the father/son reunion, however, was the dedication of the script and film of *Homicide*. It simply reads "to the memory of my father."

After their marriage, Mamet and Pidgeon moved to Boston's South End on Dwight Street in the neighborhood known as Eight Streets, described in his essay "My House" from *The Cabin*. It accompanies a short photo essay of his home in *Elle Décor* (April 1993). The space illustrates not just his good taste but his conscious use of the old and honest with the traditional but new. A Steinway piano stands in the music room; his manual typewriter sits atop a Victorian walnut desk in the library, which also has a prayer rug from the Caucasus and a burled walnut secretary. In the dining room are five small, fin-de-siècle views of Jerusalem surrounding an oak table with Windsor chairs made by a Vermont furniture maker. In one hall is a Crimean War field table; in the living room, a bench from the Staten Island ferry acting as a coffee table. The bookcase holds the *Encyclopedia Judaica* among nineteenth-century novels. The solid kitchen table is a two- inch slab of Vermont maple cut from trees on Mamet's own land. A large sign in the kitchen reads "GOOD HOUSEKEEPING is the keynote to Safety," followed by "CLEANLINESS, ORDER and a place for everything are the essentials for SAFETY." The traditional unites with the honestly made.

Homes, of course, are important to Mamet, who has written about them as symbols of his moral, psychological and spiritual journeying in essays like "Memories of Chelsea," "The Cabin," "The Decoration of Jewish Homes," "The New House," "L. A. Homes," and "Domicile." *Oleanna* begins with the attempted purchase of a new home by the professor, John, his failure to acquire it confirmation of his social and professional collapse. In the mid-nineties, Mamet and Rebecca Pidgeon moved to Newton, Massachusetts. In Newton, they purchased a large, three-story colonial-style home on a treed corner, in a residential section on a hill, an unmistakable sign of their preference for tradition and domestic stability (DMC 234). Dominating the corner on the quiet street, the house had a classic white picket fence and a large glassed-in sun room off the living room plus an enclosed back porch.

Mamet concentrated on screenplays in the nineties, completing *Hoffa*, *The Deer Slayer* (based on James Fennimore Cooper's novel), *High and Low* (based on a film by Kurosawa), and *Ace in the Hole*, a poker film originally called *Four Queens* written for Al Pacino. He also took part in a celebrity poker game for *GQ* magazine, writing an analysis of the session with fellow players Martin Amis, Alvin Alvarez, and Anthony Holden.

Cambridge was Mamet's headquarters at this time. Harriet Voyt, a costume designer who did *Oleanna*, *The Old Neighborhood*, and later *The Cryptogram*, became his assistant. The area was familiar to Pidgeon and Mamet: she was born in Cambridge and Mamet had lived in Boston with Lindsay Crouse after they left New York. Crouse had also gone to Radcliffe, and introduced Mamet to the Cambridge artist scene, although Mamet had been aware of it since 1972 when the early St. Nicholas Company performed at the Boston Center for the Arts in the summer.

At his Eliot Street office, Mamet was only a few blocks from the American Repertory Theatre run by his friend Robert Brustein and only a short walk to the Harvard Law School where another friend, Alan Dershowitz, taught. Both would later appear in a trailer for the movie of *Oleanna*, although it was not used. Living within the Harvard-Radcliffe nexus and among the myriad of other universities and colleges in the area exposed Mamet to many of the politically correct attitudes of the late eighties and early nineties. To contest them he wrote his next play, *Oleanna*, premiering on the Harvard campus at the Hasty Pudding Theater on May 1, 1992.

Like *Speed-the-Plow*, the title is confusing. It actually refers to a folk song expressing freedom from slavery, and in the printed version there is a passage from Samuel Butler's *The Way of All Flesh* celebrating the adaptability of young people to circumstances—or dying—as a preface. The short work, labeled agitprop by some, confronts the highly charged feminist atmosphere of the time with the submissive Carol reversing the male power play when, in Act II, she charges her professor John with sexism and then in Act III with sexual assault causing him to loose his tenure and university appointment. The issue presented is the challenge to the power of the male academic. The brutal language and confrontation ignited debate and controversy.

Rebecca Pidgeon starred as Carol, the student, with William H. Macy as John, the professor. Mamet directed and the play was an immediate cause célèbre, the *Boston Globe* headlining its review, "*Oleanna* Enrages—and Engages" (May 2, 1992). The *New York Times* devoted columns to debating the question of sexual harassment and the status of women after the play opened there in October 1992.[10] It ran in New York until January 16, 1994 after 513 performances and 15 previews. Pidgeon and Macy again starred, although eventually Pigeon was replaced by Mary McCann and Macy by Jim Frangione and then Treat Williams. The timing accelerated its notoriety: the first production appeared only six months after the controversial hearings for the appointment of Clarence Thomas to the U. S. Supreme Court. At those hearings, a former student of Thomas's, Anita Hill, accused him of sexual harassment.

Mamet directed, his first venture into stage direction since the triple bill of *Reunion, Dark Pony*, and *The Sanctity of Marriage* in 1979, with the exception of "Cross Patch" for the *Sketches of War* program in October 1988 in Boston. Mamet had been putting his directing energy into film, having done *House of Games* (1987), *Things Change* (1988), and *Homicide* (1991). *Oleanna*, however, was the beginning of a set of plays and projects he would direct including *Ricky Jay and His 52 Assistants* (1994), the Boston production of *The Cryptogram* (1995; Mosher directed the world premiere in London in 1994), *Boston Marriage* (1999), and *Ricky Jay: On the Stem* (2002).

At a rehearsal before the Cambridge opening, Mamet invited Dershowitz, known for his liberal views and defense of difficult cases, to attend and comment on the work. Coincidentally, Dershowitz had just taken over the case of former heavyweight boxing champ Mike Tyson, who'd been accused of rape. Mamet inquired after Tyson and Dershowitz answered that he didn't understand what's happened to him: "He's done this a hundred times before and there's never been any consequences."[11] Asked about his response to *Oleanna*, Dershowitz asked, "How did you live my life for me?" adding that, "it's like a witchhunt here at Harvard. Now I always have somebody in my office when I meet with students." But, Mamet replied, twenty years ago when he was single and teaching he didn't know a professor "who wasn't having an affair with a student." Asked if the battery and attempted rape in the play was plausible, Dershowitz explained that an indictment is not a bill of particulars, only an accusation. One could not bring this case to court as an attempted rape.

In Cambridge, Mamet likely heard various stories of sexual harassment and overbearing political correctness. One account involved a friend, a professor whose position was threatened when charges were brought against him by a student encouraged by her advisor to purse legal action. *Oleanna* in its numerous drafts was already in progress, however, although the story contributed to the immediacy of his drama (W&W 340 n.1). But sexual politics was everywhere and Mamet's topic was dynamite.

The issue between the play's two characters became one of manipulation as much as sexual harassment. Did John in some fashion take advantage of Carol as he tried to correct her distorted views of the course and what he taught? Or did she use him in some fashion that her group turns to political advantage as they accuse him, through her, of a set of "crimes," even including rape? In Act Two, Carol, confronting John, explicitly makes the situation clear, turning from the abstract to the exact:

> Carol: I don't *care* what you feel. Do you see? DO YOU SEE? You can't *do* that anymore. You. Do. Not. Have. The. Power. Did you misuse it? *Someone* did. Are you part of that group? *Yes. Yes.* You Are. You've *done* these things. And to say, and to say, "Oh. Let me help you with your problem . . . ." (OL 50).

John tries to assert *his* rights, but he's overpowered—Act III shows him abject ("I have come to instruct you," Carol announces [OL 67].) and nearly defeated. At the very end, he is faced with extortion—a set of books including his own are to be removed from the university—and then the false charge of rape. He then unleashes his rage, beating her and lifting a chair high over her as she cowers. He suddenly stops and returns to his desk to arrange his papers as she looks up and says, "Yes. That's right," then lowers her head and looks away, murmuring " . . . yes. That's right" (OL 80).

Harold Pinter, for his direction of the Royal Court production in June 1993, chose a different ending, one more psychologically devastating. Rather than threaten to hit Carol with the raised chair, John now sits at his desk and reads out loud the demands and his confession as the play ends. Through a mix-up, Pinter followed an earlier draft of the play, which was longer and had been used at the Cambridge premiere but was discarded for the New York production. According to William H. Macy, this version had a re-choreographed and longer fight. As it lengthened and grew in ferocity, the final speech was cut. Critics, however, preferred the Pinter version over the Mamet/New York revision *because* it was less physical.[12]

Reaction to Mamet's play was extreme. Dershowitz predicted audiences would be divided and among those who will love it, many will say they hate it. "I identify with your professor. And she ruined her case the moment she showed him that list (of books he had to stop teaching)" said Dershowitz. "He could take that to the tenure board and say this woman is extorting me." Replacing the sexuality of the first act is the anger of the second. "Seeing something is so different from having it explained."

From the first, the play was explosive, inciting feminists and others to protests, shouting and even threatening the actors during productions. Mamet himself got swept up in the melees that often occurred outside the stagedoor, at one point engaging in hostile comments with several feminists from Brown University after a dress rehearsal in late April 1992. The next morning, he called Harold Pinter to relay his vocal encounter, telling him he "nearly lost it" (W&W 340 n.2). At another performance, cadets from the U. S. Coast Guard academy stood and cheered when John hit Carol. Early in the Cambridge run, a group of Harvard professors stood up and booed at the end. In New York on press night, some audience members were so upset they approached the stage and shouted obscenities at Pidgeon. "Misogynist" was a common epithet hurled at Mamet and others supporting the play. And premiering in Cambridge was "like doing 'The Diary of Anne Frank' in Dachau," Mamet said (Stayton 45). But power, not sexual harassment, Mamet insisted, was its subject (W&W 342 n. 6.)

~

Mamet now felt he wanted to acknowledge the intricacies and disappointments of rural life. *The Village*, his 1994 novel, reflects this. It tells the story of Henry, who in an epiphany realizes the uselessness of his life and his inability to change it. Daily life in the small community brings dark thoughts. Only in a set of self-made dramas do the characters live. The twelve sections of the novel cover roughly a year in a remote but unidentified Vermont town. Nature, hunting, and guns are the focus of the mostly male characters who admire the animals they track because they live by instinct. Seeking to understand the natural world is their gesture toward some form of spiritual unity. Process, however, holds meaning for these characters, who are also fearful of the unknown: "every certainty concealed its opposite," he writes (VIL. 56). Chekhov and Hemingway influence the text, the minimal dramatic action occurring off stage, whether it is the disappearance of a woman, a boy falling to his death, or a marriage that dissolves. Elliptical thoughts and speech describe the work, in which unspoken experience seems the purest in a world where identify only takes the form of pronouns. Full ideas never seem to emerge and clarifying moments are few.

Rebecca Pidgeon easily took to the outdoor, small-town life of Cabot and the regular visits to antique fairs, neighbors, and the River Run Café in nearby Plainfield. This institution in the tiny village (pop. 1,300) is one of several artisanal eateries in the area, a center for bakers, organic farmers, and cheese makers. The best bakery, for example, is that of a former Goddard philosophy professor, Jules Rabin. An Argentinian-born puppeteer, New York refugees from the specialty grocer, Zabar's, and a New England novelist were everyday visitors to the River Run, which has been a post office, speakeasy, and barbershop.[13] Mamet's comfort in a world of post-and-beam houses made of first-growth pumpkin pine, hand hewn and framed without nails is genuine. But he acknowledges a conflict. In the city, language is profane and swaggering, but in the country one is to say what one means. But these different two worlds, Chicago and Cabot, are necessary for his work.

For Mamet, the establishment of a Jewish life and marriage gave him a new freedom and confidence to confront Jewish issues, from anti-Semitism to Zionism, which had remained unsettled for him. He addressed them in a number of works in the late nineties, beginning with *The Cryptogram* (family), *The Old Religion* (anti-Semitism), and *The Old Neighborhood* (the past), continuing with *Five Cities of Refuge* (the Torah), *Romance* (Arab/Israeli peace), and *The Wicked Son* (Jewish self-hatred).

But throughout this period, Mamet relished the idea of the tough Jew. Mamet did not invent this notion but capitalized on it in terms of imagery if not fact. In his Jewish characters—think of Bobby Gould, the Hollywood mover and shaker in *Speed-the-Plow*—he promotes the idea of the aggressive, in-your-face Jew who will not back down. A tough Jew is not a victim, but an active, potentially violent figure, a position Mamet has increasingly assumed and defended. His recent collection of essays, *The Wicked Son*, reaffirms this posture. Jewish endurance, which so impressed Nietzsche, has been surpassed by an aggressive, physical Judaism. It is no surprise Mamet wrote the screenplay for the HBO film *Lansky* (1999) starring Richard Dreyfus, a work about the Jewish mobster. Preceding it was *Hoffa*, a 1992 film about the Detroit teamster, incorporating the renegade dynamics of masculine power underlined by a new, Jewish violence. Danny DeVito directed, making several changes to Mamet's script ("I got David to finish his sentences."). Jack Nicholson starred. The analysis of American life in the film is clear. Hoffa asks a young truck driver, "What does everybody want?" but before he can answer, Hoffa shouts, "ALL THERE IS" (Hoffa 5).[14]

The image of the tough Jew originated with the Maccabees and continued to the Mossad—in biblical terms, moving from Joseph, Moses, Joshua, Samson, and David to the present. Chicago was part of its modern origin, the home of the legendary Jewish boxer and world lightweight and welterweight champion, Barney Ross, as well as the Jewish gangster Earl "Hymie" Weiss, killed in October 1925 in an ambush organized by Al Capone. More recently, the loan shark Herb Blitzstein continued the tradition: starting in Chicago, he moved his operations to Las Vegas, where he died in January 1997 after taking three bullets to the head.[15]

Chicago's West Side, with Maxwell Street its center, was often thought the heart of the Jewish crime scene. A 1906 account reports that "from Maxwell come the smoothest robbers, burglars and thieves of all kinds." Al Capone's financial adviser Jacob "Greasy Thumb" Guzik was a Maxwell Street graduate (Fried 90, 116). Being Jewish and a gangster meant the ultimate acceptance: "my uncle . . . use to be a gangster. You can't get any more assimilated than that" says a Jewish writer in an Ishmael Reed novel.[16] That Mamet should have written the screenplay for *The Untouchables* should come as no surprise. The Chicago journalist Ben Hecht wrote the prototype, *Scarface* (1932).

But if the tough Jew was part of Mamet's past, so was the family, which *The Cryptogram* (1994) re-opened. As Donny explains to the young boy John, "things occur. In our lives . . . the meaning of them . . . is not clear" (CRP 49). The focus is the fragile unity of the family, something Mamet experienced, but which he was trying to restore through his relationship with Rebecca Pidgeon, who was pregnant with their first child, Clara, at the time. Clara was born on September 29, 1994, exactly three months to the day after *The Cryptogram* had its world premiere in London. Secure in his newly discovered love with Pidgeon and the start of a new family, Mamet is able to dramatize its opposite, a world of faithlessness and deception. Chicago 1959 is the setting (the actual year his parents divorced) as the play reveals adult betrayal through a child's eyes. The subject becomes the double deception of the child and the mother.

The Old Religion (1997), Mamet's novel of the real life Southern lynching of Leo Frank, the Jewish manager of an Atlanta pencil factory where Mary Phagan, a white twelve-year-old factory worker, was raped and murdered, outlines many of the issues he was confronting with his renewed Judaism. Rabbi Larry Kushner is the dedicatee. It is an elliptical account of the New York born Frank's adjustment to the South and his arrest and trial (the actual Frank was born in Texas and grew up in Brooklyn). Most important, perhaps, is the hero's own rediscovery of his Jewishness. Mamet opens in 1868 with the newspaper story of a Jewish child in Spain baptized for its protection and echoing the plot of Mamet's early play, *Marannos*. Tales of anti-Semitism throughout the South instigated by the Ku Klux Klan frame the narrative of Frank's life in Atlanta and his half-hearted attempts to understand his Judaism initiated at a Passover seder. A domestic rather than dramatic novel, Mamet nonetheless intercuts questions of Jewish identity and an almost idyllic portrait of family life, with moments during Frank's trial (OR 26).

Uncertainty, however, vies with undercurrents of anti-Semitism as Mamet builds the tension. At one point Frank thinks "we cloth ourselves in rectitude to hide our shame" (OR 35). At another moment, he recognizes the irony in the name National Pencil Company, inappropriate for a company that has set up business in the South. Advertising, writing, even the typewriter become elements of communication that occupy Frank's mind. Another current is the justification of the actions of the vigilante group, even when they violate the law, something Mamet links to the need to belong (OR 56–7, 186; in *The Wicked Son* he will repeat this view). Running throughout the novel is a sense of fate, as Frank questions which of his actions led to his arrest, trial, and eventual murder. Indirectly, Mamet recounts the events, sustaining the drama by keeping it mostly "off stage," as is the action, which largely occurs in Frank's mind. But as the trial begins, when Frank knows he is assumed guilty even before it starts, we sense his fate. Mamet then introduces a rabbi to guide Frank's rediscovery of Judaism underscored by his study of Hebrew (OR 85–87, 137–9, 164–70).[17] Yet the "ritual torment" continues until its violent but surprisingly truncated end when he is kidnapped from a prison hospital, castrated and lynched. The final indignity is a photograph of the hanging body turned into a postcard and sold throughout the South (93, 193). Frank was officially cleared of any wrongdoing in 1986.

Mamet's use of a flat style and placid tone deemphasizes the violence and brutality of Frank's life, while actually increasing the tension. Matching this is the novel's "patient" structure, one that slowly steps toward its known end: Frank pays remarkable attention to minutiae, whether it is tea or texts: "Who would know that the dot had not been placed on the i at the time the word was written?" (OR 157). His reading reflects Mamet's, consisting of a Hebrew primer, *Les Misérables*, the Torah in Hebrew and English, and three novels by Trollope. In a way, but with less anger and romanticism, *The Old Religion* is another version of Mamet's *Native Son*, both texts equally focused on racial violence and discrimination.

The novel is engrossing not only for the treatment of the Frank case but for the way it offers a glimpse of the dilemma of Judaism: "How can those who are not Jews understand Jews?" Frank asks (OR 178). Mamet's own state of Jewish desire and awareness find expression in the novel. Mamet tells the story in a kind of stream of consciousness manner, paying more attention to reactions than events. Frank's attempts to reconcile his own fragile faith and Judaic teachings with the injustice of the situation becomes the focus. Jewish life in the South, rather than actual history, takes precedence with Chekhovian exchanges of conversation and action. Interspersed with background events are flashforwards to the trial and its aftermath. Bigotry, injustice, and fear dominate Mamet's account.

Mamet broadens his novel through his focus on the American economy and its growing consumerism. Frank, for instance, considers the impact of advertising, its appeal "to the fear that one is to be excluded" (OR 48). Frank contemplates his life as a Jew in a Christian culture, the ironic ending stressing his transformation into a commodity, an object on the consumer marketplace: his photograph "sold for many years in stores throughout the South" (OR 194). Mamet titles one chapter "The power of advertising," its equivalent the representation of the press in Richard Wright's novel. More important is Frank's reevaluation of his own spiritual identity as he examines his life and his relation to Judaism. To believe that logic and justice will prevail is nothing but naive, he realizes: racism and anti-Semitism are unavoidable. The forceful topic with its elements of victimization and abuse were suited to Mamet's moral vision as Frank emphasizes that "'there is no certainty. None at all. None. . . . Our shame of our lack of worth. It's all chance. All of it'" (OR 34–5).

The novel had a modest critical reception, although Alfred Kazin, an astute critic of American literature, took issue with the book and Mamet's inventions. Kazin called the book "a terrible work of Jewish jingoism," "maddingly nationalist."[18] Kazin pointed out that the Southern demagogue Tom Watson was responsible for Frank's murder, Watson a rabid hater of Jews, blacks and Catholics. His weekly magazine contained relentless attacks on Frank but neither Watson nor the perjured testimony that led to Frank's death sentence appear in Mamet's novel. Nor the mass panic that seized the Jews of Atlanta at the time.

In Mamet one gets more drama than novel because he sacrifices any social or historical context that might explain Frank's demise. "Gulps of dialogue" intensify the fragmented narrative. Because most of the story is told through Frank's mind, it allows Mamet to make "grandiose indictments," notably of the American legal system and the Gentile world (Kazin 36). All the novel stresses is the Jew as a victim expressed through a simplified consciousness. He also makes errors of fact. Citing a Nineteenth-century case of a Jewish child in Bologna secretly baptized by his nurse and claimed by the Church, Mamet's hero wonders why the Spanish government does not act. Why Spain? Italy was where it happened. Mamet even gets the date wrong: the baptism occurred in 1858 not in 1854 as he writes. Mamet also says Mary Phagan was murdered in 1915. She was killed in 1913.

Mamet's "paranoid vision of the non-Jewish world" seems to absolve him of creating real characters writes Kazin (37). This effects the very core of the novel and its overriding theme: Christians are not to be trusted by the Jews; neither is the U.S. government. Jews can only trust the old religion. Jewish chauvinism in the work, Kazin concludes, is at best unacceptable, at worse repugnant.

The Old Neighborhood (1997) is parallel in that it also dramatizes Mamet's reengagement with his Jewish past. The three plays—"The Disappearance of the Jews," "Jolly," and "Deeny"—confront (and at times exaggerate) the loss and then renewal of Jewish faith he himself was undergoing while exposing the doubts, contradictions, and coverups that had previously defined his family and spiritual life. Joey in the play believes the *shtetl* would have made him happy; Bobby corrects his romantic vision by reminding him about its deprivations. Joey then recalls Chicago "when my folks came here . . . to Orchard Street . . . you know, to Maxwell Street . . . to pushcarts . . . to . . . ." The realistic Bobby cuts him off with "we wouldn't have liked it" (ON 21). Conversation then turns to Hollywood and its Jewish studio heads and who was, and who wasn't, Jewish. It concludes with Joey frustrated: "I can't get it up. I'm going to die like this. A schmuck. *(Pause)* All of this stuff I'd like to do. I'll never do it." Bobby matches him, saying he invents ceremonies but can "never keep them up" (ON 24, 26). Desire meets disappointment, which in the second and third plays gestures toward resolution. First performed in Cambridge in 1997 with Rebecca Pidgeon as Deeny, *The Old Neighborhood* later went to Broadway with Patti LuPone playing the role of Jolly.

Romance (2005) continued Mamet's preoccupation with anti-Semitism. The courtroom farce mixes obscenity and racial epithets insulting Jews, Arabs, Christians, homosexuals, and liberals. In the second scene, the defense attorney inadvertently reveals his anti-Semitism (he's defending a Jewish chiropractor) when he refers to "this sick Talmudic, Jewish . . . " (ROM 37). He quickly apologies but faces a virulent attack by his client and a series of scatological references interrupted by the bailiff asking if they want lunch (ROM 39). The exchange continues ("Fuck *you*, you Rug Merchant, Greasy, Hooknosed, *no*-dick, Christkilling, son-of-a bitch sacrilegious . . . " provides some idea of the tone [ROM 41]). The purpose of the exchange, against the backdrop of possible peace talks between the Arabs and Jews, is to remind audiences that anti-Semitism and racism are real.

Mamet's aggressive Judaism, developed further in *The Wicked Son*, may be symptomatic not only of his cultivation of the tough Jew stance but a reaction to the paranoia that the whole world wants the Jews dead. But the paranoia and the Jewish world view merge. Jews must either die or kill. "Violence is a lovely and legitimate expression of Jewish identity" and Mamet is one of a "long line of Jews who owe their Jewishness entirely to anti-Semitism" writes Leon Wieseltier.[19] Mamet makes it more virulent, however, by adding a gender primitiveness to an ethnic primitiveness. Only Jewish men, it seems, can achieve this triumph. Jewishness is not for sissies in Mamet's world. It is another form of virility. But as Wieseltier points out, this identification with the oppressed is "really an identification with the oppressor."

Mamet's visit to Israel in July 2002 as guest of the Jerusalem Film Festival—he had been there in 1991 when he presented *Homicide*—is a fulcrum for many of his ideas. In his article "'If I forget Thee, Jerusalem,'" he details his reaction to the country, beginning with the visible separations that surround the Old City. Concern over the second intifadah creates worry. At a Shabbat lunch with friends from Newton, Massachusetts, now in Israel, he meets Michael B. Oren, author of *Six Days of War: June 1967* and of an article he had just read on Orde Wingate, philo-Semitic British officer. Mamet is "overcome by a sense of grief" as the group talks of Jerusalem, the war, and a sister-in-law killed in a recent bombing.

Mamet then focuses on the critical and oft-repeated question of how can a Jew remain in the Diaspora given the significance and constant threats to Israel? "How, I wonder, can I not be here; and how is it possible that I did not come here in my youth . . . instead of wasting my time in show business? I am full of grief . . . ."[20] The trauma of nostalgia reveals, however, an inability to face the present, which he harshly sees as "an aging Diaspora Jew on a junket, and that my cheap feelings of personal loss could better be expressed as respect and homage." Israel is, and always has been, at war he concedes, but "Israel, at war, looks very much like Israel at peace." Life, however, does go on and 9,000 attended the opening of the Jerusalem Film Festival. Mamet, invited to the podium for the official opening, offered "*Shalom, chaverim*" ("Hello, companions") to the crowd.

In Israel, even the old look young to him. He tours bomb sites, meets relatives of the founders of the first art school for the state, and travels through Jerusalem with the then mayor and now prime minister, Ehud Olmert. At one point they stand outside the Sbarro pizzeria on King George Avenue where a suicide bomber killed fifteen people in August 2001. He recalls posters with British soldiers in khaki charging off but in the foreground another soldier uses his bayonet to free a Jewish prisoner. "You have let me free; now let me set others free" reads one caption. But the superscription in one poster in English, the other in Yiddish reads, "Jews love liberty and will fight for it," but below is the directive that Britain expects every son of Israel to do his duty—"Enlist with the Infantry Reinforcements."

In his article, Mamet considers the divide between imaginary and real Jews. The world loves the imaginary, which include Anne Frank, the Warsaw Ghetto fighters, and the movie stars in *Exodus*. They willingly die heroically "as a form of entertainment," he writes. The plight of real Jews, however, has been more problematic. In Israel there are "*actual* Jews, fighting for their country." The Western world seems confused between the two. The true debt Jews and others of the West owe to those in Israel is one of personal accountability: "If you love the Jews as victims, but detest our right to statehood, might you not ask yourself 'why?' That is your debt to the Jews." Why, he wonders, has "the Western press embraced anti-Semitism as the new black?" His visit refocused his deeply felt identity and determination to confront prejudice.

In an interview with *The Jerusalem Post* at the Mount Zion Hotel, Mamet draws attention, not by his bravado, but by his Hawaiian shirt. He discusses his American Jewish past, an upbringing in what he calls an "Episcopal Reform Temple" where a doctor not a rabbi officiated. At the Film Forum, the reason for his visit, he began by offering Jewish jokes, but on the Sunday night of his visit, at the Khan Theatre in Jerusalem, the joking stopped. There he movingly read the entire unproduced screenplay *Russian-Poland.*[21] The time of his visit was dangerous, however. Yet despite the terror—four people had just been killed in a double suicide bombing in Tel Aviv and eight more in a bus ambush outside the West Bank—when the festival opened at the Sultan's Pool Amphitheater, the crowd overflowed and Mamet, welcomed as a sign of personal courage, disarmingly shrugged and said he "came only for the popcorn."[22]

The year after his 1991 Israel visit, Mamet began to work on *The Cryptogram*, which premiered in London in June 1994. A line in the play suggests something of the internal pressure he faced: "A human *being* . . . cannot conceal himself" (CRP 5). Engaging with domestic issues of loss, love, and home that long occupied Mamet's psyche, the play is an important text that is another measure of his increasing well-being. The play is a response to the desperate plea of Del, the middle-aged gay man and friend of John's mother, Donny, when he cries "if we could speak the truth . . . . for one instant. Then we would be free" (CRP 54). Like the domestic "tools" boxed up for the camping trip or the movers, from John's slippers to a blanket, the truth is boxed up and sealed but needs to be unwrapped. But unwrapping sometimes exposes secrets better left hidden. Donny echoes this harsh knowledge when she says, "if I could find *one man*. In my life. Who would not betray me . . . " (CRP 57).

John awaits the return of his father to take him on a camping trip. But will he come home? Will the trip go off as scheduled? Is there anything forgotten? Good intentions remain unacted and in Mamet's world do not work out. Domestic items get damaged: Donny breaks the tea pot, John may have torn a blanket, none of it intentional. A German survival knife (purchased, not won, in the war by John's father) is the most symbolic and powerful item to be "unwrapped," although it is in Del's possession, not his father's. The knife, however, creates confusing identities, although it quickly becomes apparent that Del has lied to Donny. Robert did not give him the knife when they were camping, In fact, Del was given the knife to keep him quiet about their *not* going camping. Robert, in fact, used Del's hotel room supposedly to meet a woman. Del then prompts John to return to bed, but as he finally goes up the omnipresent stairs, John sees a note on the mantle, which he gives to his mother. It is from her husband Robert saying he is leaving her. Act I ends.

The next night, John talks to his mother expressing his worry that "We don't know what's real. And all we do is *say* things" (CRP 30). Del then enters reporting that he has not found Robert. John still can't sleep, in fact doesn't want to sleep because every time he does, he sees things, and in his anxiety over his father *not* appearing asks, "what's happening to me . . . " (CRP 34)? The true story of the knife emerges, as is Robert's using Del's hotel room. Act III, one month later, shows the room nearly empty with items packed for moving. And again, Donny tries to explain to her son that "Things occur. In our lives. And the meaning of them . . . the *meaning* of them . . . is not clear . . . . but we assume . . . . That they *have* a meaning. We . . . (*Pause.*) We *have* to because . . . " (CRP 49). Del appears and returns the knife to give to John because he feels he wronged him. Thought to be a combat trophy, Donny quickly tells the boy the knife was bought in London and not a trophy at all. It, too, is a deception, its meaning a lie, symbolizing the destructiveness and emptiness of male bravado.

Donny, bothered again by John's reappearance, failure to sleep and Del's return to apologize, screams from her own self-pity that she only gives to others and that all men cheat: "You *lied* to me. I love you, but I can't like you. You lied," perhaps the central Mamet dilemma that his characters reencounter (CRY 59; the line echoes the supposed comment of Mamet's mother to his sister of loving but not liking her).

"Can't you see that I need comfort?" John then asks as his mother rejects him and he can't locate a blanket (CRP 60). At that point, Del gives him the knife so that he can cut the twine on the box where the blanket is, symbolically transferring the presence of the father to the son. But he finds little response from his mother, who may even feel that her own son has betrayed her, at least in the response to her feelings (CRP 60). The halting staccato delivery of the half-finished sentences in the play formalize the emotional restraint and coverups. But the child will never understand why he is being treated this way. For Mamet, the play might be the expression of the game Del suggests John play with his father while camping: the recollection game to see who has the best memory, but in *The Cryptogram*, all is deception.

Response to the play was at first confused. Critics complained about its underwritten quality and that it seemed all preparation and no action. Several, however, recognized the broader theme of how we seem to be held spiritually captive by evasions and disguises and identified certain autobiographical elements. Michael Billington in the *Guardian* made comparisons to Pinter's *Betrayal*. Mosher's direction succeeded in creating a great deal of tension, with the minimalist material achieving a fluidity of performance that often eludes Mamet when he directs. Mosher knows how to remove clunky conversational mannerisms, wrote Ian

Stuart in *Newsday*, although not the clichés that often litter the text, words becoming as dysfunctional as the people.[23]

Mamet himself directed the play in its North American debut seven months after London at the Walsh Theatre in Boston, later opening in New York at the Westside Theatre/Upstairs. The expressionless delivery and exaggerated pauses that defined his acting style, however, were criticized, although they did emphasize even greater distances between the characters. His direction was described as cool, formal, and rigid as he emphasized a cadence that was almost operatic in its ordered recitation and formalized tableaux of the characters on the stage. Nonetheless, Felicity Huffman won an Obie Award for her performance of Donny, showing both the injustice and just cause of her character's condition. The Edward Hopper-style set gave dark omniscience to the staircase John variously ascended and descended.

Mamet said of the play that it was "a message in code . . . my idea was that memory is a message in code, like a dream is a message in code, and also a play is a message in code" (DMC 150). Previously, he thought the domestic scene was "best left to anyone else but me . . . . [but] as I started cruising into middle age, I thought, well perhaps I would address that, that galaxy as the psychologists say, a little bit more directly" and sought to decode "the message of one's childhood" (DMC 151). The origin of the play was in fact not the young boy but the breakup of the marriage, concerned first with the relationship between the woman and her friend and then the boy and his sleeplessness. Asked if he was drawing from his own experiences in writing the play, Mamet coyly answered, "I don't know. I, I seem to have had a childhood . . . " (DMC 151). He does acknowledge, however, that deception is at the core of the work and that "every tragedy's based on deception; that's the meaning of . . . the tragic form . . . something has been hidden and can only be uncovered," but at a cost (DMC 153). Critics of a 2006 production at the Donmar Warehouse in London starring Kim Cattrall (of *Sex and the City* renown), praised the intensity and honesty of the play.[24]

"Take the knife and go" are Del's final words to John at the end of *The Cryptogram* (CRP 61). And in a sense they are directions for Mamet, who four years later titled his lectures on theatre *3 Uses of the Knife, On the Nature and Purpose of Drama* (1998), originally delivered as the Columbia [University] lectures on American Culture that year. Given Mamet's preference for cutting texts *and* his habit of collecting knives, the choice of his title is not unusual. What he attempts in the lectures is an extension of his work of the year before, *True and False, Heresy and Common Sense for the Actor*. That collection offered a set of unorthodox ideas on theatre practice, including:

> The audience will teach you how to act and the audience will teach you how to write and to direct (TF 19).
>
> The study of acting consists in the main of getting out of one's own way . . .
> and being comfortable being uncomfortable (TF 19–20).

An actor should never be looking inward (TF 111).
In life there is no emotional preparation for loss, grief, surprise, betrayal, discovery; and there is none onstage either (TF 33).
Show business is and has always been a depraved carnival. Just as it attracts the dedicated, it attracts the rapacious and exploitative . . . . (TF 50).

Advice to young and experienced actors balances with comments on auditions, agents, Hollywood, and the fundamental role of the audience and how they create pleasure for an actor. Uplifting as well as exhortative, in *True and False* Mamet tells his reader/actors, "it is not necessary to barter your talent, your self-esteem and your youth for the *chance* of pleasing your inferiors" (TF 50). Idealistically, he challenges them to go their own way: "form your own theatre company . . . write and stage your *own* plays . . . make your *own* films." Why? Because only in that way will you have a greater chance of "presenting yourself to, and eventually appealing to, an audience by striking out on your own." Only by doing your own work will you make an impact. But as the book goes forward, Mamet loses interest in the techniques of acting and grows more preoccupied with the theatre person as an individual. Joe Mantegna, Mamet acting pro, expressed many of these ideas when he said of Mamet's directorial style, "you invent for yourself who those people [on stage] are" (Man 253). Mamet doesn't waste hours on explanation.

3 Uses of the Knife (1998), Mamet's February 1997 lectures given to packed audiences at Miller Theatre and Low Library, Columbia University, varied from the authorship of Shakespeare's plays to the nature of the problem play—dark, realistic dramas dealing with social issues or, in Mamet's words, "melodrama cleansed of invention" (THR 14). Politics, nationhood (especially Israel), and war all contribute to his worldview: "we live in an extraordinarily debauched, interesting, savage world, where things really don't come out even." "The purpose of true drama," he adds, "is to help remind us of that" (THR 20–1). He then enigmatically writes that tragedy is a celebration of the truth, not individual triumph: "it is not a victory but a resignation" (THR 21).

Throughout *3 Uses of the Knife*, Mamet declaims his ideas on social power and theatrical purpose. He prefers a contrarian's position ("I don't believe reaching people is the purpose of art" [TRH 27]) and, while some of the observations are trenchant, others are commonplace ("Politics . . . sticks closer to traditional drama than does The Stage itself"; "Our time in the theatre . . . is precious"; "The purpose of art is not to change but to delight" (THR 23, 25, 26). He again privileges the audience, writing that never has he met an audience "that wasn't collectively smarter than I am, and didn't beat me to the punch every time" (THR 25). Truth in drama is also secondary to elements germane to the hero's quest, the ineffable object sought by the protagonist (THR 29–30).

Allusions and reference are diverse: Beckett, O. J. Simpson, Aristotle, Disneyland, Tolstoy, Hitchcock, Brecht, and foreign policy. But they also distract from creating any sustained argument. His self-assured manner presides, as well as his belief that "a good writer throws out the stuff that everybody else keeps"—revised to read "a good writer keeps the stuff everybody else throws out" (THR 51).

3 Uses of the Knife is essentially a forum for Mamet to present his views on culture, society, and playwriting, especially the challenges of the second act. Interspersed among the declarations, however, are occasional insights: "it is not that great art reveals a great truth, but that it stills a conflict—by *airing* rather than rationalizing it" (THR 46). His essential critique is that art has become entertainment in a culture that values control. The desire to create becomes the wish to amuse (THR 53). Self-censorship reigns and it must be opposed. In the name of information, we accept ignorance and illiteracy (THR 55). The information age is centralizing knowledge and making it liable to despotic control; consequently, there can be no art in information, as there is no love in the arms of a prostitute (THR 59).

Only in his final lecture, "3 Uses of the Knife," does Mamet return to language and the natural use of iambic pentameter in dialogue (THR 66). Here, he gets to the three uses of the knife, beginning with Leadbelly's song that you first use a knife to cut bread so that you'll have strength to work; you next use it to shave to look nice for your lover; and you finally use it cut out her lying heart when you find her with another man (THR 66). The knife equals the bass line in music, for it is that line, not the melody, that gives music strength and that moves us. The treble is arbitrary, unless coupled with the bass.

The purpose of theatre is not to repair the social fabric but "to inspire cleansing awe" (THR 69). It is also ritual, necessary to our survival. The goal of drama should be truth, previously overlooked or disregarded. The audience at the end remembers the earlier thwarted or misdirected attempts to find a solution and how they had been wrong. Until the end. Then all is made whole and we see that the accidental was essential. Digressive, diverse, and at times distracting, *3Uses of the Knife* defends drama's ability to resolve conflict and in so doing, renew our own sense of self and ability to confront and overcome challenges.

As a director, however, Mamet was criticized for doing more with less: Mamet the playwright was now in the grip of Mamet the director, argued some critics. And the plays, especially since he had turned his creative energy to film, were getting the worst of it—that is, he was turning out minor work without the edge of his earlier drama. The playwright, however, seemed to know more than the director, the crucial secret that "all meaningful plays are mystery plays." But his direction works to demystify his plays offering performances that are stilted, fixed, uninvolving. Ironically, he commented that directors are superfluous and "most often get in the way of the actors" (DMC 213). The social reality of getting heard, even for the unsayable, overrides the mystery. Even violence itself is said rather than enacted, *Edmond* a possible exception. Mamet the playwright seems to know things that Mamet the director does not, although they both seek the elliptical in plot and dialogue. This becomes a means of involving the viewer: "I'm always trying to keep it spare" in order to let the audience figure it out. As the editor of his first film said, "'you start with a scalpel and you end with a chainsaw.' I think that's true of writing too. For me the real division between a serious writer and an unserious one is whether they're willing to cut."[25]

In *The Cryptogram*, the mysteries of the photograph, the blanket, and even a tea kettle, cut off from their history, become puzzles that Mamet never explains. Their significance can only come about through the accretion of one with another, not alone. Their individual meaning escapes because language inadequately conveys their significance, which Mamet's direction also obscures because of its flatness. Stand and speak is the reductive expression of his technique. Or in Mamet's words, one must only "open the mouth, stand straight, and say the words bravely—adding nothing, denying nothing, and without the intent to manipulate anyone: himself, his fellows, the audience. To learn to do that is to learn to act" (TF 22). For Mamet, the claim of nonmanipulation has a psychological as well as theatrical origin. He grew up in a manipulative home that he grew to detest; in seeking to rid himself of it, he initiated a theory of acting free from such behavior. Acting had to be honest, immediate, and rely only on the text without emotional input.

Mamet's approach does not eliminate actors, but they must be themselves: do not "*pretend* to the difficulties of the written character," he insists. Such acting is dishonest. The actor must forge a character within oneself because in the end it is "*your* character which you take onstage" (TF 22, 39). The actor is only "to communicate the play to the audience. That is the beginning and the end of his and her job" (TF 9). Clarity in acting, "living truthfully under the imaginary circumstances of a play," is Mamet's goal (PHA 8).

On stage the actor should receive a minimal amount of direction, nothing more than the prerequisites of enunciation without pretense. Mamet believed that the through-line, understood by the actors, should be enough. Acting, he writes in "Realism," as well as direction, should "consist only of that bare minimum necessary to put forward the action" (WR 132). Understandably, this makes audiences uncomfortable, turning his productions into acted-out writings, words without emotion. There is little in Mamet's staging that is ambiguous or suggestive; rather, it's economical and clipped. An emotional flatness rules as his direction of the American Repertory Theatre's (ART) production of *The Cryptogram* (February 1995) showed.

Rather than express a confused and angry woman, as the script suggests, Donny in the ART production became cold and narcissistic, although more the center of the play than in its London premiere. There, the child was the focus. But in this production, Felicity Huffman, as Donny, carried the emotional weight, displaying a precise if not fierce assurance when she spoke the elliptical lines, perhaps the epitome of a Mamet-directed character. A figure in J. B. Priestley's *Dangerous Corner*, which Mamet also directed in 1995, identifies what Mamet opposed in his acting and directing style. The character remarks that "we . . . spend too much of our time telling lies and acting them." Mamet's goal is to eliminate the lies by revealing the truth of the actor, although it may be "about as healthy as skidding round a corner at sixty."[26]

Discrepancies between Mamet's principles of acting and film, however, are evident in his film version of *Oleanna* (1994). In his directing, the actors seem "staged," the feeling claustrophobic, the action undramatic. Mamet seems to have neglected his own advice from *True and False*: "The classroom will teach you how to obey, and obedience in the theatre will get you nowhere" (TF 19). Paradoxically, Mamet's obedience to drama has freed him from the theatre, but the practice of film has not broadened his art. In the film of *Oleanna*, the cut and thrust of the dialogue, the intensity of the limited action, has been diminished. Mamet seems not to realize that his concept of directing, "that bare minimum necessary to put forward the action" avoiding "embellishment," does not work in film (WR 132). The visuality of the screen demands more to see. He also seems to contradict his notion that movement is the core of acting; in *Oleanna*, his characters are almost always idle (WR 133). The reliance on uninflected jump cuts to produce juxtapositions of meaning results in a neutral experience for the viewer (ODF 2). Furthermore, telling a story in film by contrasting images without visual explaining, a principle borrowed from Eisenstien, creates gaps if not fissures. Viewers need orientation.

Acting in the film follows Mamet's imperative to "act before you think," but the result is monochromatic, unexciting. Replacing a pregnant Rebecca Pidgeon in the film was Debra Eisenstadt, understudy to Pidgeon for the stage production. She knew the part but not how to perform it. Macy, Mamet's key male actor, embodied the "practical aesthetics" method but the "truth of the moment" principle offered little sustained action, as scene rather than sequence controlled the structure (TF 20). A limited budget and tight shooting schedule did not enhance the production.

Mamet has written that in his experience as a screenwriter, "a script usually gets worse from the first draft on" (SF 136). The shooting script of *Oleanna* may not be an exception as he added three outside scenes: John at his empty postparty house; John disheveled in a hotel bedroom scribbling notes on the tenure committee report, and Carol at a duplicating center having copies of John's "confession" made. She also asks for enlargement of a manifesto beginning with "It is the right of all students to be treated with respect" adding one of two visual but not spoken texts to the film. The second appears when John makes tea for Carol: it is an inscription running at the top of the committee room wall that she reads. It says, "we will be judged by that least involved of magistrates: history," a portentous forecast of what is to come.

In these moments, Mamet comes closest to his ideal of a silent film. In *On Directing Film* he writes that "the perfect movie doesn't have any dialogue" (ODF 72). But this theoretical ideal is a practical impossibility, as least for *Oleanna*, whose very subject is language. He also noted that he originally conceived *House of Games* as a silent movie, one where he could "reduce the meaning of each of the sequences to a series of shots, each of them clean and uninflected" (SF 120). *Oleanna*, however, does not take advantage of the freedom presented by film, which explains its weakness. Mamet relies too much on the viewer to fashion the progress of the story as he relies on his audience to sustain the illusion of his action in the theatre. Exchanges of dialogue, Mamet argues in *True and False* and in *On Directing Film*, should be purposefully artificial, but in film this is a fault because its visual grammar requires some animation of language. The images and setting cannot alone be expected to generate emotion. To listen to dialogue in film is also to see it. A static camera reflecting the unvarnished "action" and language of the characters actually works against the dramatic involvement of the viewer with the story. For film, visual detail and nuance of movement do a better job of illuminating character than language (TS 9).

Space in film also works against Mamet. Many of his directorial principles work well for the confined space of the stage, but not the screen, where the camera can easily create fluidity and a shifting perspective. The camera can also move above or below the horizon line. It can constantly shift perspective. Mamet has been forceful on how to direct film, notably in his 1989 essay "A First-Time Director" and in *On Directing Film*. Although *Oleanna* was his fourth effort, it was his first attempt at directing one of his own plays in this medium. Since then, he has gone on to direct eight other films including two for TV. Among the better known—*Homicide, The Spanish Prisoner, State and Main, Heist*, and possibly *Spartan*—the camera generally remains flat and controlled even though the films emphasize plot more than character. Motivation, depth, or complexity of character seem to escape him or rather are presented so flatly as either to be immediately understood by the audience or immediately rejected because characters appear to be so one dimensional. He has acknowledged a limited visual sense and added that he seems to have a knack for dialogue "independent of whatever skill I may or may not have in construction" (ODF 72, DMC 152).

Mamet shoots most scenes as if on a proscenium stage, with the action flat against a curtain. But ironically, what generates complexity in films like *Homicide* is enclosed space, much like a stage. When the characters are physically trapped, they reveal themselves in unexpected ways, as in the jail cell fight between Bobby Gold and the arrested Welles in *Homicide*, or at the end when the wounded Gold confronts the cornered killer, Randolph. Ironically, even when he parodies the film world as in *State and Main* or in *Wag the Dog*, Mamet hesitates to draw on the full potential of film, although with *Spartan*, his action drama, critics felt he was "looser" with the camera. Theoretically, the materiality of move-making undermines the dramatic power of Mamet's plays, most evident when he films his own work. He treats the grammar of film as rhetoric. He wants his movies to be films but treats them as plays.

Mamet has a love/hate relationship with the movies, or more specifically, with Hollywood. For almost two decades, he has concentrated on film rather than the stage, although this has surprisingly not diminished his antagonistic relationship with Hollywood, excoriated in *Speed-the-Plow*, parodied in *State and Main*, and vilified in "Bambi v. Godzilla," a June 2005 essay and the title of a set of essays on the movies. In the original essay, covering business, politics, trade, democracy, corporations, and power, Mamet matches the greed and rapacity in each institution to the vile actions of producers. The tone is hostile as he supports the isolated dramatist/writer in the face of rapacious Hollywood. Producers, critics, casting agents, and others spring into action only "to oppose and feed upon" the "dramatist," he argues.[27] But opposition always defines the creator's life.

For Mamet, producers shadow the artist to promote the illusion of success. They are sycophants who counsel no more than "adaptability and compliance" to the prevailing, corporate norms. But it's a desperate situation: "the producer struggles for power; the artist, for power and fulfillment. The artist must lose" (Bambi, 37). Furthermore, according to Mamet's own experiences, "every financial interchange with Hollywood ends with an accusation by the corporation of theft." The corporation even objects to the artist seeking recognition in any form, while to them, the audience "is composed of ignorant natives" who must be transformed into consumers. In a preemptory ending, Mamet decries a new tragedy: "that of the Artist in Hollywood and his sick marriage with the corporation" (Bambi 37)—expressed earlier in *Speed-the-Plow* and his essay "Film, A Collaborative Business."

But Mamet's diatribe raises three broad questions: 1. Why does he continue to work with Hollywood under these conditions? Has the money, recognition, and pride of Hollywood captivated him? Has he found its flattery, excesses, and indulgences irresistible? Or does he so enjoy directing and the control it brings that he will happily divert his energy from the theatre to film? Might he also think he's working a con, using the industry to further his own goals in some fashion? 2. What is the impact of Hollywood on his dramatic work? Does it explain why genres begin to dominate his writing, satire for example controlling *Boston Marriage*, farce governing *Romance*? 3. Is he beginning to mimic himself? Has his life become an inverted parable of his work? If not, why did he move to Los Angeles from Massachusetts if not to signal his commitment to the movies and their world? On one hand, Mamet condemns the exploitation and complicity of the dramatist for joining Hollywood, but on the other, he has chosen to play their game.[28] Could Mamet have found theatre no more than entertainment and the world of film—writing, directing and producing—man's work?

In the mid-nineties, Mamet turned to yet another form of creativity, songwriting. He collaborated with Rebecca Pidgeon on the lyrics for five songs on her solo album *The Raven* (1994) as she sought to renew her musical career while awaiting the birth of their first child. She actually had not stopped her singing career when she resettled in New York in 1990 to be with Mamet. He had earlier contributed lyrics to the Ruby Blues Album *Down from Above*, released in July 1990. While she performed in the New York production of *Oleanna*, she did several sessions with the guitarist Anthony Coote. *New York Girls' Club* followed the next year with a song written by Shel Silverstein and Mamet, "Word Around Town."[29] A further album, *The Four Marys*, a collection of traditional Celtic folk songs, appeared in 1998. In October 2005, she released *Tough on Crime*, which featured Billy Preston on keyboards.

In 1995, Mamet wrote the book for *Randy Newman's Faust*, an unusual, satirical musical performed at the La Jolla playhouse and then in 2001 at the Goodman in Chicago. Newman did the music and lyrics; for the recording, he used Don Henley as Faust, James Taylor as God, Linda Ronstadt as Margaret, and Bonnie Raitt as Martha. It begins with a rollicking number, "Glory Train," a song by the Lord and a large backup group. When it ends, Lucifer enters with a single word, "Bullshit!" He's banished to Hell, where we shortly see him at his desk stamping various forms: "Burn (Stamp) Bake (Stamp) Fry. (Stamp)." This is Mamet.

Mamet in the nineties continued to write screenplays, completing a first draft version of *Lolita* for the director Adrian Lyne in November/ December 1994, revising it by March 1995. The 138-page revision was rejected, however, partly because it was the least faithful to the novel, radically restructuring the plot with roughly two thirds of the script covering only the first third of Nabokov's work. Humbert Humbert appears much less sympathetic in Mamet's version because he has eliminated scenes of any moral doubt. Mamet even adds to the script with an invented scene in the psychiatric ward of a hospital. Mamet, it should be noted, succeeded Pinter on the scriptwriting ladder for this film which eventually used a screenplay by Stephen Schiff, the fourth attempt to translate Nabokov's work to the screen. This last became the shooting script for the film, which would star Jeremy Irons as Humbert.[30]

Pitching movies, however, did not get any easier for Mamet, despite his success. An example is *The Edge* (1997). Art Linson moved to Fox and wanted to do a film with Mamet and informed the studio. They expressed dismay. Linson replied he hadn't asked him yet. At the time, Mamet was spending months in Vermont and in the woods. When Linson did speak to him, Mamet said he had an idea for an outdoor adventure. Linson told him great, but make sure it has "'a great big grizzly bear or an Englishman's penis.' So I flipped a coin and the bear won."[31] With the working title of *Bookworm*, the film was presented as two guys (one a book collector) and a bear; they get lost in the wilderness and have to learn to survive together, even though one guy was trying to kill the other and take his young, beautiful wife.[32]

Mamet and Art Linson were to pitch Tom Jacobson, newly appointed head of film production at Fox. Linson, who had called Mamet six weeks earlier in order to kick-start his exclusive deal with Fox, encouraged anything Mamet might suggest. Linson hoped to extend their working professional relationship: "*You get me a lot of money, I get you a good script*" said Mamet (What 25). The two had bungled, however, *Ordinary Delights* at Warner, Mamet's script of the autobiography by Andrew Potok about going blind. Money, meetings, and misery resulted (What 26).

Their pitch meeting for *The Edge* was anxious and tense, Linson aware that the executive who might buy the script probably wouldn't even have his job by the time, or rather if, the movie got made. Mamet began his pitch in the nervous atmosphere with a description of the wealthy and refined bookish man in New York married to a young fashion model who has an assignment in Alaska. A young and attractive photographer and her husband are invited along and competition soon emerges between the two men for the girl. Indeed, the photographer might want to do away with the husband, but before any plan can be enacted, the two survive a plane crash while scouting locations and, amid other problems, encounter a bear. The executive then interrupted: can an audience root for a man with money? Yes, was Mamet's curt reply—but everyone was thrown off the beat. Mamet's spirit had darkened and he quickly ended the description. Everyone left, with Linson thinking it went well. "What happens when it goes bad?" Mamet asked. "They tell you *no* in the room," Linson replied (What 31). Unexpectedly, they got the deal, although Jacobson was out and Tom Rothman, a lawyer, was in by the time production started.

But they lacked a director and a star. Harrison Ford was considered, as well as Dustin Hoffman. Next was Alec Baldwin, who had been in *Glengarry*. He tentatively said yes to the photographer's part, but the studio felt he couldn't carry a film, and he had difficulty warming to the director, Lee Tamahori. Then the search for the second star, the aging bookworm, began. De Niro? Perhaps, but he wanted a reading (a read through of the script by an actor). It took place on a Saturday afternoon at the Peninsula Hotel in Beverley Hills. Mamet did not attend. Baldwin did and so did De Niro, although he arrived late. As Linson noted, Mamet's dialogue is "very different from standard Hollywood fare. Not every actor can find a way into it to make it sound real and unforced" (What 52). Green (Baldwin) and Morse (De Niro) did not click, partly because Baldwin naturally gravitated to Mamet's language and De Niro did not, nor did he like the bear subplot.

The movie, now re-titled *The Edge*, did get produced, made possible because Anthony Hopkins wanted the De Niro part. Canmore, Alberta, in the Canadian Rockies was the location of the shoot, which took fifty-five days, although the film nearly shut down over a dispute concerning Alec Baldwin's beard, unsuited for the part. Only a fight over the film's title loomed larger, Mamet insisting *Bookworm* was right, Fox marketing declaring it was wrong. A list of possible alternatives was drawn and read to Mamet, who could only mutter, "Oh, God" (What 79). *The Edge* stayed and the opening weekend gross was \$7.8 million on 2,150 screens, putting it third among new releases. Its monthly take was about \$30 million, not a smash but respectable. The studio, however, thought they would lose \$10 million on the production.

~

The Spanish Prisoner (1997), the fifth film Mamet wrote and directed, had equal funding challenges but was more successful in visualizing his characteristic themes: deception, conspiracy, and self-delusion; in short, the con. In the "Preface" to the screenplay, Mamet calls the work a "Light Thriller," citing Hitchcock's *The Lady Vanishes* and *Young and Innocent* as prototypes. Hitchcock featured a protagonist "enmeshed" in a situation not of his own doing, while discovering that supposed "foes are friends and vice-versa." Film is "*essentially* melodrama," Mamet adds, and *The Spanish Prisoner*, with its title evoking a traditional con game (beautiful sister and fortune held hostage in Spain freed only through investment of personal funds and energy), is no exception (SPR xi).

In the film, jeopardy and comedy join forces, Mamet explaining that movies about confidence tricks are *always* intriguing: "you see the first trick, you expect a second but you don't see the third" (Gritten). Drama (and film) essentially work because the audience tries to understand the "play" that goes on. Such preoccupation and concentration, however, enables the confidence man or magician to misdirect them. "Somerset Maugham once said drama isn't a craft, it's a trick. I understand what he meant" (in Griffin). As Mamet also explained, all confidence games "play on, or exploit, a desire of the victim's pride and ego." The hero of *The Spanish Prisoner* wants to be well thought of but finds himself increasingly isolated as he learns the lesson told to him by a secretary, "y' never know who *anybody* is" (SPR 23).

The film originated when Mamet and his wife were vacationing in Jamaica and spotted an elegant yacht with a helicopter landing pad moored in the harbor. He began to imagine who might live on such a yacht and how that boat came to be there. Soon, a plot evolved and he answered his question about the owner with the name, Steve Martin. After the financing was in place, a cast began to form including Martin, Ben Gazzara, and the "Mamet mafia": Ricky Jay, Felicity Huffman, Rebecca Pidgeon, Harriet Voyt, Neil Pepe, J. J. Johnston, Tony Mamet, Scott Zigler, and Jonathan Katz. Martin and Gazzara had long been Mamet favorites and he especially admired Martin in Gregory Mosher's production of *Waiting for Godot* at Lincoln Center, co-starring Robin Williams and directed by Mike Nichols. He also had a slight acquaintance with Martin through Ricky Jay.

Thorstein Veblen, Mamet's "hero," partly explained the theme of the film, Mamet claimed. It was he who "said that behavior at the top of the food chain and behavior at the bottom . . . is exactly the same" (DMC 228). Using the corporate environment to demonstrate this behavior was Mamet's intent. The elaborate plot of the movie begins with the inventor of a mysterious "process" flown to a Caribbean island for a presentation to a group of large investors in the company, but his boss (played by Gazzara) has little interest in cutting the inventor (named Joe Ross and played by Campbell Scott) in for any of the profits. The inventor then begins to question the plan and accidentally, or perhaps not, meets on the beach an entrepreneur named Jimmy Dell (Steve Martin) and *they* make a plan to meet in New York where Ross confides his troubles to Dell and the latter offers to help. But relations sour and Ross begins to distrust everyone who surrounds him, despite their pledges to help. The script elaborates this sense of distrust:

Susan: Who in this world is what they seem . . . ?
Jimmy: People aren't that complicated, Joe. Good people, bad people, . . . they generally look like what they are . . . .
Ross: Then why are so many people having difficulty?
Jimmy: That is the question baffles me. (SPR 25, 46)

Joe is chased, grilled, and pursued, forced to go on the run by often unidentified sources, much like Joseph in Kafka's *The Trial*, which had as its original German title, *Der Prozess*.

Mamet created a fictional island, St. Estephe, for the film. To sustain the con that it was a real place, he prepared and issued a weekly newsletter for his cast and crew. Called the *St. Estephe Intelligence*, this mimeographed booklet contained gossip and news about his crew. They loved it.

Jean Doumania, producer, adopted a novel approach to promoting the film, at least in Chicago. For the premiere, he invited sixty Chicago criminal investigators to solve the mystery in the film. At the opening, he stopped the film six minutes before the end and had the professional sleuths describe how they thought the film would conclude. There were multiple theories and proposals clarified only by the completion of the showing. The audience was fascinated and the event generated the anticipated press. The visual flair of the film earned it the March 1998 cover of *American Cinematographer Magazine*. The box office was also strong, earning $10,162, 034 in the U. S. alone. The release date was April 3, 1998.

Exceeding the battle for both *The Edge* and *The Spanish Prisoner* was the financing for *Heist*. Linson again took it on, now having gone the route of an indie producer. He did the reading act again with De Niro, who once more turned him down. A few weeks later, however, Mamet and Linson got a call from an agent at the CAA agency reporting that both Gene Hackman and Danny DeVito had read the script and wanted to do the movie. But it would be expensive, the most costly Mamet ever did. His reputation for being artsy and classy might mean fewer tickets at the box office, but if it had a larger budget, he could deliver, Linson argued.

Soon, a potential backer made it clear the movie had to be shot in Canada and in forty-five days; fifty-five, Mamet countered (What 174). The backer's key to success was pre-selling the film to foreign markets for more than the cost of the movie, leaving him no risk. It worked. By the time the lunch meeting was over in which this was decided, Mamet was granted fifty days for shooting and confirmation of what he already knew: "The decisions were made before the meeting began" (What 179). Warner Bros. distributed domestically and it soon became Mamet's most financially successful film, grossing $23.5 million with $7.8 million on opening day. *The Spanish Prisoner* was his second at $10.2 million.[33]

A critical as well as financial success, *Heist* showed how Mamet was able to balance writing mainstream films like *The Untouchables* (and later *Wag the Dog*, *Ronin*, and *Hannibal*), while pursuing a parallel career of modestly budgeted films written and directed by himself. *Oleanna*, *State and Main*, and *Spartan* are examples. At the same time, he continued to offer trenchant criticisms of Hollywood and its system. Movies may have competed with Mamet's playwriting at the start of the nineties, but by the end of the decade, his preference was clear: "I use to be a rather committed gambler and I always wanted to play at the Big Table. And the Big Table is the movies."[34]

8

BOOK OF GAMES

I got to *close* this fucker or I don't eat lunch, or I don't win the *Cadillac.*

Mamet, *Glengarry Glen Ross*

To get the Cadillac, you must play the game. Richard Roma and David Mamet both know this, having studied, it seems, *The Compleat Gamester* (1674).[1] One of the earliest guidebooks to games, tricks, deceptions, and other mysteries involving cards, dice, and gambling, it is a prototype to Mamet's own contemporary lexicon of games: his plays, essays, novels, and films that form a manual to gaming as survival in America. This is the con plus the tricks and dodges necessary to succeed—the *only* way to win the Cadillac.

Deception rules in all of Mamet's genres. His work, whether the early *American Buffalo* or the more recent *Romance*, exposes the conniving and dishonesty required to do business in a society operating from the premise Anna offers in *Boston Marriage:* "Men live but to be deceived" (BM 79). Even Mamet's extravagant and undisciplined novel *Wilson* (2000) acknowledges the need to accommodate a world of dishonesty. Recognizing that "you may have *been* deluded, cheated, mistreated in every possible way . . . *yet,* is it still upon you *to close the* sale" (WIL 67). The novel is a handbook on gaming but one that is so energetic and diverse that it overflows its pages and loses its grip on plot. Blank pages, footnotes, and stop-and-start narratives undermine the consistency of the text. But this energetic treatment of form reflects one of the gamester's favorite ploys, satire, which dominates much of Mamet's work at the end of the nineties. Personally secure, he is able to step away from himself to look critically at society.

Wag the Dog (1997) is a prime example. This mainstream political satire, which received three Golden Globe and two Oscar nominations, including one for best screenplay, exposed the fakery and political motives of a corrupt presidency, soon to be reflected in reality. Mamet actually did not originate the film. Robert De Niro's company Tribeca bought the rights to Larry Beinhart's novel *American Hero.* Assigned the task of adapting it to the screen was Hilary Henkin who had done *Fatal Beauty* (1987) and *Romeo is Bleeding* (1994). The screenplay was then given to Dustin Hoffman by Tribeca as a potential directing project, but he turned it down. The director Barry Levinson also rejected it. It held no interest for him except for the subplot of faking a war. But when his larger project, *Sphere*, was delayed because of Warner Bros.' hesitation over its budget, he thought he could do a lower budget film quickly.

Levinson called Mamet and began to discuss the project, focusing on the media, Hollywood and marketing. Mamet outlined the story that had evolved into the script of *Wag the Dog*, something entirely different from the Henkin screenplay, which was an adaptation of the book. Mamet, in fact, never saw Henkin's adaptation, but that did not prevent a later disagreement. Two major drafts and revisions resulted in the final shooting version, but a dispute over second writer's credit erupted and had to be settled by the Screen Writers Guild.[2] They found in favor of Henkin, despite a detailed scene-by-scene breakdown of the two scripts showing Mamet's input. He ended up with second screen credit, while Levinson threatened to resign from the Writers Guild.

Nevertheless, the satire in *Wag the Dog* and the construction of the fake war, orchestrated by the Hollywood producer Stanley Motss (Dustin Hoffman), is masterly and Mamet's. His sense of the abuses of American politics is exceeded only by his portrait of Hollywood excess. The satire is devastating. Convinced by the Washington PR man and "spin doctor" Conrad Brean (Robert De Niro) to aid the president, Stanley Motss suddenly sees the theatrical possibilities of fabricating a war to deflect attention from the sex scandal uncovered just eleven days before the president's reelection bid. And to Brean, it's anything but a war:

Brean: It's not "war." It's a pageant. It's a pageant . . . like the Oscars . . . why we came to you.
Motss: I never won an Oscar.
Brean: N'it's a crying shame. But you *Staged* the Oscars.
Motss: Yes. Indeed I did.

The chance for Motss to finally make his name by staging a war in which Albanian terrorists reportedly have a suitcase bomb in Canada and are trying to infiltrate the U.S. is precisely the deflection necessary for the president and his campaign. The creation of the war and its consequences define the satiric thrust of the movie, but the war, as Motss reminds everyone, is nothing more than "a teaser!" Hoffman was having trouble with his role. During shooting, however, he realized that the character combined the behavior of his father and of the famed Hollywood producer Robert Evans (for Hoffman's impression of Evans, see the end of the autobiographical documentary *The Kid Stays in the Picture* [2002]). But Hoffman may not have the funniest line in the movie: that belongs to William H. Macy as the CIA operative, Young. He enters saying, "Two things I know to be true: there's no difference between good flan and bad flan and there is no war. Guess who *I* am."

Upon its release in December 1997 the film did well but not sensationally. Then in late January 1998, the Bill Clinton/Monica Lewinsky scandal broke and the box office went straight up as the film became a kind of cultural icon of presidential chicanery. It also became a commercial success: on a cost of $15 million, it grossed $43 million, becoming one of the most profitable movies of the year.

Mamet had a similar but more controversial battle the following year over screen credit for *Ronin* (1998). Hired as a script doctor for this action film directed by John Frankenheimer about a group of former intelligence agents who team up to steal a mysterious metal case, it starred Robert De Niro. Mamet contributed a rewrite to the original script by J. D. Zeik. The dialogue especially reflects this. "One can get a terrifically clean shave off his [Mamet's] writing," a critic offered, giving this example: "Have you ever killed anyone?" an agent asks Sam, the De Niro character. "I hurt someone's feelings once," he replied.[3] The script, bought by United Artists in turnaround from TriStar Pictures, reflects Mamet's skill in having characters saying everything and nothing at the same time. But a legal battle ensued concerning top screen credit and the Writers Guild refused Mamet's claim, supported by Frankenheimer, that he should be the recognized writer. "We didn't shoot a line of Zeik's script" Frankenheimer said, although Zeik's attorney insisted that Mamet only enlarged De Niro's role, added a female interest, and rewrote several scenes. To protest the Writers Guild decision, Mamet refused to allow his name to be used, substituting a pseudonym, "Richard D. Weisz."[4]

The title of the film refers to a Japanese samurai who had no master, and the movie makes a lengthy reference to the classic Japanese story of the forty-seven Ronin. The film itself is notable for a set of car chase scenes, the last occurring through the streets and tunnels of Paris, all sequences filmed live, not digitally. In a Mamet move, the contents of the metal case, the object of the chase, are never removed nor identified, an example of what Hitchcock called "the MacGuffin"—when the sought-after object is never revealed and best identified through the imagination of the audience.

State and Main (2000) continued Mamet's use of satire, an early draft of which existed in 1995, before Mamet worked on *Wag the Dog*. Set in a fictitious Waterford, Vermont, but actually shot in Manchester-by-the Sea and Dedham, Massachusetts, the film narrates the trials and more importantly the tribulations of a Hollywood film crew trying to shoot on location. Already kicked out of a New Hampshire town for the star's misbehavior with an underage girl, the crew sets up in the Vermont town and a set of overlapping stories begin, including that of the writer Joe White (Philip Seymour Hoffman) trying to survive his first film while coming up with rewrites and a new title when they discover that the town's Old Mill, the basis for the title of the film, burned down years ago. His struggle with honesty and his romance with Annie, the local bookstore owner (Rebecca Pidgeon), are set against the behavior of the pragmatic director, Walt Price (William H. Macy) and manipulative Hollywood producer, Marty Rossen (David Paymer), who will do everything and anything to get the film made.

Mamet has great satiric fun with the foibles of screen people, from the actress (Sarah Jessica Parker) who won't bare her breasts unless she's paid an additional $800,000, to the costume designer whose work is constantly rejected. Questions of what is the truth both in the film and in the lives of the characters, especially relating to the star, played by Alec Baldwin, and a compromised young woman, are at the heart of the film. Joe, the writer, for example, says he can write only on a manual typewriter, but his has been lost. He then confesses that's a lie; he can actually work on an automatic. Walt is sympathetic: "It's not a lie, it's a gift for fiction" (S&M 15). Later, when Joe tells him he has to tell the truth concerning the car accident he witnessed with the star and a young girl, Walt glibly answers, "that's just so *narrow* . . . (S&M 106)."

Everyone affiliated with the movies can be bought off in this world—if not directly, then through a con. The ambitious but meddling local lawyer/politician, Doug, determined to prove statutory rape against the male star, suddenly reverses himself on TV while holding a satchel of money, just out of camera range, to help his run for political office. To satisfy Joe's dilemma about telling the truth or not, he's ordered to court, where he actually perjures himself, only to learn later that the courtroom was a con. The court scene was a fake, a movie set, and all the officials were local actors, not surprising given that the locals begin to read *Variety* and discuss weekend box office grosses.

Acting itself comes in for satiric treatment. No one, for example, can ever learn their lines. When Walt asks the star Bob Barrenger if he knows his lines, he emphatically says yes: "I just don't know what *order* they come in" (S&M 89). Producers fare no better, as we see with Marty Rossen, a man determined to solve every problem on and off the set. To Doug, the erstwhile politician who threatens to close the set and arrest Marty, he threatens *him* in a linen closet by shouting the "two scariest things in the world [are] a black man with a knife and a Jew with a lawyer. Now, I am a lawyer, and I am *The* Jew, and you continue ONE MOMENT with this slanderous shit here in this public place, I'm going to have your ass over my mantel place" (S&M 85).

Mamet's preference for jokes on the set did not diminish, possibly encouraged by the cast, which contained a large number of the so-called Mamet Mafia: Macy, Pidgeon, Ricky Jay, J. J. Johnston, Patti LuPone, Tony Mamet, Chris Kaldor, Jonathan Katz, and Linda Kimbrough. His Cambridge, Massachusetts, friend and real estate developer, Dick Friedman, played the postman and went through a particularly difficult time on the set. Moments before shooting his single scene with his one line of dialogue, Mamet gave him approximately ten pages of new script to learn, telling him his part had been rewritten. The problem? It was in Shakespearian verse. "Take twenty minutes to learn the lines. I'll stop shooting but don't take too long; it's a union crew and it's costing me money." A nervous Friedman hid behind a tree but after twenty minutes went in a distraught state to the director to admit he was getting nowhere. "What? If you take more time, I'll have to close the set and it's costing me money," Mamet told him. "Get on with it!"

Ten minutes later a now frantic Friedman returned and admitted he just couldn't do it and would have to leave. At that point, Mamet revealed the joke. Friedman nearly fell on his knees in thanks.

There is a great deal of joking on any Mamet set, and he often prints the takes of various screwups, showing them to the cast and crew at the end of the day. One occurred while filming *Oleanna*. Macy was to go to a bowl of candy, lift it, and offer it to Carol. Mamet had the bowl epoxy-ed to the table so it couldn't move no matter how hard Macy tried, and at one point he lifted the table into the air, to the laughter of the director and crew.

Preceding the self-conscious satire of *State and Main*, Mamet confronted the past in two historically related works that demonstrate his attachment to history—a particular history: that of the Edwardian period. *The Winslow Boy* (1999), his feature film remaking Terrence Rattigan's 1946 play, and *Boston Marriage*, opening in Cambridge in June 1999.[5] Both reflect Mamet's concern with the past, effectively presenting history in both detail and theme. Morality and truth are again at the center: in *The Winslow Boy*, does the father believe his son when he denies stealing a 5-shilling postal order? And if he does, how can he prove the boy's innocence and reinstate his reputation and that of the family? In *Boston Marriage*, does Anna's Protector know he's being deceived? Does Claire's paramour-to-be understand the nature of their proposed relationship? Do Anna and Claire ever tell each other the truth?

Mamet did not have any problem in remaking his source text when he adapted Rattigan's successful drama based on the actual legal case of George Archer-Shee, asked to leave the Royal Naval College at Osborne for allegedly stealing a postal order in 1908. So inflammatory was the situation that the House of Commons debated the public issue of clearing the young man's name. The remarkable thing about Rattigan's play, which he wrote *after* Anatole de Grunwald, screenwriter, and Anthony "Puffin" Asquith, the film director, turned down Rattigan's proposal for a film about the event, is that he succeeded in creating a drama without the presence of a single courtroom scene. The four-act play was an immediate success, playing the Lyric Theatre in the West End of London for more than a year and recording 476 performances.[6] Alexander Korda, noted British film producer, quickly bought the film rights and by 1948 the film was released, directed by Asquith with a screenplay by de Grunwald adapted from Rattigan's play.

Courtroom dramas long fascinated Mamet, beginning with his early, Academy Award-nominated screenplay, *The Verdict*. The dramatic setup of a courtroom is a natural theatre in which protagonist, antagonist, and chorus (the jury) are fixtures. *The Verdict* showed how carefully one can manipulate the situation to sustain drama until the final few moments. He continued this interest in his short play *An Interview*, about a lawyer who faces judgment to determine where he will spend the rest of eternity. Mamet's *Romance* (2005) makes extensive use of a courtroom. Ironically, Rattigan's *The Winslow Boy* is a courtroom drama without a courtroom scene; more important is the movie's theme of injustice and victimization.

Three other attractions of Rattigan's play for Mamet were: its well-made quality; its logical development; and its precise language, which has long characterized Mamet's best work, a feature partly drawn from the example of Pinter. Another appeal was the play's rendering of Edwardian England, evoking its Victorian inheritance. Mamet for some time had been enamoured with the period, reading and rereading a set of Victorian novelists including Thackeray, Trollope, and George Eliot; a quote from Trollope's *He Knew He Was Right* is the epigram to Mamet's *On Directing Film*, and he often quotes Kipling from memory. A violated world of order searching to restore its balance is a frequent theme in Mamet's own work, which Victorian fiction constantly explores. Rattigan, who sets his play over a two-year period preceding World War I, captures the world of Edwardian England, which Mamet evokes through his detailed 1912 setting.

But if the period is late Edwardian, the attitudes are Victorian, marked by class awareness, gender differences, social hierarchies, and social embarrassments. Proper moral behavior and highly fixed attitudes also define the action. Recreating these features required the authenticity of time and place to validate the authority of moral law confirmed at the end of the play and the film by a biblical sense of "right," not "justice," a distinction reiterated by the impressive barrister, Sir Robert Morton, in the closing lines of the work. Underlining this dimension of the conflict is a question that has absorbed Mamet for some time, one that crosses principle with the selfish interests of the individual: "when does a fight for justice become an arrogant pursuit of personal rectitude . . . at what point does one give up the fight for an abstract principle?" Contradicting the high principle of Sir Robert is the seemingly personal pursuit of Arthur Winslow to clear his son's and his family's name, although he shares Sir Robert's determination to triumph. In a line Mamet added to Rattigan's script, Sir Robert declares, "It's only important to *win*," repeating a mantra of Mamet's father, a Chicago labor lawyer, often repeated at the dinner table.[7]

For Mamet, the issue was not restructuring but consolidating the original four-act play to ninety-nine minutes of drama, while creating a single, seamless film. "Someone once said, 'the better the play the worse the movie it's going to make' so a lot of my work here has been lifting passages of narration that can be better explained through montage and by dramatizing the purely narrative," Mamet explained to an interviewer on the set.[8] He elegantly achieves this in visual as well as verbal terms, confirming his understanding of the period as much as the formal properties of the two genres, drama and film, that must be divided in order to fulfill the expectations of each.

Surprisingly, Mamet kept much of the original language intact and introduced none of his trademark profanities. A comparison of the screenplay with the drama finds extraordinary similarities of expression. To cite one passage from the end of the play, Mamet quotes Rattigan almost exactly when he has Sir Robert explain to Catherine Winslow that "To fight a case on emotional grounds, Miss Winslow, is the surest way to lose it. Emotions cloud the issue. Cold, clear logic wins the day"

(WB 208). Rattigan writes, "to fight a case on emotional grounds, Miss Winslow, is the surest way to lose it. Emotions muddy the issue. Cold, clear logic—and buckets of it—should be the lawyer's only equipment" (R176). Mamet values the precision of Rattigan's language, editing and updating only selective expressions in the play-text.

Mamet did open out the play in a spatial sense, however. Where it was principally set in the drawing room of the Winslows, Mamet provides scenes in Parliament, the Horse Guards, a Suffragette's Headquarters, and Sir Robert Morton's office. But like the French director Robert Bresson or indeed Chekhov, Mamet places the key events of the drama offscreen which intensifies their impact, while introducing a world beyond the suffocating interiors that dominate a good deal of the film.

Mamet shot the film on location using an Edwardian townhouse on the edge of Clapham Common in the London borough of Wandsworth. Shooting began in March 1998, less than a year after Mamet and producer Sarah Green (*The Spanish Prisoner*, *Oleanna*) brought the project to the copresidents of Sony Pictures Classics during the Toronto Film Festival in September 1997. Mamet had actually been trying to produce the play at the Atlantic Theatre Company in New York, but then realized it would work better as a film.

The cast included Mamet regulars such as Colin Stinton, who plays the family lawyer Desmond Curry, long in love with Catherine Winslow (Rebecca Pidgeon). Her brother Matthew plays her brother Dickie in the film. Nigel Hawthorne (*The Madness of King George*), who had many years earlier performed in "The Shawl" for BBC Radio, played Arthur Winslow. Jeremy Northam was Sir Robert Morton. Neil North, who is the First Lord of the Admiralty, surprised Mamet at the audition when he revealed that he played the part of the original Winslow Boy in the 1950 film.

The Winslow Boy adopts a Victorian attitude toward crime—a moral rather than physical act involving the violation of a social order with a lie. Deception, deceit, betrayal, and dishonor are the operative concepts, with punishment a powerful public rather than legal act. Reproducing the Edwardian world in the film meant that social rather than judicial punishment was more effective. In *The Winslow Boy*, punishment through admission of wrong is "visited upon" those institutions (the Admiralty and the Crown) that threatened to ruin the individual. Eliot Ness may have needed a machine gun to fight crime in Mamet's *The Untouchables*, but Sir Robert Morton, the heroic barrister and MP in *The Winslow Boy*, needs only words.

In his notebooks, the Victorian writer Samuel Butler wrote, "Truth consists not in never lying but in knowing when to lie and when not to do so," later extended to the view that "if a man is not a good, sound, honest, capable liar, there is no truth in him." Anticipating Wilde in tone if not concept, Butler adds, "I do not mind lying, but I hate inaccuracy." Even Robert Louis Stevenson could see the ambiguities attached to lying: "it is possible to avoid falsehood and yet not tell the truth," adding that "the cruellest lies are often told in silence."[9] Mamet shares this late-Nineteenth-century view; indeed, his many characters who lie express only half lies. Bobby in *American Buffalo*, Del in *The Cryptogram*, Claire in *Boston Marriage*, and Bernard in *Romance* are four characters who quickly come to mind, paralleling the many liars who appear in *House of Games, The Spanish Prisoner* and *Heist*.

Lies and the question of truth are at the center of Rattigan's play, which Mamet saw first as a film in Chicago as a youngster, not discovering the play until about 1979. Then, in approximately 1994, when he was doing some revisions for an Off-Broadway production of J. B. Priestley's *The Dangerous Corner* for the Atlantic Theatre, he became excited by Rattigan's reconstruction of the late Victorian period and its cadenced but exact language. What appealed to him was its "drama of manners" and its emphasis on fighting for what one believes is right.[10]

Challenging the Admiralty and the Crown, who have supported the accusations by the Naval College against young Ronnie Winslow took courage. But a father who defends his son and has his family's backing was a theme Mamet admired (and perhaps subconsciously longed for). Despite the social cost—the family's finances shrink, the father's health deteriorates, the elder son must leave Oxford because of the expense, and the daughter, Catherine, loses her fiancé because of the unfavorable publicity and her suffragette ideas—their commitment to the truth and belief in the "Winslow Boy" displays a heroism rooted in the family, ultimately recognized by society through the courts. The gentility, honour, and accountability in the play are virtues Mamet has repeatedly tested, but in the film are clearly upheld.

For Mamet, whose characters are often shady figures for whom the truth is malleable and lying frequently the only means to survive, the clarity of morality in *The Winslow Boy* was a welcomed change. He had previously written, however, several upright characters, notably Eliot Ness in Brian DePalma's *The Untouchables* and Gino, the honest Italian who refuses to lie but still convinces a mob boss that he is *il capo di capo* in *Things Change*. In that film, the first he directed from material not his own, Mamet displayed a kind of quiet, individual heroism that triumphs over institutions.

How did Sir Robert know Ronnie Winslow told the truth? The mystery is revealed in Mamet's film when, in response to Catherine Winslow's question of what had happened in the examination to make Morton sure he was innocent, Sir Robert explains: Ronnie made far too many damaging admissions, which a guilty person would have worked to cover up; he failed to fall into a trap he set and then did not escape through a loophole Sir Robert also outlined (WB 176). The only remaining question was the unaccounted-for twenty-five minutes when the theft took place. What happened during that period? The ever suave Sir Robert teases Catherine that she should have guessed what happened because she, too, indulges in this "crime"—smoking (WB 176–7).

At the end of the film, right triumphs over justice in a speech underscoring the moral center of the screenplay. Hasn't justice been achieved, Catherine asks Sir Robert? "No. Not justice. Right. Easy to do Justice—very hard to do right," he states, explaining no more (WB 209). Mamet also says no more, preferring the economy of statement to the distraction of explanations. To overexplain is to undermine the power of the scene, a principle Pinter made clear several years earlier in an interview concerning his screenplay for Joseph Losey's film, *Accident:* "it is the mystery that fascinates me: what happens between the words . . . when no words are spoken." "In this film," he continued, "everything happens, nothing is explained." Mamet's view is similar. In his short study, *On Directing Film*, Mamet writes, "you always want to tell the story in cuts. Which is to say through a juxtaposition of images that are basically uninflected." Mamet elaborates this in *True and False*, his guide to acting: "Great drama, on stage or off, is not the performance of deeds with great emotion, but the performance of great deeds with no emotion whatever."[11] Rattigan, however, felt the need to explain fully, and has a further sentence in the play defending Sir Robert's emotionalism in court: "Unfortunately, while the appeal of justice is intellectual, the appeal of right appears for some odd reason to induce tears in court. That is my answer and excuse."[12]

Lying is offensive because it betrays language, invalidates morality, and destroys honor. This is what upsets Mamet. The Victorian and Edwardian periods shared this outlook and confirmed their own urgency for the truth that Frank Galvin neatly summarizes in *The Verdict* when he tells Laura, "we become tired of hearing people lie." Mamet agrees and has written that the theatre is exceptional because it "affords an opportunity uniquely suited for communicating and inspiring ethical behaviour." This moral space should not be abused, but when an actor deviates from the "through-line" of a piece, "he creates in himself the habit of moral turpitude; and the *play*, which is a strict lesson in ethics, is given the lie."[13]

Mamet is a lie detector who challenges and yet understands that language is a sign of cultural and moral decay. Sir Robert in *The Winslow Boy* accepts the truth of what Ronnie Winslow tells him because the simplicity, directness, and consistency of his language confirm that the young boy *is* telling the truth, logically balancing Arthur Winslow's instinctive belief that his son has always told him the truth. Neither Sir Robert nor Arthur Winslow need further proof, and while they may doubt the overall success of the case, they never question the honesty of young Ronnie. The attraction of Mamet to the work may in fact originate in his own family's opposite behavior: linguistic deviousness and manipulation.

When word arrives that they have won, first with Violet, the housekeeper, and then Sir Robert, Arthur Winslow accedes to the demands of the press now at his door to make a statement. He faces them with Sir Robert's sarcastic but truthful answer to the question, "what shall I say?" ringing in his ears: "Whatever you say will have little bearing on what they write" (WB 205). The film closes with a sharp but revealing exchange between Sir Robert and Catherine that contains unacted sexual overtones (added by Mamet) that may or may not continue between the characters. In a world without lies, romance may thrive.

The Winslow Boy was released in June 1999; five months earlier, Mamet's son, Noah, was born. That same year Mamet published "The Story of Noach" in a collection of essays entitled *Genesis: As It is Written, Contemporary Writers on Our First Stories.* Mamet's contribution is of interest because he blends Freudian notions of manifest and latent dreams with the Tower of Babel story which he understands as the manifestation of God's determination to destroy the world through a flood. Critical of those who band together in groups because it easily leads to demagoguery, Mamet then offers a distinctive reading of Noah and the Flood as redemption from the desire to murder and kill: "the double-encrypted wish-dream in the Noach story is the memory of the desire to renounce/forget murder." The trope of Noach is that "one cannot have what one wants . . . " although the message of the Torah is that we must constantly conquer our lower nature. Its constant reassertion, however, defines what it means to be human. Despite the building of Babel and the emergence of idolatry, the Torah reminds us that there is a story "beneath the story and that the very fact of its encryption should compel our interest and study."[14]

~

Henrietta (1999), a children's book about a pig, is another story beneath a story. The occasion was the death of Dick Friedman's pet pig on his Nantucket farm. The book is a fable about a self-educated pig who is at first rejected from attending what is likely Harvard Law because she lacks the necessary credentials but then accidentally meets and helps the president of the university, who is so impressed by her knowledge of Shakespeare, Fielding, and Thoreau that he oversees her admission. She does splendidly, becoming valedictorian and subsequently rises to the U.S. Supreme Court, extolling the virtues of social justice. Whimsical watercolors by Elizabeth Dahlie add to the charm of the outrageously successful pig.

The theme of self-reliance is fundamental and empowering as the porcine heroine ascends the social scale. The language is advanced, however, and children may not easily understand the formal syntax, as in the opening about Boston setting "itself up as our Seat of Learning—and have not the Luminaries in all fields issued from there these last three hundred years?" Mamet, however, may be more in jest than young readers might realize. The self-mocking voice is not unusual for him, with one critic noting that Mamet might be "too grownup to write a good story for kids."[15] Mamet's characters' search for vengeance, the desire to correct a wrong; admittedly disguised but not unnoticed in his work, it finds its way not only in *Henrietta* but in the pies thrown in the face of the Aunt in his children's play *The Poet and the Rent* and the pogrom described by the grandmother in *Passover.* Additionally, *Warm and Cold,* his first children's book, written for his daughter Willa, is a grownup's attempt to recreate a childhood he never experienced.

That same year Mamet published *Bar Mitzvah*, with illustrations by Donald Sultan, who earlier illustrated *Warm and Cold*. *Bar Mitzvah* continues the theme of a troubled young boy seeking the advice of an older, admired individual, in this case a rabbi and Talmud reader in preparation for his Bar Mitzvah. The grandfather figure wants to convey to the young boy what it means to be Jewish and does so through the example of an old watch, which the boy realizes reminds one of times past. The old man then elaborates his story through the Holocaust and humanity's connection to God. One always searches for meaning in life, but it does not always make sense, he explains. The illustrations by Sultan of watches, geometric patterns, barbed wire, and bullets establish a parallel narrative to Mamet's understated text. Most crucially, the old man tells the boy that the test of being a good Jew is only through one's actions.

Two key Mamet themes emerge: the first is the necessity of learning from earlier generations and the role of fathers (or grandfathers) as teachers, perhaps an expression of what Mamet missed in his youth. Second, the story underscores the importance of action as the measure of belief, echoing his Aristotelian view that character is action. *Bar Mitzvah* expresses Mamet's search for a Jewish identity within the frame and burden of Jewish history. Richly illustrated, the story incorporates personal as well as spiritual themes in Mamet's life.

Not especially political, although he has contributed for years to Democratic Party candidates and the Democratic National Committee, in January 1999 Mamet testified with Mike Wallace and Neil Rudenstein, then president of Harvard, in the U. S. District Court of Boston on behalf of Kaveh Afrasiabi. An Iranian political scientist and writer, Afrasiabi was suing two former members of the Harvard Center for Middle Eastern Studies and a Harvard police officer after charges of extortion and threats supposedly made by him were dropped due to lack of evidence. The civil rights lawsuit filed in the federal court in 1996 came to trial in 1999 in a ten-day litigation. The original issue was his dawn arrest by Harvard police on allegedly fictitious charges intended to silence his criticism of a Jewish professor of Middle Eastern Studies at Harvard who had previously "smeared" Afrasiabi and the journalist Mike Wallace. At the time, he was a professor of American government. The *Boston Globe* reported extensively on the trial.

Preceding the June premier of *Boston Marriage*, Mamet participated in a two-day (April 10–11) Hemingway conference to mark the one hundredth anniversary of the writer's birth, at the Kennedy Library at Harvard, which is now the repository of one of the largest Hemingway archives in the world. Although Mamet always deflected comparison with Hemingway, parallels exist, from their writing styles to their love of the outdoors, including hunting. At the start of the conference, Mamet introduced a Hemingway double-feature of *To Have and Have Not* and the 1946 version of *The Killers* at the Brattle Theatre in Harvard Square. Others attending the conference were Saul Bellow, Derek Walcott, Chinua Achebe, and Annie Proulx.

Boston Marriage (1999), opening at the Hasty Pudding Theatre, Cambridge in an American Repertory Theatre production in June, like *The Winslow Boy* deals with lying (which might be thought of as a satire of honesty) in its story of two unmarried women and their maid, who have lived together in a likely gay relationship. As the play opens one of the women, Anna, now has a lover—referred to as a Protector—while the other, Claire, is trying to establish a new relationship with a younger woman. The title is a slang term from nineteenth-century New England referring to a lesbian couple living together, although it could also mean two women in a living arrangement independent of men. Mamet formally called the work "a comedy of manners about two ladies of fashion at the turn of the century, and their maid" (DMC 234).

The three-hander is not unlike *Speed-the-Plow*, where the temp provides a pivot for the action. In *Boston Marriage* the maid, named Catherine and from Scotland, but variously and humorously called Bridey, Mary, Nora, and Molly and constantly thought to be from Ireland, is the source of a plot to correct a wrong. A good part of the malevolence in the play, when not occurring in the sarcastic exchanges between Claire and Anna, is the latter's tirades on the Irish:

Anna: Cringing Irish Terror, is it? What do you want? Home Rule, and all small children to raise geese? O . . . Ireland, each and all descended from kings who strode five miles of lighted streets in Liffey whilst the English dwelt in Caves. Is that the general tone, of your Irish divertimento? (*Pause*) Eh?

Maid: I'm Scottish, miss. (*Pause*)

Anna: Are you? (*Pause*) (BM 9–10)

Mamet mimics the conventions of British drawing room comedy throughout the play and shows the humor at being very un-PC.

The play also records sexual and linguistic warfare as the register of language radically alternates between high and low, a post-Jamesean world of formal locutions and semi-modern street talk that often makes fun of itself through contemporary expressions and Wildean echoes. When Claire responds to Anna's overreaction to her announcing a new, if untested, love by saying "how ill your disordered state becomes you,." Anna replies with, "Tell it to the Marines" (BM 23). When Anna bargains to be a witness to the proposed assignation in their parlor between Claire and her new friend, she also offers to bake a pie. Claire's answer is quick: "I am concocting a seduction. I do not require a pâttissière" (BM 35). And after a particularly colorful description of events involving a necklace and the daughter's discovery of her mother's jewel, Claire archly asks Anna, "Have you taken up Journalism?" "What a vile thing to say," she replies (BM 47).

Mamet experiments with language in this play, as he maintains differences, but not collisions, between nineteenth-century melodramatic, sensational, and journalistic diction, with passages of excessive formality, interspersed with plain, direct, and surprising street talk. "Do you garner the thrust of my declaration?" Anna asks Catherine, the maid, at one point, disguising a possible sexual interest in her. Catherine answers clearly. Later, when Claire asks Anna if her seams are straight, she answers abruptly, if mischievously, "Euclidean" (BM 41, 87). When the two women decide to use the tales the maid Catherine has been telling them in their proposed séance, the language ricochets between the polite, impolite, and sensationalist:

Claire: We want you to help us plan a sort of party.
Maid: Waal, I don't know.
Anna: What don't you know?
Maid: . . . after th' things you've said . . .
Claire: Oh, bullshit. Sit down, or we'll throw you in the streets to starve, pox-ridden and pregnant.

A few moments before, Claire has asked Anna, as they hatch their plan, "but could such a Byzantine rodomontade restore the girl to me? Could it convince the father?" Anna replies that men want to be deceived (BM 84, 79).

One of the themes Mamet expands in the work is the lie. All three characters commit lies at one point or another in the play, the maid lying when she must go to get candles when in fact she is meeting her lover. Claire "lies" in her supposed affection for Anna, who feels hurt in the face of new sexual competition, and Anna lies in explaining the source of her Protector's gift. All three work up a lie as they prepare for a séance to convince the Protector, his daughter (who turns out to be the new love of Claire), and the girl's mother that they can contact the spirit world. The maid plays an important part in this unfolding and then unraveling of the story, echoing *The Shawl* with its pseudo-clairvoyance. Only the reality of a lawyer's letter threatening action if the necklace is not returned and the departure of the Protector and his family from town prevent the séance from occurring. However, the loss of the Protector's money, recovery of the misplaced necklace, and the renewed love between Anna and Claire result in a certain self-contentment that they accept at the end with continued employment for the maid. The Nineteenth-century plot seems to combine Flaubert with Trollope's *The Eustace Diamonds* (1872) and the earlier *Lost Brooch* (1842) by Harriet Mosley, the sister of Cardinal John Henry Newman.

Starring in the premier of his first all-women drama were three Mamet regulars: Rebecca Pidgeon, Felicity Huffman, and Mary McCann. Huffman played the brittle Anna, every gesture and word exaggerated. Pidgeon played the more restrained Claire, who could still match Anna in pointed one-liners. McCann played the maid with comic flair. Rehearsals went smoothly at ART, the three, under Mamet's direction, meshing well. The set was a pastiche of pastel washes and chintz effects. Redecoration is in fact the opening gambit, Claire unsure if she has the right address when she enters because the room looks so different. The dialogue is straight Wilde:

Claire: I beg your pardon. Have I the right house?
Anna: What address did you wish?
Claire: Two forty-five.
Anna: The number is correct in all particulars.
Claire: Then it is the décor which baffles me. (BM 1)

Critics were less sympathetic toward the radical registry of language, finding Mametspeak in conflict with more effete locutions. The register seemed uneven, the directness of "You Pagan slut," or "kiss my ass" in conflict with "the couture of the paranormal does not well withstand the gaze of day" (BM 36, 53, 85). There was also criticism of Mamet's direction, self-consciously artificial. The result was a kind of deadpan acting with rhythmic delivery and too much attention to the right tone of voice rather than the creation of believable emotional connections. Pidgeon, in particular, was criticized for her lack of nuance, her actions more like "deadly exercises in actorly obedience and rote memorization."[16] Mamet's stiffly controlled directing style may be at odds with maximizing the resonance of his language, although he does not seem to think so. His best actors—Mantegna, Macy, and Huffman—provide themselves with a certain latitude, treating his stringent restraints with some elasticity.

Ironically, although his first all-women cast was gaining positive attention, Mamet faced a legal battle with a New York theatre company who wanted to switch the gender of characters in a set of Mamet plays. At first, he granted and then refused permission to the all-women's QuintEssential Theatre Company, who chose as its inaugural production seven short plays from *Goldberg Street* at the Limelight Theatre, in New York, under the title *Mamet Bare*. Rights from two publishers were granted but a few weeks before the January 6, 1999, performance they were told that the pieces were not intended for an all-female cast. They began to rehearse other Mamet pieces, but the day before opening night, the cast was ordered by the publisher Samuel French to cease and desist. The shows were canceled. Mamet's about-face attracted media attention (including *Time Magazine*) because he withdrew permission over the production's intent to portray all the characters as women.

Mamet at the time of *Boston Marriage* continued to write about theatre practice, preparing the foreword and contributing to Karen Kohlhaas' *The Monologue Audition, A Practical Guide for Actors* (2000). This book divides the process into directing, acting, and auditioning your monologue according to the Mamet method. Reinforcing ideas in *A Practical Handbook for the Actor*, this book is another Mamet acting manifesto. Explicit statements on the need for an acting objective, comments on action as the defining mode of character, and detailed remarks on Practical Aesthetics all broaden Mamet's approach. Several comments remain controversial, such as: "after you choose an Action for your monologue, you can then let each line mean anything it needs to mean for you to achieve the Action."[17] Not many directors would agree. Nonetheless, the book is pragmatic, with chapter 5, "Acting in the Moment," the pivot, combining Mamet's ideas with those of Stanislavsky and Meisner. *The Monologue Audition* is a useful expansion of many ideas in *True and False, Heresy and Common Sense for the Actor.*

Displaying Mamet's directorial skill at this time was his direction of a film of Beckett's short play *Catastrophe* (2000). Starring were Harold Pinter, Rebecca Pidgeon, and John Gielgud, in his last performance. Produced for Irish television as part of a comprehensive *Beckett on Film* project, other episodes were directed by Neil Jordan (*Godot*), Atom Egoyan (*Krapp's Last Tape*), Karl Reisz (*Act without words*), and Anthony Minghella (*Play*). The works were also shown on PBS in the States in September 2003. Mamet's selection for *Catastrophe* was inspired, since it dealt with the handling of a single figure for a single performance. The 1982 play lasts only seven minutes; the work, dedicated to Václav Havel, deals with the problem of an individual's oppression. It is singularly moving, as a Protagonist (Gielgud) stands on a podium while, with the help of a female assistant (Pidgeon), a Director (Pinter) helps prepare him for a theatrical spectacle. He is treated like an object, not a human being. Molded into a pose, he is presented like a prisoner, preparing for his final moment or "catastrophe." The Assistant suggests that the Protagonist might raise his head, if only for an instant, at the end. The Director objects, but as the blinding light shines on the figure, he *does* raise his head, stilling applause with his defiant and independent act.

Mamet directed with characteristic simplicity and precision, Pinter moving deliberately, although not always fluidly, followed by Pidgeon, who in a comic, expressionless manner, keeps repeating "I'll make a note" every time Pinter offers a suggestion. At one point, the Director almost mimics Mamet's method when he angrily responds to the Assistant's suggestion of a little gag in the mouth of the object: "For God's sake! This craze for explication! Every 'I' dotted to death! Little gag! For God's sake!" Equally satiric is his repeated phrase, "Light!" meaning a mini-flashlight so he can consult an equally mini-notebook. The circulating camera follows Director and Assistant about the theatre until the Assistant warily approaches the Protagonist to make adjustments.

Mamet warmly lights the set, a small Victorian London musical hall, and provides especially flattering and seductive light on Rebecca Pidgeon, noticeably at the end when she alone claps after the Director shouts to the lighting technician, "Now . . . let 'em have it" as the lights abruptly darken, leaving only the bowed head of the Protagonist lit. The Director then concludes, "Terrific! He'll have them on their feet."[18] As the sound of Pidgeon's clapping is heard and the light shines on her smiling face while she looks at the camera, Mamet cuts for an instant to the Protagonist who, hearing the quiet clapping, slowly, in a gesture of defiance and assertion of his humanity, raises his head. He is an effigy come alive, Mamet choosing to light only the forehead and sunken eyes. The mouth remains in darkness. Mamet actually deemphasizes the overt politics of the play in favor of the humanity of the Protagonist and the seeming inhumanity of the Director. It is effective, although the focus is on the theatrical rather than the metaphysical or political. But importantly, almost four generations of theatre history coalesce in the production, moving from Gielgud to Pinter to Mamet to Pidgeon. Gielgud died on May 21, 2000 at age ninety-six, shortly after the filming of *Catastrophe*.

~

Mamet's *Wilson: A Consideration of Sources* (2000), a book of pseudo-scholarship, errata, and footnotes to footnotes, is a novel that further embodies Mamet's focus on satire. Set in the year 3000 after the Cola Wars, the novel satirizes historical fiction in line with Laurence Sterne or John Barth. Phenomenology as fiction or fiction as phenomenology becomes Mamet's obsession in the book which his agent characterized as "unpublishable, his wife as impenetrable and his British editor a modern-day *Tristram Shandy*."[19] Faber did publish it, however, the following year. Dropping the historical orientation that dominates *The Old Religion* and the rural/realistic focus of *The Village*, Mamet transports the reader to a futuristic fictional dystopia of competing influences and commodities The work exhibits the tattoos of postmodernism—a de-centered narrative organized into fragments with an indeterminate plot written upon by intruding references. He rejects the conventional form of his two earlier novels in favor of parodic encounters with e-zines, neural nets, and Boolian logic.

The cover of *Wilson* introduces the satire. The illustrations create a *trompe l'oeil* effect of spinning plants and flying saucers complete with coffee stains and a pile of comic books, all without dates. A balding intellectual figure looks out of the top left corner. The earth recedes in the distance, while a blurb on the Faber edition of the book continues the gag, one line ironically describing the text as one in which "nothing is certain except the certainty of academics." Mamet constantly disproves the statement in the work, contradicting it through footnotes and annotations that supposedly stabilize the text. However, the cacophony and density of ideas intercutting and cross-referencing each other, colliding and damaging each other, obscures rather than displays knowledge in the work. The form of the book shapes itself more like an unedited film than a novel, joining several other texts published at that period displaying similar attention to visual form. Two examples are Mark Z. Danielewski's *House of Leaves* (2000) and Jeff VanderMeer's *City of Saints and Madmen* (2002).

Unreliability is the signature feature of the book, which attempts, through its referencing, to provide a grid for the Cola Wars. But the footnotes are as questionable as the text itself which parodies extravagant fictional undertakings ranging from Carlyle's *Sartor Resartus* to Nabokov's *Pale Fire*. Parodies also appear with their own "in-jokes." A six-line parody of a Shakespearean song ends with an allusion to Mamet's friend, Ricky Jay. "Bongazine" replaces magazine and suddenly the text includes letters to the editor, feature stories, and profiles. Chapter titles are themselves spoofs, mixing history with biography and meta-commentary, as the title on page 131 illustrates. It reads, "The Halfway Point," but it's not. Others sport titles like "The Uses of Inaccuracy," "A Disquisition on the Uses of Narrative," and "The Missing Page." Three sections broadly divide the text, but the thematic organization is not at all clear.

Neither is the plot. The novel essentially deals with life after the accidental destruction of the Internet in 2021, which has wiped out knowledge in the latter half of the Twenty-first century. A group of pedantic editors of "Bongazine" then attempt to recreate the lost literatures through fragments, which appear to originate in the confused and down-loaded memories of Ginger Wilson, wife of the former U.S. president whose name provides the work with its title. The published book is the product of the editorial labors of Ginger's misremembered thoughts, supplemented with seemingly endless footnotes crammed with various misquotations, misattributions, and dreadful puns. Dogs, music, and comic references dominate. Poetry, codes, and capsules are other devices of the story. The novel is equally erudite and mischievous, drawing from Swift, Pope, and even Gibbon. But it also expresses Mamet's double nature: intellectual and practical, a man of ideas and one who objects to mixing Coke with Pepsi.

The theme of *Wilson*, were one bold enough to claim one, would be Mamet's assault on the idea that "all things were alike, that polarities were unities," a myth reinforced by the revolutionary discovery that "Coke and Pepsi were one" (WIL 19). The result was the Cola Riots and attendant intellectual upheaval culminating in the accidental erasure of the Internet. Mamet's all-out attack on the commodification not only of culture but information is equal to his attack on the hyperintellectualism of literary study. Disjointed and in pieces, *Wilson* nevertheless, is a claim for the need to build alternate information systems. The novel is a Swiftian satire whose very form contains its own answer of what is to be done: reject the homogenized for the individualized. Reception of *Wilson* was uniformly negative, one reviewer declaring that "the whole thing flew so far over my head, I didn't even hear it pass. In fact I didn't even understand the blurb." Enigmatic, digressive, and challenging to one's sense of narrative logic, the novel stands apart, but it cannot be dismissed. In it, Mamet battles the postmodern and its properties to a draw.

At this same time Mamet became involved with a work that was a cautionary tale about excess: Faust. Long absorbed by the theme, and responding to a request by Jude Law to "punch up" the Christopher Marlowe text for a possible Broadway and Los Angeles version of his March 2002 Young Vic production in London directed by David Lan, Mamet could not resist. Law was also tentatively set to star in Mamet's remake of *Dr. Jekyll and Mr. Hyde* but had pulled out when the financing evaporated coinciding with an offer from Anthony Minghella to be in *The Talented Mr. Ripley*. In response to the Marlowe work, Mamet supposedly said, "I can do better" and chose to write his own *Faust*, a curious and verbose failure, stressing the expository at the expense of the dramatic. Recognized as overly rhetorical—audience members supposedly walked out of the 92nd

Street Y in New York when Mamet read long passages from the play in March 2002—it is entirely premised on deception and the con.

Dr. Faustus, re-titled by Mamet as *Faustus* in its printed version, had its world premiere at the Magic Theatre in San Francisco on February 28, 2004. Mamet directed a cast consisting of Colin Stinton (to whom Mamet dedicated the play) as the Friend, David Raiche as Faustus, Dominic Hoffman as the Magus (replacing Ricky Jay, who dropped out), and Sandra Linquist as the Wife. The lobby of the Magic Theatre was distinctly Mametesque, decorated with stills from the production and several large posters of Mamet's latest film *Spartan*, which opened in mid-March (and disappeared with remarkable haste, suffering from what the *New York Times* called too much "Mametude"). Started in Berkeley in 1967 with early contributions by Michael McClure and Sam Shepherd, the Magic was well-established near the Presidio in the second story of a set of massive, reconditioned naval warehouses above boutiques, restaurants, and a bookstore.

Mamet dispenses with many of Marlowe's features in favor of a more abstract, philosophical play that concentrates on epistemology rather than metaphysics. Mamet streamlines the source text, although not the language. In Marlowe, for example, the context for the hero's decision to join forces with Mephistopheles has a full explanation. In Mamet, we are told of Faustus' skills and power, but in Marlowe we see them displayed through the use of the fantastic. Devils dance, the seven deadly sins report, and Lucifer himself appears. Nothing except some simple magic tricks occur in Mamet. Furthermore, Marlowe's language equals his on-stage displays becoming both elaborate and complex:

Had I as many souls as there be stars,
I'd give them all for Mephostophilis.
By him I'll be great emperor of the world,
And make a bridge through the moving air
To pass the ocean with a band of men;
I'll join the hills that bind the Afric shore
And make that country continent to Spain,
And both contributory to my crown.[20]

Mamet's language seems prosaic and stilted by comparison:

Faustus: Do I transgress a magical divide? Do I encroach upon the netherworld . . . ? Shall I avert my unschooled gaze lest it be seared by the mysteries . . . ? Poor uninitiate, to wander, sightless in the sacred grove (F 48–9).

Where Mamet's Faustus seemingly, but only verbally, agrees to follow the precepts of the Magus (it's more a "show me and then perhaps I'll believe you," rather than "Yes! I'll join up!"), Marlowe's hero signs his soul away in blood with his arm becoming, itself, a text inscribed in blood (see 28–30). The hero displays his necromancy and power and conjures up wild beasts. And where Mephistopheles provides Faust with a magic book of spells and promises, Mamet's Faustus has written a book, not of spells, but one that supposedly answers the fundamental philosophical questions of mankind.

Mamet's *Faustus* presents the story of Faustus the day he completes his magnum opus. It focuses on periodicity and a numerical explanation of the universe: "All is reducible to periodicity. To cipher, to a formula, expressed in number; and that number signifies not quantity . . . not quantity. But a progression." As he then explains, "there is a generalized periodicity . . . Which, once revealed's encountered everywhere" and if given enough scope could plot the concordance of nature and "supposed acts of will" (F 27, 28).

His friend Fabian visits to produce yet another skeptical newspaper account of his career, followed by the appearance of a Magus or magician whom Faustus at first rejects. Various tricks begin to convince him of his power, however, although when the Magus tells Faustus there is an error in his great work and that he has likely cribbed the explanation from another, the incensed Faustus makes his pact, swearing on the lives of his wife and child, that he did not steal any answer and that the work is entirely his.

Act II begins with the consequences of his promise: a desolate, Beckettian landscape of grey ruin in contrast to the elegant Venetian home in Act I. Now a blind and decrepit Fabian wanders before Faustus to tell him that his son died of illness and that his wife has committed suicide. Disbelieving, Faustus soon meets both. The language alters from its pseudo-Eighteenth-century formality to something more modern but prosaic. Interrupted by his wife to visit their ailing son, for example, Faustus pauses and then falls back on formal rhetoric as he explains a further principle to his friend, Fabian:

> One moment. (*Pause*) Do I vex you? Do I confound? All of your adjurations, to recant, are but reminders to speak hypocritically, as all men speak. (*Pause*) You fear the impending limit of the circumscribed. You cling to: tradition, reason, custom, common sense, an intelligent submission. And I ask: to what? (F 35)

When questioned what is not to be despised, Faustus answers, "immortality" (F35). At the end of the play, Faustus appears at first to angrily "denounce the Devil" (F 94)—as Faust in Marlowe's play also does—but discovers his son before him asking for his father's atonement, although the son does not recognize the father. Recalling the poem the son wrote for the father is an attempt to renew their bond but, in what he believes to be the discovery of "the secret engine of the world," regret, he also triumphantly believes he, like his work, has been "completed": "I am become as God," he cries; "As, My Lord, am I," the Magus replies as the play abruptly ends (F 44, 102).

Just before the conclusion, however, Faustus realizes his son's poem is the unconscious source of the formula for the completion of his tract (F 86–88). Accused as a plagiarist, he admits that the conclusion to his work is not his own and seeks amends from the Magus while confessing his regret (earlier declared the secret engine of the world), demeaning his work as only "the toy of an overfed mind" (F 87). Faustus contrition, to be enacted by slitting his throat (note Mamet's use of a knife again), suddenly halts when his wife emerges from Hell to castigate him: "You envied ["hated" reads the original ts.] all fame but your own, and basked in the self-awarded mantle of simplicity. And we who loved, indulged you. To your cost" (F 92). Here at the end, Faustus projects the dilemma of Marlowe's Faust, who as early as Scene V in that play questions the commitment to the devil—although by the end, Mamet's Faustus renounces his renunciation and makes a final pact with the Magus in hopes that he has become, as he says, complete.

That Mamet should at this point in his career confront the Faust story is telling. Could it be that at fifty-seven he was reexamining his own pact with the devil of success—Hollywood? Has his search for popular recognition come at the cost of artistic integrity, which he "solves" by writing his own *Faust?* Could it be that in his pursuit of both theatrical and cinematic success, he is admitting that while the former remains for him still "pure," the latter does not? Is his treatment of Faust an admission of his own faults, or a projection of how he understood his relationship with his own father in some fashion—someone who would not recognize his merits? There are no clear answers, and *Faustus* remains a coded, inaccessible play in which the secrets get in the way and the audience remains emotionally distanced from the work.

Faustus, however, confirms Mamet's repeated use of the past in his work. Having employed pseudo, turn-of-the-century language, costume, and setting for his characters in *Boston Marriage* and having earlier displayed an absorption with Edwardian and late-nineteenth-century life in *The Winslow Boy*, it is not surprising to find his new work historically and even philosophically centered in the past. Drawing from Marlowe and Goethe, *Faustus* appears to reflect Shaw, while Beckett hovers just off-stage. The strong exposition, however, restricts the action, especially in Act I. The narrative in Act II is similarly only reported. Faust's exclamation in Marlowe's play, "Sweet Analytics, 'tis thou hast ravish'd me," applies with equal and ironic force to Mamet, whose exposition and moralizing interferes with the dramatic potential of the work (Marlowe 6).

But Faust is not a new theme for Mamet. Many of his plays consist of failed or unsuccessful pacts with the devil, sometimes satirically as in "Bobby Gould in Hell." The deal-making that goes on in his work is essentially the search for a Faustian pact that, naturally, never pays off. *Faustus* may be the culmination of that move or strategy. Teach never gets to take "the shot"; Shelly Levene doesn't get away with his crime (despite making pacts with disreputable figures, beginning with Williamson); and John gets trapped by Carol in *Oleanna* in spite of his efforts to "settle" their misunderstandings. Morality is of the moment in Mamet, as

Levene tells Roma in *Glengarry:* "What we have to do is *admit* to ourself that we see that opportunity . . . and *take* it. (*Pause*) And that's it" (GGR 72). Richard Roma, the amoral Magus of the play, also rejects an absolute set of rules, substituting the immediate for the future, the now for tomorrow: "I say *this* is how we must act. I do those things which seem correct to me *today*. I trust my self" (GGR 49). But throughout his work, Mamet's trickery is either exposed or stopped: in *The Shawl*, the clairvoyant is uncovered; in *Boston Marriage*, the séance never occurs; in *Heist* the end is ambivalent.

Edmond is perhaps Mamet's most Faust-like play before *Faustus*. Its situations and themes anticipate those of *Faustus* and the consequences of such a pact with the devil. His essay "Corruption" in *Some Freaks* develops a similar theme as Mamet examines the misuse and temptations of power, compressed in lines from Marlowe: "Hell hath no limits, nor is circumscrib'd / In one self place, but where we are is hell, / And where hell is there must we ever be" (Scene V. 31). Mamet identifies this theme, but Marlowe makes it the center of his work. In Mamet's *Faustus*, however, the inflated language and inaction restrain any dramatic action.

What to make of the work? Thematically and linguistically, connections to his previous plays are clear, but unlike them, it lacks theatrical force. The language is stilted and distant, the action negligible, although the articulation of ideas are of interest. Faustus' comment to the Magus in Act II is ironically and critically exact: "Strong, striking verbiage, yet hardly discourse" (F 79). The work also lacks humor, missing the sense of play that Marlowe's *Faust* possessed: "Oh I'm not omniscient—but I know a lot" Mephistopheles, for example, tells Faust in Goethe's version (Goethe 55). "You wonder why you are pursued? For entertainment" is a further exchange in Marlowe (81). This is definitely not the case for Mamet. In his version, Faustus comes up with the supposed all-time formula to explain human behavior—only to have it revealed that he merely copied his son's arithmetic doodling. This trivializing of his discovery, another form of the con, reduces Faustus' achievement, as well as the impact of Mamet's play.

Mamet does not trivialize history, however, in his adaptation of Harley Granville-Barker's 1905 play *The Voysey Inheritance* which premiered March 23, 2005, at American Conservatory Theatre in San Francisco, and remounted at the Atlantic Theatre in New York in December 2006 to positive reviews. Deception again lurks beneath the late-Victorian pretense and wealth through the discovery of another con, this time of a family defrauding clients for several generations of their capital and living off their income. The entire meaning of trust comes under review as Edward Voysey, the son about to succeed his father, discovers the financial deception and tries to right the wrong by convincing unwilling family members to return their embezzled monies. Mamet's world of rationalized illegality emerges when another Voysey son explains that "the more able a man is the less the word 'honesty' bothers him . . . and Father was an able man" (VI 47). At one point, the father is even called an artist for his skill in mismanaging the money of others entrusted to him and not getting caught (VI 56).

Edward, the moral son, is initially puzzled by the behavior of his father, a "gifted criminal." But the son's sense of right and wrong will not be compromised—echoing the attitude of Arthur Winslow in Mamet's *The Winslow Boy* (VI 47). The impact of Edward learning that his admired father has for years been misappropriating funds overturns the stability of the Voysey family. But instead of agreeing to make restitution, the family first looks for ways to mitigate the impact, from doing nothing to partly righting the errors through re-investment. Bankruptcy, which Edward sees as the only step, is rejected.

The various schemes prompt Edward to offer a statement of the characteristic Mamet dilemma couched in nineteenth-century syntax: "It's strange the number of people who believe you can do right by means which they know to be wrong" (VI 61). But even Edward is "trapped" into restoring funds he does not have when George Booth, the best friend of the elder Mr. Voysey, demands the return of his capital. Edward then prepares to sacrifice himself to the courts. His lover Alice, however, tells him he should stop acting heroically, that moral righteousness has no purchase on self-protection: "That's the worst of acting on principle . . . one begins thinking of one's attitude instead of the import of one's actions" (VI 65). This is quintessential Mamet, pulling together what he believes defines character (action) and undermines character (thought). Mamet's adaptation restates his indictment of capitalism and moral corruption, themes that have engaged him since his earliest work.

In the New York production, the sumptuous Edwardian set, with every space in the library covered by oil paintings, was itself a shell. There were no walls behind the paintings, a metaphor of the falseness of the Voysey family. "Business nowadays is a confidence trick," a statement of the elder Voysey, summarizes Mamet's take on the collapse of values or, inverted, a pithy celebration of what *House of Games* calls "the American Way." Mamet reduced the original five-act play to two, downplaying the original struggle between father and son. Mamet's comment on money alludes to the core of the play: on one hand, you can say it's meaningless and doesn't really exist "and so everything is really all about trust. You can also say that means it's all about crime."[21]

Mamet's concern with moral right, politics, and the law found even stronger representation in his satire *Romance* (2005), a work that occupied him throughout most of 2004. His first original play since *Boston Marriage* and first composed (at least in part) in California, it furthers his exposure of hypocrisy and pseudo-social morality against the backdrop of Mideast peace talks. "Peace. Is that not the theme of the week?" the judge in the play comically asks (ROM 7). The play is politically incorrect from start to finish and turns into a kind of Marx Brothers movie if written by Mamet. Displaying sophistry at its fullest, the play is set in a New York courtroom where a distracted judge (Larry Bryggman in the premiere at the Atlantic Theatre) tries to rule. The action becomes a burlesque of courtroom procedure with the judge increasingly disoriented by his allergies and medicine as chaos, not justice, overtakes his courtroom.

As the son of a lawyer, Mamet easily grasps the formalities of legal procedure and undisciplined prejudice. The defendant, a Jewish chiropractor, and his attorney soon insult each other because of anti-Semitic remarks the lawyer made in anger. Mamet does not hold back, defusing the situation only when the Bailiff interrupts with a crossword puzzle.

Defendant: Fuck you.
Baliff: Prehistoric fish. Ten letters.
Defense Attorney: Is, that, do I take that to mean . . . ?
Defendant: Fuck you.
Defense Attorney: Fuck me? Fuck *you*, you Rug Merchant, Greasy, Hooknosed *no*-dick, Christkilling, son-of-a bitch sacrilegious . . .
Baliff: The judge says . . .
Defense Attorney: Fuck the Judge, and fuck *you*, and and *you*, you mocky sheeny *cock*-sucker . . . when I've missed taking Little Tommy to Church Youth Hockey, because I'm stuck in here listening to your sniveling, sick . . . (ROM 41).

Hyperbole vies with insult throughout the play in a battle of racist epithets. A sample: "you people can't order a cheese sandwich . . . without mentioning the Holocaust" (ROM 44). The comic treatment of the harsh language negates its impact, however. There is surprise, but not shock.

Across town, the prosecutor and his thong-clad boyfriend are also hurling insults at each other. He's burned the roast and an argument ensues just as the defense attorney calls to ask for a continuance because his defendant has discovered a way to bring peace to the Middle East. The prosecutor angrily dismisses the idea, turning to his lover Bernard with this exchange:

Bernard: Tell him to go with God.
Prosecutor: Fuck you.
Bernard: Fuck you, too,
Prosecutor: And fuck you, *too*. You little two-bit piece of fucking INTELLECTUAL FLUFF.
Bernard: Oh, oh, oh, did you marry me for my *mind*?
Prosecutor: Fuck you.
Bernard: So that we could discuss *Proust*? Was that what had you GLUED TO THE SMALL LEATHER-GOODS COUNTER AT SAKS, DAY AFTER DAY? (ROM 58–9).

Mamet's ear is right: he gets the tone, the rhythm, and the sound of such dialogue, as when Bernard, hurt and having lost his contact lens, orders the Prosecutor back to his "priceless" phone call.

Go, go on with your "if it please the court," sick Macho *bullshit:* Mumbo Jumbo, Habeas Gumbo . . . I've lost my contact . . . Put the World in Prison. Maybe that will compensate you for your lack of self-esteem. I'm done. I'm done . . . I've burned the roast. *You* clean the fucking pan. I'm sorry for you (*He exits*). (ROM 61).

Scene Four continues the courtroom mayhem with the judge entering and asking the Bailiff what time it is: nine A.M., he replies: "At night?" is the response (ROM 63). Insults continue as when the Defendant tells the court that Shakespeare was a Jew. Contradicted by the Prosecutor, the Defendant replies, "no Christian can write that good." "What do you say to that?" the judge suddenly intervenes but before the Prosecutor can answer, the Bailiff interrupts to declare that Shakespeare was "a Fag." The judge is incredulous and the audience in stitches while the question remains unanswered: "Was Shakespeare a Jew? You go first. Whaddaya say?" asks His Honour (ROM 72–73, 101). The supposed confession that the judge himself is Jewish is another source of confusion, since he then learns that if his mother was not Jewish, he is not. Havoc overtakes the final scene as a doctor appears to administer a drug to the besotted judge, who in his final words manages to utter, "This court is adjourned" (ROM 118).

Critics were wary when they viewed the world premiere at the Atlantic Theatre in March 2005: "Mamet lite" did not seem to jive with the writer of *American Buffalo* or *Oleanna*. Few could explain his turn to farce with premises such as the readjustment of vertebrae restoring mental balance to world leaders. Other critics objected to the foul language, calling it a "frontal assault on the limits of taste."[22] Audiences, however, loved it, from the very announcement of the play, a printed subpoena with Mamet declaring he is not the plaintiff nor the defendant but the playwright, to the energetic direction of Neil Pepe. Rehearsals of the play carefully blocked the action and timing of the comedy, although at one point, the cast was unsure about a particular joke. Pepe was also uncertain. The solution was to "call David!" which he did. Moments later, Pepe returned from a hallway folding his cellphone and announcing the verdict: "keep the fucker in!" The cast cheered.

Romance recalls the *Hellzapoppin* farce of the original *Lone Canoe* (1972, Goddard College), with scenery falling and actors skidding across the stage. During an interview days before *Romance* began previews, Mamet remembered a question Macy would often ask: "Why do you write this lugubrious bullshit that puts everyone to sleep?" He would answer, "What about your acting?" The exchange went on for decades, but now, Mamet explains, *Romance* and its farcical actions is his "riposte in dramatic form to Billy Macy."[23]

Mamet's interest in violence linked to the con remained transparent during the nineties, finding its clearest expression in films like *Hoffa* (1992), *Rising Sun* (1993), a Sean Connery action film set in Japan, *Ronin* (1998), and *Lansky* (1999; screenplay and executive producer for HBO TV). Ridley Scott's *Hannibal* (2001), a sequel to *Silence of the Lambs*, was another appealing project: hired to write the screenplay as part of the "supercrew" that included Scott and Anthony Hopkins, Mamet's first draft failed to impress the producers and they couldn't agree on changes (Mamet's resistance to rewrites was well-known). Mamet then chose to work on *State and Main* rather than revise *Hannibal* and Steve Zaillian, who worked on *Schindler's List*, was brought in to revise the script, although the one-liners about cannibalism in the film may be Mamet's. And given his effortless movement among the educated and wealthy, Hannibal Lecter may be the ultimate Mamet con artist.

Satire seems to best define Mamet's theatre work in the late nineties, aligned with his persistent determination to expose hypocrisy, moral uncertainty, and exploitation. His film work blended action with his fascination with the con in one form or another. Only one place seemed right to pursue both, the modern equivalent of Mephistopheles' hell: Hollywood. Mamet moved there in 2002.

9

ARCADE AMUSEMENT

People tell stories . . . cinematically.

David Mamet, *On Directing Film*

Movies quickly became Mamet's focus, paradoxically allowing him an element of artistic freedom while under studio control. He realized this when he added two scenes and one critical monologue to the screenplay of *Glengarry Glen Ross* that were not in the stage version. The monologue, featuring Alec Baldwin as Blake (a new character), is known as "Coffee's for closers."[1] Increasingly, Mamet understood what differentiated plays from films. A play, he said, is "like an airplane. You don't want to have any extra parts" but a movie is "more like a car; it can probably sustain a couple [of] extra parts to make it look pretty." Fortunately, he explained, he did not "come from a theoretical background, the point to me was not how to use the soft currency of my playwriting expertise and make the movies eat it, but rather to learn how to write movies."[2]

He contradicts himself in the same interview, however, saying that he had done a lot of theoretical readings, especially of the Russians like Pudovkin and Everinov and Eisenstein. Mamet then outlined what the Russians taught him: "that a movie is ideally a succession of uninflected shots which, when juxtaposed, create a third reality in the mind of the viewer such that when these third realities are added together they create a scene, and that similarly, the scene, when cut together, creates the third reality in the mind of the viewer" (Katz 198).

Articulate on the process of directing and shooting a film, Mamet also remains unrepentant in his criticism of the industry. On the movies' interest in backstory, for example, he's clear: "it's important for Hollywood because it allows a lot of unemployable people to earn their living saying this to writers" (Katz 195). In Hollywood, the artist has no choice: he must collude with the studios. The artist has no chance because agents, producers, and the studios control everything and the artist always loses, in part because the studios treat the audience only as consumers.

But writers have something to learn from Hollywood, and Mamet gives several examples. During the shooting of *The Winslow Boy*, his producer, Sarah Green, was on the set and "doing the board, the day-by-day what do you shoot on each day" listing. But when she boarded out a lot of the scenes, she noticed that a number of them had the same "log line," that is similar action. Perhaps the action in one or more scenes is superfluous, she suggested. "That's the smartest thing I ever heard—give me back that script,'" Mamet commanded (Katz 200).

Film for Mamet is "an arcade amusement." It is pleasure, not work, as it removes the audience from the everyday. He recounts that when he was working on his play about the universe and meaning (presumably an early draft of *Faustus*) and talking to Macy about it, Macy reacted strongly: "You stupid motherfucker. I need to lock you in a room and show you the films of Preston Sturges" (Katz 200–1). He specifically had *Sullivan's Travels* in mind. The film stars Joel McCrea as a man who thinks he wants to save the world but realizes that all people want to do is to laugh at Mickey Mouse. "I'm one of them," a world saver, Mamet lamented (Katz 201).

Mamet's highest grossing movie, *Heist* (2001), displays many of his best moviemaking qualities. It's no surprise it was a hit—not only because of the way he succeeded in the fluidity of composition and perfection of the gangster film, but through the performances of Gene Hackman and DeVito. The tight, film-noir script also helped, ending with Gene Hackman memorably standing over a critically wounded Danny DeVito, answering DeVito's plea, "D'ya want to hear my last words?" by blowing him away while muttering, "I just did." The scene echoes Margaret Ford in *House of Games* when she shoots the conman, Mike, while he facetiously says, "Thank you, sir, may I have another?" (HG 70). She lets him have it.

Mamet drew on his repertoire of cons for *Heist*, a film critics described as "high-grade fun from beginning to end," a reflection of Hackman's ability to dispel "the Mamet chill, the portentous and equivocal atmosphere" seen in *House of Games* or *The Spanish Prisoner*. The seventy-one-year-old actor provided a dynamic presence and seemed "to liberate David Mamet from David Mamet."[3] In the film, Hackman heads a small band of thieves including Ricky Jay (Pinky), Rebecca Pidgeon (his young, hip wife), and Delroy Lindo (a violent accomplice). Seeking to retire, they pull one last jewelry heist only to be told by their fence, Danny De Vito, they have to do one *more* job—steal $50 million in gold bars—before being paid off. De Vito's character, who enjoys betraying people, sends his violently ambitious nephew to join the crew and various cons are pulled on him. Like the audience, he is never sure if an actual heist occurs or if it is a scam. Reversals become the fundamental building blocks of the film. Several complicated jobs come off while Mamet, more so in this film than in any of his others, entertains his audience, paying more attention to physical action and the paraphernalia of deception, as when a cup of coffee is used to smuggle a gun past a metal detector.

The artistry of the con rules and we witness the crafty illusions that surround but eventually destroy the characters. Hackman's gang steals more jewelry, then the gold, but spends more time tricking the nephew, "Jimmy." Reviewing the film, David Denby summarized the complex function of the con for Mamet as "the distilled essence of movies and theatre—dramatic forms designed to convince people that the illusion that holds them is the truth" (Denby 139). Or as Mamet so often says (quoting Meisner citing Stanislavsky), in the theatre one must "live truthfully under imaginary circumstances" (SMA 136). But his ambivalence possesses an underlying hostility, his obsessiveness suggesting that "he requires us to be taken in but also despises us for being such suckers" (Denby 139). Mamet's world is one of true lies. What makes *Heist* work, however, is his determination to put "the audience in the same position as the protagonists, led forth by events, by the inevitability of the previous actions" an approach he outlined as early as 1981.[4]

The world premiere took place at the Toronto International Film Festival in the fall of 2000, with the cast and Mamet present. At a press conference, he admitted that the similarity between the confidence game and the motion picture industry was strong: "in fact, the older I get, the more everything in the world looks like a confidence game." Ricky Jay's influence on him, going back to *The Shawl, House of Games*, and *Things Change*, has shaped his sense that the basis of much theatre and film is deception, which the audience willingly wants to believe in. "Everyone loves to be fooled" Mamet said. Yet what the press conference also conveyed was the sense of male camaraderie among the actors: "it's just all this guy stuff" said the actor Sam Rockwell, who played the nephew, Jimmy: "it was a bunch of testosterone."[5]

The success of *Heist* and interest in developing Rebecca Pidgeon's career, plus work on a new film, *Spartan*, took Mamet to Hollywood, specifically to Santa Monica where he and his family moved in 2002, exchanging his Newtown, Massachusetts, colonial home for a large California house. California would also allow him to be closer to his two daughters from his first marriage and to his sister Lynn Mamet, with whom he would soon be working on a new and successful TV series. To an interviewer he admitted that he spent more time on film scripts than plays, partly because changes in the urban landscape meant that the once stable theatre audience, necessary for a flourishing theatre, had diminished—and moved to the suburbs. Directing, he added, is particularly appealing because it is social and at the same time isolating: "It's like going on safari" and you are in charge.[6] Mamet may, in fact, be the successor to Graham Greene: no author of comparable distinction has been so involved in the movies, although Mamet directs and Greene did not, and where Greene focused on spies, Mamet concentrates on conspiracies—which led one critic to allege that "Mamet has the most deeply imagined paranoid worldview of any American dramatist—and that paranoia is global, societal *and* interpersonal."[7]

Spartan (2004), starring Val Kilmer, the ninth film Mamet wrote and directed, presents the paranoid Mamet world: tough men involved in Special Operations dealing, in this instance, with the kidnapping of the president's daughter by Arab terrorists. Double-crosses and conspiracies lead to a dangerous country, while a subplot traces the antagonistic bond between a mentor (Scott, played by Kilmer) and his protégé Curtis (Derek Luke). William H. Macy lends a sinister hand and it all involves planes, guns, and explosions, while indicting the White House and national leaders. Critics focused on the film's "Mametude," as A. O. Scott called it in the *New York Times*: the way language becomes staccato, tough talk with wise-cracks and "spiky tough-guy koans," noting that Mamet's language is "not meant to express a character's thoughts or emotions, but to deflect attention from them."[8] One example is Scott's curt response to a would-be volunteer before he can give his name: "Do I need to know? If I want camaraderie, I'll join the Masons. There's just the mission." *Spartan* was a modest box office hit, perhaps because audiences had tired of the search and destroy genre, although Mamet displayed greater fluency and momentum with the camera than in his earlier films. There are also a series of marvelous scams in the film, which he expanded from earlier work.

Val Kilmer, the stoical hero, made several important points about working on a Mamet set, beginning with the family atmosphere and energy. Mamet, he emphasized, was also thorough in his research, although he was often a "fantastic liar. If he doesn't have the answer he just vamps better than anybody . . . and you find you're saying your lines and they haven't changed but suddenly you believe them. I'm convinced he takes a lot of ideas from his children."

Mamet's precision, however, requires a great deal of concentration because of the particular rhythm he imparts to the dialogue. He was also concerned about the idea of a modern "warrior" and discussed ideas extensively with Kilmer. Additionally, he removed a number of scenes that seemed crucial to understanding the story but made one end up understanding it in a different way, Kilmer noted. Mamet was also interested in the classical elements that made up the hero's journey, and thought of the film as a mythic quest. The hero is, first, put on the wrong track, then his superiors lie to him. But when he finds out the missing girl is not dead, he starts over and gets her back, which is the second act of the movie. Mamet is also tough with his actors, wanting a particular performance. And he's courageous, Kilmer said: "to still wear a beret in 2004, you have to have guts." But in Mamet's world, at least in *Spartan*, "few acts of decency go unpunished." A winner in Mamet's country "would have to be a gold medalist in the Machiavellian Olympics."[9]

One consequence of working on the film was Mamet's meeting Eric L. Haney, a retired sergeant-major and author of *Inside Delta Force: The Story of America's Elite Counter-terrorist Unit* (2002). Mamet read this account of Delta Force while working on *Spartan* and called the Special Ops veteran after he had written a draft of the film, inviting him to be his technical advisor. Haney quickly agreed and proved to be a fascinating figure, teaching Mamet, the costumers, armorers, and actors on proper Special Ops techniques, including the unofficial name of the group, "The Unit." One day while wrapping *Spartan* and having lunch with Haney and Shawn Ryan, writer/producer of the TV series *The Shield* for whom Mamet was directing an episode, Mamet and the other two decided to develop a show inspired by Haney's book. One original element would be its fifty/fifty split between the fighting men and their wives, life in the field, undercover, and life at the base upholding the need for right conduct and rules. But the women have "issues" and add to the complexity of the show through infidelity, drinking, or bad judgment. But they are also part of the con, since they don't really know what their husbands do. The Unit itself seems a con: its existence is not acknowledged by the military or the U.S. government.

The result was the TV series *The Unit* starring Dennis Haysbert of *24* fame, Scott Foley from *Felicity*, and Robert Patrick from *The X-Files*. Regina Taylor, a noted stage actor, plays the alphafemale in the series, a real estate agent not above making mistakes. But why would Mamet do such a show? Part of the answer is the production speed and professionalism of TV and part is his belief that "the military form is . . . one of the universal staples of drama, etc. See Homer, Shakespeare, John Wayne, etc.. Doing TV is just like doing movies while skiing,"[10] he explained. Another appealing element of the series, he believes, is that "the electronic campfire," TV, allows us to sit around and join a clan that might be policemen, doctors, members of the White House, or the military. This restores a sense of belonging to a special group. Finally, he conceived of the first season of thirteen episodes as a novel, each episode a chapter in an effort to maintain cohesiveness. An ensemble cast also insured continuity.

The Unit premiered March 7, 2006, a mid-season replacement that from the first scored in the top ten ratings every week. The episodes of the first season ranged from Afghanistan to Idaho, choosing to mask the operation as the 303rd Logistical Studies Unit. Mamet directed two episodes and wrote three the first season, one, entitled "Security," with a Jewish theme (could one of the agents sent to monitor a Russian-Iranian meeting be Jewish, insulting the Muslim hosts?). Each episode divides its story between the wives and their drama and the adventures of the men off on secret missions, usually in foreign countries. The tense opening episode had the team deal with a highjacked plane of foreign diplomats that landed in a remote airfield in Idaho. The dialogue is clipped "Mametspeak" matching the action:

Bob Brown (Scott Foley): You've got a reputation for being difficult.
Jonas Blane (Dennis Haysbert): Yeah, it means I'm not dead yet.

Asked why he doesn't watch the news, a young man in one episode replies, "No truth in news and no news in truth." Another line with the Mamet tone is a warning from Jonas Blane to one of the men in his unit: "If you see an Indian, be careful. If you don't see an Indian, be doubly careful."

An exchange Mamet was particularly proud of occurred in episode six. The character Tiffy has been having an affair with the commanding officer, who realizes how wrong it is and wants to leave her. Mamet had prepared a long speech for Tiffy in response to the colonel's question, "What do you see in me?" But at the last moment, while filming, Mamet threw it away and told the actor, Abby Brammell, to turn and simply say, "I get a man who loves me more than his dammed hobby. Now *you* tell me that makes me a tramp." The episode illustrates, as Mamet emphasized, what Chekhov did when preparing *The Three Sisters*. When a character asks "How's your wife?" another character was to answer with a long comment about how when he wakes up in the morning she is like a rose and at mid-day she blossoms in to . . . and so on. The night before the opening, however, Chekhov telegraphed the theatre with instructions that when the first actor asks how's your wife, the response should only be, "a wife is a wife." Are you willing to cut or will you risk boring the audience? For Mamet that is the test of a great writer; or as he said in a recent interview, "in drama it's the great line which time after time kills the good scene; it's the great scene time after time which kills the good play."[11]

Several of the episodes are a family affair. Lynn Mamet (also a supervising producer of the show) wrote episode thirteen, "The Wall" (May 16, 2006), with Eric L. Haney. Her brother directed. It tells the story of a self-centered and not very competent French commander who attempts to arrest a former Yugoslavian general. A botched attack by the French leads to the Unit actually capturing the general, although the French general acting for the UN takes the credit. Later, the Yugoslavian general escapes and seeks revenge for the death of his wife in the earlier battle. In the final scene, he and his group somehow manage to get to the Unit's celebration of the colonel's wedding. A bloody shoot-out erupts at the reception, but our heroes prevail. The colonel, well played by Robert Patrick, has decided to play it straight by marrying the character played by Rebecca Pidgeon who, in a moment of wicked triumph, returns to Tiffy her love letters to the colonel when she comes to give her flowers to "welcome" the colonel's new wife to the base.

But the series can't seem to release itself from the con. In the October 31, 2006, episode, "Old Home Week," Mamet, who wrote and directed the segment, has the con work for the military side of the equation. Jonas and a fellow member first steal some smuggled diamonds in Italy and then trick a series of West African diamond suppliers so that members of The Unit can attend an auction in order to get near to a sheik who is the center of a terrorist operation. With the help of a third agent who supplies weapons, they kill the sheik and other operatives. But the character played by Scott Foley notices that not all the diamond packets were turned over to the watchful CIA. The missing packet turns up in a semisecret hideout of The Unit on the base, where it is passed on to a retired member who keeps it as insurance to cover expenses and assist families should any fighting member be killed. The Army itself is conned.

The retired "Unit" member in charge of the diamonds is the Chicago actor Meshach Taylor, the original Bigger Thomas of Gregory Mosher's 1978 *Native*

Son. Rebecca Pidgeon rounds out the cast with an appearance at the end of the episode, which contains a Mamet twist: a rediscovered love letter by a soldier killed in the Battle of the Bulge is thought to be to his wife—it's addressed to Midge—but it turns out to be to his comrade, who survived and with whom he had been in love. Mamet doesn't reveal this until the final moments of the episode, when the now eighty-year-old veteran on stage for "Old Home Week" at the base interrupts the presentation of the letter to his dead comrade's wife with the words "I'm Midge."

TV is the not the only current exposure for Mamet. A film version of *Edmond* starring William H. Macy, Rebecca Pidgeon, and Joe Mantegna was released in July 2006 to critical favor. Set in L.A. rather than New York and directed by Stuart Gordon, it sustains the strong language, pseudo-machismo, violence, and bigotry, as well as the suspense, candor, and crackling language of the stage version. Unlike the films Mamet directs in which the overly stylized line readings tend to dry out the emotion or the material is treated reverentially, Gordon balances dark comedy with the hurricane temperament of Edmond. Gordon also succeeds in playing the dialogue against the context of a horror-suspense movie. Macy himself introduced the film in Chicago in late July.

Current events, especially of an anti-Semitic nature, continue to draw Mamet's voice. Seeing himself as a public artist, he feels responsible for commenting on public affairs. An article in the *Chicago Tribune* of August 6, 2006, for example, identifies the lengthy fight for Israel's survival; Israel not as the initiator of aggression but the defender of its existence in the face of Arab attacks. The press, he states, misinterprets the conflict with Lebanon and Hezbollah: it's not a desire to invade Lebanon but to stop Hezbollah from killing Jews. It's not bad PR that is creating a negative image of Israel but anti-Semitism. In response to Mel Gibson's outburst against Jews, also part of the column, he finds his comments repugnant but his apology acceptable. "Good for him," Mamet concludes with a tone of sarcasm. Such interest presaged a new essay collection, published in October 2006.

Entitled *The Wicked Son, Anti-Semitism, Self-Hatred and the Jews*, the 187-page book contains thirty-seven short pieces expressing the intensity, anger, and focus of Mamet as he takes aim at those who hypocritically profess their Judaism but know little about it. He also attacks apostates for thinking that they could ever escape their Jewishness. He criticizes those Jews who might weep at the film *Exodus* but "jeer at the Israeli Defense Forces" (WS xi). He squares off against Jewish hatred, sentimentalizing the Holocaust and those Jews who might educate themselves about radical politics, extremist history, or cultural behavior but know next to nothing about their own religion.

Mamet's premise is that the world hates the Jews, but at the same time, he systematically confronts their misrepresentation by anti-Semites. The self-loathing Jew is a particular anathema to Mamet, although in his assault he often gets sidetracked into discussing American politics or the question of who wrote Shakespeare's plays. Reclaiming and sustaining Jewish identity is the most persistent and coherent subject in the volume, at times inverting logic: Jewish guilt, he claims, is not a side effect of being Jewish but of being "insufficiently Jewish." "Our problematical longevity taxes the world," he writes (WS 46, 50). The burden and challenge of being a Jew troubles Mamet, whose response is to fight, resist, and reject those who criticize or undermine the religion. The energetic if occasionally fragmented essays express Mamet's well-defined if aggressive positions, which alternate between antagonism and abuse. The book is a provocation disguised as a warning.

Mamet's Judaism remains on high alert. In a short essay in a new collection edited by Alan Dershowitz on the topic of what Israel means to a group of writers, Mamet eviscerates Noam Chomsky for his opposition to the existence of the State of Israel. He then criticizes Chomsky's opposition to its occupation of Arab lands, which Chomsky calls a "new anti-Semitism." Mamet counters by emphasizing that Israel is a free society where "the rights of the minority, the oppressed, indeed of the criminally foolish are protected." And while free to promote his ideas in the U. S., Chomsky would be prosecuted as a Jew in any Arab country. And if prosecuted, it would be, ironically, Israel that would offer him a home under the Right of Return: "This," Mamet concludes, "is what Israel means to me."[12] Yet, Mamet cannot resist the con. A picture of him wearing a kefiyah, a heavy cotton scarf that has become a symbol of solidarity with the Palestinian cause, appeared in the *New York Times.* He explained his garb as a bargain from a used army surplus site, suggesting it was a deal too good to pass up.

~

Mamet values the past because of its celebration of traditional skills and virtues, and he often expresses this in his love of honestly built furniture, old-fashioned tools, and old movies. His decision to direct Priestley's *The Dangerous Corner*, Rattigan's *Winslow Boy*, and Granville-Barker's *The Voysey Inheritance* reaffirms his admiration for a structured past of defined moral values. He even set his production of Beckett's *Catastrophe* in the past, Wilton's, a Victorian London musical hall, and dressed his actors in a sort of fifties style, the human object/prisoner in the play outfitted in Victorian long underwear.

Mamet acknowledges the past fully—when it's not his own. His 2002 visit with Ricky Jay to the almost ninety-nine-year-old Al Hirschfield for a sketch turned into a welcomed tutorial by Hirschfield of Broadway's vaudeville past in preparation for Jay's show, *On the Stem.* Mamet's celebration of encounters with Roland Winters, who played Charlie Chan, or meeting Lillian Gish, who talked to him about D. W. Griffith, is another. Working with eighty-year-old Don Ameche on *Things Change* brought him in contact again with cinema's past. Jose Ferrer, Denholm Elliot, Samson Raphaelson (who wrote *The Jazz Singer*), are others he has met and respected. As Mamet noted, "I was fortunate to come up in the years when every performer entered show business through the stage" (TF 126). To this and his value of tradition he relates the well-made work, whether a play, set design, direction, or performance. He knows that to convince, it must be true. His pursuit of theatre history reflects his desire to know a subject thoroughly.

Mamet is above all a moralist, and constantly educates his audience on the differences between the true and the false. Theatrical tradition is essential for him; he has learned from it and discovered one of its most important lessons: that the barometer of theatrical success can only be the audience. It is *their* reaction that measures the success or failure of a work and their approval that gives him the freedom to construct and write his plays the way he does. "Only when the artist renounces the desire to control the audience will he or she find true communication with the audience—not power *over* them, but power *with* them" (SF 96). Yet this differs from his practice because the participation of the audience encourages the deployment of the con.

Pauline Kael, the film critic, understood this nearly twenty years ago when commenting on Mamet's film, *Things Change*:

> Mamet cons the audience. He brings it into a hip complicity with him. He gives people the impression that in making them wise to the actor's games he's making them wise to how the world works—that he's letting them in on life's dirty secrets. And flatness of performance seems to be part of the point. Mamet's minimalism suggests a knowingness, disdain for elaboration or development . . . . People can feel one up on the action . . . .[13]

By linking the con to his directorial style, Kael identifies how Mamet coopts the audience into his work. The supposed flat style is a way of clearing a path so that the directness of the delivery reflects the directness of the language, unelaborated, unemotional. The irony is that Mamet's control can go only so far. A William H. Macy or Mike Nussbaum or Felicity Huffman or Joe Mantegna cannot be erased. Their character, even if reduced, combines with a Mamet text to create a singular Mamet style. A further irony is that his love of the Nineteenth-century past is a love of the elaborate, enlarged, and rhetorically strained. Kipling is a writer known for verbal excess, as is Trollope, Thackeray, and others he favors, including Dreiser.[14]

Like the nineteenth-century heroes he admires, Mamet's characters speak digressively, not discursively. They don't talk about themselves as he rarely talks about himself. To a recent interviewer who asked about his processes of revising *The Voysey Inheritance*, he replied, "I think it's chutzpah for me to inquire into my own mental processes. I try not to think about it."[15] His characters, like himself, prefer action to introspection, fulfilling the Aristotelian claim he favors that character is habitual action. Indeed, to another interviewer he said he never writes character, just dialogue, the language of action (KCRW). For Mamet, character only reveals itself by what it does. But the task for the writer is to find drama where no apparent drama exists.

Mamet involves contradictions, beginning with his combination of the Midwest with New England, Dreiser with Thoreau. Independent, outspoken, direct, an outdoorsman who reads the Stoics, he is also a theatrical "terrorist" who chooses to bring his pupils to idyllic Vermont; a writer of city life who actually composes his works in a country cabin; a teacher who would fine late students a dollar a minute and then burn the money in front of them; a cigar-smoking, foul-mouthed acting teacher who would pause at the sight of a deer herd silently crossing the lawn of the state capital in Montpelier, Vermont, at midnight.

When he lived in Boston, Mamet outfitted himself as a traditionalist—not only in the decoration and furnishings of his home—weathered and honest American antiques (see his essay on Gregory Mosher's table, "Domicile," in JAF)—but in his chosen environment. Shawmut Avenue in his Boston neighborhood he called "the most beautiful street in America," a street defined by its traditional, proportioned style. This side of him, reflected in his use of late-Nineteenth-century social and linguistic locutions, balances his rough-and-ready image and profanity in his better-known, urban plays. A drama of manners (*The Voysey Inheritance*) is as important to him as the violence of *Edmond*. In many ways, the world of *The Winslow Boy* and not *American Buffalo* defines Mamet today.

But what of his influence? How strong is it? Surprisingly, it may be more important in Britain than in the U. S. This may have started with the strong reception given to *Glengarry Glen Ross*, which had its world premiere in London. Conor McPherson, the Irish dramatist and author of *The Weir* and most recently *Shining City*, seems to confirm this. Written in a stylized, stop-and-start dialogue pioneered by Beckett, refined by Pinter, and intensified by Mamet, *Shining City* is about two Dubliners in crisis: in the first scene, a businessman confesses to his therapist that he has been seeing the ghost of his dead wife. The therapist, a lapsed Roman Catholic priest, is dealing with his own ghosts after leaving his child and girlfriend, who helped him through a spiritual crisis.

McPherson (compact and slender as Mamet is compact and broad-shouldered) became interested in theater at University College, Dublin, where he completed a Master's Degree in philosophy: "I started drifting into plays after reading '*Glengarry Glen Ross*.' I remember thinking, 'All that swearing. I could do this." He later added that "the day I read *Glengarry Glen Ross*, that was it. I knew exactly what I was going to do."[16] Like Mamet, his early plays were sets of monologues and short scenes, as in *The Lime Tree Bower*, a comic trio of monologues that include a portrait of a degenerate, drunken academic. His next play was *St. Nicholas*, which introduced audiences to a vile character, a theatre critic who socializes with vampires (the allusion to Mamet's St. Nicholas Theatre Company may not have been accidental). *The Weir* broke the monologue method (as *American Buffalo* did for Mamet): it's about a group of patrons in an isolated Irish pub who trade ghost stories. It ran for eight months on Broadway after winning an Olivier Award in London. McPherson's newest play, *Seafarers*, is about a poker game in which one of the five players is the devil. Mamet, poker, and Mephistopheles seem to blend in the new work, which opened at the National in London in September 2006.

Martin McDonagh is another playwright directly influenced by Mamet. He first went to the theatre in August 1984 at fourteen to see Al Pacino in *American Buffalo* in the London production at the Duke of York's. Pacino's manic, self-mocking performance and Mamet's "demotic arias in which banal squabbles acquire an epic momentum" overwhelmed him.[17] McDonagh went on to write a series of cruel but brutally honest plays like *The Lieutenant of Inishmore*, with its graphic depiction of torture, murder, and dismemberment within a framework of farce. It offers a savage critique of Irish-nationalist terrorism and was intended to provoke: "I was trying to write a play that would get me killed" McDonagh said (NYKR 45). He previously had written *The Beauty Queen of Leenane*, produced at the Atlantic Theatre, another link to Mamet.

The American Neil LaBute, author of *In the Company of Men*, is another young writer affected by Mamet and who, like him, mixes drama with film. First a play and then a surprisingly successful film, *In the Company of Men* draws on many of the Mamet tropes, beginning with its male camaraderie and misogynist attitudes. Born in Detroit but raised in Spokane, LaBute presents edgy portraits of human relationships, while working with ensemble casts including Aaron Eckhart and Ben Stiller. *The Mercy Seat* was one of the first major theatrical reactions to 9/11, the story of a man who missed work at the World Trade Center that morning because he was with his mistress. Believing that his family thinks he was killed, he considers running away to start a new life with the woman. Ben Younger, writer/director of the film *The Boiler Room* about an underground brokerage house, is another new voice in the Mamet mold. Brooklyn-born and a former policy analyst for New York City, he's turned to film writing since 1995, following *Boiler Room* with the romantic comedy *Prime*.

Mamet has not lacked imitators. Frederick Stroppels's "The Mamet Women," premiering in a 1992 Los Angeles production, presents two women in an exaggerated display of Mamet's most typical characterizations. Upset over a babysitter canceling, Sally first discounts her husband as a candidate because "a man is only a thing, and a husband is less than a thing." Her friend Polly responds:

Polly: What are you thinking?
Sally: I'm thinking about thinking. I'm doing the preliminary work.

The comic scene ends with what seems like a deal—her friend will baby sit—and then no deal. As the two women overplay language in the Mamet mode with echoes of *Glengarry*, their agreement falls apart:

Polly: You're not listening.
Sally: I'm listening.
Polly: You're not *hearing*.
Sally: Am I hearing? I'm hearing.
Polly: So you're not listening. Listen when you hear.
Sally: Speak when you talk.[18]

Mamet has, of course, acknowledged influences on him: Pinter, Beckett, and even Arthur Miller. One of Beckett's crucial roles was to confirm the principle of cutting or subtraction in a text. As he later described to his biographer James Knowlson, Beckett famously realized during a rare visit to Ireland, that "Joyce had gone as far as one could in the direction of knowing more, [being] in control of one's material. He was always adding to it; you only have to look at his proofs to see that. I realized that my own way was in impoverishment, in lack of knowledge and in taking away, in subtracting rather than in adding."[19] This led, of course, to the minimalist and powerful drama of his fictional trilogy, *Molloy, Malone Meurt* and *L'Innommable*, as well as *Godot*, *Krapp's Last Tape*, and *Ohio Impromptu*—and is reflected in Mamet's realization that cutting is the clearest way to improve a text. His frequent remark to throw away the best work is an extension of Beckett's policy that less *is* more, Mies van der Rohe's modernist claim.

The death of Arthur Miller prompted a short article by Mamet recalling, first, their meeting backstage after Dustin Hoffman's performance in *Death of a Salesman* and the importance of that play and the *Crucible*. He notes that we are freed at the end of those two major dramas not because there is a solution but precisely because Miller "has reconciled us to the notion that there is no solution . . . and that no one is immune from self-deception."[20] This parallels Mamet's own thinking. In "Meritocracy" he writes, "it is not a sign of ignorance not to know the answers. But there is great merit in facing the questions" (TF, 127). For two hours in the theatre we lay aside the delusion that "we are powerful and wise," he writes. Speaking at Miller's eightieth birthday party, he quoted Kipling and the need not to retreat from the tasks fate has provided for us.

Pinter, of course, was particularly central, especially his "demotic language," Mamet citing *Review Sketches*, *A Night Out*, and *The Birthday Party* as key texts (DMC 219). Mamet especially sensed how Pinter's use of the pause became part of the dramatic line, conveying just as much meaning as the words. It is bad drama "to have everyone say what they think because in real life people never say what they think. They speak to gain something from the other person." Language for Mamet is not performative but "exhortative" or "manipulative" (DMC 219).

Inflexible, truculent, uncompromising: Mamet's behavior in and out of the theatre has often exasperated, yet his fierceness, bolted to a sense of purpose and determination to overcome obstacles through hard work, form the unassailable core of his writing and life. The disparate sources that have shaped his life reinforce his self-confidence, especially through the support of his students and ensemble companies. His multiple identities as actor, playwright, director, screenwriter, children's author, poet, essayist, religious commentator, and novelist do not conflict—nor do the apparent differences between macho writer and theatre practitioner, nor reversal from critic of Hollywood life to happy resident of the corrupt "City of Angels." The "trash ethics" of Hollywood both repulse and attract Mamet, as his essay collection *Bambi vs. Godzilla* reconfirms.[21] His shift from the bearded, Chicago guerilla look of the seventies to the Brechtian swagger of the cigar, clear glasses, and brush cut of New York in the eighties, to the quasi-country gentleman in his 4x4, wearing jeans and boots in the nineties to the clean-shaven TV writer/film director of Hollywood today reflects a change in outlook as well as attitude.

But Mamet can also laugh at himself. A December 1991 parody written to honor Gregory Mosher mimics his own style. Mike Nussbaum tries to read a script composed of the letter "I" but wonders if there is a misprint because one of the letters is lower case. A debate between Mamet, Nussbaum, and Mosher begins, Mamet impatient, Nussbaum serious, and Mosher trying to negotiate between the two. Macy appears and is jealous. He, too, wants a misprint in his script. At one point, the meticulous Nussbaum again expresses his thought that it's a typo. An exasperated Mamet shouts, "I DON'T CARE IF IT'S A TYPO. TELL HIM, GREG, JUST TELL HIM SAY IT ANYWAY. Macy then interrupts with " . . . is this part of the etude"? The comedy is in the way Mosher must repeat Mamet's comments to Nussbaum, especially when Mamet realizes it is a typo and Nussbaum doesn't *have* to say it. Mike: "Well, why couldn't you have told me that before I memorized it?" is the reply.[22]

Mamet's importance and popularity is unquestioned. The playwright, director, screenwriter stands at the pinnacle of contemporary American drama by his intensity and volume. The dark, edgy, streamlined language of his work, centered in the world of hucksters, con artists, and scammers, reflects not only a contemporary fascination with the dangerous and deceptive but is a startling voice recording contemporary mores.

Mamet's reputation, however, has gone up and down. After the meteoric beginning with *Sexual Perversity in Chicago* and *American Buffalo*, there seemed to be a dip in his success until *Glengarry Glen* Ross, and then a lull until the controversial *Oleanna*. His films have never been box-office hits, but he has been steadily developing a strong following. Jonathan Kalb summarized this when he wrote that Mamet has been "consistently able to parlay big-screen fame into Broadway marketability," reversing the usual emphasis from theatrical to cinematic achievement. His productivity, however, has been exceptional, although some would argue the very cause of his weakness: trying too much in too many genres. One ungenerous critic summarized his career by saying Mamet's theatre work since *Glengarry* "has been mostly mediocre. Now sixty, Mamet is a major dramatist turned minor film director."[23]

Venerated for his early poetic naturalism, criticized for his foul language and supposed inability to portray women, Mamet nonetheless relishes the enigma, which he repeatedly displays in interviews. When questioned by strangers, he can be monosyllabic, but with friends, on movie sets, and in the theatre he is garrulous and social, remembering everyone's name and thanking all, often with gifts. Similarly, in synagogue he is friendly, involved, and delighted to dance as well as sing. Yet, he can't (or won't) lose the tough-guy image, always ready to express something unacceptable but honest: "he goes into the men's room and comes out with a script," one critic quipped.[24]

Mamet may be the ultimate artistic grifter, shifting from form to form, conning audiences and genres alike. He can encompass love and violence in the same sentence and might subscribe to the view that compares the human gene "to a successful Chicago gangster" offered by the socio-biologist Richard Dawkins. In *The Selfish Gene*, Dawkins writes that if we were told a man lived a long life in the world of Chicago gangsters, we might guess what sort of figure he was. He would have the qualities of "toughness, a quick trigger finger, and an ability to attract loyal friends." These are not infallible deductions but "you can make some inferences about a man's character if you know something about the conditions in which he has survived and prospered," an explanation of biography, as well as of Mamet and his persona.[25]

In person, Mamet's a witty jokester and deeply religious, romantic yet with a public reputation for misogyny. But he has always been hardworking in the Chicago tradition, appropriating this to acting, where, he has argued, "the only talent you need . . . is a talent for working" (PHA 5). A lonely and alienated childhood may have affected the anger that he channeled into his drama, now tempered by maturity and success. But his drive and creativity continue as he works in various genres, adding television to his list of triumphs. But loyalty to ideas is as strong as his loyalty to friends: "I've always been more comfortable sinking while clutching a good theory than swimming with an ugly fact" ("Pen").

Nonetheless, Mamet's acting ideas remain controversial. Statements like "there is no such thing, for the actor, as characterization," which is "as Aristotle reminded us is just habitual action," or, "a good writer gets better only by learning . . . to remove the ornamental . . . the narrative, and especially the deeply felt and meaningful" bring rebuke (SF 61; WR xv). The result is often unsympathetic reaction to his directing in both the theatre and on screen. But Mamet is unwavering: he believes his principles and like his hero Aristotle emphasizes "doing" more than thinking. He also knows that we withhold judgment of someone's character "until we see *how they act*" (SF 62). Mamet doesn't hesitate or quibble, which is both his strength and weakness. Actors and audiences know where he stands, which for some brings discomfort and others satisfaction. But he is never indefinite or unsure, a quality exhibited in his early years at Goddard as a student and teacher.

Now sixty, recognition and awards have begun: in February 2005, he won the Screen Writers Guild of America West Screen Laurel Award at the Guild's 57th Annual Ceremony. Given for work that has advanced the literature of the motion picture and made an outstanding contribution to the profession of the screenwriter, the award had been previously presented to Billy Wilder, Preston Sturges, Joseph L. Mankiewicz, John Huston, and Mel Brooks. The citation noted Mamet's body of work and uncompromising vision, and that perhaps more than other contemporary writer today, Mamet "has influenced the way we speak on film, on the stage and television and even in our own lives."[26] The announcement even refers to the apocryphal story of Mamet using a metronome in rehearsal to sharpen the precise delivery of his staccato lines.

In March 2006 he was fêted at a six-week Mamet Festival at the Goodman Theatre in Chicago, where over the years more than a dozen of his plays have been produced. The festival featured full productions of *A Life in the Theatre, Romance*, and the children's play *The Revenge of the Space Pandas*. In addition, there were three evenings of one-act plays including *The Shawl* directed by Mike Nussbaum and *The Disappearance of the Jews* directed by Rick Snyder. There was also a special thirtieth anniversary reading of *American Buffalo*, an "acting Mamet" panel discussion, and even a Mamet Write-Alike contest, the winning scripts read by Goodman actors.[27] Even a Mamet Slam was planned.

A highlight was not only the T-shirt and caps that read "'#@!%*' David Mamet Festival," but an evening with Mamet himself chaired by Richard Christiansen, held on March 27, 2006. Warm applause from a full house greeted Mamet when he walked on stage in a dark blazer, tie, and light pants, setting the tone for his generous and often lengthy responses to Christiansen's questions. Mentioning that he and his eighteen-year-old daughter Zosia had just come from the Twin Anchors, one of his favorite North Side Chicago restaurants, Mamet launched into a seventy-five-minute chat about his early theatre life, foregoing his abrasive and uninformative manner for one of relaxed reminiscing. He ranged from his days at the real estate office at Lincoln and Peterson Avenues to midnight children's shows at Hull House Theatre, and William H. Macy as Puck at the Oak Park Shakespeare Festival in the mid-seventies. He also alluded to Mike Nussbaum, in the audience, as the inspiration for the older and sentimental actor in *A Life in the Theatre*, adding that, "I'm not saying Mike was like that in real life. Although he was and is."

Mamet explained that a well-structured play addresses three questions: "Who wants what from whom? What happens if they don't get it? Why now?" a distilled formulation of his overall aesthetic presented in *True and False*. Asked why he came back to Chicago after graduating from Goddard and before he returned to take up teaching acting there, he answered, "I didn't know where to go. I didn't have any money. I didn't have any skills." He also spent a good deal of that time "perched on the edge of a poker table." He ended the evening by distinguishing between New York and Chicago writers. New York writers were always writing about "What does life mean? Who the hell cares?" Chicago writers focused on doing life. Yet he still feels like an outsider, not only because he is Jewish but because he is a writer, more pointedly a Chicago writer. "The question is not how to get into the country club," he surmised, but "what's going on here?"[28]

A second Chicago celebration of the playwright occurred in October 2006 when he received the 2006 Carl Sandburg Literary Award given by the Chicago Public Library Foundation. The award is presented in recognition for work and a career that has enhanced "the public's awareness of the written word." The 2005 winner was John Updike; past winners include Kurt Vonnegut, Joyce Carol Oates, and David McCullough. The ceremony took place on October 12, 2006 in the ninth floor Winter Garden atop the block-long Harold Washington Library Center on Chicago's State Street. The afternoon of the award ceremony Mamet gave an interview in which he complained about the difficulty of writing, the gift of writing dialogue, the importance of Hemingway and Kipling and their war writing, and his upcoming agenda which includes a musical with Patti LuPone.[29]

Preceding Mamet to the podium that evening and symbolically marking his hometown return was Mayor Richard M. Daley, Jr., to receive an award for support and commitment to the Chicago public library system. In his short acceptance speech, Mamet—for the first time in years clean-shaven—alternated fond memories of reading authors such as Sinclair Lewis and Willa Cather in the third floor reading room of the old main library on Randolph Street (now the Chicago Cultural Center) with a call to rallying around the freedom to think and freedom to read. He underscored, in particular, the importance of Dreiser, because he wrote of things Mamet was experiencing: "loneliness, the need to find work, to make money, to fight my way in, in short to *understand*."[30] His heroes, he stressed, were the "freethinkers, the shade tree mechanics or philosoph[ers], who stripped it down to the metal and could explain their ideas in a paragraph" (Sand 2).

In referencing Chicago as a city of "working people living in a workers' town," he also recalled his father's love for the city, as strong as a father's love for his family (Sand 1, 2). But in an aside, he remarked that the media exists today only to entertain and inflame. He then offered a simple test of character: how one behaves on the job, which, if conduct is respectful, leads to the free exchange of ideas that is at the center of America's development (Sand 3).

The next day, Mamet offered a commentary on his life and career at a noon forum at the library with the journalist, radio commentator, and friend, Rick Kogan. Stories, anecdotes, and theatre history, mixed with Hollywood comment, were his focus, with people like Mike Nussbaum in the audience to correct him on dates or incidents in the past. He also offered his view of making it in showbiz, explaining that talent is not enough: only persistence wins out in the end. And will he ever forgo his Chicago identity? He answered by citing the closing lines of Kipling's poem "The Virginity": "We've only one virginity to lose / And where we lost it there our hearts will be!" As a token of gratitude, the library gave a beaming Mamet their original index card from their catalogue for *Glengarry Glen Ross*.

His library appearance suggested the importance of an archive, one that contains a writer's accomplishments as well as false starts and failures. For years Mamet has been amassing one, which is now housed at the Harry Ransom Humanities Research Center at the University of Texas, Austin. Journals, play drafts, produced and unproduced screenplays, production files, and correspondence form the bulk of it. In a statement to mark its April 2007 acquisition, Mamet acknowledged the range of the material and his writing process, both longhand and typed drafts. He "eschews" (a typical Mamet word), the computer. He also notes his contradictory position: he has no interest in seeing his early drafts because they remind him of the effort, if not pain, of writing, but he has also never thrown anything away. Someone might find diversion, if not benefit, from reviewing the material. Such is every parent's fantasy, he says, that those who would come after would actually "care."

But can he explain his creativity and his work? Not likely, he answers. No artist, he offers, can pinpoint the origin or meaning of their creations: "That's why the product is art, which may connect the unconscious of the artist to that of the audience." But to now have his material in the hands of archivists fulfills the fantasy of both the parent and the artist, who, though absent, "might envision a cost-free colloquy with a perfect interlocutor."[31]

Mamet remains active, directing, for example, the Los Angeles premiere of *Boston Marriage* at the eighty-four-seat Geffen Theatre (January 31- March 19, 2006). The production starred the film actors Mary Steenburgen, Alicia Silverstone, and Rebecca Pidgeon. Marking his continued attachment to the Geffen, affiliated with UCLA's School of Theatre, Film and Television, was his direction of the remounted *Ricky Jay and His 52 Assistants* (November 2006-January 2007) and the early 2007 production of *Speed-the-Plow* directed by Randall Arney, former Artistic Director of Steppenwolf Theatre in Chicago. In 2000 he began to publish cartoons in *Boston Magazine* in a feature called "Dammit Mamet." This expanded to a blog at www.huffingtonpost.com/davidmamet, consisting mostly of political or social cartoons with an occasional comment. A collection of these satiric works that often showcase visual and verbal puns, titled *Tested on Orphans*, appeared in 2007 (he blames Shel Silverstein for the book because Silverstein told him Thurber couldn't draw either.). The title originates in a cartoon of a bottle with a label boldly stating "Not Tested on Animals" but below, in smaller type, "tested on orphans."

A collection of essays on the movie business, entitled *Bambi vs. Godzilla*, and partly drawn from his film columns in the *Guardian*, appeared in February 2007. This 262-page book dedicated to his long-time film editor Barbara Tulliver—she did *Homicide* as well as *Heist, State and Main, Spartan*, and other Mamet films—is a discussion of his principles and practices of movie-making, from screenwriting to location shooting. Mamet identifies himself here as a filmmaker rather than segregating himself as a screenwriter or director. It is one of his most sustained and successful essay collections, which alternates between problems in financing to the behavior of "stars," with its expected indictment of producers and studios for emasculating writers and their creativity.

In a chapter wryly called "(Secret Bonus Chapter) The Three Magic Questions," Mamet sets out one principle and three questions. The principle is that "no one can write drama without being *immersed in* the drama," suggesting that the writer has to go through what the "antagonist" undergoes. He then analyzes drama, filmed or on stage, as "a succession of scenes," each to end with the hero thwarted in pursuit of his goal so that he is forced to go on to the next scene. The audience then watches with the hero as he progresses. But to write a successful scene one needs to answer these three questions:

1. Who wants what from whom?
2. What happens if they don't get it?
3. Why now? (BVG 85–6).

Writers naturally avoid these questions, but they must be addressed. Few studio executives or producers pay attention to such matters, but one group does: the audience.

In *Bambi vs. Godzilla*, Mamet pays particular attention to the audience, those who, in fact, actually shape the work. He always writes with them in mind. Unlike the studios or producers, who see the audience as a commodity, he acknowledges the audience as an associate, an adjunct to creation (BVG 122). Consequently, he always seeks to "err on the side of the audience" (BVG 115). They are the only arbiters of taste and artistic success or failure. He supplements this discussion with a set of guidelines, including "*stay with the money*" (shoot the star), "*burn the first reel*" (always throw out the first ten minutes), and always *cut* if you think you should cut: "in film, *less* is always better" (BVG 114–15). And as he likes to repeat, you "get to make a movie three times: when you write it, when you shoot it and when you cut it" (BVG 109).

The role and authenticity of the audience is in contrast to the hucksters and confidence men who started and maintain the movie business, which was originally "the *cosa nostra* of arcade hustlers" (BVG 9). Opposing this strain, however, is the "rampant American love of workmanship," a persistent Mamet theme (BVG 7). For a filmmaker, this value overrides the hypocrisy, avarice, and ignorance of producers and explains why one would put up with such distractions. It is the love of the well-made that Mamet has elaborated in many earlier collections and does so again in "The Development Process" (BVG 25–6). The importance of the well-made, he declares, is at the core of every serious filmmaker and, indeed, of every well-made play.

He also displays his admiration for the work of Preston Sturges and a series of older films including Sturges' *Lady Eve*, Alfred E. Green's *The Al Jolson Story*, and Roberto's Rossellini's *General della Rovere*. Mamet displays a thorough knowledge of movie history in the collection, but can't quite free himself from the allure of crime, beginning his chapter "The Development Process" with this sentence: "The artist is, in effect, a sort of gangster." He enters the "guarded bank of the unconscious in an attempt to steal the gold of inspiration." The producer is like the getaway driver "who sells the getaway car and waits outside the bank grinning about what a great deal he's made" (BVG 23). The artist as criminal or thief is a persistent Mamet motif, his way of embodying his knowledge that the writer will always be an outsider at the same time he seeks to be accepted as a "worker" embedded in society. Mamet seeks to replace the status of "artist" with the word "maker."

When dealing with topics other than the technical features of moviemaking, Mamet's tone is acerbic. He begins "Jews in Show Business," for example, with this sentence: "Let me see if I can offend several well-meaning groups at once" (BVG 19). Mamet as a Jacobin summarizes his stance, subversive, bracing, and challenging the status quo, like his drama.[32] Replacing the theoretical is "the thing itself," which can be understood "only through experience" (BVG 109). His book is a passionate and cohesive poetics of the movies that becomes an invigorating summary of his current film and theatre aesthetic. Several days before its publication, Mamet held forth on the movie business in Manhattan at a New York Times Talk with Frank Rich.

Mamet's high-octane productivity has continued. A second season of *The Unit* ran throughout the fall/winter of 2006/07 receiving strong ratings. He also directed two ads for the Ford Motor Company that premiered on Fox's *American Idol* in April 2007. The script, which he approved, imitated his clipped, brawny style, although his persistent indictment of American commercialism made his unexpected involvement highly ironic. More characteristic is his next film, a $10-million production for Sony Pictures Classic set in the Jiu-Jitsu fight world. Based on an original screenplay by Mamet entitled *Redbelt* and to star Chiwetel Ejiofor, as well as Rebecca Pidgeon and Ricky Jay, it contains the classic Mamet blend of machismo and the con. The plot centers on how a cabal of movie stars and fight promoters con a Jiu-Jitsu master who is no longer prizefighting but operating a self-defense studio in Los Angeles. To regain his honor, he must reenter the ring. Set in an underworld inhabited by bouncers, cage fighters, cops, and special forces operatives, *Redbelt* is quintessential Mamet. Production began in May 2007 with Mamet directing; it was released to favorable reviews in May 2008.

In the film, Mamet managed to blend the B-movie conceit of good man versus bad world by balancing old Hollywood and Greek tragedy according to the *New York Times* (May 2, 2008). In an essay on fighting, he explained that it's the sadness in the faces of fighters that he admires citing three films: *Night and the City* (1950), *The Killing* (1956), and *The Seven Samurai* (1954). All fighters and fight films are sad Mamet remarks. In the same essay, he upholds film noir as "tragedy manqué:" "the gods still win, but good's triumph gets an asterisk" (Mamet, "Hard Lessons Learned in the Ring," *New York Times*, April 27, 2008: AR 19).

Another new development is *November*, a political comedy set to open on Broadway in January 2008. This is Mamet's first world premiere on Broadway since *Speed-the Plow* in 1988. Joe Mantello, who directed the Tony-Award-winning revival of *Glengarry Glen Ross* on Broadway in 2005, will direct. Nathan Lane is to star. Inspired by the absurdity of presidential pardons for Thanksgiving turkeys, *November* is about a single day in the life of a president shortly before an election in which he is running as an incumbent. It involves civil marriage, gambling casinos, lesbians, American Indians, presidential libraries, questionable pardons, and campaign contributions according to the show's producers. Also announced is a double bill at the Kirk Douglas Theatre in Culver City, CA to open in May 2008 of *Duck Variations and Keep Your Pantheon,* a stage version of what was originally a BBC radio play. Neil Pepe, Artistic Director of the Atlantic Theatre in New York, is to direct.

As if to bookend this study, *Keep Your Pantheon*, originally broadcast on BBC's Radio 4 in late May 2007, is another encounter with life in the theatre. This time, however, the stage is ancient Rome. The forty-five minute radio play comically recounts the adventures of a failing company of actors in conflict with an autocratic military rule. By accident, they have entered the wrong door of an Armory where the Tenth Legion is holding a solemn funeral ceremony for Fallen Comrades. This is no place for stand up comedy and they are quickly arrested. Strabo, their actor-manager, and who has struggled to keep the company afloat, at one point offers his jailer a marvelous defense of his profession: "I am an actor, a man whose life at best is a series of shams. We make nothing . . . . we are despised . . . by those who toil in the world—but for that moment, that one moment on the stage, when we are permitted to make them laugh or cry in sympathy, not even with ourselves, but for that better being we impersonate. For we ourselves are nothing."[33] The speech resonates with "Mametian" concerns. But can Strabo and his players act their way out of a death sentence?

The jailer is moved but not deceived. He recognizes the plea for mercy as an imitation of Plautus' *Metathon*; speaking from the heart, the actor is still a counterfeit. Typically for Mamet, the speech itself is a con. Mamet has also invented the name of the Plautus play and the dialogue. *Keep your Pantheon*, Mamet's Roman farce about deception and perception, is itself a con, condensing numerous Mamet themes and situations. And like Face and Subtle in Ben Jonson's *The Alchemist*, Strabo has little to redeem him except his talent for deception. Nevertheless, gags and catchphrases sustain the humor of this new work which extends the world of *A Life in the Theatre* by reimagining a theatrical past.

Mamet's America has been an imaginary and romanticized world of tough-guys, the last *real* American men. It is a world of seedy respectability that seems to have peaked between the end of the 1940s and 1960s. In this world, according to Sean Wilentz, "men rub up against certain supposedly eternal American verities: that morality is phony; that everyone is on the take; that anyone who won't admit as much is either an idiot, a liar or a weakling." Facing these realities, "tough-guys confront their own twilight."[34] Mamet's through-line has been how competition drives the American dream ironically producing deceit if not sinister behavior. Betrayal, violence, and death are often the result, features that have defined his work from *American Buffalo* through *Redbelt*. The con, breeding distrust and malfeasance, becomes the primary mode of survival *and* betrayal.

Stanislavsky anticipated this behavior. In *An Actor Prepares*, he writes, "every *action* meets with a *reaction* which in turn intensifies the first." Counteraction is natural "because its inevitable result is more action. We need that clash of purposes, and all the problems to solve that grow out of them. They cause activity which is the basis of our art."[35] The "clash of purposes" is the catalyst at the center of Mamet's inner landscape and theatrical world.

Mamet's versatility, like his wry humor, is to be admired. Few contemporaries can match his ambition. Mantegna understood early that Mamet didn't build a career on only one thing, nor did he sit back after the success of a Pulitzer Prize and slowly bring out new material. "What's so great about this guy is that he puts it on the line every year, every day" and "whether you like it or not, it's out there. That takes guts" (Man 263–4). For Mamet, there is no separation between acting and social behavior. As Robert claims in *A Life in the Theatre*, "our aspirations in the Theater are much the *same* as man's . . . we *are* society" (ALT 35–6). The language of Mamet's world may be raw, the atmosphere highly charged, the actions cruel, the expressions broken, but if asked to explain himself, Mamet's likely retort would be unequivocal: "It's kickass or kissass . . . and I'd be lying if I told you any different" (AB 74).

AFTERWORD

Competing with David Mamet's work since the appearance of this biography in 2008 has been his politics. Although he premiered a new play—*Race*[1]—and published a new collection of essays on the theatre, attention has focused on Mamet's newly announced conservatism expressed with characteristic fervor, if not stridency, in *The Secret Knowledge, On the Dismantling of American Culture* (2011).[2] Despite his continued output of plays, essays, and films that repeatedly assault political bias, racial prejudice, and theatrical boundaries, Mamet has introduced a more pronounced and vocal political agenda. While alienating him from his liberal admirers, it has created a puzzle, if not a paradox, for his fans.

The roots of Mamet's conservatism, some pundits opine (now *that's* Mametspeak: recall his swings between arcane diction and slang in *Boston Marriage*), can be found in his early plays that do not skewer misbehavior and rapaciousness as much as expose the dark side of character and narcissism. In the politics of action, which might characterize *American Buffalo*, *Glengarry*, and *Edmond*, he addresses chicanery, greed, and race capped by urban violence. But beneath the exposure of these vices and reliance on the con is a preference for a secure, conservative sense of settled values: security, wealth, and family. His 2008 *Village Voice* essay "Why I Am No Longer a 'Brain-Dead Liberal'"[3] outlined his change.

In that essay, now a keynote for his politics, Mamet confesses that in the sixties he believed that government was corrupt, business was exploitative, and people were generally good at heart. But those naïve beliefs began to shift with his experience. He soon revised his view: people are not generally good, and in circumstances of stress, they can "behave like swine," which is the only fit subject of drama. Suddenly, he realized the free-market understanding of the world meshed more exactly with his experiences than "the idealistic vision I called liberalism." Milton Friedman, Friedrich Hyak, and others facilitated this change. But was it actually a shift? For years, Mamet favored militarism, social order, and independence, as well as the "tough Jew" stance expressed by the lawyer Marty Rossen in the film *State and Main*. Confronting the local councilman Doug Mackenzie, Rossen shrieks that "there's an old saying, the two scariest things in the world, a black man with a knife and Jew with a lawyer. Now, I am a lawyer, and I am *The* Jew, and you continue ONE MOMENT with this slanderous shit here in this public place, I'm going to have your ass over my mantleplace." *Speed-the-Plow's* Bobby Gould furthers the image of the abrasive, demanding, and often-bellicose Jew displayed by Mamet when he excoriated all self-hating Jews in his 2006 collection, *The Wicked Son*, a study of anti-Semitism.

Oleanna and *Romance* were similarly antagonistic political works, the former challenging the excesses of political correctness with the victimized professor fighting back, the latter a satire of the politically incorrect. The emergence of the TV series *The Unit*, a glimpse at the macho military world of a Special Ops unit, solidified Mamet's rightward, militaristic leanings. To say he was never a political playwright is to simplify the case. To some critics, *American Buffalo* and *Glengarry* were clearly allegories of a heartless country ruled exclusively by markets and capital. It was a Hobbesian jungle, taken to its extreme, perhaps, in *Edmond* and gentrified in *Boston Marriage* where commercial values override moral. Even his film *The Winslow Boy*, based on Terence Rattigan's play, reinforces the exchange between politics and justice.

But it was writing the political satire *November* (2008) that prodded the re-consideration of his politics Mamet explained in his *Village Voice* essay. The play became "a polemic between persons of two opposing views," pitting the "conservative (or tragic) view and the liberal (or perfectionist) view" against each other. The conservative view, expressed by the president in the play, is for government to stay out of people's way because government intervention interferes with free-market economics and personal liberty.

As he narrates, after many decades, Mamet reversed a set of inherited liberal views, partly because everything was "not always wrong." How could he have thought, in fact, that things were wrong when people were basically good? This led him to a re-evaluation and a new understanding that the Constitution is what holds the contradictory behavior of Americans together. It assumes people are swine and act in a self-interested manner (which should have been no surprise to the creator of Teach from *American Buffalo*, Ricky Roma from *Glengarry*, or Bobby Gould from *Speed-the-Plow*). As a result, the Constitution separates power into three branches to thwart any single entity from control. This led him to revise his view of corporations, George Bush, and the military. They, too, are susceptible to corruption and mismanagement, but the conservative view asks how could things be better and at what cost? Liberals avoid such questions.

But can we work things out on our own? "Yes" is Mamet's emphatic answer: experience proves it. Take away the director from a staged play, he argues, and things improve (anticipating his position in *Theatre* [2010][4]). Similarly, through deliberation and good intentions, people work things out, whether it's a school system or a jury he optimistically writes—not perfect, but acceptable solutions and workable to the community. Suddenly, he realized that America is a marketplace not a schoolroom and a set of new heroes emerged: Thomas Sowell, philosopher, Milton Friedman, economist, Paul Johnson, historian, and Shelby Steele, social critic. With these conservative scholars and others, he realized that "a free-market understanding of the world meshes more perfectly with my experience than that idealistic vision I called liberalism."

Reaction to Mamet's *Village Voice* declaration was surprise if not shock, cynics convinced he was taking up this new position to re-gain what he had lost: attention, perhaps our scarcest resource according to *The Attention Economy* by Thomas H. Davenport and John C. Beck. Being heard, with its political, moral, economic, and social implications, was critical. The theatre community reacted to his new conservatism in two opposite ways: his politics would certainly not interfere with the meaning or production of his plays; or, we always knew he was a crypto-conservative. Attending a soldier of fortune convention, as well as collecting knives and guns, merely confirmed this opinion.

To his credit, Mamet has never hidden his views. On the Charlie Rose Show in January 2008, when *November* opened, he explained that his politics were no better than anyone else's. But the *Village Voice* essay allowed him to explain that his previous political ideas were reflexive and not thought-out. He now understood that the liberal imagination had dried up and that corporations were actually good for public and private life. Even the military was honorable. As the speechwriter in Mamet's play *November* explains to the corrupt president, we are not a nation divided but a democracy of decent people who may have differing opinions. "Decent" is the key term, although the president complains that the liberal agenda sacrifices the happiness of real people "to protect some cockamamie, dumb idea of 'justice'" (*November* 103). And when at the end of the play an Indian chief who attempted to kill the president asks for a pardon, as well as Nantucket Island *and* a casino, the cynical president responds with "Jesus I love this country" (*November* 120). Government, Mamet shows, is no more than a con job run by con artists.

More recently, in a lengthy interview in the neoconservative *Weekly Standard* (May 23, 2011), Mamet elaborated his move to the conservative camp. The interview opens with a reminder of Mamet's attack on higher education at Stanford University in January 2009. Higher education, he declared, was an elaborate scheme to deprive the young of their freedom of thought. Four years of college was no more than a lab experiment where students learned to recite received and often unexamined ideas. Their reward was a grade or a degree. He then went on to defend capitalism, blasting high taxes and the redistribution of wealth. He denounced affirmative action and celebrated business, repeating these ideas in his essay "Culture, School Shootings, the Audience and the Elevator" in *The Secret Knowledge*. There, he writes that college only delays "the matriculation of the adolescent into society" (22). *His* aim is to make education practical (an offshoot in political terms of his earlier theatrical concept of Practical Aesthetics): "[I]n my racket, show business, one learns through doing and through watching" (21).

What he soon realized, he states in the interview, was that he was "Talking Left and Living Right," a common condition among American liberals, he thought.

These are individuals who shelter their income but advocate higher taxes, or vote against school vouchers, while sending their children to private schools.

Following the 2004 election, Mamet encountered a hatred for George Bush that he couldn't understand. And how could the country function so well when it faced all of its challenges? His answer? Again, the Constitution. The separation of powers, guarantee of property, freedom of speech, and freedom of religion made American society workable.

Mamet's attitude toward the Hollywood writers' strike of 2007–08 crystallized his discomfort with the liberal point of view he explained in his *Weekly Standard* interview. He saw that the union risked the jobs of countless others from drivers and scene painters to cameramen and grips. And the union, he believed, did not even know what it wanted. The question for him became "what do liberals do when their plans have failed?" One thing they do not want to do is admit they failed.

He began to break away from the herd, disdaining consensus or so-called received wisdom that gives his essay collection *The Secret Knowledge* its bite. What he realized, he tells his interviewer, is that perhaps "the left flattens people, reduces people to financial interests" in the words of Mordecai Finley, Mamet's Southern California rabbi who began to send him books. One was *A Conflict of Visions* by Thomas Sowell, and its impact was strong. His unconstrained vision of man's endless improvement informed Mamet's understanding of what conservatism meant. Shelby Steele, author of several books on race, also became a favorite and a friend (he dedicated *Race* to him). Among Steele's titles are *The Content of Our Character, a New Vision of Race in America* (1990) and *White Guilt: How Blacks and Whites Together Destroyed the Promise of the Civil Rights Era* (2006). Steele, in talking to Andrew Ferguson for the *Weekly Standard* profile, said Mamet likely "might have always been a conservative without knowing it. All that happened was he finally found a politics that suited his values."[5] Breaking away from the herd—Mamet had earlier studied and admired William Trotter's 1916 *Instincts of the Herd in Peace and War*—has become not only his new mantra but also his lasting cry.

Accompanying the new politics, however, is an old aesthetic, re-stated in interviews, and a 2010 collection simply titled *Theatre*. In February 2008, for example, Mamet reiterated his firm views of style in film and in writing. Elaborating his belief that the cut is the most important part of a work because it rids the text or the film of the rhetorical or the digressive ("a good writer gets better only by learning to cut, to remove . . . the deeply felt and meaningful" [*On Directing Film* xv]), he tells one interviewer that you throw out everything that is not the plot "because that's all the audience cares about." Asked if he's thrown out good material, he responds with:

> I hope so. That's what makes you strong. Not throwing out the bad scene, but throwing out the great scene that kills the good play. That's the difference between an amateur and a professional writer. The ability to do that.

He then repeats his claim that writing can't be taught: "[A]nybody who is going to learn how to write is going to teach himself how to do it".[6]

In *Theatre*, a collection of twenty-six short essays plus an introduction, Mamet repeats his discomfort with Stanislavsky and Brecht, as well as the academic study of acting, the inadequacy of theatre schools, and the role of the director. *Writing in Restaurants* (1986), *On Directing Film* (1991), and *True and False, Hersey and Common Sense for the Actor* (1997) address similar if not identical topics with much of the language in the new book sounding like the old. "It's not the actor's job to be emotional—it is the actor's job to be *direct*" (*On Directing Film* 71) sounds close to "Nobody cares what you, the actor feel. You are expected to do you job, which is to show up and say the lines" (*Theatre* 38).

But there is a difference, and it's in Mamet's working definition of theatre, a distinctly conservative definition: "The theatre is a magnificent example of the workings of that particular bulwark of democracy, the free-market economy." If a play fails, it is replaced. Furthermore, theatre

> is the province not of ideologues (whether in the pay of the state and called commissars, or tax subsidized through the university system and called intellectuals) but of show folk trying to make a living (64–65).

This market-driven assessment, which often leaves actors and playwrights out of work, is to be valued, he believes. Only the deserving survive, which is OK with him. Theatre grants, he believes, are pernicious and only prop up the incompetent whose work would otherwise not attract an audience (97–99). Such playwrights always begin with a conclusion and award the audience for applauding its agreement. True theatre is the opposite: it should challenge and even threaten the audience.

His comments on theatre teaching are similarly caustic: "Most of that which passes for acting training is an exercise in confession" (108). The only group that will teach the writer *and* the actor is the audience. In fact, the only role of the playwright is to "make the audience wonder what is going to happen next. That's it" (125). How to do this? Through the structuring of plot, the only thing the audience cares about (126). In a remarkably prescriptive and yet simplistic manner, Mamet explains that one book alone will teach you how to construct good plot: Aristotle's *Poetics* (127). Presentation rather than explanation is the core of drama he emphasizes, similar to what he achieves in his finest plays (although human nature is shown to be consistently unethical, cutthroat, and unreliable). Show don't tell expresses his position; let action alone reveal character.

Mamet's emphasis is on audience. Theatre, he explains, is not about "the communication of ideas but rather the inculcation in the audience of the instincts of the hunt." Such instincts supersede even the verbal (18). Repeating himself (as he does frequently in the book), he writes that the audience is not "involved in sharing the *ideas* of the drama, but rather experiences the thrill of the communal hunt" (19). A play, he suggests, doesn't celebrate a hunt, it *is* the hunt. To correct the folly of the hero's (and the audience's) assumptions of the world is a further goal.

In the new collection, Mamet declares that the job of the actor is to "inhabit the part:" "to stand still and say the words—in order to accomplish something like that purpose indicated by the author. That's it" (33). He goes further and declares that there is nothing called character—it is "only a few words of speech delineated on the page" (55). Earlier, in *True and False* he writes, "the actor is onstage to communicate the play to the audience . . . there is no character. There are only lines upon a page" (9). In a risky remark, he claims in the new book that the "immemorial dream of the talentless" is "that a sufficient devotion to doctrine will produce art" (58). To be free of doctrine, he implies, will assert your independence and display your essentially conservative but honest nature. And you shall succeed.

Reaction to the collection was indifferent at best, unsympathetic at worst. Most critics understood it not so much as a playwright complaining about what's wrong with the profession as perhaps someone in the back of the theatre having a tantrum. His belief in directorless theatre is one of the sillier statements claims the former drama critic of the *Boston Globe*, Ed Siegel. Mamet's work, he points out, is entirely dependent on good direction. A well-directed production leads you to think Mamet is one of America's most gifted playwrights; a poorly directed production might "make you conclude that he's more dated than daring" (Boston.com May 13, 2010). Method actors, European stage theories, and critics are similarly attacked by Mamet. And while he reviles method actors, his favorite actor is Brando because "the quiddity of Brando came not from his deep examination of his own feelings but from his odd, essential nature as a human being" (113).

In advance of the opening of *Race*, Mamet published "We Can't Stop Talking About Race in America" in the *New York Times.*[7] In the piece, he suggested that race has preoccupied Americans for the past 230 years, from the First Continental Congress through the Equal Employment Opportunity Commission. His new play is to further the debate, adding as an aside that as a Jew "there is nothing a non-Jew can say to a Jew on the subject of Jewishness that is not patronizing, upsetting or simply wrong." The same holds true among African Americans, he adds. His new play deals with this dilemma and the issue of lying. "All drama is about lies. When the lie is exposed, the play is over," he asserts.

Race, he declares, is like sex, "a subject on which it is near impossible to tell the truth." Self-interest and desire make the truth inconvenient to share even with oneself. Drama, he explains, can be used to "buttress" popular beliefs, but tragedy should strive to uncover unacceptable beliefs that have become repressed. But their resolution always ends in tragedy. Contemporary debate on race is no more than sanctimony he writes, therefore the best drama must ask "what are the lies?" This is the very substance of his new play. And let us admit, he adds, that there has always been a degree of hate between blacks and whites. But we are working it out, although no one knows when it will be over until "fatigue, remorse and finally forgiveness bring resolution." For Mamet, faith in being able to work it out overshadows any prejudice, bias, or dislike. The article, a bracing set of incomplete, and some would say naïve, statements, nevertheless offers some insight into Mamet's truncated sense of drama and the nature of his new play—plus his soon-to-be fully disclosed conservatism. Condensed, the column anticipates the ideas expressed in his nonfiction collection, *The Secret Knowledge*.

But *Race* (2009), Mamet's first post-conversion play—that is after his March 2008 political declaration in *The Village Voice*—failed to display any new perceptions emerging from his new conservatism. A didactic presentation of two celebrity lawyers, one white (Jack) and one black (Henry), they must decide whether or not to defend a white millionaire accused of raping a black woman. Surprisingly, there is no dramatization of political points; instead, heavy-handed expositions replace presentation, the very thing Mamet criticized in weak dramatists. It opens with a mini-lecture on misperceptions of blacks and moves on to a Mametian/Hobbesian view of the world: people are self-interested and "will exploit every advantage they may have" (21). The law is not "an exercise in metaphysics. But an alley fight"(8). Society, or competing sides in a lawsuit, do not want the truth but to "prevail." Lying is the natural state of the litigants (9).

Reinforcing this view is the ethos of the play, which Jack explains to the accused, Charles: "There are no 'facts of the case.' There are two *fictions*. Which the opposing teams each seek to impress upon the jury" (14). Everything that the accused, Charles, has taken for granted will land him in jail, "guilty or not" (14). In many ways, this expresses Mamet's realization that all he had accepted as a liberal did not make him a better man or citizen. When Charles says he's innocent, Jack bluntly responds with "nobody fucking cares" (15). And echoing a line from Mamet's first film, *House of Games*, is this exchange: when Jack tells his partner Henry that their client's "married to another woman, [but] he's fucking the *black* girl . . . ," Henry responds with "Alright, that's the American Way. We *understand* that" (20). In *House of Games*, "the American Way" phrase also appears but it means conning people out of their money.

Susan, the black junior lawyer of the two principals, lends another perspective, the feminine. She suggests that Charles is likely guilty because he acts guilty and need to atone not for the act but for being caught. Much of the first act is spent arguing back and forth among the lawyers about the proposed defense of the accused and how to play, or not, the black/white card. The case is only about narrative and which story will dominate the minds of the jurors. Entertainment, not innocence or guilt, rules (26). But they reverse their decision not to take the case when they find they have received a sizeable retainer and inadvertently become the Attorneys of Record because of an exchange with the D.A. (District Attorney). And as the three in the law office debate the merits or demerits of the case, scene one ends with a restatement of Mamet's point that there is no difference between sex and race. They're the same:

Susan. This isn't about sex, it's about Race.
Jack. What's the difference? (37)

Scene two continues the office discussion, focusing on the absence of sequins in the hotel room from the dress the assailant supposedly ripped from the victim. Their strategy will clearly focus on evidence and not race. Mamet then introduces a discussion of herd mentality suggested in his *Village Voice* article and elaborated in *Theatre*. People instinctively form groups whether it is a race, a jury, an audience, or even a mob. The job, however, is to get the jury to believe in a new definition of "group," no longer whites or blacks but "The Audience:" "We're going to put on a show," Jack excitingly tells Susan (41).

Cross-examination of the accused, however, leads to new details beginning with the accuser being a prostitute who received gifts from the accused. And now he wants to confess to immoral behavior but only because he is white. The lawyers reject this and plan to restage the assault on a mattress in the courtroom to show that the woman consented to the sex because if she hadn't, there would be red sequins from her dress thrown about the room. But then Susan, the junior, accidentally discovers that her firm investigated her before she was hired because she was black. Another lecture follows, this time Susan berating Jack: "There is nothing. A white person. Can say to a black person. About Race. Which is not both incorrect and offensive. Nothing. I know that. Race. Is the most incendiary topic in our history" (52). Mamet's fragments, broken by periods, emphasizes the delivery and import he attributes to the moment and illegality of Jack's action.

Jack responds by asserting that "might not [she] exploit being Black? Or that any human being whatever might not, when pressed, exploit whatever momentary advantage he or she possessed" confirming that we are all greedy and self-interested (55)? Justice, he believes, lies "only in the imperfect, and mutually unacceptable result of . . . interaction"(55). The third and final scene continues in the office, now with a postcard written years ago suggesting the client's racial bias initiating a tedious back and forth about why Charles's friend saved the postcard. Again, the lawyers must explain that their job is to get the accused acquitted, not to explain why he holds certain attitudes. But an unexpected report appears, overturning their plans: red sequins *were* found under the bed, which invalidates the proposed defense. Race then exposes itself in the firm as Henry tells Jack he's been racist in his attitude to Susan. He's exploited her and only allowed her to work because she received "dispensation because of [her] race . . . [but] she sold us out. Because of the Race of our client. Who is innocent" (70). Susan, it becomes clear, believes the client is guilty. The setup of Susan is similar to that of *Speed-the-Plow* and the treatment of the secretary Karen who ends up reading a rejected script and successfully argues that it could be a major movie. But to move up the ladder of success, she has had to sleep with one of the two studio executives.

Mistrust of Susan becomes one of the several issues at the end of the play (essentially three scenes with four characters), not the least her belief that white men exploit black women. Susan is then accused, again, of selling out their client by contacting the prosecution just as further evidence mounts confirming that the accused *did* rape the black woman. Accusations fly as the play moves toward its indecisive ending, while claims of betrayal continue. Susan, however, never admits to any of the accusations and exits declaring that the white client *is* guilty. Curtain.

The absence of Mamet's scalpel-like language and ineffective verbal jousting in the play baffled most critics. The rape itself disappeared from the drama as does the situation of Charles, the accused. The play doesn't appear to end but deflate. Reviewers labeled the work a "dud" and unfocused, lacking the energy, spit, and drive of his earlier work. Mametspeak became Mametshout *Time Magazine* wrote (January 11, 2010) as thematic statements seem imposed rather than expressed. *The New York Times* noted the lack of provocation and disturbance, underlined by the self-conscious standing ovation on opening night. Mamet directed the production, which Ben Brantley in the *Times* labeled "slack" because there was no dramatic tension (NYT December 7, 2009). The play neither sings nor stings, he quipped. *Romance* (2005) contains a more effective satire of lawyers and a courtroom, while *Oleanna* (1992) offers a more serious presentation of sexual politics. Prejudice and the abuses of the legal system are more brutally front and center in both works.

But in spite of its tame racial politics, *Race* was a Broadway hit, earning back its initial investment of approximately $2.5 million following a five-month run, one of the few shows on Broadway in 2009–10 that did. This was possible because of the actor James Spader, formerly of TV's *Boston Legal* and the film "Pretty in Pink." But the work also anticipated a number of the ideas Mamet would expand in his "reading" of the dismantling of American culture, *The Secret Knowledge*.

In preparation for the release of his new book of essays, Mamet did a series of interviews, one of the most important with John Gapper of the *Financial Times* (June 11–12, 2011).[8] Meeting at the Knickerbocker Bar & Grill in New York's Greenwich Village, while scouting locations for his new HBO movie on Phil Spector starring Al Pacino and Helen Mirren, Mamet and Gapper initially discuss Mamet's belief that Spector was not guilty, that there was reasonable doubt. The remark was controversial. Within days of the interview, friends of murdered Lana Clarkson wrote to Mamet and to HBO concerned that Mamet would exonerate Spector in the death. "Please refrain from rewriting history for 'creative license,'" they asked.[9] The deputy district attorney in Los Angeles who prosecuted Spector released a statement underlining that even an appellate court upheld Spector's conviction.

Mamet continued the Financial Times interview by launching into his political mistakes, which he has now exposed and seeks to correct in *The Secret Knowledge*, having earlier cited John Maynard Keynes's comment that "when the facts change, I change my mind." Voting for big government was one of those mistakes he admits. Asked what prompted his new conservative outlook, Mamet repeats the impact of the Hollywood writers' strike of 2007–08 and its effect on *The Unit*, his Special Ops TV Show. Because of the strike, his show was suddenly off the air and his entire team, from stagehands to costume designers, was out of work. The unions screwed him as much as helped him, which is ironic, since he dedicated *The Secret Knowledge* to his labor-union lawyer father, Bernie Mamet. He began to read the work of free-market economists (Friedman, Hayek, and Adam Smith), as well as John Stuart Mill and Thomas Hobbes. The result is his new book that dismisses global warming, objects to government intervention, and attacks liberalism, nothing more than "a parlor game, where one, for a small stipend, is allowed to think he is aiding starving children in X or exploited workers in Y," he exclaims. Mamet also disparages the tax system (SKnow 141).

When the conversation veers toward writing in the interview, Mamet responds with his declaration on plot and its difficulty because it must be both surprising and inevitable as Aristotle demanded. He returns to politics focusing on the Middle East and his sense that the American left has betrayed Israel and that the British are fundamentally anti-Semitic. Eliding criticism of Israel with anti-Semitism, however, seems not only wrong but also glib, the reporter interjects—although Mamet "has a knack for combining character assignation with dry wit, as if only half-serious." Obama, Mamet adds, has sold out America, while Sarah Palin fascinates him.

In an interview for the *New York Times* Sunday magazine (May 27, 2011), Mamet offers similarly facile answers: "[O]f course I'm alienating the public! That's what they pay me for. . . . When the government starts deciding what's absurd, you're on the road to serfdom." Balancing tautologies with incomplete reasoning, he tries to uphold a number of dubious claims: "[I]t's appalling what the government has done to the great African-American community in the last 50 years"; the Middle East conflict is no more than "entertainment." Response to the interview ranged from quick assessments of his downhill slide following *Glengarry* to a critique of his position as just anger. Plus this retort: "It's just as I suspected: sobriety and ignorance lead to quoting Milton Friedman. I think I'll stick with the red wine, my PhD and reading the N.Y. Times."

The Secret Knowledge, with its enigmatic, almost Kabbalistic title, appeared at the same time as Ann Coulter's *Demonic: How the Liberal Mob Is Endangering America* (2011) and Laura Ingraham's satire *Of Thee I Zing, America's Cultural Decline* (2011), reflecting a trend in exploiting liberal weaknesses and the seeming decline of American values, which conservatives believe they can reconstitute.[10] Blurbs on the book jacket from three leading conservatives—Shelby Steele, Victor Davis Hanson, and Melanie Phillips—reinforce Mamet's new conservative credentials with two of the three from the Hoover Institute.

The topics in the book itself range from political choice to diversity, from Chicago to bumper stickers. But despite an announced topic, Mamet never feels obliged to stick to it; one is never sure where the essay is going or which direction it will turn other than "right." His piece on the game-show host Monty Hall, for example, becomes an exercise in mathematical choice and that the odds in choosing the right door on *Let's Make A Deal* were only 2 to 1 not 50–50. Misconstruing the choice can lead to disastrous mistakes, which he then applies to mathematics, Middle East politics, apologies, and race. "Alcatraz" begins with a reference to the former prison but quickly shifts to failure, university education (or rather un-education), power, capitalism, and the evils of big government. "Maxwell Street" becomes an essay on the liberal state and governmental power without a single reference to the west side Chicago street thought to be the heart of the Jewish crime scene in the 1920s.

Mamet also displays a curious antipathy to facts and accuracy. "My job, as a dramatist, was not to write accurately, but to write *persuasively*," he states as a curious defense in the essay "The Political Impulse" (5). This may justify a certain license in his plays but not his essays. Errors abound undermining the certainty of Mamet's position. Citing Dambisa Moyo, a Zambian economist, he identifies her as a Gambian. Criticizing American health-care reform, he declares that only 20 million are uninsured when the latest estimates suggest just over 50 million. Other unqualified statements include Karl Marx never working a day in his life, that America won the Vietnam War in 1973, and that America is a Christian country, largely on the basis that the Constitution is the distillation of the thought of Christian men. One of his most incorrect statements is that Bertrand Russell, one of the first to criticize Lenin in a report from Moscow, was a fellow-traveling dupe and tourist of the Jane Fonda type (SKnow 98).

Instead of Sowell or Friedman, Mamet might have glanced at *How Well Do Facts Travel? The Dissemination of Reliable Knowledge*, edited by Peter Howlett and Mary S. Morgan (2011) or Mary Poovey's earlier work *A History of the Modern Fact* (1998). The distribution of facts can, as Mamet's work confirms (although he doesn't seem to acknowledge), easily be distorted, dissimulated, and dissembled. And his inclusion of a bibliography must be more visual than substantial, as a sign that he's either glanced at these titles or would like us to believe so. None of his earlier nonfiction works, including *The Wicked Son*, his study of anti-Semitism, contain such a listing.

Discontent mildly defines Mamet's outlook; anger might be stronger. Show business has "killed itself" (76); government intervention creates bloated bureaucracies; only a free-market world will self-correct inefficiencies; the end product of government is only waste (77). Such attitudes, coupled with his belief that all people are venal, "politicians doubly so by profession," led to what he calls his "love letter to America," his play *November* (5–6). But generalities demand clarification. To write that "most legislation aimed at eliminating unhappiness and discontent has resulted in misery" conveniently disregards such successes as the Civil Rights Law (71). And this hyperbole causes a double take: "What is Big Government but the Executive's cocaine dream . . ." (77)? What irks Mamet are taxes that only fund programs "that proved failures decades ago" while new programs exist only to correct "the errors of their predecessors" (188). Ironically, in his last essay, he reveals that "there is no secret knowledge. The Federal Government is merely the zoning board writ large" (223). Arguing that "Leftist thought" has devolved "from reason to 'belief' in an effort to stave off powerlessness," Mamet concludes by restating more government power is bad, less is good, reminding one of New Hampshire's curt state motto: "Live Free or Die."

The Secret Knowledge is purposefully polemical and strident and largely unconvincing as numerous reviewers remarked. The *Economist* summed up many views when it called the book a "tedious and simplistic rant." Christopher Hitchens in the *New York Times Book Review* referred to it as "extraordinarily irritating" (June 16, 2011; June 19, 2011). Losing your faith, he continued, does not mean you've found your reason. Avoiding irony, Mamet "prefers his precepts to be literal and traditional," which, coupled with the incompleteness of argument, results "in a straw book" of little merit.

Other readers suggested that his recantation of liberalism is part of a tradition of similar turns to the right, particularly among Jewish intellectuals à la Irving Kristol, Norman Podhoretz, and Nathan Glazer. But unlike Kristol, Podhoretz, or Glazer, who had strong convictions and were immersed in the political life of their times, Mamet seems self-centered and disingenuous in his presentation of history, culture, and politics. No existential or political soul-searching is present, nor a broader sense of social perception. And for Mamet, villains abound, from FDR ("he dismantled the free market") to Lord Beaverbrook, newspaper magnate (identified as a Jewish courtier like Disraeli, which would have surprised the Canadian son of a Scottish-born Presbyterian minister, facts again contradicting Mamet's claims).

Rather than experience a political conversion, *The Secret Knowledge* may only be a rewrite, a new script for a new character. Jon Voight, thanked by Mamet in the book, may have had a role in the process in that he gave Mamet *Witness*, Whittaker Chambers's autobiography recounting *his* conversion from Communism to a Christianity that permitted him to testify against Alger Hiss. Mamet's change allows him to flaunt a new politics in the face of his clearly weak-kneed liberal, Hollywood friends. But as some critics have argued, Mamet has no political ideology except personality, the only foundation, it seems, needed for either politics or ideology. Another name for personality as the touchstone for reality might be celebrity. As *MacLean's Magazine* summarized, Mamet has written "what amounts to a high-class version of Fox News" (June 20, 2011).

More than sixty years ago in *The Liberal Imagination*, Lionel Trilling[11] wrote that the word liberal "is a word primarily of political import, but its political meaning defines itself by the quality of life it envisages" (ix). In the United States at that time, he added, "liberalism is not only the dominant but even the sole intellectual tradition" (vii). "There are no conservative or reactionary ideas in general circulation," he added, possibly true for 1950 but certainly not today (vii). But the form and practice of culture Trilling identifies is not very different from Mamet's: "[E]xistence is struggle, or at least debate—it is nothing if not dialectic," Trilling wrote (7). In a reasoned way, Trilling proceeded to expand the idea of a liberal imagination expressed in literature and culture countering the tone and attitude of Mamet. Criticism's job, he noted, was "to recall liberalism to its first essential imagination of variousness and possibility which implies the awareness of complexity and difficulty" (xii). At one point, he cites John Stuart Mill's remarks in his essay on Coleridge asking that the conservatives "sharpen their wits, give acuteness to their perceptions . . . and clearness to their reasoning powers. We are in danger from their folly, not from their wisdom" (in Trilling viii). Trilling quotes this as a challenge to liberals to sharpen their own game and re-examine their values. It may also stand as a reaction to Mamet's posturing, rhetoric, tautologies, and misrepresentations in *The Secret Knowledge.*

II

Research on Mamet has not slowed, and with his extensive archive now available at the Harry Ransom Humanities Research Center at the University of Texas at Austin, it is likely to increase. The 2007 acquisition includes more than 300 boxes containing manuscripts, journals, production files, correspondence, and multiple drafts of each of his works. Unpublished as well as abandoned work is also part of the collection. Among the most valuable items are 175 journals ranging from 1965–2001, each 150–200 pages. They contain the germ of many works, as well as his reflections and experimental writings. Notebooks, where he would write his first drafts in longhand, supplement the journals. Correspondence in the archive includes lengthy exchanges between Mamet and the actor Joe Mantegna, the magician Ricky Jay, and the director Gregory Mosher. Letters between Mamet and Pinter, as well as Mamet and Mike Nichols, also exist.

Critical studies continue to appear from Steven Price's useful *The Plays, Screenplays and Films of David Mamet* (2008) to Johan Callens edited volume, *Crossings: David Mamet's Work in Different Genres and Media* (2009). This last is a wide-ranging collection of fifteen essays dealing with Mamet and intermedia, naturalism, film, and language. It also suggests a shift to comparative studies: Mamet and Chekhov or Mamet and Pinter represent this emphasis. Christopher Collard's "Chekhov Among Friends: Mamet's *Vanya* or Adaptation through a Russian Looking Glass" in *Crossings* or my 2011 article "Boxing with Brecht: Bertolt Brecht and David Mamet" in the *Journal of Dramatic Theory and Criticism* are examples. Drawing parallels between Mamet's work and others, as well as Mamet in context, highlight both his continuation of certain traditions and yet divergence from his predecessors. And Mamet's treatment of masculinity, Judaism, and violence continues to fascinate critics.

Mamet and film also remains an important focus with new and important documents turning up such as his October 19, 2005, memo to writers of his TV show *The Unit.* In it, he concisely outlines his dramatic principles for storytelling and good writing. Addressing the divide between drama and information, he opts for drama that is "THE QUEST OF THE HERO TO OVERCOME THOSE THINGS WHICH PREVENT HIM FROM ACHIEVING A SPECIFIC 'ACUTE' GOAL." And if a scene is not dramatically written, it will not be dramatically acted. Expositional scenes must go. "THE JOB OF THE DRAMATIST," he tells his staff, "IS TO MAKE THE AUDIENCE WONDER WHAT HAPPENS NEXT. *NOT* TO EXPLAIN TO THEM WHAT JUST HAPPENED OR TO SUGGEST TO THEM WHAT HAPPENS NEXT." Learn to tell the story in pictures and constantly ask yourself if the scene is dramatic, essential, and advances the plot (to read the full document, see http://www.slashfilm.com/a-letter-from-david-mamet-to-the-writers-of-the-unit/).

In March 2007, Mamet was a guest film programer for Turner Classic Movies and his four choices indicate his taste: first was *In Which We Serve* (1942), Noel Coward's war drama that celebrates heroism in combat and at home. Mamet emphasized Coward's multiple roles as actor, screenwriter, and codirector (with David Lean). *Le Jour Se Leve* (1939) was his second choice, a film about a killer holed up awaiting a dawn assault by the police. Jean Gabin starred in what Mamet called a "crime tragedy," not a crime romance representative of similar American films. Guilt not freedom is the focus. *Island in the Sky* (1953), directed by William Wellman, was his third choice, a work Mamet calls "one of the great flying films." It's about a U.S. bomber going down in Labrador on its way to England. It stars John Wayne along with James Arness, later of *Gunsmoke* fame. *The Killing* (1956) is Mamet's final favorite, a work he calls "the world's greatest film noir." Praising the director Stanley Kubrick—it was only his third film—he notes the effective use of voiceover and the tight script written by Kubrick and the hard-boiled writer Jim Thompson: "[T]his film is so good it makes perfection seem tawdry," he added.

Mamet continues to be produced, whether in Nottingham, Santa Barbara, New York, or London, often in outstanding productions. *Speed-the-Plow* at London's Old Vic starring Kevin Spacey and Jeff Goldblum is one example. The "near-peerless pairing" of the two American actors for the February 2008 production led to unanimous praise.[12] This, the third major production of the play in London since its 1989 debut, which included the young Rebecca Pidgeon, whom Mamet later married, is the first to actually feature two Hollywood stars. From the opening beat, Goldblum as Bobby Gould and Spacey as Charlie Flox launch into a high-octane struggle for survival. The production was a smash hit.

A Broadway production of the same play in October 2008 was destined for similar praise. Starring the Emmy-winning Jeremy Piven of TV's *Entourage* fame, along with Elizabeth Moss from *Mad Men*, and the experienced Raul Ezparza, the Atlantic Theatre Company's production, directed by Neil Pepe, opened to strong reviews. But the unexpected departure of Piven in December—despite his hope of being nominated for a Tony Award—because of supposedly high mercury levels and possibly the Epstein/Barr virus led to disappointment, which Mamet turned into a wisecrack: "I talked to Jeremy on the phone and he told me that he discovered that he had a very high level of mercury," Mamet told *Variety*. "So my understanding is that he is leaving show business to pursue a career as a thermometer." The producer, Jeffrey Richards, was not so lighthearted and the mix of money, ego, and talent led to accusations and legal action resulting in a forty-four-page arbitrator's decision ruling in favor of the actor and his medical condition that made it impossible for him to continue in the production.

Ironically, this occurred as Broadway had been relying increasingly on "high wattage stars from film and television" to sell tickets to its nonmusical plays the *New York Times* reported (October 9, 2009). But Mamet knew that back in 1988 when Madonna was cast in the original New York production of *Speed-the-Plow*. Despite Piven's absence, the play continued with two replacement actors in succession and the production recouped its initial $2.26 million investment. It closed as scheduled in February 2009, although only Mr. Piven's co-star, Raul Ezparza, received a Tony nomination.

The first Broadway production of *Oleanna* opened on October 11, 2009, starring Bill Pullman and Julia Stiles. Originally produced by the LA Center Theatre Group at the Mark Taper Forum in June 2009, it transferred to New York in the fall but received mixed reviews. The *Times* complained that the production lacked the explosiveness of its original Off-Broadway production: stasis, not action, defined its new incarnation, eliminating the tension. The problem may have been that Mamet directed the original New York version starring William H. Macy and Rebecca Pidgeon but not the Broadway revival. As a "text-driven" director, he believes that if the actors just say the words, the play will take care of itself. But what was a war of words for Mamet in the original production, has become an exercise in motivation and consideration in the new production. Language, here, is not a conditioned reflex but a considered, thoughtful statement, definitely anti-Mamet. But technically, for a very short time, Mamet could claim two shows running simultaneously on Broadway since *Race* opened on December 6, 2009, the date of *Oleanna's* last performance (it was originally to close on January 3, 2010). But after fifteen previews and sixty-five performances, declining ticket sales forced *Oleanna's* early close. Nevertheless, the December closing, in the words of the producer Jeffrey Finn, allowed for a modest distribution to investors.

Another early Mamet work, *A Life in the Theatre*, opened in New York in October 2010 with the same producers as *Race*: Jeffrey Richards, Jerry Frankel, and Steve Traxler. But the play was generally dismissed as a sentimental work about theatre life that could not bear the weight of Broadway. Yet regardless of quality, all plays seem to come to Broadway, one critic wrote, "if they have starry names attached." Patrick Stewart (*Macbeth, X-Men*) and T. R. Knight (of *Gray's Anatomy*) were the two attached to this production directed by Neil Pepe. The elegant words of the older Robert (Stewart) seem blunted and less probing than a typical Mamet work, while T. R. Knight, as the younger John, seemed bland, the language between them lumbering. According to the critics, the plays within the play were not seriously funny but, rather, cartoons. "Ponderous" was the consensus of critics and audience. It was to close January 2, 2011, but poor audience attendance meant a November 28, 2010, curtain, prompting the critic Susan Hughes in *The Independent* to ask "Is Broadway's Love Affair with Mamet Over"(November 23, 2010)? She recalled that in 2008 a New York production of *American Buffalo* starring John Leguizamo closed after a week and *Oleanna* closed a month early. While *Race* went on to 297 performances, critics such as John Lahr in *The New Yorker* complained that it offered "nothing but cynicism." Perhaps, she suggests, Mamet's increased involvement with TV and film had blunted his dramatic style.

But Mamet's new work continues, most excitingly, perhaps, his HBO film on Phil Spector. Mamet has written and directed the story of the former record producer, now serving a prison sentence of nineteen years to life for the 2003 murder of the struggling actress Lana Clarkson in the foyer of his mansion. Filming began in the summer of 2011 in Mineola, Long Island, re-fashioned to look like Los Angeles, and Brooklyn. A new play, *The Anarchist*, is to debut in London in the fall of 2012 to be directed by Rupert Goold. It is a prison drama dealing with a lifer who battles for parole. Unexpectedly for Mamet, the two lead characters, a prison governor and the prisoner, will be women, echoing *Boston Marriage*. And there is rumored a new screenplay about a girl who applies to Harvard and is turned down—until she declares herself an Aztec intending to test affirmative-action practices.

Challenging, controversial, abrasive: such terms still apply to Mamet, although at a level more diminuendo than fortissimo. But he still commands notice. Mamet has learned, as he instructed actors in *Theatre*, to "stand at an angle. Diagonals are powerful," reminding them also to "take the scene off with you" (83).

NOTES

INTRODUCTION

1. David Mamet, "Hearing the Notes that Aren't Played," *New York Times*, July 15, 2002: E1.
2. David Mamet, telegram of April 28, 1977, to the St. Nicholas Theatre Company, Theatre Collection, Chicago Public Library; WR 20, 14. For his essay on *A Life in the Theatre*, see WR 103–106.
3. Joe Mantegna in Leslie Kane, "Interview with Joe Mantegna," *David Mamet: A Casebook* , ed. Leslie Kane (New York: Garland, 1992), 264, 251. Hereafter "Man."
4. Mamet in Susan Bullington Katz, "A Conversation with . . . David Mamet," *Conversations with Screenwriters* (Portsmouth, NH: Heinemann, 2000), 196.
5. Mamet in Christopher Porterfield, "David Mamet's Bond of Futility," *Time*, February 28, 1977: 54+. Review of *American Buffalo*. JAF xiii. Jafsie was a shadow figure in the Lindbergh kidnapping who volunteered to act as a go-between but may, in fact, have been part of the crime.
6. David Mamet in Chris Jones, "Mamet talks Mamet during rare visit home," *Chicago Tribune*, March 29, 2006: Section 5:1. Mamet was participating in a question-and-answer session with retired *Chicago Tribune* drama critic Richard Christiansen at the Goodman Theatre on March 27, 2006, part of a month-long Mamet Festival. He repeats his formula in BVG 86–7.
7. John Heilpern, for example, titles his 1995 review of *Cryptogram* "Mametspeak," which he identifies as an "oblique, disjointed" dialogue. See Heilpern, "Mametspeak," *How Good is David Mamet, Anyway?* (New York: Routledge, 2000), 220.
8. David Mamet in Brian Case, "Hard and Fast," *Time Out*, January 5, 1989: 29. Hereafter "Case." Sherwood Anderson, *Sherwood Anderson's Notebook* (1926. Mamaroneck, NY: Paul P. Appel, 1970), 195.
9. The structural features of the con function as a means to express, through deception, plot changes and unexpected surprises, a feature in Chekhov as much as in Mamet. His early love of poker (Chekhov also enjoyed gambling) was the practical expression of this pleasure with the con, bluffing a favorite posture. "If I had money to spare, I would spend the whole year gambling" Chekhov wrote in 1891. Chekhov in Philip Callow, *Chekhov, The Hidden Ground* (London: Constable, 1998), 166.

   It is no surprise that one of his closest and long-time friends is the master "con" and magician Ricky Jay. Mamet directed two of Jay's most successful Broadway entertainments, *Ricky Jay and his 52 Assistants* and *On the Stem*.

10. David W. Mauer, *The Big Con, The Story of the Confidence Man*. Intr. Luc Sante (1940; New York: Anchor Books, 1999), 2. Confidence men are dramatists, Mauer emphasizes, and in the Big Con always perform theatre. See also Luc Sante, *Low Life, Lures and Snares of Old New York* (New York: Farrar Straus Giroux, 1991).
11. Gregory Mosher in Leslie Kane, "Interview," *David Mamet, A Casebook* (New York: Garland Publishing, 1992), 233.
12. *Romance* satirically represents this theme. At one point the defendant, the exact charge against whom we never learn, in the midst of firing his attorney largely because of an anti-Semitic slur, exclaims, "God forgive me, what have I done? I hired a Goy lawyer! It's like going to a straight hairdresser." Rejecting the lawyer's plea to submit to the court, he unleashes his own insults: "You fucken, brain-dead, white socks, country club, plaid pants, Campbell's soup fucken *sheigetz* Goy. Submit. That's fine. Take the example of Your Lord" (ROM 43). Judaism, Mamet has said, is "not a religion or a culture built on faith. You don't have to have faith. You don't have to believe anything; you just have to do it" (AOT 74–5).
13. Mamet in Josh Kun, "Carry the Weight," *San Francisco Bay Guardian*, February 18, 2004. Hereafter Kun.
14. See Heilpern, *How Good is David Mamet, Anyway? Writings on Theatre and Why it Matters* (London: Routledge, 2000), 220–28 and, for a contrasting view, Leslie Kane, *Weasels and Wisemen, Ethics and Ethnicity in the Work of David Mamet* (New York: Palgrave, 1999) Hereafter W&W.
15. Mamet in Rick Groen, "The Interview," *Globe and Mail*, June 11, 1999: C3.
16. Mamet in Esther Harriott, "Interview" (August 1984), *American Voices: Five Contemporary Playwrights in Essays and Interviews* (Jefferson, N. C.: McFarland, 1988), 79.
17. Robert Falls in Chris Jones, "The Truth about Mamet," *Chicago Tribune*, February 26, 2006.
18. Mamet is also echoing Beckett's minimalist practice. To his biographer in 1989, Beckett explained that Joyce's style was about adding material and that his was about taking it out. Beckett in James Knowlson, *Damned to Fame, The Life of Samuel Beckett* (New York: Simon and Schuster, 1996), 319.

CHAPTER 1 CITY OF FACT

1. Mamet was born at 12.31 A.M. at the Michael Reese Hospital in Chicago on November 30, 1947. In an interview held at the Chicago Public Library on October 13, 2006, Mamet refers to Fifty-third and Dorchester as his birthplace. However, the Chicago phone directory lists Bernard Mamet at 928 East Hyde Park Boulevard that year. By 1949, the family would move to Park Forest.
2. According to Ellis Island records, "Mamets" began to arrive as early as 1892 with a larger influx in 1902/1903 and then 1909 through 1922. Itzik Mamet from Ostiluk, Russia, and Mattule Mamet from Grubiczow, Russia, both arrived in 1909. Later Mamets came from Luck, Poland, Lyon, France, and Paris.
3. Mamet in Hannah Brown, "Schmoozing with David Mamet," *Jerusalem Post Magazine*, July 26, 2002: 16.

4. Mamet in Kenan Heise, "Bernard Mamet, lawyer for many labor unions," "Chicagoland," *Chicago Tribune* (July 4, 1991): 8. This is Bernie Mamet's obituary.
5. For Mamet's early piano experiences, see Mamet, "Hearing the Notes that Aren't Played," *New York Times*, July 15, 2002 E1. Years later, he would compose songs for Rebecca Pidgeon, his second wife, on her 1996 album, *New York Girl's Club*. In a 1987 interview, he acknowledged the importance of his piano lessons and his father's obsession with semantics as sources for his ear and for his combative language (IOW 132).
6. Lynn Mamet in Samuel G. Freedman, "The Gritty Eloquence of David Mamet," *New York Times Magazine* (21 April 1985: 46) Hereafter Freedman.
7. It went "If a duckling could say 'what a beautiful day' he wouldn't mean sunny and fair, 'cause a duck looks at things in a different way; he would mean it was wet everywhere.'" Citing this in a 1977 interview, Mamet joked that he would put it on his tombstone. His attentiveness to language, however, led the writer Jack Kroll to remark that "Mamet's ear is turned to an American frequency." Mamet in Jack Kroll, "The Muzak Man," *Newsweek* (February 28, 1977): 79.
8. Lynn Mamet, "The Lost Years," unpublished. 6. Hereafter LY.
9. Lynn Mamet in "David Mamet," www.filmakers.com/artists/mamet/biography/page2.htm
10. Mamet, in an interview with Rick Kogan, Chicago Public Library, October 13, 2006, WBEZ Chicago Public Radio Amplified series, repeated his love of Riverview. Hereafter Kogan CPL. Mamet writes about the amusement park in "A Party for Mickey Mouse," SF 78–9.
11. For Howells and Mencken, see the Chicago writer Richard Stern's "The Chicago Writer's City," *What Is What Was, Essays, Stories Poems* (Chicago: Univ. of Chicago Press, 2002), 99. Stern links the novelists to the rise of journalism and Chicago columnists like George Ade, Ben Hecht, Mike Royko, and Studs Terkel, whose heroes were "the abused and the abusive" (100). Stern provides an incisive "reading" of Chicago in this essay. Hereafter Stern.
12. Mamet in Minty Clinch, "Mamet Plots His Revenge," *Observer* (January 24, 1989).
13. Freedman, "The Gritty Eloquence of David Mamet," *New York Times Magazine* (21 April 1985: 46).
14. Court documents filed with the Circuit Court of Cook County, Illinois, dated January 12, 1959, January 13, 1959 and January 19, 1959.
15. David Mamet in Clinch, "Mamet Plots His Revenge," *Observer* (24 January 1989).
16. Macy in "The Man Behind the Curtain, David Mamet," *On Stage* (Chicago: Goodman Theatre, March 2006), 12; Schachter in Freedman, 50.
17. David Mamet on the Charlie Rose Show in 1994, in Leslie Kane, "'It's the Way That You are with your children:' The Matriarchal figure in Mamet's late Work," *Gender and Genre, Essays on David Mamet*, ed. Christopher C. Hudgins and Leslie Kane (New York: Palgrave, 2001), 151.
18. Willa Cather, "Lucy Gayheart" in *Lucy Gayheart & My Mortal Enemy* (Boston: Houghton Mifflin Company, 1938), 24–5. Hereafter LG. For later changes in mood and the city, see LG 119, 127.
19. Uncle Henry was also supposedly an actor who had a bit part in *Panic in the Streets* with Richard Widmark, although scrutiny of the film did not turn him up. Uncle

Henry also did some modeling; Mamet remembers a photo of a snappily dressed figure standing next to a 1941 Packard (DMC 95).

20. From 1922 to 1956, groups like the Yiddishe Dramatishe Gezelschaft performed plays relating to Jewish life at the Jewish Peoples Institute on Douglas Boulevard. Among early and important Yiddish actors were Muni Weisenfreund, who began acting as a teenager in his family's Pavilion Theatre on Twelfth near Halsted but by the 1930s was in Hollywood winning an Oscar for *The Story of Louis Pasteur* as the better-known Paul Muni. He would also star in the 1932 Chicago gangster film *Scarface*, written by another Jewish Chicagoan, Ben Hecht. Bernard Schwartz played Yiddish theatre for many years in Chicago before moving on to the movies as Tony Curtis. A measure of this awareness of Jewish drama was the 3,500 singers, dancers, and actors organized by the Jewish Community for *Romance of the People* performed on July 3, 1933, at Chicago's Century of Progress Exposition. The pageant drew 125,000 people to Soldiers Field, many to hear the principal speaker Chaim Weizman, later the first president of Israel. Mamet's parents and grandparents may have attended. Another important Jewish pageant was *We Shall Overcome*, performed at Chicago Stadium on May 19, 1943. Ben Hecht and Kurt Weill wrote the work, narrated by John Garfield and Burgess Meredith. It focused on the slaughter of Jews in Europe.
21. For Mamet's Yiddish expression see "David Mamet," The Cranky Critic, www.cranky-critic.com/qa/davidmamet.html. For an account of the Bellow dinner see Mamet, "A Meal with Mamet," www.nextbook.org/cultural/ feature.html. On the influence of Yiddish on his work, see Kane, *Weasels and Wisemen, passim*. On Yiddish theatre in Chicago see Irving Cutler, *The Jews of Chicago from Shtetl to Suburb* (Urbana: Univ. of Illinois Press, 1996), 90–94. There are also several useful pages in Christiansen, TOO.
22. Other items included a map of the U. S. made out of pickles, a knight sculpted out of prunes, and the Statue of Liberty carved out of salt. Canada contributed a 22,000 lb. cheese. See Erik Larson, *The Devil in the White City* (New York: Vintage, 2004), 247–8 and *passim*.
23. Algren, Hemingway in Carla Cappetti, *Writing Chicago, Modernism, Ethnography, and the Novel* (New York: Columbia Univ. Press, 1993), 146.
24. Mamet in Chris Jones, "Mamet talks Mamet," *Chicago Tribune* (March 29, 2006): Sect. 5: 1.
25. Mamet in Hedy Weiss, "David Mamet: The Quintessential Voice of Chicago Theatre," "Weekend," *Chicago Sun-Times* (March 10, 2006): 13. Mamet appears on the cover of the weekend magazine behind the headline "King David."
26. Marie Kirchner Stone, *The Progressive Legacy, Chicago's Francis W. Parker School 1901–2001* (New York: Peter Lang, 2001), 144. Hereafter Stone.
27. Graduates of the Parker School include the artist/illustrator Edward Gorey, the journalists David Dunlap and Jonathan Alter, the composer Philip Moll, and the actors Daryl Hannah, Jennifer Beales, Anne Heche, and Billy Zane, as well as Mamet.

CHAPTER 2 SOUTH OF THE NORTHEAST KINGDOM

1. M. Clinch, "Mamet plots his Revenge," *Observer* (January 24, 1989).
2. Mamet in C. Gerald Fraser, "Mamet's Plays Shed Masculinity Myth," *New York Times* (July 5, 1976: 7).

3. In a 1987 interview, Mamet misremembers the title and publisher of the book but not the plays. See IOW 135; rpt. DMC 72.
4. The play became the longest-running musical in history, opening on May 3, 1960, and after 17,162 performances, closing on January 13, 2002. It reopened at the Snapple Theatre in mid-town New York in August 2006.
5. In his essay "Hotel Lincoln," Mamet recounts his admiration for Boleslavsky's slim, 122-page book, which he later inscribed and gave to a young actor with his $170.00 receipt for his monthly rent at the Hotel Lincoln, where he lived in the early seventies (CA 95).
6. Vera Soloviova describes her program at the Moscow Art Theatre, with classes in singing, diction, recitation of prose and poetry, fencing, and body movement (classic ballet, Dalcroze, and the Isadora Duncan method) in "The Reality of Doing: Interviews with Vera Soloviova, Stella Adler and Sanford Meisner" in *Tulane Drama Review* 9 (1964): 136–37. The issue is the first of two devoted to Stanislavsky in America.
7. Harold Baldridge in *Acting Now, Conversations on Craft and Career*, ed. Edward Vilga (New Brunswick, NJ: Rutgers Univ. Press, 1997), 13–14.
8. MBT 34. Other New York adventures involved Mamet's roommate at the time, a dance student at Julliard, who often returned with lovely young ballet students. Two young women, one a flier in the circus and the other Irish, lived across the hall. But he was lonely and dislocated, even when he took minor acting jobs in summer stock and then left the city, although it still had mystery for him: at midnight on New Years' Eve 1967, for example, he came upon a snowball fight between a policeman and kids in Washington Square. Nostalgically, he recalled life in New York at that time, with afternoons at the Café Figaro and Steve Martin at the Bitter End, in a number of later essays.

   He also recalled other incidents: Thompson Street, in bed with a woman and how they let the candle burn down until he woke up to discover the walls, an Indian bedspread on the walls, and the mattress were in flames—"and we were out on the street naked and shivering" (JAF 11); visits from his father, coming down once or twice and going out to hear jazz with him at the Top of the Gate after *The Fantasticks*, "some of the fine times I remember that we had together" (JAF 11).
9. David Mamet in David Witz, "The David Mamet Interview: Sex, Ducks, and the Big Apple," *Chicago Theater*, February 1977: 2.
10. Mamet, "Preparing Camel," "The Camel Document" (unpub.) [1]. Hereafter CD.
11. Mamet in Kate O'Hare, "'The Unit' Catches Fire," www.zap2it.com/tv/news, March 14, 2006.
12. Chekhov, Letter to A. S. Lazarec, November 1, 1899.
13. A January 15, 1970, court document between his divorced parents refers to his psychiatric care and its expense. "Maladjusted"—today it would read "adjustment disorder"—is the term used to mean depression. The document further states that he was under the care of a psychoanalyst. Reference is also made to his applying for post-graduate work at the University of Chicago.
14. Glenna Syse, "E/R restores Organic Health; Mamet in Clover," *Sunday Sun Times* (Chicago) July 24, 1983.

15. There are more than 175 journals in the Mamet archive beginning in 1966 and running to 2001. They are his working mss., journals, and personal diaries and contain notes on his residences and weather, as well as pages of dialogue or story outlines. Some journals are devoted to single projects but most include notes drawn on for many projects at different stages or completely discarded. Occasional drawings or ts. leaves affixed or loosely inserted exist throughout. The materials deal with all aspects of his writing, including his films.
16. *Lakeboat* then remained unperformed for nearly a decade until the Milwaukee Repertory discovered it in 1979. Its first full production in a revised text was by the Court Street Theatre, a project of Milwaukee Rep, on April 24, 1980.
17. Mamet in C. Gerald Fraser, "Mamet's Plays Shed Masculinity Myth," *New York Times* July 5, 1976.
18. William H. Macy in "The Man Behind the Curtain, The Story of David Mamet," *On Stage, Goodman Theatre* (March 2006), 12.
19. William H. Macy in Michael Phillips, "Macy brings his memories back to town," *Chicago Tribune* July 28, 2006.
20. Robert Falls in Robert Loerzel, "Maximum Mamet," *Pioneer Press* (February 23, 2006: B3).
21. Gordon Gayer, "Saint Nicholas Theatre in Delightful Performance," *The Times-Argus* (Barre-Montpelier, VT), May 4, 1972.
22. The title of this work was *Sexual Perversity on Clark Street*, but the series of blackouts dealing mostly with comments about sex was considered by the critic in *Boston After Dark* to be thin.
23. Bonnie Jacob, "Of ducks and sex in Chicago," *Boston After Dark* (July 25, 1972), np.

CHAPTER 3 OFF-LOOP

1. Linder Winer, "Life and death with fowl perspective," *Chicago Tribune*, October 13, 1972: B6.
2. Mamet in C. Gerald Fraser, "Mamet Plays Shed Masculinity Myth," *New York Times*, July 5, 1976: A7.
3. Mike Nussbaum in conversation with the author at the Goodman Theatre, March 29, 2006.
4. Fraser, "Mamet's Plays Shed Masculinity Myth." See n. 2 above.
5. Mamet in Les Bridges, "Openers," *Chicago Tribune*, December 15, 1974: H8.
6. Linda Kimbrough to the author, Chicago, June 5, 2006.
7. R. Dettmer, "*Squirrels* overrun with Obscurity," *Chicago Tribune*, October 14, 1974.
8. Tanya Akason, "Squirrels and St. Nick," *Triad Guide*, October 1974, 79–82.
9. Michael ver Meulen, "In Your Town," radio script. Special Collections, Chicago Public Library.
10. Mamet in Yurl Rasovsky, "On the fallacy of Romanticism," *Chicago Sun Times*, February 9, 1975.
11. Jack Hafferkamp, "An Organic Ghost Story," *Chicago Daily News*, December 16, 1976.
12. 2851 N. Halsted, despite its theatrical history, was demolished in the spring of 2006. A celebration of the building occurred on April 9, 2006, with performers, friends, critics

and board members enjoying a champagne farewell. Richard Christiansen chaired a panel discussion. See Jonathan Abarbanel, "Final Bow for Historic Off-Loop Venue," at www.performink.com.

13. J.J. Johnston in Samuel G. Freedman, "The Gritty Eloquence of David Mamet," *New York Times Magazine*, April 21, 1985: 50–51.
14. Steven Schachter, director's notes, Goodman Archive, Special Collections, Chicago Public Library; Linda Winer, "A Silly but Sweet Dream," *Chicago Tribune*, July 25, 1975; Richard Christiansen, "Bard meets the Marx Brothers," *Chicago Daily News*, July 16, 1975; *Chicago Reader*, July 1975.
15. Douglas L. Lieberman and William H. Macy in Kane, *Weasels and Wisemen*, 321 n. 4.

CHAPTER 4 SOUTH SIDE GYPSY

1. David Mamet, "Foreword," *American Buffalo*. Illustrated by Michael McCurdy (San Francisco: Arion Press, 1992), 7. For another account of Mamet's poker game, see "Gems from a Gambler's Book Shelf," MBT 9–10. The entire essay is a wonderful summary of the con in its many guises.
2. Gregory Mosher, "Introduction," *American Buffalo* (New York: Grove Press, 1996) ix. Hereafter "Intro. AB"
3. Mosher, interview with author, December 27, 2004.
4. Gregory Mosher, "Mosher on Mamet: An Interview," *Lakeboat, Goodman Guide* (Chicago: Goodman Theatre 1982), 31–2.
5. Mantegna in Leslie Kane, "Mantegna acting Mamet," *American Theatre* Vol. 8 (September 1991), 21. Rpt. in *David Mamet, A Casebook* , ed. Leslie Kane (New York: Garland Publishing, 1992), 249–69.
6. Mamet, *American Buffalo* Ts. Special Collections, Chicago Public Library, 1–2. Hereafter AB ORD.
7. Mamet in Ron Powers, "A Playwright with the Chicago Sound," *Chicago Sun-Times*, January 7, 1976.
8. Bury St. Edmund, "Like A Play, Only Longer," *Chicago Reader*, October 1975.
9. Richard Christiansen, "Bravos for a play and a theatre," *Chicago Tribune*, December 1975; Linda Winer, "A timely move by St. Nicholas," *Chicago Sun*, December 1975.
10. Claudia Cassidy, "American Buffalo," WFMT; Glenna Syse, "American Buffalo Needs More Work," *Chicago Sun-Times*, October 24, 1975.
11. Mamet in Willimja Raidy, "Will success buffalo DM? Are you Kidding?" *Chicago Daily News*, April 2–3, 1977. Second City in particular would offer a number of satires of Mamet's work. Frederick Stroppel's *The Mamet Women* (1992) is another example. Imitating Mamet's style has itself become a contest initiated in San Francisco in 2005 at the American Conservatory Theatre and more recently in Chicago during the Goodman Mamet Festival (March 2006) with the "David Mamet Write-Alike" contest.
12. David Witz, "David Mamet Interview, Sex, Ducks and the Big Apple," *Chicago Theater*, February 1977 [1–2].
13. Mel Gussow, "St. Clement's Presents 3-character Play," *New York Times*, January 28, 1976: 28.

14. Richard Christiansen, "Mamet Scores a Hit with Broadway Critics," *Chicago Daily News*, ca. February 18, 1977.
15. Mamet in Christopher Porterfield, "David Mamet's Bond of Futility," *Time*, February 28, 1977: 54+.
16. Cited in Gary Houston, "Vital Arrogance," *Re-setting the Stage* (Chicago: Chicago Public Library, 1990), 20. This is an exhibition catalogue on Twentieth-century Chicago theatre. On St. Nicholas and the acting style of Mamet stressing a studied *flatness* and anti-musicality of delivery, see p. 20.
17. Witz, "David Mamet Interview," *Chicago Theater,*, February 1977 [1–2]; Polly Ullrich, "Mamet: He's still a Chicagoan," *Chicago Sun-Times*, February 6, 1977.
18. Richard Christiansen, "Mamet's Touching Fable, A Life in the Theatre," *Chicago Daily News*, February 4, 1977; Mel Gussow, "Mamet Wins with 'Life in Theater,'" *New York Times*, February 5, 1977: 22.
19. Mel Gussow, "The Water Engine," *New York Times*, May 14, 1977.
20. Walt Jones, "Interview," June 4, 2001 (San Diego, CA); Mamet in William B. Collins, "Mamet's *A Life in the Theatre*," *Philadelphia Inquirer*, October 21, 1979, M1: 17.
21. Mamet in Terry Curtis Fox, "Bringing the Theatre back Home," *New Times*, December 11, 1977. Terry Curtis Fox was involved with the Doc Film program at the University of Chicago. He became a playwright then film critic, filmwriter, producer, and most recently an academic. He wrote *Cops* in 1978, produced at the Organic with Dennis Franz and Joe Mantegna. He then became film critic of the *Chicago Reader* and the *Village Voice* before going to Hollywood, where he became a screenwriter and then a producer. He did scripts for *Hill Street Blues, JAG*, and *Stargate G-1*.

    Mamet was to collaborate with Terry Curtis Fox on *Cops*, but they differed on how they thought the play should go. It deals with three policemen in a late night Chicago diner playing practical jokes on customers, but a new customer misunderstands and a hostage drama ensues.
22. Marilyn Preston, "The dream rises to top in Mamet theory," *Chicago Tribune*, November 16, 1977. Section 2.
23. Richard Christiansen, "Mamet New Play in Uneven Debut," *Chicago Daily News*, November 17, 1977: 35; Richard Eder, "Mamet Expands Range in *Woods*," *New York Times*, November 30, 1977: C 19; Sherman Kaplan, "The Woods," WBBM Radio.
24. Lindsay Crouse in Bruce Smith, "Lindsay: honing the family edge," *Daily News*, October 16, 1979: 27; Lindsay Crouse, "The Actor's Job," *Chapin Alumnae Bulletin* (1979): 15–16.
25. Henry Kissel, "David Mamet: A voice from the side pocket heralds an era," *Women's Wear Daily*, October 19, 1977. Hereafter Kiss.
26. Mosher in *Chicago Daily News*, April 25, 1977.
27. Gregory Mosher, Leslie Kane, "Interview," *David Mamet, A Casebook* (New York: Garland, 1992), 232.
28. For an account of the Wright-Green and then Wright-Houseman scripts, see Hazel Rowley, *Richard Wright, The Life and Times* (New York: Henry Holt, 2001), 213–25.
29. David Mamet, "Misguided, excessive and true," *Guardian*, July 17, 2003; Mamet, "In Every Generation," MBT 206–07.

30. Richard Wright, "Introduction," *Native Son*, Restored Text Est. by the Library of America (New York: Harper Perennial, 1998) xv.; Mosher, "Memo," Goodman Theatre Archive, Production History File, 1978/79, Special Collections, Chicago Public Library. Box 49.4. This is also the source for the typescript of the play cited in the following pages.

    Earlier, in January 1978, Joseph Papp produced *The Water Engine*, a play of violence but within the frame of a radio program, in New York, transferring to Broadway in March (although it ran for only sixteen performances). It premiered at the St. Nicholas in May 1977. During this time, and as a sign of Mamet's ascendancy, Second City titled its annual review *Sexual Perversity among the Buffalo* and included a parody of Mamet's style.
31. Interestingly, the national press was not invited to review the show because of a possible lawsuit. They had made a new "text" out of Wright's words, although they credited the Paul Green text. No one, it seemed, bothered to compare the two to see the differences. Mosher assumed the production would get him fired when it was discovered what he (and Mamet) had done.
32. Michael Billington, "Wiles in Windy City," *Guardian*, June 29,1978: 12; Michael Coveney, "American Buffalo," *Financial Times*, June 29, 1978: 12.
33. Jack Helbig, "American Icon," "Time Out!," *Daily Herald* (Chicago), February 24, 2006: 36. Helbig was unofficially enrolled in Mamet's course and attended all nine weeks. Another influence at the time was Bruno Bettelheims' *The Uses of Enchantment*, published the year before *Lone Canoe*.
34. Gregory Mosher in Kane, "Interview," *David Mamet, A Casebook*, 235.
35. Mamet, *Lone Canoe or The Explorer*, TS., Goodman Theatre Archive Productions, Special Collections, Chicago Public Library, Box 49 File 12.
36. Twenty-six years later, Mamet would recall the earliest version of the work very differently from its Goodman production: rather, an "out-and-out *hellzapoppin'* farce about the scenery falling down, called *Lone Canoe*." This was a 1972 draft he labeled the "Goddard Version," which lost its comic edge when he began to revise it in 1978 and add a libretto. See Mamet in Logan Hill, "Funny Peculiar," *New York Magazine*, February 28, 2005.
37. Linda Winer, "Uneasy laughter greets Mamet's new play 'Canoe,'" *Chicago Tribune*, May 25, 1979; Roger Ellis, "Lone Canoe," *Theater Journal* 32 (1980): 257.
38. Richard Eder, "Lone Canoe or The Explorer," *New York Times*, May 26, 1979: 16.
39. Ellis, "Lone Canoe," *Theatre Journal* 32 (1980): 256–7. For Mamet on the drunken critics, see Mimi Leahey, "David Mamet, The American Dream Gone Bad," *Other Stages*, November 4, 1982: 3. Hereafter Leahey.
40. Mel Gussow, "Stage: 'Reunion,' 3 Mamet Plays," *New York Times*, October 19, 1979; Jeremy Gerard, "Theatre in our Town," *Our Town*, November 4, 1979; Mamet on critics in William B. Collins, "Mamet's A Life in the Theatre," *Philadelphia Inquirer*, October 21, 1979.
41. DMC 142; Mamet in Chris Chase, "At the Movies," *New York Times*, March 26, 1981: C 6. In the *New York Times* interview, Mamet offers several comments on his past and his parents, noting that his "mother and father are very happy. They're especially happy

because they haven't spoken to each other for the last 20 years. They're both remarried." He also comments that he's supported himself from the time he got out of college and that success still seems unreal: "When I see 'Help Wanted' signs on bulletin boards, I have to stop myself from taking down the phone numbers" (*ibid).*

42. Mamet in Michael Earley, "Playwrights Making Movies: David Mamet," *Conversations on Art and Performance*, ed. Bonnie Marranca and Gautam Dasgupta (Baltimore: Johns Hopkins UP, 1999), 259. Hereafter "Ea." The interview was conducted in 1981.
43. Mamet in Dan Yakir, "The Postman's Words," *Film Comment* (March/April 1981): 21.
44. See Roger Ebert, "Postman Rings Twice," *Chicago Sun-Times*, January 1, 1981 and Vincent Canby, "A New Postman Always Rings Twice," *New York Times*, March 20, 1981, for representative comments.

CHAPTER 5 THE AMERICAN WAY

1. Mamet, "'Misguided, excessive and true,'" *The Guardian* July 17, 2003: 16–17.
2. Richard Wright, *Native Son* (1940; New York: Harper, 2005), 105. Nicholas de Jongh in the *Evening Standard* wrote, "no modern piece of theater offers a more fearful moral-health warning than David Mamet's *Edmond*, " calling it "disturbingly topical" (July 19, 2003). Michael Coveney in the *Daily Mail* praised the "musical" element of the work, "the rhythm and pace" of the production directed by Edward Hall that matched Richard Eyre's Royal Court production of 1985 (July 18, 2003). Charles Spencer in the *Daily Telegraph* stressed the moving glimpse of "redemption and common humanity that ends the play," adding that *Edmond* "sends you out into the night with a conviction that spiritual possibilities may somehow survive in a corrupt and fallen world" (July 18, 2003). Branagh was universally praised. A 2006 film featuring William H. Macy met with only a modest reception, however; the material, was, perhaps, still too harsh for general acceptance.
3. Don Shewey, "David Mamet puts a dark new urban drama on stage," *New York Times*, October 24, 1982: Arts: 2.
4. Richard Christiansen, "Mamet's *Edmond* Savage but Compassionate," *Chicago Tribune*, June 7, 1982, sec. C: 14; Glenna Syse, "*Edmond* A superb Odyssey of Raw Rage," *Chicago Sun-Times*, June 8, 1982: Living: 54; Mamet in David J. Blum, "David Mamet's Wealth of Words," *Wall Street Journal*, June 11, 1982: 25. On the 1996 production at the Atlantic Theatre see Ben Brantley, "In Mamet's *Edmond* A Man on Empty," *New York Times*, October 2, 1996: C13. For a comment on Branagh's performance at the National Theatre, London see Michael Billington, "*Edmond*: Kenneth Branagh uncaged," *Guardian* July 19, 2003. On the film see Anthony Lane, "Men at Sea," *New Yorker* July 24, 2006: 83.
5. Mamet in Blum, *Wall Street Journal*, June 11, 1982. Mamet is always seeking a constituency. In a shoe store to buy a pair of boots, the sales clerk recognized his name and said, "I've seen some of your plays." "Why haven't you seen all of them?" Mamet asked. "I didn't like all of them," she answered. He didn't respond. *Ibid.*
6. Mamet in Mimi Leahey, "David Mamet, The American Dream Gone Bad," *Other Stages*, November 4, 1982: 3.

7. Sidney Lumet in Joanna E. Rapf, "Interview with Sidney Lumet," *Sidney Lumet, Interviews*, ed. Joanna E. Rapf (Jackson: Univ. of Mississippi Press, 2006) 178. Also see Mamet in Jack Kroll, *Newsweek*, October 19, 1987.
8. Lumet in Don Shewey, "Sidney Lumet, The Reluctant Auteur," *Lumet Interviews*, ed. Rapf, 112–113.
9. The 156-page *Malcolm X* screenplay, originally drafted in July 1982, has November 1983 as the last dated revision.
10. Mamet in Kane, *Weasels*, 264. Mamet worked on the script the same time he was writing his first film, *House of Games*, released in 1987.
11. Frank Rich, "Review/Theatre: Mamet's Tasteful Hell for a Movie Mogul," *New York Times*, December 4, 1989.
12. Mamet, "A Beloved Friend Who Lived Life the Chicago Way," *New York Times*, October 14, 2001: Sec. 2, 7.
13. Mamet in Glenna Syse, "Theaters brace for 'ripping openings," *Chicago Sun-Times*, January 29, 1984: 8.
14. Benedict Nightingale, "American Buffalo Proves its Quality," *New York Times*, November 6, 1983: Arts and Leisure Sect. 3.
15. Mamet to Mosher, February 20, 1984. Private collection.
16. Clive Barnes' review is symptomatic of the positive take on the play, stressing that the nasty amoral world in the work has a "passionless objectivity" that gives the play its power. Its cruel humor is unconscious and these "brochure bandits, peddlers of false dreams" are little more than paranoid American businessmen created by the system. They are crooks that have forgotten "that what they are doing is crooked." Barnes, "Mamet's *Glengarry*: A Play to See and Cherish," *New York Post*, March 26, 1984: sec. 2, 15+. Others, like James Cook in *Forbes*, praised its accurate depiction of sales, differentiating it from Miller's *Death of a Salesman* in which the blame is on the system. Mamet focuses on the life of the salesman. "Always be closing" is the mantra, even if you hate the job. Cook, "Life of a Salesman," *Forbes*, May 21, 1984: 56.
17. For a comment on the opening Goodman production, see Bury St. Edmond, "Mamet's Prime," *The Chicago Reader*, February 17, 1984: sect. 1, 40. Bury St. Edmond is the pseudonym of the Chicago critic Lenny Kleinfeld.
18. Jordan Lage, "Boot Camp with David Mamet," *American Theater* 21:1 (January 2004): 38+. Lage was a student of Mamet's at both NYU and the Vermont summer school and became a member of the Atlantic Theatre Company formed at Mamet's urging. Among other productions, he was in Mamet's 1995 staging of J. B. Priestley's *Dangerous Corner*. His article is part of a special section on "Technique/Acting Practice." Hereafter Lage.
19. This summary is partly taken from Dennis Carrol's *David Mamet* (London: Macmillan 1987), 6. For the debate on Mamet's blend of acting sources, see Don S. Wilmeth, "Mamet and the Actor," *The Cambridge Companion to David Mamet*, ed. Christopher Bigsby (Cambridge: Cambridge UP, 2004),138–53. For a highly critical analysis of Mamet's *True and False, Heresy and Common Sense for the Actor*, see Bella Merlin, "Mamet's Heresy and Common Sense," *New Theatre Quarterly* 16 (August 2000): 249–54.

20. Macy suggested this idea in Samuel G. Freedman, "The Gritty Eloquence of David Mamet," *New York Times Magazine*, April 21, 1985: 64.
21. Neil Pepe in Steven Drukman, "Go Form a Company, Mamet Said, So they Did," *New York Times*, November 7, 1999: Arts , 8.
22. The transfers include the Tony Award winning production of *The Beauty Queen of Leenane* and *Lieutenant of Inishmore*, both by Martin McDonagh. The premieres include Mamet's *Romance*. The Atlantic dedicated its fifteenth season to the work of Mamet, producing five of his plays including a series of one acts in 2000.
23. Mamet to the Atlantic Theatre Company, July 21, 1985: 1.
24. John Guare, *Rich and Famous* (New York: Dramatists Play Service, 1977) 7. The play was originally produced in 1974. Mel Gussow, "David Mamet's Latest Microcosm," *New York Times*, December 4, 1977: D3. Gussow writes about *The Woods*.
25. Mamet, "Program Note," *The Cherry Orchard*," *Stagebill* (Chicago: Goodman Theatre, 1095): 15.
26. For an account of these changes and the origin of the New Theatre Company see Richard Christiansen, "What's New? Goodman's company in a company," *Chicago Tribune* March 3, 1985, Sect. 13: 11–12. The NTC lasted only a few months. Following Mosher's departure for New York, it folded. The Goodman then turned to Robert Falls as artistic director who officially took over in the spring of 1986. The theatre itself moved into new facilities in October 2000 on North Dearborn Avenue. For an account of the creation of the space, now with two theatres, see Tom Creamer, *et al*, *Robert Falls, At Goodman Theatre, The First Twenty Years* (Chicago: Goodman Theater, [2006]), 143–49.
27. Richard Christiansen, "New Cherry Orchard is the pits," *Chicago Tribune*, March 15, 1985: Sect. 2: 5. Glenna Syse, "Mamet, Mosher replant *The Cherry Orchard*, " *Chicago Sun-Times*, March 15, 1985: 47. Robert Brustein, "Robert Brustein on Theater, Musical Chairs," *New Republic*, April 29, 1985. Brustein also notes that the halting speech with hints of crudeness and inarticulateness creates problems: Mamet makes everyone sound alike. His adaptation enjoys a unified style at the cost of Chekhov's theme and characters, the acting reinforcing the idea that class distinctions are being ignored. The language introduces a sense of democratic leveling that Chekhov had anticipated but not realized in the play. Brustein also observes that Peter Brook did a chairless *Cherry Orchard* in Paris.
28. Mamet in Glenna Syse, "Mosher and Mamet Build a New Tradition in Drama," *Chicago Sun Times*, March 3, 1985: 6–8.
29. Nancy Coons, "Lindsay Crouse, Broadway Baby now a Star," *Daily Herald*, March 21, 1985. Interestingly, Crouse had studied at the Stella Adler school and with Uta Hagen and then with Sanford Meisner.

CHAPTER 6 SOLDIER OF FORTUNE

1. Mamet, "Conventional Warfare," *Esquire*, March 1985; Hereafter "CON." Mamet reprints the article in *Some Freaks*, 34–44. The text cited is the passage found on p. 36.
2. On cutting off sentences at the pass, see Katina Alexander, "Two Mamet Plays are Quirky," *Southtown Economist*, April 28, 1985: 8; Anthony Adler, "Lindsay Crouse," *Chicago Reader*, May 10, 1985: 46.

3. Persi Diaconis in Mark Singer, "Secrets of the Magus," *New Yorker* 69 (April 1993): 64. This is a full and revealing profile of Jay.
4. Ricky Jay's other roles for Mamet include Silver in *Things Change* (1988), Aaron in *Homicide* (1991), and the inventor in the TV production of *The Water Engine* (1992).
5. Orson Welles in Margo Jefferson, "Myth, Magic and us Mortals," *New York Times*, Arts and Leisure, May 26, 2002: 4.
6. On Renaissance cons see Wayne Rebhorn, *Foxes and Lions, Machiavelli's Confidence Men* (Ithaca: Cornell UP, 1988), 1–44; for American examples, see Karen Halttunen, *Confidence Men and Painted Women, a Study of Middle-class Culture in America, 1830–1870* (New Haven: Yale UP, 1982). Melville's allegorical novel *The Confidence-Man, A Masquerade* appeared in 1857.

   The term "confidence man" originated in an editorial of *The New York Herald* in 1849. See Johannes D. Bergmann, "The Original Confidence Man," *American Quarterly* 21 (1969): 560–77. Italian writers of the Renaissance preferred *beffatore* and the *beffa*, words employed by Boccaccio, the *novella* writers who followed him, and Machiavelli (Rebhorn 7). From Boccaccio to Molière and beyond, confidence men have flourished: Felix Krull in Thomas Mann's *Felix Krull, Confidence Man* and Yossarin in *Catch-22* are two more recent examples. For a partial genealogy of the early confidence man, see Rebhorn, 11.
7. Ricky Jay in Margo Jefferson, "Myth, Magic and us Mortals," *New York Times*, Arts and Leisure, May 26, 2002: 4. The first show won the Lucille Lortel and Obie Awards for Outstanding Achievement. The second ran for seven months but actually started before *52 Assistants*. The genesis was a show called "The Man Who Does Everything," which Jay and Mamet worked on in the mid-eighties, in which Jay would exhibit every performance skill possible. Mamet, however, thought it more fun to limit it to New York, making it revolve around the city and the idea of New York entertainment. Revised, it became *Ricky Jay: On the Stem*, essentially a history and demonstration of Broadway tricks and characters ("on the stem" is pre-Broadway slang for the main drag in town).
8. Crouse in Anthony Adler, "Lindsay Crouse," *Chicago Reader*, May 10, 1985: 46. Hereafter Adler.
9. Mamet in Art Linson, *A Pound of Flesh: Perilous Tales of How to Produce Movies in Hollywood* (New York: Grove Press, 1993), 67. Hereafter Linson.
10. Among those auditioning for a part was Joe Mantegna as Capone, recommended by Mamet. Mantegna didn't take it seriously, however, and when he walked in the room, he looked at De Palma and said "'I'm not going to waste your time. You know and I know that you're going to have De Niro gain fifty pounds and play this part.' We all 'ha, ha, ha' laughed and that was six months before they cast the movie." Mantegna in Kane, "Interview," *David Mamet, A Casebook*, 268.
11. Mamet "The Untouchables" in Gay Brewer, *David Mamet and Film* (Jefferson, NC: McFarland & Company, 1993), 119–20. Hereafter Brewer.
12. Mamet in Glenn Lovell, "David Mamet keeps his Multifaceted Career Speeding Along," *Chicago Tribune*, 28 October 28, 1988: sec.E:7. Mamet also "improved" the story: "That something is true does not make it interesting. There wasn't any real story. Ness and Capone never met . . . . so I made up a story . . . ." Mamet in Richard Corliss, "Shooting up the Box Office," *Time*, June 22, 1987: 78.

13. On the process of making the film see Mamet, "Introduction, A First-Time Film Director," *House of Games* (New York: Grove, 1987), v-xviii; ODF 2, 32.
14. David Denby, "What's in a Game?" *New York Magazine*, October 19, 1987:101.
15. Mike Medavoy, *You're Only as Good as Your Next One*. With Josh Young (New York: Pocket Books, 2002), 169. Hereafter Medavoy.
16. Mamet in Ray Greene, "Confidence Man," Boxoffice online, Cover Story, http://www.boxoff. com/apr98story2html.
17. Jack Kroll, "The Profane Poetry of David Mamet," *Newsweek* October 19, 1987. Hereafter Kroll.
18. Mamet in David Savarn, "Trading in the American Dream," *American Theatre*, September 1987: 18.
19. Mamet in David Gritten, "Prepared for Anything," *Daily Telegraph* (London) March 7, 1998.
20. Howard Kissel, "No, She Can't Act," *New York Daily News*, May 4, 1988; Jack Tinker, "Settling Some Old Scores," *Daily Mail*, January 26, 1989.
21. William A. Henry, III, "Madonna Comes to Broadway" *Time*, May 16, 1988: 74–5.
22. On the play's New York production see David Kaufman, "Desperately Seeking Audiences," *Independent*, May 9, 1988; Edith Oliver, "Mamet at the Movies," *New Yorker*, May 16, 1988: 95. On Madonna's supposed departure see "Madonna, you can't be serious," *Daily Mail*, June 25, 1988.
23. Christopher Edwards, "Speed-the-Plow (Spoleto Festival)," *The Spectator*, July 16, 1988: 38.
24. Pidgeon in "An American Pinter sticks his pen in the White House," *Sunday Times*, August 1, 2004.
25. Michael Billington, "Hollywood or bust," *Guardian*, January 26, 1989; Tony Dunn, "Speed-the-Plow," *Plays & Players* (March 1989), 34, 35.
26. Sandy Lieberson, "True life drama," *Evening Standard*, January 19, 1989.
27. It's the first of several children's books Mamet would write, the others being *Passover* (1995), *The Duck and the Goat* (1996), *Bar Mitzvah* (1999), and *Henrietta* (1999).

    Despite personal difficulties, nineteen eighty-eight would be a significant year: Mamet's second child, Zosia, was born on 2 February; *Uncle Vanya* opened at the American Repertory Theatre in Cambridge in April; *Speed-the Plow* opened in New York in May; he directed *Sketches of War* in Boston in October; *Things Change* was released in October.
28. A similar statement appears in Lynn Mamet's unpublished play, *The Lost Years*. The troll remark appears in Nan Robertson, "Lindsay Crouse Keeps up a Family Stage Tradition," *New York Times* (2 January 1981) C:3.
29. Mamet, in Anton Chekhov, *Uncle Vanya*, adapted by David Mamet from a literal tr. by Vlada Chernomordik (New York: Grove Press, 1989),19. Hereafter UV.

    Mamet's adaptation was the basis of Louis Malle's 1994 film, *Vanya on 42nd* Street starring Wallace Shawn as Vanya and Julianne Moore as Yelena. Its opening is memorable: the actors walk the streets of New York, one-by-one entering the run-down New Amsterdam Theatre engaging in familiar talk, but, before the viewer realizes it, the dialogue has transitioned into the Chekhov play. For a brief commentary see

Steven Price, "On Directing Mamet," *Cambridge Companion to David Mamet*, ed. Bigsby, 154–5.

Mamet's version of *The Three Sisters* by the Atlantic Theatre opened in 1991 at a theatre festival in Philadelphia, the text similarly updated with Mamet's characteristically direct language.

30. Mimi Kramer, "Double or Nothing," *New Yorker*, December 25, 1989: 79.
31. Thorstein Veblen, *The Theory of the Leisure Class, An Economic Study of Institutions* (New York: Modern Library, 1934) 278, 276.

CHAPTER 7 A JEW IN THE NINETIES

1. In this essay, Mamet also offers his objections to *Schindler's List*, calling it "emotional pornography" (MBT 141). It exploits rather than reenacts the horror of the Holocaust and panders to the audience. In another essay, he writes that, "reason is not a defense against anti-Semitism. The least appearance of race hatred is a questioning wedge whose end is murder" (MBT 206). More recently, Mamet expresses his aggressive Judaism in *The Wicked Son, Anti-Semitism, Self Hatred and the Jews* (2006).
2. See for example, "The Jew for Export," "Minority Rights," and "In Every Generation" in *Make-Believe Town*; "The Decoration of Jewish Homes," in *Some Freaks*; *The Wicked Son* (2006) consistently demonstrates this approach.
3. Macy in Michael Joseph Gross, "Leading Lady," *Boston Magazine*, June 1999: 91. Lynn Mamet in John Lahr, "Fortress Mamet," 81.
4. Rebecca Pidgeon in Gross, "Leading Lady," *Boston Magazine*, June 1999, 117. Hereafter Pidgeon.
5. *Luftick*, the adjective, means one who is nimble, "cool," airy. In 1987, Mamet published *Three Jewish Plays*, containing *The Disappearance of the Jews, Goldberg Street*, and *The Luftmensch* (New York: Samuel French, 1987).
6. For a thorough discussion of Jewish elements and influences in Mamet's work, see Leslie Kane, *Weasels and Wisemen, Ethics and Ethnicity in the Work of David Mamet* (New York: Palgrave, 1999). The Judaic foundation of Mamet's moral thought might be another way of describing her detailed discussion.
7. Orion Pictures withdrew financing and only when the independent producer Edward R. Pressman (*Wall Street, Reversal of Fortune*) stepped in with $6.5 million could the project go ahead. Bruce Barton, *Imagination in Transition, Mamet's Move to Film* (Brussels: Peter Lang 2005), 181.
8. Mamet in Hannah Brown, "Schmoozing with David Mamet," *Jerusalem Post Magazine*, July 26, 2002: 16.
9. Rabbi Larry Kushner, in conversation with the author, May 2, 2003. Mamet's continued joy in Judaism was evident when the author attended Shabbat services with him and Rebecca Pidgeon at their new Los Angeles synagogue, Ohr HaTorah. Rabbi Mordecai Finley officiated, the dedicatee of *The Wicked Son*.
10. See six responses to the play in "He Said . . . She Said . . . Who Did What?" Arts and Leisure, *New York Times*, November 15, 1992: 6. Two different playbills were printed

for the production at the Orpheum Theatre in New York, one showing a male seated with a target on his chest, the other a female.

11. Alan Dershowitz in Richard Stayton, "David Mamet meets Alan Dershowitz," http://www.mindspring.com/~jason-charnick/mamet-museum/dershowitz.html. Hereafter Stayton.
12. William H. Macy to the author, at the Atlantic Theatre, April 11, 2000. For a discussion of the two productions and different endings, see Ira B. Nadel, "The Playwright as Director: Pinter's *Oleanna*," *Pinter Review* 11 (2001): 121–8.
13. See Mamet's Foreword to *River Run Cookbook, Southern Comfort from Vermont* (New York: Harper Collins, 2001), ix–xi.
14. DeVito in Sean Wilentz, "Tales of Hoffa," *The New Republic*, February 1, 1983: 55. The article also contains a useful account of the film's historical and dramatic inconsistencies.
15. On the topic of tough Jews see, Paul Breines, *Tough Jews, Political Fantasies and the Moral Dilemma of American Jewry* (New York: Basic Books, 1990) and Warren Rosenberg, *Legacy of Rage: Jewish Masculinity, Violence and Culture* (Amherst, MA: Univ. of Massachusetts Press, 2001). For a specific discussion of Mamet in these terms see Rosenberg 209, 233–46.

    On Jewish gangsters see Albert Fried, *The Rise and Fall of the Jewish Gangster in America* (1980; New York: Columbia 1994), Rich Cohen, *Tough Jews: Fathers, Sons and Gangster Dreams* (New York: Simon & Schuster, 1998) and Rachel Rubin, *Jewish Gangsters of Modern Literature* (Urbana: Univ. of Illinois Press, 2000).
16. *Wicked City: Chicago* was the title of a 1906 study by Grant Stevens. *Chicago and the Cess Pools of Infamy* (1910) was a work by Samuel Paynter Wilson. Sergio Leone's film about Jewish gangsters in New York, *Once Upon A Time in America*, appeared in 1984. For commentary on *The Untouchables* and *Hoffa* see Gay Brewer, "*Hoffa* and *The Untouchables*: Mamet's brutal orders of authority," *Literature Film Quarterly* XXVIII (2000), 28–34. Ishmael Reed, *Reckless Eyeballing* (1986; New York: Atheneum, 1988), 16.
17. Not knowing Hebrew is an important sign of Bobby Gold's inert, atrophied Judaism in *Homicide*.
18. Alfred Kazin, "Oy Gevalt!" *The New Republic*, November 3, 1997: 36.
19. Leon Wieseltier, "Machoball Soup," *The New Republic* , April. 24, 1995: 46.
20. Mamet, "'If I Forget Thee Jerusalem': The Power of Blunt Nostalgia," *Forward* 27 December 2002; rpt. in *Those Who Forget the Past: The Question of Anti-Semitism*, ed. Ron Rosenbaum (New York: Random House, 2004). I write this while Israel experiences the eighth day of fighting Hezbollah in Lebanon, July 2006. The danger to the country does not change, made more frightening by the presence of my son there. But by phone he tells me "there is no other place I would rather be," a gesture of reassurance and commitment.
21. Mamet in Brown, "Schmoozing with David Mamet," *Jerusalem Post Magazine*, July 26, 2002: 16.
22. Mamet in David Horovitz, *Still Life with Bombers, Israel in the Age of Terrorism* (New York: Knopf, 2004), 25.
23. Michael Billington, "The Cryptogram" *Guardian*, June 30, 1994; Ian Stuart, "A Puzzle of Portent from Mamet," *Newsday*, July 1, 1994: B2.

24. See for example Charles Spencer, "Bitter truth exposed by cracking family code," *Daily Telegraph*, October 18, 2006. Cattrall's acting, along with the script, was especially praised.
25. Mamet in Richard Corliss, "The Gamut of Mamet," *Time Magazine*, April 6, 1998.
26. J. B. Priestley, *Dangerous Corner* (1932; New York: Samuel French, 1959), 14, 15. Mamet's production of the Priestley work, based on his revision of the text, occurred at the Atlantic Theatre in the fall of 1995 staring Rebecca Pidgeon, Felicity Huffman and Mary McCann. Mamet cut the psychological drawing room comedy set in the 1930's from three acts to two. Vincent Canby in the *New York Times* wrote that the "production matches the text, being economical and clipped though resonant." He goes on to praise Mamet's method of finding the meaning of the work not by "broadening its context, but by stripping the play down to its bare bones." Canby, "Priestley Crosses the Sea and Becomes Mamet," *New York Times*, October 12, 1995.
27. David Mamet, "Bambi v. Godzilla," *Harper's Magazine*, Vol. 310 (June 2005), 36.
28. When asked "why Hollywood" in 1997, Mamet glibly answered, "it's screaming good fun. It pays very, very well . . . I'm not an ascetic. I'm greedy and ambitious like everybody else." Mamet in Bruce Webber, "At 50, a Mellower David Mamet may be ready to tell his story," *New York Times*, November 16, 1997, Arts and Leisure : 3.

    The counterpoint to Mamet's attitude is Woody Allen. Living in New York, he has maintained a certain professional independence from Hollywood, quite different than Mamet's.
29. In 1995 Mamet wrote a six-stanza satire entitled "Keep Me Out of L.A." A whimsical complaint against the comic foibles of west coast culture—"Gimme the seasons and the winter chill/ Lemme keep some semblance of my own free will"—the song nonetheless highlights what Mamet and Pidgeon would accept once they moved there in 2002: a culture "with an eye on the mirror and an ear to the phone."
30. The first screenplay for Lyne was by James Dearden dated 1991. See Christopher C. Hudgins, "'Lolita' 1995: The Four Filmscripts," *Literature/Film Quarterly* 25 (1997):23–30.
31. David Gritten, "Prepared for Anything," *Daily Telegraph*, March 7, 1998. Hereafter Gritten.
32. Art Linson, *What Just Happened? Bitter Hollywood Tales from the Front Line* (New York: Bloomsbury, 2002), 23. Hereafter What.
33. *State and Main* is Mamet's third most successful film at $6.9 million followed by *The Winslow Boy* at $4.1 million and then *Things Change* at $3.5 million. *Homicide* is next at $3.0 million, followed by *House of Games* at $2.6 million. His least successful film is *Oleanna*, earning only $125, 000.
34. A few years earlier, Mamet was more hesitant:

    Playboy: At the end of the day, do you ever get a sense that you should go back to your room and to your real work, which is writing plays; that maybe movie making is a lesser form?

    Mamet: I don't think it is a lesser form. I do, however, feel absolutely that the theatre is my real work, and when I'm making movies I sometimes feel like I'm playing hooky. (DMC 128)

CHAPTER 8 BOOK OF GAMES

1. The full title is "THE COMPLEAT/ Gamester: OR,/INSTRUCTIONS/ How to play at BILLIARDS, TRUCKS, BOWLS,/ and CHESS./ Together with all manner of usual and MOST Gentile Games either on/ CARDS or DICE./ To which is added The ARTS and MYSTERIES/OF/ RIDING, RACING, ARCHERY,/and COCK-FIGHTING." (London: Printed at A.M. for R Cutler and to be sold by Henry Brome at the/ Gun at the West-end of St. Pauls. 1674. 232 pp. Written by Charles Cotton, co-authored with Iszak Walton of *The Compleat Angler*, *The Compleat Gamester* contains what is thought to be the earliest rules for cards and the earliest reference to poker. Until 1850 there were no printed rules for poker. Interestingly, a fever for gaming infected the Seventeenth-century, to which *The Compleat Gamester* was a response. Anyone in society ignorant of the rules was thought to be low-bred "and hardly fit for conversation," writes one contemporary commentator (Richard Seymour, "Preface," *The Court Gamester*).
2. October, December 1996; January 1997. For a discussion of the script's evolution and issues regarding the making of the film, see Tom Stempel, "The Collaborative Dog: *Wag the Dog* (1997)," *Film & History* 35.1 (2005): 60–64. Note 12 p. 64 cites the Mamet drafts.
3. Chris A. Bolton, "Ronin," www.24freamespersecnd.com/reactions/films/ ronin.html.
4. John Frankenheimer in "Mamet Removes His Name from Film," "Studio Briefings," *Variety* (August 5, 1998).
5. Interestingly, his HBO film about the Jewish gangster Meyer Lansky, starring Richard Dreyfus, also appeared that year, suggesting, again, Mamet's attraction to both the street-wise and educated, mobsters vying equally with the British upper-middle class.
6. Geoffrey Wansell, *Terrence Rattigan* (London: Fourth Estate, 1995), 160. On the development of the play and changes to the actual events, see 152–60.
7. Mamet in Nick James, "Suspicion," *Sight and Sound*, n.s. 8 (October 1998): 23, 24. Mamet, "The Winslow Boy," *The Spanish Prisoner and The Winslow Boy, Two Screenplays* (New York: Vintage, 1999), 165. Hereafter WB.
8. Mamet in James, "Suspicion," *ibid.*, 23.
9. Samuel Butler, "Truth and Convenience," *Notebooks*, ed. Henry Festing Jones (London: A.C. Fifield, 1912), 248; Robert Louis Stevenson, "Truth of Intercourse," *Virginibus Puerisque* (London: Kegan Paul & Co., 1881), 79, 81.

   For an analysis of Victorian morality, see Walter E. Houghton, *The Victorian Frame of Mind* (1957), Peter Gay, *The Bourgeois Experience, Victoria to Freud, The Education of the Senses*, Vol. I (1984), and Herbert F. Tucker, ed. *A Companion to Victorian Literature and Culture* (1999).
10. Mamet in Renee Graham, "Mamet with Manners," *Boston Globe*, May 2, 1999: N1; rpt. DMC 230–34.
11. Harold Pinter in John Russell Taylor, "Accident," *Sight and Sound* (Autumn 1966) quoted in Steven F. Gale, *Butter's Going Up* (Durham, NC: Duke Univ. Press, 1977), 242.

    David Mamet, *On Directing Film* (New York: Penguin 1992), 2. In the "Preface," he writes that "a good writer gets better only by learning to *cut*, to remove the ornamental, the descriptive, the narrative, and *especially* the deeply felt and meaningful," xv.

Mamet, *True and False, Heresy and Common Sense for the Actor* (New York: Vintage, 1999), 13.

12. Terrence Rattigan, "The Winslow Boy," *Plays: One*, Intr. Anthony Curtis (London: Methuen 1999), 177.
13. Mamet, *The Verdict*, unpublished screenplay, 119; Mamet, *Writing in Restaurants* (NY: Viking, 1987), 26, 25.
14. Mamet, "The Story of Noach," *Genesis: As It Is Written, Contemporary Writers on Our First Stories*, ed. David Rosenberg (San Francisco: Harper Collins, 1999), 62. Other contributors include Francine Prose, Leonard Michaels, Robert Pinsky, Grace Schulman, and Arthur Miller. Rpt. JAF 112–16.
15. Mamet, *Henrietta*, Elizabeth Dahlie (Boston: Houghton Mifflin, 1999), 1. On the grownup Mamet, see Thea Diamond, "Mamet, *Henrietta*," *David Mamet Review* (Fall 2000): 11.
16. Jonathan Kalb, "Two Marriages," *New York Press*, Arts & Listings, June 23–29, 1999: 24. John Lahr makes an interesting case for the comedy of the work in the articulation of the lines: "If the actors get the rhythms right, the very intakes of air necessary to speak the words at speed force them into the vain, strutting posture that is their characters' hilarious essence." Here, Mamet's language is all surface. Lahr, "Lust be a Lady, David Mamet Makes Merry," *New Yorker*, April 2, 2001: 94. For other critical reactions see David K. Sauer and Janice A. Sauer, *David Mamet, A Research and Production Sourcebook* (Westport, CT: Praeger, 2003), 78–90.
17. Karen Kohlhaas, *The Monologue Audition, A Practical Guide for Actors*. Foreword by David Mamet (2000; New York: Limelight Editions, 2002), 69.
18. Samuel Beckett, "Catastrophe," *Collected Shorter Plays* (New York: Grove, 1984), 299, 300–01.
19. Leslie Kane, "New and Forthcoming," *David Mamet Review* Vol.7 (2000). The review had been the single most complete source of productions and new work by Mamet.
20. Christopher Marlowe, *Doctor Faustus*, ed. John D. Jump (Cambridge: Harvard Univ. Press, 1965), 22–3. Hereafter Marlowe.
21. Mamet in Charles McGrath, "An Edwardian Drama Gets a Mametian Makeover," *New York Times*, Arts & Leisure, December 10, 2006: 9.
22. Hap Erstein, "'Romance' not the Best Mamet," *Palm Beach Post*, January 13, 2007: 4D. Erstein did admit there were some very funny lines in the play, however.
23. Mamet in Logan Hill, "Funny Peculiar," *New York Magazine*, February 28, 2005.

CHAPTER 9 ARCADE AMUSEMENT

1. In addition to Baldwin's monologue, Mamet added a scene of Shelley Levene visiting an uninterested client and a scene involving phone calls. He also changed the ending, omitting Roma's turning on Shelley to grab 50 percent of his commissions after he leaves the room. The film release was 1992.
2. Mamet in Susan Bullington Katz, "A Conversation with . . . David Mamet," *Conversations with Screenwriters* (Portsmouth, NH: Heinemann, 2000), 198. Hereafter Katz.

3. David Denby, "Illusions," *New Yorker*, November 12, 2002: 139.
4. Mamet in Dan Yakir, "The Postman's Words," *Film Comment*, Mar–Apr. 1981:22.
5. Pam Grady, "The Art of the Con," www.reel.com/reel.asp?node=features/*interviews/heist*.
6. Mamet in David Elmer, "Cine side of the Street," *Times* (London), August 5, 2004.
7. David Edelstein, "The Man with two Brains," *Slate*, March 11, 2004. This is a review of *Spartan*. Hereafter, Edelstein.
8. A. O. Scott, "The Thriller According to Mamet," *New York Times*, March 12, 2004.
9. Val Kilmer, "Commentary," *Spartan* DVD. 2004. Edelstein.
10. Mamet in Luaine Lee, "Mamet tries his hand at television with 'The Unit,'" *Chicago Tribune*, March 2, 2006.
11. Mamet to Elvis Mitchell, "The Treatment," KCRW (Santa Monica), April 5, 2006. The show is archived on their website. Hereafter KCRW.
12. David Mamet, "What Israel Means to Me," *What Israel Means to Me*, ed. Alan Dershowitz (Hoboken, NJ: John Wiley & Sons, 2006), 258–60.
13. Pauline Kael, "The Current Cinema: Unreal," *New Yorker*, November 14, 1988: 128.
14. On Thackeray, see *In Their Own Words*, Savran, 137; on sending Trollope's *The Way We Live Now* to Art Linson, see *Pound*, 46. On his collecting old knives, guns, visiting antique fairs, and more, see his various essays in *Some Freaks, The Cabin*, and *Jafsie and John Henry*.
15. Mamet in McGrath, "An Edwardian Drama Gets a Mametian Makeover," *New York Times*, Arts & Leisure, December 10, 2006: 9.
16. Jason Zinman, "Death, No. Redemption, Maybe," *New York Times*, Arts and Leisure, May 14, 2006: 10. McPherson in Maddy Costa, "'Human beings are animals,'" *Guardian*, September 13, 2006.
17. Fintan O'Toole, "A Mind in Connemara," *New Yorker*, March 6, 2006: 43.
18. Frederick Stroppel, "The Mamet Women," *Single and Proud & Other Plays* (New York: Samuel French, Inc.), 41, 44. A later example of "the Mamet effect" is the low-budget film *Frogs for Snakes* (1999), written and directed by Amos Poe. Starring Barbara Hershey, John Leguizamo, and Ron Perlman, it deals with a group of unemployed New York actors who double as part-time money collectors. The actors satirize Mamet's clipped language. Al Santana is their loan shark who owns an Off-Broadway theatre and moonlights as a theatrical impresario seeking to stage a production of *American Buffalo*. The joke is that the small-time hoods would kill for the role of Teach, and do, as competitors for Teach's part are continuously knocked off.
19. Beckett in James Knowlson, *Damned to Fame, The Life of Samuel Beckett* (New York: Simon and Schuster, 1996), 319.
20. Mamet, "Attention Must be Paid," *New York Times* , February 13, 2005.
21. The phrase "trash ethics" appears in Toby Zinman, "So Dis is Hollywood: Mamet in Hell," *Hollywood on Stage: Playwrights Evaluate the Culture Industry*, ed. Kimball King (New York: Garland, 1997), 103.
22. Mamet, "The Greg Scene," December 19, 1991: 3, 4. Unpublished.
23. Jonathan Kalb, "Casting New Light on the Most Visible of Playwrights," *New York Times*, November 7, 1999: AR 8; Bill Marx, "Playwright Envy," WBUR (National Public Radio) Boston, December 15, 2006.

24. "An American Pinter sticks his pen in the White House," *Sunday Times* (London), August 1, 2004. Hereafter Pen.
25. Richard Dawkins, *The Selfish Gene* (London: Oxford Univ. Press, 1976), 2.
26. "Screenwriter and Playwright David Mamet to Receive Screen Laurel Award at WGA 57th Annual Ceremony," News Release, Writers Guild of America West, January 7, 2005.
27. The impact of this event can be seen in the satire by Randy Gener, "Mametogram, or How to Write Like David Mamet," *American Theatre* , (March 2006): 12–13.
28. Mamet in Chris Jones, "Mamet talks Mamet during rare visit home," *Chicago Tribune*, March 29, 2006.
29. Mamet in Bill Zwecker, "Work has Mamet on Pins & Needles," *Chicago Sun-Times*, October 14, 2006.
30. David Mamet, "Carl Sandburg Award Speech," Ts., Chicago Public Library, October 12, 2006. Hereafter Sand.
31. David Mamet, "For the Harry Ransom Center," March 2007, www.hrc.utexas.edu/news/press2007/davidmamet.html.
32. A Jacobin was a member of a radical political club with republican tendencies in the period of the French Revolution; see BVG 67.
33. Mamet, "Keep your Pantheon" in Andrew Billen, "A talent for deception," *New Statesman*, June 4, 2007.
34. Sean Wilentz, "Tales of *Hoffa*," *The New Republic*, February 1, 1993, 55.
35. Constantin Stanislavsky, *An Actor Prepares*, tr. Elizabeth Reynolds Hapgood, Intr. John Gielgud (1936; New York: Theatre Arts Books, 1959), 263.

AFTERWORD

1. Mamet, *Race*. 2009. New York: Samuel French, 2010.
2. Mamet, *The Secret Knowledge, On the Dismantling of American Culture*. New York: Sentinel, 2011.
3. Mamet, "Why I Am No Longer a 'Brain-Dead Liberal,'" *The Village Voice*, March 11, 2008.
4. Mamet, *Theatre*. New York: Faber and Faber, 2010.
5. Andrew Fergusson. "Converting David Mamet," *Weekly Standard*, May 23, 2011.
6. Garcia, Chris. "Interview: David Mamet," *Austin American-Statesman*, February 17, 2008.
7. Mamet, "We Can't Stop Talking about Race in America," *New York Times*, September 13, 2009.
8. John Gapper, "'Liberalism Is an Expensive Habit,'" *Financial Times*, June 11–12, 2011.
9. Howard Blume, "Writer David Mamet Criticized for Phil Spector Remarks," *Los Angeles Times*, June 16, 2011.
10. Alan Ackerman's *Just Words: Lillian Hellman, Mary McCarthy, and the Failure of Public Conversation in America* (New Haven: Yale Univ. Press, 2011) does a much more substantialjob in exposing the limitations of public discourse.
11. Lionel Trilling, *The Liberal Imagination, Essays on Literature and Society* (1950; Garden City, NY: Anchor Doubleday, 1953).
12. Matt Wolff, "Jeff Goldblum and Kevin Spacey Are a Near Perfect Duo in Mamet's Speed-the-Plow," *New York Times*, February 19, 2008.

INDEX